# IN THEIR FOOTSTEPS

# IN THEIR FOOTSTEPS

## MORMON PIONEERS OF FAITH

**DONALD G. GODFREY**

Published by the Religious Studies Center, Brigham Young University, Provo, Utah, in cooperation with Deseret Book Company, Salt Lake City.
Visit us at rsc.byu.edu.

© 2018 by Brigham Young University. All rights reserved.

Printed in the United States of America by Sheridan Books, Inc.

DESERET BOOK is a registered trademark of Deseret Book Company.
Visit us at DeseretBook.com.

Any uses of this material beyond those allowed by the exemptions in US copyright law, such as section 107, "Fair Use," and section 108, "Library Copying," require the written permission of the publisher, Religious Studies Center, 185 HGB, Brigham Young University, Provo, Utah 84602. The views expressed herein are the responsibility of the authors and do not necessarily represent the position of Brigham Young University or the Religious Studies Center.

Library of Congress Cataloging-in-Publication Data

Names: Godfrey, Donald G.
Title: In their footsteps : Mormon pioneers of faith / Donald G. Godfrey.
Description: Provo, Utah : Religious Studies Center, Brigham Young
    University, in cooperation with Deseret Book Company, 2018. | Includes
    bibliographical references and index.
Identifiers: LCCN 2017033988
Subjects: LCSH: Mormon pioneers--Canada--History. | Mormon pioneers--United
    States--History. | Mormons--Canada--History. | Mormons--United
    States--History.
Classification: LCC BX8611 .G64 2018 | DDC 289.3092/2 [B] --dc23 LC record available at https://lccn.loc.gov/2017033988

**DEDICATED TO**

*My wife, Christina Maria Godfrey;
my children; and my grandchildren*

*Also the families of
Kenneth, Arlene, Marilyn, Lorin,
and Robert Godfrey*

"The heritage of the past
is the seed that brings forth
the harvest of the future."

*—Wendell Phillips (1811–94)*

# CONTENTS

| | |
|---|---|
| ix | PREFACE |
| xv | ACKNOWLEDGMENTS |
| xvii | PROLOGUE |

| | |
|---|---|
| 1 | **PART 1:** From The Victorian Age to the Canadian West, 1800–1887 |
| 3 | Chapter 1: Victorian England |
| 35 | Chapter 2: On the American Frontier |
| 71 | Chapter 3: Into the Canadian West |

| | |
|---|---|
| 99 | **PART 2:** Travelers in the American & Canadian West, 1839–1906 |
| 101 | Chapter 4: On the Western Frontier |
| 129 | Chapter 5: Mormons Moving into Southern Alberta |
| 173 | Chapter 6: Families Follow to Alberta |

| | |
|---|---|
| 189 | **PART 3:** Bridging the Western Frontier & the Modern West, 1887–1980 |
| 191 | Chapter 7: Frontiers Coming Together |

| | | |
|---|---|---|
| 251 | Chapter 8: The Modern Canadian West |
| 285 | Chapter 9: Small-Town Business |
| 315 | Chapter 10: Service in Cardston |
| 335 | Chapter 11: Canadian Gospel Service |
| 357 | Chapter 12: Taipei, Taiwan |
| 389 | **PART 4:** IN THEIR FOOTSTEPS |
| 391 | Chapter 13: Footprints |
| 401 | Epilogue |
| 405 | SELECTED BIBLIOGRAPHY |
| 415 | INDEX |
| 431 | ABOUT THE AUTHOR |

# PREFACE

*In Their Footsteps* is the story of pioneers across four generations who lived in many communities and countries. These men and women lived from the early 1800s into the 1980s. They lived in Bristol and Liverpool, England; Nauvoo, Illinois; North Ogden and Logan, Utah; and Cardston, Alberta, Canada. This story reflects the foundations of the Mormon presence in Canada and LDS life in the small communities that spread their influence across the nations.

Authors today often write only about leadership and celebrity, but even in ordinary lives "extraordinary things begin to happen."[1] Most people live outside of the limelight, but they often accomplish uncommon things. Thomas S. Monson, President of The Church of Jesus Christ of Latter-day Saints, noted that "history turns on small hinges, and so do our lives."[2] For the past three decades, public historians have sought to link local historical perspectives together. "Based on the premise that people [and their environments] are active agents in creating history,"[3] public history works to bring historical studies of pioneering communities, cultures, and individuals together. Local and community history provides the framework and the contributions of these ordinary citizens.

---

1. Ransom Riggs, *Miss Peregrine's Home for Peculiar Children* (Philadelphia: Quirk Books, 2011), 12.

2. Thomas S. Monson, "Follow the Prophets," *Ensign*, January 2015, 5.

3. Paul Ashton and Hilda Kean, eds., *People and Their Pasts: Public History Today* (New York: Palgrave Macmillan, 2009), 1.

It examines the past and the fabric of individual life experiences from within the context of historic events.[4]

When public history began, there was a significant distinction between "amateur and professional historians." The prevailing wisdom was that amateurs reworked people and local history while "professionals were more concerned with national and world history."[5] Today, the public history approach to historical research works to change that perception. In a Grace A. Tanner Lecture in Human Values, British historian Asa Briggs suggested that "the greatest excitement for the historian is to bring back to life people of different centuries. . . . The historian restores life." He suggested that historians "examine not only whole societies, but the intimate personalities of men and women."[6] Like the traditional approach to history, LDS publications include biographies on all the prophets, but they have few accounts that reflect local people and history. Kent F. Richards provides insight with *A Family of Faith: An Intimate View of Church History through the Journals of Three Generations of Apostles*.[7] While it centers on a personal approach, the people are most certainly of leadership stature. The work covers about three generations similar to "families everywhere who are striving to live after the manner of happiness, 'believing' and passing the legacy of faith from generation to generation."[8] Closer yet to the public history approach and the common Latter-day Saint, *Four Zinas: A Story of Mothers and Daughters on the Mormon Frontier* chronicles four generations of women. Drawing from personal and family papers, their story provides a gendered history of women in their different

---

4. D. Glassburg, *Sense of History: The Place of the Past in American Life* (Amherst: The University of Massachusetts Press, 2001), 210. See also R. Samuel, *Island Stories: Unraveling Britain* (London: Servso, 1998), 223.

5. David E. Kyvig and Myron A. Marty, *Nearby History: Exploring the Past around You* (Nashville: The American Association for State and Local History, 1892), ix–xx.

6. Asa Briggs, *Social History and Human Experience* (Cedar City, UT: Grace A. Tanner Center for Human Values, 1984), 4–5.

7. Kent F. Richards, *A Family of Faith* (Salt Lake City: Deseret Book, 2013), x.

8. Richards, *A Family of Faith*, x.

environments.⁹ The book reflects what Gordon B. Hinckley, former Church President, urged when he stated, "It is good to look back to the past to gain appreciation . . . for the future . . . for strength for whatever lies ahead . . . [for the] great harvest of which we are the beneficiaries."¹⁰ Similarly, Elder William R. Walker, formerly of the Quorum of the Seventy, echoed the same sentiment, emphasizing that it is through our ancestors and the personal lives of others that the faith of all Saints is fortified.¹¹

People are the foundation of history and community life. They offer inspiration and commanding motivations. The biographies of Church leaders provide some history, but unfortunately most histories of the common Latter-day Saints are anthologies of sorts; they are self-published collections of stories and photos, mixed with genealogical sheets. Their audience is limited. Yet they could be significant public histories if brought together, telling of the times, societies, and families of historical eras. Each family creates history one individual, one family, and one community at a time. These are the seeds from which public history and personal heritage grow. They are a magnifying glass through which we can acquire a personal glimpse of history. *In Their Footsteps* is one such history. It is the story of pioneering men and women from the Joseph Godfrey and Charles Ora Card families. The framework of this history began more than two hundred years ago in Charles Dickens's England and leads into twenty-first-century America. Ancestors from Victorian England migrated to the New England colonies, moved on to Nauvoo, scattered into the Great Salt Lake Basin, and moved northward into Canada. This work tells the story of the men and women woven together by circumstance, with love for each other, a familiar faith in the gospel of Jesus Christ, and a determination to "hold to the iron rod" no matter how many turns

---

9. Martha Sonntag Bradley and Mary Brown Firmage Woodward, *Four Zinas: The Story of Mothers and Daughters on the Mormon Frontier* (Salt Lake City: Deseret Book, 2000), vii–xxii.

10. Gordon B. Hinckley, "The Faith of the Pioneers," *Ensign*, July 1984, 3.

11. William R. Walker, "Fortifying Faith with Ancestors' Stories," *Church News*, 13 April 2014, 20.

their lives took.¹² They crossed the Atlantic, rode wagons, and walked barefoot across the plains to Zion. Lives were lost. Families suffered the results of angry mobs. They knew the prophets—Joseph Smith, Brigham Young, John Taylor—and contemporary Apostles N. Eldon Tanner and Hugh B. Brown. They endured the terrors of persecution. They hid in the Mormon Underground. They grew and flourished in the regions of the Salt Lake, Weber, and Cache Valleys in Utah; Star Valley, Wyoming; and the prairies of Alberta, Canada. They were the first settlers into southern Alberta. They were faithful Latter-day Saints contributing to their communities and their Church in common and uncommon ways.

*In Their Footsteps* draws on a rich collection of personal papers. These men and women saw the value in keeping journals, diaries, notebooks, handwritten autobiographies, reminiscences, photographs, and oral histories. The diaries of Charles Ora Card, from 1871 to 1903, and his letter copybooks portray life in Cache Valley and Canada at periods critical in history. The journals of Floyd and Clarice Godfrey detail the experiences of the first LDS couple missionaries in Taiwan, the Republic of China. The letters between Clarice Card, the oldest, and her youngest sister, Melva Card-Witbeck, chronicle decades. The family organization newsletters record family activities over four decades. Oral histories were conducted and preserved by more than a dozen living ancestors.

In addition to personal records, the research for *In Their Footsteps* utilized the LDS Church History Library in Salt Lake City, Utah; Brigham Young University's L. Tom Perry Special Collections in Provo, Utah; the Courthouse Museum and Archives in Cardston, Alberta; the Town of Cardston public records; the Magrath Museum in Magrath, Alberta; the Galt Museum in Lethbridge, Alberta; the Glenbow Museum in Calgary, Alberta; the North Ogden Museum in Ogden, Utah; and the Utah State Archives in Ogden, Utah. Documentation from these archives provided detailed collaboration and contextualization.

---

12. See 1 Nephi 15:23–24.

The work is carefully framed within the time periods. National and local sources provide this framing, which is interwoven throughout the manuscript in narrative, at the head of each part of the manuscript and within extensively annotated footnoting. The primary national scholars include multiple texts from Leonard Arrington; F. Ross Peterson, *A History of Cache Valley*; Kenneth W. Godfrey, *Logan Utah*; Joel E. Ricks, ed., *The History of a Valley*; and Richard C. Roberts and Richard W. Sadler, *A History of Weber County*. Conway B. Sonne, *Ships, Saints, and Mariners* provided information on Atlantic Ocean crossing. Lowry Nelson's *The Mormon Village* provided public history–styled patterns of early settlement techniques. Works of Canadian scholars such as Brigham Y. Card, *The Mormon Presence in Canada*; Hugh A. Dempsey, *Red Crow: Warrior Chief*; A. A. Den Ottor, *Civilizing the West: The Galts and the Development of Western Canada*; and Donald G. Wetherell and Irene R. A. Kmet, *Town Life: Main Street and the Evolution of Small Town Alberta, 1800–1946* all provide Canadian framing to growing southern Alberta communities. Helpful community historical society publications included Magrath's *Irrigation Builders*, vols. 1–2; *Cardston and District*, vols. 1–3; Floyd J. Woodfield, *A History of North Ogden: Beginnings to 1985*; and Jeanette Shaw Greenwell and Laura Chadwick Kump, *Our North Ogden Pioneers, 1851–1900*.

The research and writing were all accomplished within the standards of acceptable scholarship. The author's traditional approach to history is grounded in the methodology of Arthur Marwick's *The Nature of History*, and Allan Niven's *The Gateway to History*. Personalizing this traditional approach, Earnest J. Wrage and Barnett Baskerville's *American Form* and *Contemporary Forum* frame the historical questions that were debated from 1788 into the twentieth century. With Baskerville's *The People's Voice*, the issues and oratory advanced societal values and altitudes of the time. John Collier Jr. and Malcolm Collier's *Visual Anthropology: Photography as a Research Method* provided a methodology for examining the human values reflected in the visual technology of the times. Finally, David Kyvig's *Local and Community History* and *Nearby History: Exploring the Past Around* provided insight into approaching the specializations of public history. Methods of research and documentation, which were guides for a traditional scholarly approach, followed the author's own works in *Methods of Historical Analysis in Electronic Media*.

# ACKNOWLEDGMENTS

As always, a book is never the work of an author in isolation. My appreciation goes to my immediate and extended family, friends, and archivists who have supported this work over the years. I extend my love and special appreciation to my wife, Christina Maria, who patiently supports all of my writing.

A special thanks to Fran Matera, professor at the Walter Cronkite School of Journalism and Mass Communications. She more than any individual has inspired improvements, reading my manuscripts and providing counsel and direction. I thank LaDawn Dalton, archivist of the Prescott Museum, for helping me with the manuscript and for encouraging me along with the concept of putting green leaves on the family trees. Archivists and historians Wendy Coleman, of the Magrath Museum; LaVern Cottrell, of the North Ogden Historical Museum; and Joan Shaw, of the Courthouse Museum and Archive, all opened doors and understanding of regional and family history. I thank Paul Godfrey for his trips to the Alberta Provincial Archive in my behalf, and Lorin Godfrey with Marilyn Pitcher, who read early drafts of this manuscript.

Thanks to Thomas A. Wayment, Joany O. Pinegar, Brent R. Nordgren, Devan Jensen, Tyler Balli, Leah Emal, Kimball Gardner, Allyson Jones, Lauren Whitby, and Carmen Durland Cole of the Religious Studies Center.

Finally, I thank the family of Floyd and Clarice Godfrey. Kenneth F. Godfrey, Arlene J. Payne, Marilyn Pitcher, Lorin Godfrey, Robert Godfrey, and Douglas Godfrey all kept a continuing flow of communication and supply of family documents, photos, and opinions coming my way.

# THREE GENERATIONS OF GODFREY AND CARD HISTORY

*Generation One*

**JOSEPH GODFREY (1800–80)**
**SARAH ANN PRICE (1842–1928)**

   John
   Sarah Jane
   Margaret Ann
   Jemima Helen
   Charlotte Emily
   Jeremiah
   Josiah
   *Melvin*
   Josephine

**CHARLES O. CARD (1839–1906)**
**SARAH J. PAINTER (1853–1936)**

   Matilda Francis
   *George Cyrus*
   Lavantia Painter
   Pearl Painter
   Abigail Jane
   Franklin Almon

*Generation Two*

**MELVIN GODFREY (1887–1956)**
**EVA JONES (1878–1963)**

   Bertrand Richard
   Parley Melvin
   Lottie
   *Floyd*
   Mervin "J"
   Joseph
   Norris
   Douglas

**GEORGE CARD (1880–1958)**
**ROSE E. PLANT (1879–1959)**

   Leland Plant
   *Clarice*
   Cyrus Henry
   Glen Charles
   Amy
   Melva Rose

*Generation Three*

**FLOYD GODFREY (1906–92)**
**CLARICE CARD (1907–80)**

   Kenneth Floyd
   Arlene Janet
   Marilyn Rose
   Lorin Card
   Donald George
   Robert Melvin

# PROLOGUE

From the beginning, let's pretend we are barefoot, walking in the footprints of individuals making history. We feel the outline of their impressions as we stand on our own feet within their soles. Perhaps they wore sandals, boots, hand-me-downs from an older brother or sister, or just rubber cut from a worn boot or an old tire. Maybe they wrapped their feet in cloth or animal hide and tied it around at their ankles. Perhaps they walked barefoot. Can you feel the sores on their feet? Their feet hurt as they walked and walked, stepping on the thorns and sharp rocks of life's trials. They are out of breath and cold, but they continue pressing forward. They bathe their tired feet in the cool, clear running water of the streams along the prairies and the mountains. Weary, hungry, scared, and exhausted, they keep moving forward. They placed one foot in front of the other, determined to hold on, moving forward—never back. Then, their footprints disappear. Why? Were they riding a horse, wagon, train, or maybe one of the nation's first gasoline automobiles? When we stop to imagine and *feel* these footprints, they are inspirational even in their trials.

Are your footprints shaped like theirs? They grew strong and supple in their childhood and youthful years, then wrinkled and scarred with age. Still their footprints enterprisingly pressed forward through eras of transition, celebration, and war.

And now, while you walk in their footsteps, you also create your own. May our prints offer a clear path—strong, never-ending, and faithful—linking the past to the future for those generations yet to come.

Part 1

# FROM THE VICTORIAN AGE TO THE CANADIAN WEST

1800–1887

# VICTORIAN ENGLAND

###### Chapter 1

Four generations ago, in England's Victorian Era, Queen Victoria reigned on the throne of Great Britain (1837–1901) and the British Empire covered the globe. It was an era of domestic peace, prosperity, economic and industrial growth, global migrations, and, at the same time, one of increased social awareness.[1] Prosperity contrasted with child labor in the factories and mines.[2] Charles Dickens, born in 1812, created fictional characters most picturesque of this era.[3] As a journalist, Dickens would later describe the Latter-day Saints boarding a ship to America. The Bristol Channel provided the primary thoroughfare for worldwide shipping and flowed from England's second-largest port at Bristol to the Atlantic Ocean. Industry sprung up around the port as ships sailed the world, returning with a bounty of imported goods: tobacco, rum, cocoa, sugarcane, slaves, spices, and whale oil. Ships sailed in and out on the waterway's extreme high tides until locks were installed in the Bristol Harbour, luring companies that had used the larger harbor at Liverpool.

---

1. See Christopher Hibbert, *Queen Victoria: A Personal History* (London: Harper Collins, 2000).

2. See George Behler, *Child Abuse and Moral Reform in England, 1870–1908* (Stanford: Stanford University Press, 1982).

3. See Michael Slater, *Charles Dickens: A Life Defined by Writing* (London: Yale University Press, 2009).

In the Victorian Age, childhood was an experience dependent upon family status. The children of aristocrats enjoyed the new fortunes of the time, whereas childhood barely existed for those born to poor families. Youngsters were expected to work, and some children as young as age five were contributing to the livelihood of their family. They worked in the factories, in the mines, and on the farms twelve to sixteen hours a day in unimaginable conditions. They crawled under new manufacturing machinery into spaces too small for adult workers. They cleaned the residue from the machines and the floors so that the machinery could churn nonstop. It was dangerous work. There were no child-labor laws protecting them. Working children who were lucky undertook apprenticeships, leading to respectable trades and domestic service for the rich. The others were consigned to a lifetime of poverty.

This was the time within which young Joseph Godfrey grew into childhood. He was born circa 14 March 1800, forty miles south of Bristol and in the vicinity of North Petherton, Somerset, England—a village along the Bristol Channel, which separates Wales and southern England.[4] The fifteenth-century Church of St. Mary, North Petherton, remains today. Joseph's family was poor, yet amidst his suffering, he broke free, learned the sailor's trade, and traveled the world. He could easily have been one of Dickens's children of the street had it not been for a kind, nameless sea captain.

**AN ABUSIVE CHILDHOOD**

Joseph was the son of William Godfrey and Margaret Barrows[5] and the fourth of five children. Little is known about his two older brothers

---

4. In family papers, Joseph's birth date varies from 1794 to 1806. Clarice Godfrey confirms that Joseph was christened at St. Mary Redcliffe on 1 March 1806. Primary histories include Ellen Clair Weaver Shaeffer, "Joseph Godfrey, 1806–1880: A Compilation of Various Sources," 2008; John W. Gibson, "Biographical Sketch of Joseph Godfrey," 1925, Godfrey Family Papers; Jemima Helen Godfrey, "Joseph Godfrey," handwritten document related by Jemima to Lorine Woodwan and Myrtle C. Swainston, 31 December 1955, Godfrey Family Papers; Arlene G. Payne's work, "Joseph Godfrey Our Grandfather," Godfrey Family Papers, is a fictional children's story based in fact and illustrated by her grandson.

5. Margaret's name appears as Barrows, Bauer, and Barron in differing family histories. The original parish records indicate Barrows. A later bishop's transcription

(Richard and John) and sister (Jemima). But Joseph and his younger sister Fanny cared deeply for each other. Their mother, Margaret, was missing during much of Joseph's childhood, leaving her children to struggle with their father.[6] Love and attention were absent from this single-parent home. William was a physically abusive alcoholic, so Joseph and Fanny were sent to live with their Aunt Caroline Trott. Although she likely lived in the vicinity, it is not known exactly where she lived or how long they lived with her, but their placement proved temporary, as their father wanted them home. He likely wanted them for what they could financially contribute to the household rather than out of love. Home life with their father was painful, and young Joseph suffered.[7]

One day, Joseph took a loaf of bread his father had tried to hide on a high shelf. He climbed up and retrieved it to feed Fanny, who was crying for food. Joseph found the bread, broke it open, and scratched out the center to share with his little sister. Joseph "felt so sorry for her that he had reportedly often stole bread, which his father had hidden." When William returned from work intoxicated and discovered the bread gone, he tied Joseph's hands above his head, hooked them onto a wall, and "flogged him long and hard . . . , beating him until he was in a stupor." A doctor was called in, and the boy was treated. Most family histories reflect only one incident, but there may have been more.[8]

Joseph was only eleven, but after the beating he gathered what few possessions he had and planned his escape.[9] His disappearance that first morning went unnoticed. By the next day, he had made his way

---

changes this to Barron. If these records are accurate, she would have died when Joseph was twenty to twenty-five years of age, thus further confusing the family relationships and dates. Correspondence with Marilyn Rose Pitcher, 1 June 2015, Godfrey Family Papers.

6. As of the publication of this book, no documentation was found as to why his mother was absent.

7. Arthur Meecham, "A Brief Sketch of the Life of Joseph Godfrey," 1, Godfrey Family Papers.

8. See Mary Ellen Godfrey Meacham, "Joseph Godfrey," 1, Godfrey Family Papers.

9. Melvin Godfrey, "Brief History of Melvin Godfrey," 1, handwritten document in Godfrey Family Papers. Other sources place the age at eight or nine. Eleven fits his history better, given the maturity of the thinking.

to the Bristol docks. He hid in an empty barrel that was being loaded onto a whaling ship in preparation for its departure to the North Sea. Joseph's hiding place made the barrel too heavy to be empty and just before they set sail, he was discovered by the ship's first mate.

At the same time, his father, now searching the harbor streets, rushed to the wharf, yelling for his son.[10] On board, Joseph pleaded with the captain not to return him to his father and showed the captain the fresh wounds on his back. The captain listened. Calling out to William, the captain told him Joseph was leaving with them and that William would never again abuse his son.[11] As the ship left harbor, Joseph watched his father walking along the wharf. It must have been a difficult moment in both of their lives—an emotional assortment of love, fear, anger, agony, relief, and anticipation.

The captain was kindhearted, and over the years he raised Joseph as his own son. Working as a cabin boy, Joseph won the hearts of his shipmates and over many years learned the working trades of the seamen. It was years later before the ship returned to Bristol. Even then, Joseph made no attempt to contact his family. Once when the ship was in port, Joseph saw his father at a distance, but he chose not to reach out to him.[12]

**SAILING THE WORLD**

Joseph grew to maturity under the watchful eye of the captain and progressed through the ranks of a British sailor. It was the captain who taught him to read and write, "how to splice a rope, box the compass, and in fact how to be a good sailor."[13] He sailed to the northernmost outposts of the Atlantic, hunting for whales in Eskimo country. This

---

10. Lois Lindsay Anderson, untitled sketch on the life of Joseph Godfrey, Godfrey Family Papers.

11. As of the publication of this book, the name of the captain or the ship was not discovered in any of the sources.

12. Anderson, untitled sketch on the life of Joseph Godfrey.

13. Quoted from Joseph's grandson J. Arthur Meecham, "A Brief Sketch of the Life of Joseph Godfrey," 1, Godfrey Family Papers.

was not casual labor and could be quite dangerous, as evidenced by the sinking of the *Essex* in 1820 by a sperm whale. When the crew sighted a sperm whale, the sailors dispatched in small boats to harpoon the whale, tie it alongside the larger vessel, and begin the grisly process of cutting it into pieces. The pieces were boiled to extract the oil, which was then stored in barrels. Joseph's responsibilities during the whale hunt are unknown, but he no doubt knew about the dangers of the profession.

Joseph sailed east around South Africa's Cape of Good Hope and into the Indian Ocean. On another trip, he sailed west, around South America's Cape Horn into the Pacific. These were trade ship voyages, carrying precious cargo from the foreign ports back to Britain. He sailed into the principal ports of the world, reportedly before the mast of the English seas for almost thirty years in the days when the sun never set on the British Empire.[14] During his life at sea, Joseph, as well as the ship, captain, and rest of the crew, was sequestered into the British Navy likely as a cargo vessel. Joseph reportedly told his family of the Battle of Trafalgar and the death of Lord Nelson.[15] However, the ship was primarily a hunting and cargo vessel. Trade and cargo ships paid much better than those sequestered into navy service.

As the captain aged, many of the ship's crew thought Joseph would assume the helm. However, when the captain became seriously ill and died, Joseph's fortunes changed dramatically. It was the rule of the sea that the first mate had the senior claim of the captain's position. Conflict fostered talk of mutiny between those supporting the first mate and those supporting Joseph. Seeing the potential trouble, Joseph chose not to fight for the captain's helm and prepared to depart the ship. The new captain grew jealous of the crew's loyalty to Joseph and

---

14. Reports of Joseph's time at sea range from nineteen to thirty-one years.

15. See Arthur Meecham, "A Brief Sketch of the Life of Joseph Godfrey," 1. Meecham was a grandson giving a history lesson about his grandfather's life. Meecham indicated that Joseph remembered the Crimean War. This is unlikely, as this conflict occurred from 1853 to 1856, when Joseph lived in North Ogden. If Joseph remembered the Battle of Trafalgar and the death of Horatio Nelson, it would have been at the very beginning of his experiences at sea, as the battle took place in 1805. Lord Nelson was a heroic British admiral who was shot and killed during the Battle of Trafalgar.

planned vengeance. As emotions escalated, the ship was making its way up the St. Lawrence River, between the Canadian territory of Quebec and the US New England states. They docked at Quebec for a time and then continued to Prescott, Ontario. Anchored off the shore, Joseph concluded that for his own safety he must leave the ship quickly.[16] So, with his staunch sea friend, George Coleman, the two started off.[17] They packed their belongings into their seaman's chests, and as they were lowering them down into a small waiting row boat, the new captain and one of his supporters dropped an iron bar through the bottom of their row boat. All of their belongings sank into the harbor. Joseph and George struggled with the chests, but realizing that it was going to be impossible to save both property and their lives, they dropped the chests, stripped off their coats and shoes, and swam for shore. They were without hats, coats, shoes, or any of the resources they had saved over the years and stashed away in the now sinking cases. They had nothing to show for their time at sea except each other, experience, and their invincible will.[18] Supporting themselves, they traded in their

---

16. As of the publication of this book, there was no documented time line for these events. To be considered for the position of captain would mean that Joseph was a mature adult when he was near the end of his career at sea. Whether Joseph debarked in Prescott, Ontario, or Quebec City, Quebec, remains a question. Prescott was a bustling town, a transfer point for cargo where travelers and settlers headed west. Travelers usually came from Montreal via stage coach. However, it is unlikely the ship sailed all the way from Quebec City to Prescott because it would have been difficult to navigate the rapids of the river without the canal system, which was not in place until 1845. Letter from Robert Dalley, general manager, port of Prescott, to Donald G. Godfrey, 30 October 2012. Jemima Helen Godfrey reports it was a "Canadian" port. See Jemima Helen Godfrey, daughter of Joseph Godfrey, as related to Lorine Goodwin and Myrtle C. Swainston, 1.

17. In order to provide verification of information and events, it has been helpful to corroborate the records of the Joseph Godfrey and George Coleman families. While both families' records are scant, there is no doubt that Joseph and George were stalwart friends: they married sisters, worked together, served in the military together, and lived parallel lives. See "Our Pioneer Heritage: The Moroni Coleman Family," Magrath, Alberta, Canada, 2009, Magrath Museum. Hereafter referred to as "Coleman Family History." George was born 2 March 1817 in Norfolk, England. "Coleman Family History," 15.

18. The Coleman family records confirm the records of Melvin Godfrey, Joseph's son, which place the ship in Canadian waters. See Melvin Godfrey, "Brief History

sea legs for those of the laborer, the militiaman, and the farmer for the next six years.

Joseph was now thirty-six years old.[19] Most of his life had been at sea. He and George's first land travels took them over the St. Lawrence River from Prescott, Ontario, to Waterton, New York, where they worked through the winter of 1836. In the spring of 1837, they boarded a steamboat across the Great Lakes to Detroit, Michigan, and worked on the Chicago Canal, which was to connect Lake Michigan with the Mississippi River.

Chicago was a rapidly growing city of approximately four thousand residents.[20] Joseph apparently "was not a lover of larger cities with their noise, and he was not too happy with the people on the canal construction crew."[21] Joseph and George returned to Canada and were drafted into the Canadian militia. They served for two years and were discharged 1 June 1839, then volunteered for an additional year at Fort Malden, Ontario. This fort was a British defense military staging area, used during the Upper Canada Rebellion of 1837–38. Here, as Canadian Loyalists, Joseph and George fought against the rebels on the Canadian frontier who supported Canadian separation from British control.

On 1 June 1840, they were discharged, and the duo made its way back to Johnson's Creek in New York. They were transient workers who labored as farm hands in western New York and New Jersey. One of these jobs would change their lives; they were hired to work the farm of James and Eunice Manning Reeves.[22] James and Eunice were parents of two daughters—Ann Elizabeth Eliza, age twenty-two, and Mary, age

---

of Melvin Godfrey;" 1. Other reports vary as to whether the port was New York or Prescott.

19. This assumes the 1800 birth date.

20. Frank Alfred Randall and John D. Randall, *History of the Development of Building Construction in Chicago* (Urbana: University of Illinois Press, 1949; repr. 1999), 57, 88.

21. "Coleman Family History," 15, 79. These records indicated they served under Colonel Rattler.

22. This name appears in two ways: Reeves and Rheese. The "Coleman Family History" uses the former.

twenty.²³ Little is known of their courtship, but in 1840, Joseph married Ann, and George married Mary. The couples eventually settled in Roseville, Warren County, Illinois, a small town some fifty miles east of Nauvoo, Illinois.

## NEWLYWEDS AMIDST TURMOIL

In the mid-1800s, the United States was struggling within itself over issues of slavery, the unification of the states, territorial expansion, and religious turmoil. These topics provided a forum for political debates on the establishment of "a more perfect union," as well as new religious sermons on liberalism as opposed to traditional orthodoxy.²⁴ This historical era opened the western frontier and ushered in the progressive growth of an industrial age.

The people's voice was being heard, but not without conflict. Three million slaves who had provided stability to a cotton-based economy in the southern states were fighting for freedom. New states of Florida and Texas were added to the nation as the union began to split apart. Lincoln and Douglas debated for the presidency. The whole of New England seemed occupied with religious debates. The Fox Sisters "cracked their toes," providing individual prophecies for those who would listen. "Peepers" scoured the New England states, hunting for lost Spanish gold. Ralph Waldo Emerson attacked the dogmatic rituals of the Calvinist doctrine. This was the environment in which The Church of Jesus Christ of Latter-day Saints was founded, causing even more religious controversy. This was the environment of our two newlywed couples—Joseph and Ann Godfrey, and George and Mary Coleman.²⁵

---

23. Ann Elizabeth Eliza was born 28 September in either 1817 or 1818. Mary was born 6 August 1820. See FamilySearch.org. Mary's marriage date was 7 November 1842. "Coleman Family History," 15.

24. See Ernest J. Wrage and Barnet Baskerville, *American Forum: Speeches on Historic Issues, 1788–1900* (Seattle: University of Washington Press, 1967).

25. For more historical background of the Church during this time period, see Leonard J. Arrington, *Great Basin Kingdom: An Economic History of the Latter-day Saints, 1830–1900* (Salt Lake City: University of Utah Press, 1993).

## CHALLENGES OF EARLY MORMON LIFE

Mormonism, or more properly The Church of Jesus Christ of Latter-day Saints (LDS Church), was blossoming in New England, and Joseph Smith, the Church's founder, was nominated as a candidate for the US Presidency on 29 January 1844.[26] As Joseph Godfrey and George Coleman moved about with their new wives, working as farm laborers from New York to Illinois, in 1843 they encountered the Mormon missionaries. Joseph and Ann were baptized by H. Jacobs.[27] George and Mary followed Joseph and Ann and were baptized on 3 April 1843 by Archibald Montgomery.[28] By late 1844, the couples had moved from New York to Hancock County, Illinois, and later to Nauvoo. Not too surprisingly, they were now treated as outcasts by family and former associates who wanted nothing to do with them because they had joined the Mormon Church. The enemies of the Church were bitter, and persecutions became more and more severe as the Church's numbers and political influence grew and polygamy began. Nevertheless, Joseph, George, and their wives worked their farms and persevered.[29]

It was a frighteningly wonderful yet challenging time to be alive. In Nauvoo, they were with the main body of the believers, Joseph having purchased farm land just outside of Nauvoo. In 1845, he was ordained a local Seventy in the Church by Benjamin L. Clapp and became

---

26. Andrew H. Hedges, Alex D. Smith, and Brent M. Rogers, eds., *Journals, Volume 3: May 1843–June 1845*, vol. 3 of the Journals series of *The Joseph Smith Papers*, ed. Ronald K. Esplin and Matthew J. Grow (Salt Lake City: Church Historian's Press, 2015), 169.

27. The only "H. Jacobs" appearing in the source materials at this time was Henry Bailey Jacobs. He was the first husband of Zina Diantha Huntington. She would later marry Joseph Smith, then Brigham Young. See Martha Sonntag Bradley and Mary Brown Firmage Woodward, *4 Zinas: A Story of Mothers and Daughters on the Mormon Frontier* (Salt Lake City: Signature Books, 2000), 111–15; Donna Hill, *Joseph Smith: The First Mormon* (New York: Doubleday & Company, 1977), 361.

28. "Coleman Family History," 15.

29. Secondary sources indicate that Joseph told stories of the mobs and his association with the prophet Joseph Smith. However, there is little detail or primary evidence of these events.

acquainted with the Prophet Joseph Smith.[30] He served as one of Joseph's bodyguards and worked on the Prophet's farm. The challenge that Joseph and George faced when they arrived in Nauvoo was that the city was at the height of bitter persecution. Missouri governor Lilburn W. Boggs had issued his infamous extermination order to rid the state of the Mormons. The extermination order was titled "Executive Order 44, issued 27 October 1838," for the specific purpose of the "extermination" of all Mormons.[31] Illinois governor Thomas Ford even visited the jailed Joseph Smith and promised protection; however, within days, a local militia group, the Carthage Greys, had attacked the jail and murdered the Prophet.[32]

In 1846, the Latter-day Saints began fleeing Nauvoo. Joseph and George left their homes and farms to the mobs and set off on a journey of unspeakable poverty and hardship. The trek would be 1,300 miles across the Mississippi River to the Great Basin of the Rocky Mountains. The Mormons had been promised they could stay in Nauvoo until spring, but the violence inflicted upon those remaining prohibited any delay. Joseph and George left with the Saints. There is nothing in source materials describing specific violence against Joseph or George; however, fear permeated the city, their leader Joseph Smith had just been murdered, and violent attacks were increasing in Nauvoo.[33]

In the middle of winter, on 4 February 1846, Joseph, George, and their families crossed the Missouri River on the ice, making their way

---

30. Benjamin L. Clapp was a member of the First Council of the Seventy from 1845 to 1859 and was later excommunicated. See *Encyclopedia of Mormonism* (New York: Macmillan Publishing, 1992), s.v. "Appendix 1: Biographical Register of General Church Officers," 1634, "Appendix 5: General Church Officers," 1680.

31. The order was rescinded in 2006 by a state resolution asking for pardon and forgiveness. See also Thomas Ford, *A History of Illinois* (Urbana: University of Illinois Press, 1995), 180.

32. Ford, *A History of Illinois*, 243–48. See Dallin H. Oaks and Marvin S. Hill, *Carthage Conspiracy: The Trial of the Accused Assassins of Joseph Smith* (Urbana: University of Illinois Press, 1975), 1–45.

33. See Marshall Hamilton, "From Assassination to Expulsion: Two Years of Distrust, Hostility, and Violence," in *Kingdom on the Mississippi Revisited: Nauvoo in Mormon History*, ed. Roger D. Laumius and John E. Hallwas (Chicago: University of Illinois Press, 1996), 214–30.

to Iowa. They relocated on a farm a few miles south of Council Bluffs. Winter hardships took their toll on the immigrants in Council Bluffs and Winter Quarters. Within a year, the two families moved again, this time to Misquote Creek near Kaysville, Illinois, and found new land for farming. They remained for three years, until 1849, working and acquiring supplies and a wagon for their trek west. Both families were poor. They scrimped every morsel of food as they saved for the journey west. Joseph and Ann lost three of their four children to cholera: sons Albert and James, and a daughter, Eliza Jane. In George's family, Mary came down with dysentery. By the time they began moving toward to the Rocky Mountains, they were two families among the "approximately 20,000 Mormons scattered on the prairies in a thin line . . . across the prairies."[34]

## MORMON BATTALION

Persecution remained severe. It is an understatement that the pioneers were significantly surprised, angered, and in a state of disbelief when their brethren were recruited by the United States federal government to engage in the Mexican-American War (1846–48). US President James K. Polk had the vision of a coast-to-coast nation, his eyes focused specifically on California. At the same time the Saints, the homeless band of believers, were leaving United States territory with the hope of creating their own independent State of Deseret, where they could worship and live free from persecution.[35] The State of Deseret would never materialize, but this was the context of the time when in July 1846 the US government asked for Mormon recruits. Church President Brigham Young encouraged the members to assist, and at this suggestion, five hundred men enlisted in what became known as the Mormon Battalion. Joseph and George drew lots to determine who would go and who would remain and care for their families, assuring

---

34. Norma Baldwin Ricketts, *The Mormon Battalion: U.S. Army of the West, 1846–1848* (Logan: Utah State University Press, 1986), 1.

35. Dale L. Morgan, "The State of Deseret," *Utah Historical Quarterly* 8 (1940): 65–251.

that they made it to Utah. The lot fell upon George, and he joined the battalion. Joseph promised his friend that he would care for George's family until he returned, to which George responded, "And if I don't come back, raise a family for me will you?"[36] Thus, Joseph was left to take charge of George's family "as far as she [Mary] would let him."[37]

The officers of George's company (Company A of the US Army of the West) were Jefferson Hunt, captain; George W. Orman, first lieutenant; Lorenzo Clark, second lieutenant; William W. Williams, third lieutenant; and "Willis," who later became captain. George was enlisted as a private in the company.[38] The battalion leaders were professional soldiers, not empathetic Mormon volunteers. Complaints from the Saints who joined the battalion chronicled verbal abuse, drunkenness, and the constant threat from the officers to leave the volunteers behind or give them extra duties if they failed to follow orders or simply fell sick.

George's company arrived in Sante Fe, 1 December 1846, but despite both cold and hunger they were ordered to continue marching. Traveling usually ten to twelve miles per day, some did fall sick and indeed were left behind. By 8 December, snow was falling, and members of the company were finally able to purchase food and supplies using their own funds. George was so hungry that he overate and did not feel at all well during the night. Dr. William Rust, one of the company men, gave him "tincture of lobelia," which was a nineteenth-century herbal aspirin and "it helped a little." The next day, Captain Willis ordered the company off again. George was still feeling poorly, so he was left behind with only a saddle and a mule. The company arrived at Pueblo mid-January, but George did not. A search party was sent back, but to no avail. His body was later found near where Captain Willis had left him. "He died sometime mid-December 1846."[39] It would be several years before his wife and Joseph would learn of his death.

---

36. "Joseph Godfrey of North Ogden Utah," 6, author unknown, handwritten document in Godfrey Family Papers.

37. "Joseph Godfrey of North Ogden Utah," 6.

38. Ricketts, *The Mormon Battalion*, 21.

39. Ricketts, *The Mormon Battalion*, 242–44. "Coleman Family History," 17, 35. These records place his death at sixty-five miles from Sante Fe, New Mexico, on 18 December 1846.

George's death would change Joseph's life forever. The story of George Coleman in the battalion spawned early speculation and folklore contrary to fact. Did George abandon his family, his friend, and the Church? The answer to these questions is a definitive no.[40]

At the same time George marched with the battalion, Joseph, Ann, and Mary trekked toward Utah. They eagerly anticipated George's return and were preparing for their own migration west. It took two years to earn sufficient funds to purchase a team of oxen and a wagon. The westward movement of the Mormons was organized into companies to better handle the growing number of converts. They operated under strict rules in terms of daily prayers, the care of their guns, guarding animals, and night-time circling of the wagons.[41] By 1852, Mary and George's only son, Moroni, had joined the Orson Hyde company. Joseph and Ann followed with the sixth company, under the leadership of David Wood. The David Wood company included 288 individuals and 58 wagons.[42]

It was an arduous journey and many just walked alongside the wagons. The European immigrants were often unfamiliar with driving a team of oxen; thus progress was slow going and continually delayed. The cattle were herded along at the side of the wagon train as they drove. Night camps were highly organized; wagons were circled for protection, with the tongue of each wagon tucked under the rear of the one in front. Food was prepared for the evening meal and the next day's journey. At night, the company entertained themselves by singing hymns of encouragement and dancing, putting their hardships behind them in preparation for the next day.

Forging the rivers was viewed as both a blessing and a challenge. It was a blessing because it provided the pioneers a place to stop, rest,

---

40. The rumors seem to stem from John W. Gibson in "Biographical Sketch of Joseph Godfrey," 2–3. John William Gibson Jr. and Sr. were contemporary residents of North Ogden. See Jeanette Greenwell and Laura Chadwick Kump, *Our North Ogden Pioneers, 1851–1900* (North Ogden, UT: Watkins Printing, 1998), 227–30. Page reference denotes the typewritten manuscript. The original handwritten document is in the Godfrey Family Papers.
41. Leonard J. Arrington, *Great Basin Kingdom*, 18–21.
42. "6th Company," *Deseret News Weekly*, September 1852, 2.

and wash the blood from their feet; however, it could be challenging if the river's currents were treacherous. Women and children were carried on the backs of the men. The wagon masters used the rivers to replenish their critical water supply. Water needed to be restocked at least every Saturday so that a proper Sabbath could be observed. The Sabbath was a day of worship even on the trail. The Wood company followed the Mormon Trail, arriving in the Great Basin in October 1852, just in time for the Church's quarterly conference.

Joseph settled his family in North Ogden, Utah. Mary Coleman and her son, Moroni, unaware of George's fate in the battalion, went to Tooele. They lived with her sister Matilda Bates and awaited George's return. Mary was desperate to find George, so in 1853 she left Moroni and returned to search for her husband. Before she left, she encouraged Moroni to "try and get along with Mr. Bates," whom she described "as a rough and harsh character."[43] Then she headed back to the Mississippi and the area of the battalion's departure to find some trace of George. She searched but returned without him.[44]

### NORTH OGDEN: DUGOUT LIVING

Joseph's first home in North Ogden was a dugout. The dugout was a simple, uncultured shelter, a temporary dwelling place for pioneers and frontiersman moving west. It was built by excavating the ground from the face of the side of a hill or by simply digging a hole into the ground. To call these homes simple is an understatement. They had dirt floors, dirt walls, and dirt ceilings. A rock or adobe fireplace provided warmth and heat for cooking. An animal hide covered the hole, which served as a door, and a cotton sheet on the opposite side of the dwelling sometimes covered another hole as a window and provided cross ventilation. Pioneer-styled air-conditioning for summer heat consisted of

---

43. Francelia, "The Story of May Reeve's Life," 6, in Godfrey Family Papers.

44. Lucy Brown Archer, "Women of the Mormon Battalion: Wives and Daughters of the Soldiers, 1846–1848," The Life, Times, and Family of Orson Pratt Brown, http://www.orsonprattbrown.com/MormonBattalion/women-children1847mb.html.

replacing the hide that covered the windows with burlap, which, when soaked with water, created a cool breeze through the structure.

Homes and lifestyles were basic by today's standards. The pioneers ate what they raised on the farm and harvested from their gardens and from the wild. A cow, pig, and chickens provided protein, and sheep offered wool for clothing. The women worked both on the farm and in the home long before the term "working women" took on a political posture. They assisted in planting and harvesting, tended to the farm animals, and made all their own clothing—spinning wool from the sheep and making the yarn from which cloth was woven. Joseph's daughter remembers "seeing her [mother] spin day after day walking [rocking] back and forth at the old spinning wheel," making yarn for clothing from the sheep's wool.[45] Joseph too had a hand in household affairs. He held to the stern discipline of a sea captain and was strict with his children and how they dressed. He allowed no extravagance or showiness, such as ruffles on his daughter's clothing.[46]

The farm and large gardens yielded grain, hay, vegetables, fruit, calves, pigs, and chickens in a good year. There was little or no money. Purchases were made "in kind," meaning goods of equal value were exchanged. If the harvest was poor, families went without and were at the mercy of others. The disadvantaged later became Joseph's responsibility when he was called into the bishopric of the North Ogden First Ward and put in charge of caring for the needy.

### HOME LIFE IN NORTH OGDEN

Joseph's dugout soon became a food cellar when he purchased thirty-three adjacent acres and constructed his first home. Ann sold her priceless china for the land. The dugout became the cellar underneath the home, where food was stored. The Mountain Water Ditch, part of a hand-dug irrigation system, carried fresh spring water and

---

45. "Coleman Family Papers," 25.

46. Jemima Helen Godfrey, as related to Loraine Goodwin and Myrtle C. Swainston, 3.

snow runoff through the northern boundary of Joseph's acreage.[47] The western border was along what today is 600 East, or Barrett's Lane.[48] The south end is today's 2100 North and was called by the locals Orton and Woodfield Lanes.[49] The eastern boundary today is the LDS Church building's property line. There was a water well dug in the northeast corner of the acreage. A canal cut diagonally through the farm is where the children learned to swim in the summer. The soil above the canal was rich and ideal for growing onions and garden vegetables. The soil below the canal was used to grow hay for the farm animals.[50]

The new home was a two-story structure with a rock foundation and the dirt cellar for food storage. The walls were adobe brick, twelve inches thick, protecting the family from the cold of winter and the heat of summer. There was nothing in the way of luxuries, no built-in closets, no cupboards, no bathrooms. However, compared to the dugout, the house would have seemed like a palace.

### BEN LOMOND MOUNTAIN

Mount Ben Lomond to the north became the sentinel of North Ogden. Joseph's children and North Ogden's John Hall each credit Joseph as being the first to name the mountain, which was named after Scotland's Mount Ben Lomond.[51] The North Ogden Ben Lomond looked so much like Scotland's—which he had often seen

---

47. Floyd J. Woodfield and Clara Woodfield, *A History of North Ogden: Beginnings to 1985* (North Ogden, UT: Empire Printing, 1886), 203.

48. See Greenwell and Kump, *Our North Ogden Pioneers*, 44–64. Today, Barrett Lane runs 600 East from 2100 North to 2550 North.

49. Greenwell and Kump, *Our North Ogden Pioneers*, 360–71, 510–816. Today Orton Lane is 2100 North from Washington to Fruitland Drive. No designation for Woodfield Lane was located.

50. Laura Chadwick Kump to the Godfrey Family, 16 November 1991, Godfrey Family Papers. This letter contains a rough diagram of the property.

51. John Thomas Hall and John Hall Sr. were contemporary residents of North Ogden. See Greenwell and Kump, *Our North Ogden Pioneers*, 251–53. Numerous histories credit Joseph for naming Mount Ben Lomond in North Ogden. See letter from Lorin Card Godfrey to Donald G. Godfrey, 14 November 2012, Godfrey Family Papers, indicating that the director of the North Ogden Cemetery suggested Joseph had indeed named the mountain.

Mount Ben Lomond, to the north of Ogden, Utah. Photo by Steven Ford, www.Fordesign.net.

as he sailed up the Firth of Clyde to the port of Glasgow, Scotland—that his continual reference gave the Utah mountain the same name.[52]

## CHURCH AND COMMUNITY SERVICE

It was but a few years after Joseph had arrived in North Ogden that he was settled and fully involved in community and church service. Brigham Young visited North Ogden on 4 March 1853 and changed their small branch into a ward.[53] Thomas James Dunn was the bishop

---

52. Port Glasgow was a trading port where ships from Europe and Britain were unloaded and taken up river to the city of Glasgow. The naming of North Ogden's Mount Ben Lomond is a debated subject. The tintype of Joseph Godfrey notes that he saw the mountain "every voyage he sailed on Loch Lomond at the foot on Scotland's Ben." This is inaccurate. When Joseph saw the mountain it would have been during the time he sailed up the Firth [Gulf] of Clyde and the River Clyde to Port Glasgow, Scotland. Author's correspondence with Genna Tougher from the University of Glasgow Archive Services; and Barbara McLean from Mitchell Library Archives, Glasgow, 12 December 2012 and 19 December 2012. See "Tintype of Joseph Godfrey," Godfrey Family Papers. Also, Jemima Helen Godfrey, as related to Lorine Goodwin and Myrtle C. Swainston, 1.

53. In Joseph's day, bishoprics served until they were released, which could mean decades of service.

of the ward, and within a few years, Joseph Godfrey became a counselor.[54] Joseph's responsibilities in the ward included caring for the poor. If families were unable to provide for themselves, the bishops' storehouse was a foundation for help.[55] If specific materials were unavailable at the storehouse, Joseph would canvas the neighborhood until he found and acquired what was needed. He was a humanitarian, kind and understanding toward the poor, and always giving more than he took. He often cared for them personally with his own resources. Joseph knew how to dress a wound and set a broken bone. He became known as the "family doctor" for his neighbors and any who were sick, dispensing medical advice learned from his sea travels.

Joseph was an entertaining storyteller, and in the evenings he kept youngsters in the neighborhood and his family enthralled with stories of his adventures at sea and around the world. The far-flung places of the earth were fantasy to the young minds, but reality to him, and he enjoyed these times with the children. Many called him "Father" or "Daddy" Godfrey. He created a unity of purpose within the community. His unique experiences gave him talents that he employed in personal service to others.

Unity did not mean that life was easy. Winters could be severe, and the winters of 1854 and 1855 in North Ogden were particularly trying. From November until March, snow piled up three to four feet and drifted over the foliage and closed all roads.[56] Farm animals were weakened and died of exposure and lack of food. After the long, cold winter, grasshoppers and crickets ate the crops, leading to food scarcities. During such times, Joseph harvested native plants: thistles, sour docks, and sego lily bulbs to sustain his family.[57]

---

54. Woodfield and Woodfield, *A History of North Ogden*, 46.

55. At a bishops' storehouse, goods are not purchased but given to those in need. It is unlike the dole in that service may be required of the recipients, the goal being independence, not dependence. See R. Quinn Gardner, "Bishop's Storehouse," in *Encyclopedia of Mormonism*, ed. Daniel H. Ludlow (New York: Macmillan Publishing, 1992), 1:123–25.

56. Gibson, "Biographical Sketch of Joseph Godfrey," 6.

57. Several varieties of wild thistle can be eaten as greens and are thought to have medicinal properties. Woodfield and Woodfield, *A History of North Ogden*, 19, mentions sourdock or sour dock as a food source. This is a sour-tasting herb, which can be

In good harvest years, food was grown in the summer and stored for the winter. Bounteous harvests produced cellars full of fresh fruits and vegetables. Nothing went to waste. Meats were cured and hung from the rafters, and summer vegetables were dried. There was little sugar, so Joseph created North Ogden's second sugarcane mill, where he crushed the cane and boiled it to extract the liquid molasses. This was the only sweetener the family had for many years.[58]

**MULTIPLE WIVES**

During the 1850s, two more children were born to Joseph and Ann: Reuben (1854) and Matilda (1856); and then tragedy struck. Ann Eliza Reeves Godfrey died (just seventeen days after Matilda was born) on 16 January 1857.[59] Ann was the first woman buried in the North Ogden Cemetery.

Joseph was grief stricken and left alone with a household of four young sons and a new baby daughter. Mary, the wife of Joseph's friend George Coleman, and her son, Moroni, were still in Tooele, Utah, and having a difficult time of their own. Mary had apparently been briefly engaged to a man named Tolman, until they separated due to Mary's melancholy over the prospects of a plural marriage and living in Tooele. When she heard Ann Eliza had died, she left to help her sister's bereaved husband and his family.[60] It is possible that Mary learned of George's death through the North Ogden's bishop, Thomas Dunn. Dunn was a member of the Mormon Battalion for two-and-a-half years and came to North Ogden in 1851. Shortly after Mary came to North Ogden, Joseph proposed marriage. He was fifty-seven, Mary

---

used in salads or cooked carefully. It had to be prepared cautiously or it could make one sick. The bulbs of the sego lily were common in Utah and eaten by the pioneers.

58. Meecham, "A Brief Sketch of the Life of Joseph Godfrey," 4. Also, Woodfield, *A History of North Ogden*, 298.

59. Greenwell and Kump, *Our North Ogden Pioneers*, 236–37.

60. See Jemima Helen Godfrey, as related to Lorine Goodwin and Myrtle C. Swainston, 2. Also, Francelia, "The Story of May Reeve's Life," 6, Godfrey Family Papers. No additional confirmation could be located relative to the relationship between Mary and Tolman.

was thirty-seven, and Moroni was fourteen when they reunited in North Ogden.

Joseph also sought to hire temporary help. He approached the neighboring Jeremiah Price family and asked if their daughter Ann could assist with his children. But Ann was engaged to be married and thus occupied in her own life, so she sent her fifteen-year-old sister, Sarah Ann, to care for Joseph's children and handle household chores. The wedding day, 7 March 1857, was an unusual day. After counseling with President Brigham Young—who had initially been hesitant to encourage Joseph to take more than one wife, until changing his position for some unknown reason—Joseph married both Mary and Sarah Ann. The marriages were performed by President Young in his Salt Lake City office. Despite her previous aversion to polygamy, Mary was now in a polygamous marriage. Mary and Joseph would have four children of their own, while Sarah and Joseph's first child was born in 1860, and eight more would follow. With everyone living in one house, it was a tight fit.

In 1868, Mary and her sister Matilda received word that their brother John died and left them each an inheritance. So the sisters left Utah and headed back east for the inheritance. Mary received $5,000 ($123,335 in today's money), which must have seemed like a fortune.[61] Mary used the money to purchase a "rock house with two lovely big bedrooms" and moved close by Joseph and Sarah's home.[62] She later moved with Moroni and her other children to Park Valley in northern Utah, near the Idaho border. Abundant grasslands in the area attracted the early settlers, including Joseph and several North Ogden families who owned land in the area.[63]

---

61. "Coleman Family Papers," 25. This is the first point at which the 2015-dollar equivalents are introduced. The inflation calculator used in this writing is http://www.westegg.com/inflation/.

62. Francelia, "The Story of May Reeve's Life," 9, Godfrey Family Papers.

63. Greenwell and Kump, *Our North Ogden Pioneers*, 238. Here, Mary's granddaughter Francelia mentions that "there was much tension in the home" and thus Mary decided to move. However, there is no other documentation that supports Francelia's claim—quite the contrary. Greenwell and Kump indicate that Joseph was a frequent visitor and they had two more children. Did Mary move because of conten-

## WAR: AMERICAN INDIANS AND THE CHURCH

The Utah War from 1857 to 1858 was a trying time. The political pressures against the Church and the practice of polygamy were growing and began to affect the daily lives of Mormon families. President James Buchanan sent the US Army to control the Mormons, who began preparing to defend against the army's invasion.[64] The proximity of the army under Colonel Albert S. Johnston prompted a temporary evacuation of North Ogden. Some residents moved to the mountain canyons, others moved south to Provo, and the few that remained in the city prepared to "torch the town," thus robbing the army of food and sustenance.[65] It was a turbulent time for the Saints in Utah, but a "free and full pardon" was eventually extended by Buchanan, and peace was restored.[66]

The relationship between North Ogden residents and Native Americans had its ups and downs. The Shoshone Indians were persistent in begging for food and often commandeered calves or food from the pioneers. One native youngster, caught stealing food, was whipped by a settler, and Joseph was called in to settle the delicate and potentially dangerous conflict. He offered the tribe fruit, meat, and a variety of vegetables, thereby defusing the contention. Afterward, the natives began calling upon him regularly, but their visits made Joseph's children nervous. One described "three large Indians that often came to our home to eat and talk with my father following him as he went about his work 'till he could hardly work."[67]

North Ogden was a long way from Church headquarters, even by horse and buggy, so settlers were encouraged by Church authorities to build a fort to protect themselves against the Indians. The North

---

tion? Or, as with many other plural wives, had she simply established a separate home as antipolygamy pressures increased? See Frederick M. Huchel, *A History of Box Elder County* (Salt Lake City: Utah State Historical Society, 1999), 364.

64. Arrington, *Great Basin Kingdom*, 170–74.

65. Woodfield and Woodfield, *A History of North Ogden*, 11–12. Richard D. Poll, "Utah Expedition," in *Encyclopedia of Mormonism*, ed. Daniel H. Ludlow (New York: Macmillan, 1992), 1500–1502.

66. Arrington, *Great Basin Kingdom*, 192.

67. "Joseph Godfrey of North Ogden Utah," 7–8.

Ogden "fort" was approximately seventy acres surrounded by a rock wall six to eight feet high. The fort was to be constructed within the boundaries of the North Ogden First Ward. However, as hostilities between the Saints and the natives decreased, plans for the fort were abandoned.[68]

Notwithstanding the pioneers' hardships, the Church members of North Ogden formed a united community. During the winters, they gathered in the school house for Church services, dances, spelling bees, plays, and debates. The debates featured rhetorical questions: Which has the greatest influence over man—women or money? Who had been treated more cruelly—"the Indians or the Negro?"[69] Which gives life the most pleasure—the pursuit or the possession? All North Ogden's fun and trials were set within a spiritual perspective. The settlers of the valley, including Joseph's family, shared one common bond—the Church.

Joseph had been the first of his family to join the Mormon faith. In his later years, it was reported that "he went back to England at one time to try and get his family to come to America." His brother and sisters were married and settled, and Joseph was reportedly "not well received by them."[70]

Joseph eventually had twenty-one children, of which six died and fifteen grew to maturity. The children who lived had the same pioneering spirit as their father. All of them moved from North Ogden, scattering throughout the West into Idaho, Montana, and Alberta. Ann Eliza's children moved to Montana, and Mary's and Sarah's children went to Idaho and Alberta.

---

68. Woodfield and Woodfield, *A History of North Ogden*, 10–11, 17. Also Gibson, "Biographical Sketch of Joseph Godfrey," 4–5.

69. Gibson, "Biographical Sketch of Joseph Godfrey," 6. These local debates were a common form of small-community entertainment, along with the traveling Chautauqua speakers, local social dances, singing, and picnics. During the nineteenth and twentieth centuries, the Chautauqua was a popular entertainment enterprise, which included vaudeville entertainers, traveling preachers, politicians, and lecturers who traveled the circuit.

70. See Jemima Helen Godfrey, as related to Lorine Goodwin and Myrtle C. Swainston, 3.

## THE MAN JOSEPH GODFREY

The man Joseph Godfrey can be characterized as a world sailor, a humanitarian, and an individual dedicated to the gospel. Joseph, once an abused runaway child, grew in experience and in stature as he learned the skills of a sailor, becoming a man of love and caring. He stood only five feet seven inches tall, weighing about 150 pounds. One can only assume that he would have been mostly muscle given his labor at sea and on land. His eyes were blue, and he had light brown hair, which was never combed. His face was rugged, with a heavy jaw line that reflected firmness and discipline. He read without glasses and had almost a full set of teeth even at age eighty. He knew the world of his day more extensively than his associates did—he had sailed around it.

Sketch of Joseph Godfrey (1800–1880). Courtesy of North Ogden Historical Museum.

Joseph was a community humanitarian and a member of the North Ogden bishopric, given the charge to care for the poor. It was said, "He could go into a group and pass a hat around, and the people would freely contribute, without saying a word or asking what or for whom it was for, all knowing that someone, whom he [Joseph] did not care to mention, was in need of help."[71] If there was a need, he was first to give. He gave away his blacksmith and carpentry tools to young settlers. He created peace with the Indians; he believed it was better to feed and befriend them than to fight. The Indians sought him out,

---

71. Thersa Chadwick Lowder, "Life of Joseph Godfrey," 3, Godfrey Family Papers. Lowder was Joseph's granddaughter.

calling him "Emigary," a native word meaning friend or peacemaker.[72] He was a sexton that cared for the aging and, when necessary, performed the responsibilities of undertaker. He was often asked to speak at the funerals of those whom he loved.[73]

Nowhere was his humanitarianism reflected more than in his family. He did not seek the responsibilities of plural marriage. His marriage to Mary Reeves, his sister-in-law, helped them both through difficult times. His marriage to Sarah Ann Price was at the suggestion of Brigham Young to ease the Price family's and Joseph's own difficulties. Sarah now had a home of her own and was no longer a dependent. To ease Sarah's labors, Joseph bought her a Singer sewing machine, one of the first in North Ogden. Joseph's family reflected the life of the times and the challenges of the pioneers.

Spiritual peace was in their hearts, but the physical trials of pioneering filled their daily lives. After Joseph's first wife, Ann, had died, Sarah was the only wife that lived in his house, as Mary owned her own home. Joseph would die prior to the Edmunds Act of 1882, but they had joined the Church at a time when persecutions against polygamous Mormons were growing. He and Ann had been driven from their home in Nauvoo in the middle of winter and lost children from resulting illnesses, but they never lost their faith.

On his eightieth birthday, his neighbors gave him a surprise party. It was a community and family picnic at his home and supplied "everything to make the heart glad." Thomas B. Helm, master of ceremonies, called the gathering to order, and after much singing and food, Joseph was asked to say a few words.[74] "He gave a brief history of his life, commencing with his early boyhood and the circumstances of his joining the church some forty years ago; his association with the Prophet Joseph [Smith]; the mobs; his starting to Carthage with the Prophet

---

72. This word is sometimes seen spelled "*H*migary."

73. "Died," *Deseret News*, 26 February 1880, 16. Frank Esshom, *Pioneers and Prominent Men of Utah* (Salt Lake City: Utah Pioneers Book Publishing Company, 1913), 892.

74. Helm was a resident of nearby Pleasant View, Utah. See Woodfield and Woodfield, *A History of North Ogden*, 125.

Joseph; his journey to Utah, and its early settlement." It was a fitting tribute to a local leader. "May Father Godfrey live to see many more such occasions," said the host.⁷⁵

Joseph was healthy, but while husking corn sometime in the late fall, he felt a sudden chill. He developed pneumonia and in a weakening state suffered a stroke. He died 16 December 1880. He was eighty years, nine months, and twelve days old. His funeral was said to have been the largest to date ever held in North Ogden. He was revered for his memories, his testimony of the gospel, his loyalty, his citizenship, and his being "a zealous, unweary, an indefatigable worker for the good of the public."⁷⁶

## SARAH ANN PRICE

Sarah Ann Price (1842–1928) became Joseph Godfrey's third wife. She was born 7 February 1842, in Rhymney, Monmouthshire, South Wales. Rhymney sits on the north side of the Bristol Channel, fifty-three miles north of the city of Bristol. In the mid-1800s, Bristol was a small ironworks factory town using the coal from the local pit mines. Sarah's father, Jeremiah Price, was a superintendent at one of the mines and considered well-off financially.⁷⁷ He owned several homes in the area that he rented out to the mine workers.

Sarah Ann Price-Godfrey (1842–1928). Courtesy of Godfrey Family Organization.

---

75. "A Surprise Party," *Ogden Standard Examiner*, 13 March 1800, 2. The article was written by an unknown subscriber. This practice was common in frontier journalism at the time as locals and travelers shared information.

76. Lowder, "Life of Joseph Godfrey," 4. "Died," *Deseret News*, 12 January 1881, 16.

77. This name appears with several different spellings in family records: Jermiah, Jeramiah, and Jermia—Jeremiah is correct. LaVerna Coleman Ackroyd, in her

Jeremiah, his son Josiah, and his daughter Sarah Ann met the Mormon missionaries in 1851. They were baptized the night of 4 December 1851 under a bridge and out of sight to avoid being seen and avert the persecution that would follow. However, when Jeremiah's employer found out that he had joined the LDS faith, he was fired. The discrimination created family hardship. He lost his salary. Funds that he had lent earlier LDS immigrants went unpaid and now they were unable to help other immigrants, let alone repay their own debts. He was shunned by his former employer, friends, and peers, unable to sell his home and belongings at a fair market price for his voyage to America.[78]

Sarah's mother, Jane Morgan Price, was a petite woman with dark hair, thick dark eyebrows, and dark skin. She apprenticed as a dressmaker and was a quick learner. She sold her dresses and clothing in the Bristol marketplace, which greatly helped with family finances. While sewing at home she displayed dresses and hats in the window and sold them out of their house. She valued a clean, neat home and scrubbed the floor of their home with sand, making the floor boards white and smooth. One day, while working in the house, their cow escaped the pasture. Jane left her scrubbing and ran to corral the cow. When she returned, she found her oldest daughter, Jane, still a baby, had somehow fallen into the bucket and drowned.[79]

Sarah spent much of her childhood with her grandmother, Margaret Liewelln Morgan. Why she lived with her grandparents is unknown, but it was five miles from her parents' home in Merthyr Tydvil.

---

untitled single-page history, indicated this was a limestone mine. Other sources indicate coal being mined.

78. Myrtle C. Swainston, "Brief History of Jane Morgan Price," Godfrey Family Papers. Myrtle C. Swainston was a great granddaughter of Sarah. "Jeremiah Price and Jane Morgan Price," Godfrey Family Papers. "Jane Morgan Price," Godfrey Family Papers.

79. Myrtle C. Swainston, "Brief History of Jane Morgan Price," Godfrey Family Papers. Myrtle C. Swainston was a great granddaughter of Sarah. La Verna Coleman Ackroyd, "Jeremiah Price and Jane Morgan Price," Godfrey Family Papers. La Verna Coleman Ackroyd is also a granddaughter of Sarah. Jemima Campbell, "Jane Morgan Price," Godfrey Family Papers.

Sarah walked the distance often and was frightened by the loud men and noise of the large ironworks factory as well as by a cemetery she passed on her journeys.[80] The family's faith had always been strong. As Methodists, they walked a short distance every week to Sunday School, singing gospel hymns along the way. When they joined the Mormon Church, the walk became five miles. Walking was their only option for transportation.

### BROTHER AND SISTER COME WEST

The Price family wanted to join the European exodus of Mormons to America and the Great Salt Lake Valley. The unemployed Jeremiah was particularly anxious, but his wife was reluctant to leave her fine two-story English brick home.[81] They decided to send two of their children first, with the remaining children and parents to join them in a few years. The two children to emigrate were eleven-year-old Sarah and her older brother Josiah, age nineteen.[82] May was afraid, as any mother would be, to let them go alone, but she relented in the end. Their journey took six weeks. They walked from their home to Merthyr, caught the train to Swansea, and sailed from there to Liverpool. They got lost wandering through the city, but eventually boarded the ship *Jersey* on 25 January 1853. Sarah celebrated her eleventh birthday while crossing the Atlantic.[83]

---

80. Jemima Campbell, "Jane Morgan Price," Godfrey Family Papers.

81. Myrtle C. Swainston, "Brief History of Jane Morgan Price," Godfrey Family Papers.

82. Swainston's history indicates Sarah was nine years of age when she came to America. The Thersa Chadwick Louder history, "Sarah Ann Price Godfrey," indicates she was ten. These appear to be errors. If Sarah was born in 1842 and sailed for the United States in 1853, then she was eleven.

83. La Verna Coleman Ackroyd, "Jeremiah Price and Jane Morgan Price." Louder, "Sarah Ann Price Godfrey," Godfrey Family Papers. At this point, Joseph Godfrey would have already been settled in North Ogden. Jeremiah and Jane would leave 17 April 1855 and arrive in North Ogden in October 1855. The cost for an adult passage was $800 ($22,432).

The *Jersey* sailed south over the Atlantic Ocean, through the Gulf of Mexico to New Orleans, and up the Mississippi River, where it landed in Keokuk, Iowa, at the state's southeastern tip. At the time, Keokuk was one of the centers used for outfitting the Mormon settlers and other westward migrants.[84] In the spring of 1853, "2,548 Saints, 360 wagons, 1,440 oxen, and 720 milk cows" came across the plains in ten different wagon trains from Keokuk.[85] Sarah and her brother were with the Joseph Young Company.

Sarah had no wagon, no handcart, and no shoes; she walked the Plains barefoot. One day, she was playing with the other girls along the Platte River, where she almost lost her life. The children had been running along the river banks "killing rattlesnakes, swinging on the vines of the trees." Each child took a turn pulling a makeshift play raft from the shore as the other children rode the water's edge. It was Sarah's turn to ride when the elders called the children to return to camp. Without thinking, the girls dropped the rope and started running. The raft, caught by a strong current, began gliding rapidly down the river. Sarah screamed for help, and the men had a difficult time retrieving the raft and pulling the child to safety. In the end, no one was hurt and Sarah was rescued.[86]

One day, while she was walking next to a wagon, an Indian from the Plains walked up, took her by the hand, and began walking alongside her. The intruder startled the company, and when "Brother Young saw the two, he ordered Sarah into the wagon, but the Indian would not let go of her hand," so the whole company stopped. They fed the

---

84. Andrew Jensen, *Encyclopedic History of The Church of Jesus Christ of Latter-day Saints*, 398.

85. William G. Hartley, "Mormons and Early Iowa History (1838 to 1858): Eight Distinct Connections," *The Annals of Iowa* 59 (Summer 2000): 217–60.

86. "Sarah Ann Price Godfrey, As Told by Herself," 29 October 1928, handwritten and typewritten copies, Godfrey Family Papers; Josephine Swensen, "Sarah Ann Price Godfrey," typewritten document in Godfrey Family Papers; Ellen Clair Weaver Shaeffer, "Sarah Ann Price Godfrey, 1842–1928," 2009, 6.

Indian, after which everyone moved on.[87] The company arrived in Salt Lake City on 10 October 1853.

Sarah earned her keep, working for room and board. She lived with several families over the next few years, all the time being observed carefully by her older brother Josiah, who helped her move each time it was required. At one time, she lived with three different families in one room. Some families were hard on her, treating her poorly, and others were kind. She was sent to school from time to time.[88] In the two years before her parents arrived, she was "bumped around from pillar to post" in a life full of uncertainty. She later described her duties as "running errands, gathering wood . . . , rocking the cradle that always seemed to be in use, or the many small things that small hands could do to help lighten the work of older folks."[89]

Sarah's parents, Jeremiah and Jane Price, arrived in the United States on 22 May 1855. It had been a heartbreaking passage. They lost a child at sea, but they did not turn back. They had sailed for Philadelphia on the ship *Chimborazo*, a journey lasting thirty-five days. The ship carried 431 people who were mostly financed with funds from the Perpetual Emigrating Fund.[90] They took the train from Philadelphia to Pittsburgh, a steamboat along the Ohio and Mississippi Rivers to St. Louis, and then they camped at Gravery, Missouri, three miles north. Here they boarded a steamboat to Mormon Grove, near Atchison, Kansas, where the company was outfitted and organized. There were 350 people and 39 wagons in the sixth PEF company. Charles A. Harper was captain. They departed between 25 and 31 July 1855 on a three-month journey before they arrived in Salt Lake City around the 28 or 31 October 1855.[91]

---

87. Josephine Swensen [daughter], "Sarah Ann Price Godfrey," typewritten document in Godfrey Family Papers.

88. Shaeffer, "Sarah Ann Price Godfrey, 1842–1928," 6; Louder, "Sarah Ann Price Godfrey," Godfrey Family Papers.

89. Shaeffer, "Sarah Ann Price Godfrey, 1842–1928," 8.

90. Conway B. Sonne, *Ships, Saints, and Mariners: A Maritime Encyclopedia of Mormon Migration, 1830–1890* (Salt Lake City: University of Utah Press, 1987), 42.

91. "Immigration List," *Deseret News*, 12 September 1855, 214–15.

Jeremiah, age fifty-one, and Jane, age forty-six, first settled in Payson, Utah. Sarah's mother continued selling her fine hand-sewn clothing as she had done in England, and they started a poultry business raising chickens and selling them in town. On 19 March 1860, while Jane was doing the washing, Jeremiah and their son John were crossing Utah Lake on the ice to deliver chickens to their customers when the ice in the center of the lake broke and they fell through. Jeremiah pushed John out of the freezing water and John ran for help. Jeremiah had frozen to death before help had arrived. It was a blow to Sarah and the family.[92]

Their son Josiah had already acquired property in North Ogden and started to build an adobe home. Sarah and her mother and family moved north—close to Joseph Godfrey's home—to be together and help one another. Sarah had already married Joseph, and now her family were their neighbors.[93]

**THE YOUNGEST BRIDE**

In comparison to the newly arrived Price family, who continued to struggle with life's tragedies, Joseph Godfrey was an established member of the North Ogden community. Josiah likely knew Joseph, and Sarah first met him when he visited her home to enlist the aid of her older sister Ann. However, Ann was engaged to Rosser Jenkins and unable to accept employment.[94] Sarah was given the offer and had three weeks to make up her mind. She accepted. She worked for Joseph and his family for a month before Joseph proposed and they were married. Joseph and the family were very conscious of the age difference between Joseph and Sarah. She was yet a teenager, fifteen years of age; he

---

92. La Verna Coleman Ackroyd, "A Few Lines About Our Grandparents," typewritten manuscript (n.d.); Jemima Campbell, "Jeremiah Price," handwritten manuscript (n.d.); "Jeremiah Price," *Daughters of Utah Pioneers, Our Pioneer Heritage* 2 (1959): 170; typewritten excerpt in Godfrey Family Papers.

93. Shaeffer, "Sarah Ann Price Godfrey, 1842–1928," 7. "Sarah Ann Price Godfrey, As Told to Her Daughter Josephine Swensen," Godfrey Family Papers.

94. Shaeffer, "Sarah Ann Price Godfrey, 1842–1928," 7–8.

was fifty-seven.[95] Their marriage, performed by Brigham Young, was to provide care for a young "daughter of Father in Heaven." Family records report that Joseph "did not live with her until she became a mature woman." Their first son, John, was born almost three years later on 12 December 1859. It was the first period of stability Sarah had in her life. She lived as a child with both her grandmother and her parents in England. She traveled across the Atlantic Ocean and walked the Great Plains. She shuffled from house to house, working for her room and board. She had lost her father in a tragic accident. The only constant in her teenage life, for almost six years, had been her older brother Josiah. As Joseph's wife, she now had an anchor and a home of her own. Her first anchor was the gospel; her second, a stable family. Her own father had been middle-aged when he had married her mother, a teenage bride.[96] Sarah lived the pioneer life with Joseph, working the farm and spending time assisting others. She was thirty-eight when Joseph died. Their youngest child was one month old.

**THE LADY**

Sarah Ann Price Godfrey was a small woman. She wore her hair parted at the center and braided down her back. She had a sharp nose and loving eyes. She always wore a black satin dress. She spent her life in church and family service. She taught Sunday School and was in the Primary presidency. She, like Joseph, was compassionate and caring. She was set apart with other sisters to "wash and anoint the sick, prepare and lay out the dead for burial."[97] The hardships of her earlier life gave her empathy for others.

---

95. Sarah was born on 7 February 1842, got married 7 March 1857, and had her first child on 12 December 1859.

96. Family records indicate Mary was eighteen when she married Jeremiah Price. Mary was born 28 January 1810, got married 20 February 1929, and gave birth to her first child in 1830. See Myrtle C. Swainston, "Brief History of Jane Morgan Price." Jemiama Campbell, "Jane Morgan Price and Clarice Godfrey," Godfrey Family Papers; La Verna Coleman Ackroyd, "Jeremiah Price and Jane Morgan Price," Godfrey Family Papers.

97. Swenson, "Sarah Ann Price Godfrey," 4.

At fifty-four years of age, she wanted to travel and spend time with her children. In 1896, she formally achieved her citizenship in the United States of America so that she could move about freely and live where she wanted.[98] By 1898, she had homesteaded 160 acres near Choteau, Montana.[99] Her children homesteaded throughout central Montana and southern Alberta. She spent a good deal of her later life with them in Idaho, Montana, Utah, and Alberta. At eighty-six years of age she recognized that her time in life was short; "she was glad that she was going" and remarked that "she would not trade her husband [Joseph] for any man on earth."[100]

At the time of her death, she and Joseph's progeny numbered nine children, seventy grandchildren, 117 great-grandchildren, and four great-great-grandchildren.[101] It was Sarah and Joseph's eighth son, Melvin, who, with several of his brothers, would eventually make the trek into Canada.

---

98. Declaration of Intention, United States of America District Court of the Tenth Judicial District of the State of Montana and for the County of Choteau, 6 March 1896, copy in Godfrey Family Papers.

99. Homestead Certificate 4505, Helena, Montana Land Office, 6 April 1898, copy in Godfrey Family Papers. Homestead Certificate 1372, Helena, Montana Land Office, 25 November 1902, copy in Godfrey Family Papers.

100. "The Life History of Sarah Ann Price," written by an unidentified granddaughter, typewritten document in Godfrey Family Papers.

101. Swenson, "Sarah Ann Price," 4; correspondence from Floyd Godfrey [grandson] to the author, 6 February 1985, Godfrey Family Papers.

# ON THE AMERICAN FRONTIER

CHAPTER 2

Joseph Godfrey's family felt the venom of anti-Mormon mobs attacking Nauvoo, Illinois, during the winter of 1845–46. They were forced to abandon their home and farm, and they lost children to illness during the cold winter months, but they continued faithfully working and saving money to make the trek to Utah. The western frontier was the new landscape of the lives of Joseph and Sarah Godfrey. They were shaped by their faith and the immigration experiences of the Mormon Trail. In Utah, they evaded most of the persecutions surrounding polygamy because Joseph's first wife, Ann, had died and his second wife, Mary, purchased and lived in her own home, leaving only Sarah in the original home. Their children, however, were keenly aware of the tensions surrounding the US marshals hunting the polygamists.

At the same time, more people were moving westward, with settlers traveling along the Oregon Trail to the California gold rush.[1] And Mormon settlements sprung up throughout the West and northward into the Canadian territories. Families moved at

---

1. See Eugene E. Campbell, "The Mormon Gold Mining Mission of 1849," BYU Studies nos. 1–2 (Autumn 1959–Winter 1969): 19–31. Also Ann M. Buttler

first to secure religious freedom, avoiding the persecution of Missouri and Illinois and later the increasing antipolygamist sentiment of the United States government. By the late 1800s, the government wrestled legal control of Utah from the Mormon Church leadership and awarded it to non-Mormons. This action created increased persecution and the division of polygamous families. Polygamist husbands were driven into hiding throughout Utah, Idaho, Wyoming, and Arizona, and even internationally in Mexico and Canada.

The Oregon Trail was used by people of all faiths and ambitions, coming from Europe and the eastern United States into farmland and the California gold fields. These movements all intersected with the Mormons. The Utah Latter-day Saints who remained in place often restocked westward travelers and freight wagons with the necessary provisions for their journeys as well as took advantage of some unique missionary opportunities as venturous travelers passed through Utah.[2] The Saints on the move also used these trails and the rapidly growing railroads to seek employment and get out of harm's way. The marshals looking to arrest polygamists focused primarily on Church leadership, but no one felt safe. The expanding population of the West created farms, new towns, and industry; aided in the building of the Mormon economy; and provided new places to hide.

US expansion spread when the transcontinental railroad was completed, followed by the north–south spur lines, transporting goods and people where they had never traveled before. Temporary railroad towns emerged and often disappeared quickly when construction ended. They provided work and refuge for the polygamous fathers. It is in this context that the Saints moved into Canada, Mexico, and throughout the West. The earliest movers had only covered wagons,

---

and Kenneth L. Holmes, *Covered Wagon Women*, vol. 1, *Diaries and Letters from the Western Trails, 1840–1849* (Lincoln: Bison Press, University of Nebraska, 1995).

2. James Henry Martineau, for example, was on his way to the California gold fields when he veered south from the Oregon Trail to see the Mormons. He ended up settling in Utah. See Donald G. Godfrey and Rebecca S. Martineau-McCarty, *An Uncommon Common Pioneer: The Journals of James Henry Martineau, 1828–1918* (Provo, UT: Religious Studies Center, 2008).

and then the railroads, to move about. Young Melvin Godfrey would be among these frontier movers.

Melvin Godfrey (1878–1956), the eighth son of Joseph and Sarah Ann Price Godfrey, was born 15 October 1878 at 11 a.m. His father was seventy-eight years old. Two years later, Josephine completed the family and was barely a month old when their father died. All that Melvin remembered of his father was being lifted by a family member to "look in the coffin" to see him.[3] Melvin and Josephine were raised by their widowed mother and their older brothers and sisters. They lived with Joseph's other children, all growing up as a close-knit family unit. They were "imbued with the pioneer spirit," bonded together in work, love, and friendship. Melvin's childhood was challenging. He was without a father. Daily farm chores required physical labor, as was the norm of rural farm life. His mother and sisters took care of the little ones as well as handling chores. They all learned the meaning of hard work—milking cows and feeding the cattle, horses, pigs, and chickens. As Melvin grew, his responsibilities included four acres of onions that needed constant weeding. Its yield was 1,400 bags per acre, for a total of 5,600 bags. This kept a boy busy. "Josiah and I done most of the

Melvin Godfrey (1878–1956). Courtesy of Melvin Godfrey Family.

---

3. "Brief History of Melvin Godfrey," Godfrey Family Papers.

weeding, crawling on hands and knees and topping the onions."⁴ They worked in the garden and the fields of hay, onions, and sugar beets. They were poor. Melvin had no clothes of his own, save for "hand-me-downs" from his brothers—"any kind of clothes . . . would do that would cover a person['s] body," he wrote. At school, he wore a pair of brass-toed boots and an old jacket hood covering his head.⁵ During these pioneering years, everyone made do and learned to make what they needed. Melvin learned rugged independence and the importance of education.

### EDUCATING THE FAMILY

Education was actively encouraged by Melvin's family, the community, and the Church.⁶ It was part of growing up. And it was important enough that schoolhouses were among the first buildings constructed in Utah communities. The older Godfrey children attended North Ogden's first schoolhouse. It was a log house built in 1851, just one year before Joseph arrived.

By 1854, there were forty-seven families in the community, and the Godfrey family was one of them.⁷ They used a second schoolhouse, built four years later using adobe brick. The school had an east–west layout, 30 x 60 square feet. The inside furnishings were handmade. Benches were pine logs hauled from the mountains and sawed in half. Children sat on them or, if they were writing, would kneel on the floor and use the flat surface of the log as a desktop on which to write. Individual chalk slate boards were used for drawing and multiplication questions. Writing quills were even made by the students, likely shaped from a feather. During winter, an open fireplace at one end of the building provided the only heat. Any classroom books were those

---

4. Josiah was Melvin's older brother, born 1874. "Brief History of Melvin Godfrey," 4.

5. "Brief History of Melvin Godfrey," 4.

6. LDS scriptures promoting education include D&C 93:53 and 88:78–79.

7. Woodfield, *A History of North Ogden: Beginnings to 1905* (Ogden, UT: Empire Printing, 1986), 65.

North Ogden school of Melvin Godfrey's Childhood. Courtesy of North Ogden Museum.

of families who had brought them across the Plains. Tuition was $3 ($80) per term and could be paid either in kind, cash, or service. Service included gathering wood from the canyons for the fire, janitorial work, or providing teacher support.[8]

Melvin and Josephine started their education in North Ogden's third schoolhouse, which was constructed in 1882. This was the same year that the Edmunds Act, an antipolygamy legislation, was passed in the US Congress. Melvin's first school year was 1885–86. His class met in the new red brick structure known as the Sage Brush Academy. It had two windows. Students still sat on the log benches, but these were cut just long enough for only two children. Heat still radiated from a stove in the middle of the room. By 1890, Melvin's class moved into the new Red Brick Schoolhouse, a major step forward, with more windows, five rooms, and a tower. The community and its children were growing.

---

8. Woodfield, *History of North Ogden*, 43–47.

Melvin and the children of North Ogden started their school days like many of the pioneer children. School began *after* morning chores at home. Then, as today, school got the kids out of the house as well as gave them an education. Children all walked to school in the sun, snow, or rain. Before class started, they played outside. At the sound of the bell, they lined up and marched inside. There were no age requirements for starting or ending a student's school experience. There were no grade levels. The curriculum focused on reading, writing, arithmetic, penmanship, memorization, and manners. Each day began with the recitation of the Pledge of Allegiance and the Lord's Prayer. Discipline was strict and swiftly administered with a hickory stick. A turn-of-the-century song depicting the discipline was written by Will D. Cobbs, "School Days." The lyrics sang, "School days, school days, Dear old golden rule days, 'readin' and 'ritin' and 'rithmetic,' Taught to the tune of a hickory stick." The stick kept the children in check. They talked only when called upon or when they raised their right hand for permission to speak. They could be excused only for a drink of water or going to the bathroom, which would have been outside. There were generally two terms in the school year: summer, from May to August, and winter, from November through April. These schools did not always see boys during planting and harvest seasons. They were needed in the fields. It did not affect their grades, as when they returned they simply picked up with the reader where they were prior to harvest.[11] Unlike today, the pioneer children were grouped according to skills and ability levels, not age or grade levels. They worked themselves through a series of readers. A "reader" was a saddle-stitched workbook which presented drills and checks on student comprehension. They were an organized series of individual progressive learning exercises. Children colored, worked the problems, and basically wrote in and all over their own individual books. When the exercises of each reader were completed and checked by the teacher, then the student advanced to the next level reader. One teacher taught all reader levels.[9]

---

9. See John C. Moffitt, *The History of Education in Utah* (Salt Lake City: John Clifton Moffitt, 1946).

Melvin was seven years old when he was given his first reader.¹⁰ His schoolmaster was John W. Gibson.¹¹ Mr. Gibson was a harsh, no-nonsense teacher. His hickory stick enforced a "no talking" rule even when students whispered to the pupil in the next seat. He allowed no one out of his or her place during school hours. Students of all ages had a great respect for him, as well as a fear of his corporal punishment with the hickory stick across a pupil's hand or hind end for even the smallest infraction. Melvin was afraid of Gibson. He dared not even raise his hand to ask to be excused. So he said, one day, "I had to fill my pants. Then he [Gibson] sure did let me out." However, these were also the days when, if a child was in trouble at school, he or she was in more trouble at home, and so he "got a good 'lickin' from [his] sister, when [he] could not [even] help it."¹²

Melvin did like his second teacher, John M. Bishop.¹³ Now eleven years old, Melvin had made it through the first four readers. His interest in learning was encouraged, and he appeared to enjoy school. Edward Joseph Davis was his third teacher, and he helped Melvin "finish up to the eighth reader learning more than I ever learned in all my schooling."

Melvin's final instructor was a young lady named Jane West.¹⁴ She was a "lovely person, quiet, gentle and loved music." She took an interest

---

10. "Brief History of Melvin Godfrey," 4.

11. Schoolmaster denotes the male gender. This Gibson would appear to be the same person who would later write a Joseph Godfrey history. See Floyd J. Woodfield, *A History of North Ogden: Beginnings to 1985* (Ogden, UT: Empire Printing, 1986), 47, 51. Also Richard C. Roberts and Richard W. Sadler, *A History of Weber County* (Salt Lake City: Utah State Historical Society, 1997), 90. Gibson was also one of the Probate Appraisers in 1898 when Joseph's estate went to the Second District Court, Weber County, Utah. No. 693, Weber Country Second District Court Probate Case Files, Utah State Archives.

12. "Brief History of Melvin Godfrey," 4.

13. John M. Bishop was the principal of the North Ogden Schools from 1892 to 1893 and again from 1894 to 1895. Woodfield, *A History of North Ogden*, 51–53. Greenwell and Kump note that the bishop and his wife were both teachers. See Greenwell and Kump, *Our North Ogden Pioneers*, 40.

14. Jane West's name appears in the records as Josie, Janie, and Jane. Jane is correct. See Greenwell and Kump, *Our North Ogden Pioneers*, 69, 150, 205, 240.

in Melvin and helped him finish his ninth and tenth readers. It was she who "finished my education."[15] Melvin was stricken with this teacher, but his success might also have had something to do with the fact that she was boarding at his home and with his family. In short, communication between mother, teacher, and student was extremely efficient.[16]

**GROWING-UP STRAINS**

Melvin and the children of North Ogden felt the increasing strain of the 1882 Edmunds Act and particularly the later Edmunds-Tucker Act of 1887.[17] They were confused about why the US Congress had passed laws deeming their families illegal. They saw the result from a child's point of view. The 1887 act awarded court jurisdiction to non-Mormons and set punishment for polygamy at six months in prison and a fine of $300 ($7,394), a fine that a family could not hope to pay. For the children, the scariest threats were from swarms of deputies who patrolled belligerently through the streets. The youngsters panicked when marshals dramatically burst into their homes unannounced. "Terror, frustration and embarrassment were multiplied many fold among all husbands, wives and children of plural marriages." Families were split. The polygamist fathers disappeared into the Mormon Underground to avoid persecution. They were forced to leave wives and children without support.

Although Melvin's polygamist father had died, Melvin knew polygamist families within this tight-knit community. It was during this time that he finished his education, worked in northern Utah, and then left home to work in Oregon's construction boom.

---

15. "Brief History of Melvin Godfrey," 5; also Greenwell and Kump, *Our North Ogden Pioneers*, 240.

16. Her boarding in Joseph's home could have provided extra income for the family and covered tuition for the children.

17. For the broad effects of the Edmunds and Edmunds-Tucker Act, see Arrington, *Great Basin Kingdom*, 358–61, 376–79.

As a teen, Melvin led a herd of horses to the grasslands of northern Utah at "the Promontory and lost every one of them."[18] The Promontory is a mountain in northern Box Elder County, almost at the Idaho border. He took a herd north for summer grazing. His family owned land in the area where the grass was reportedly "waiving around their horses' knees, and occasionally as high as the stirrups of the saddles."[19] Of the horses with him that day, Melvin "lost every one of them."[20]

Melvin reported that his horses were stolen and that he had spent the entire summer searching for them. The only thing he found was a "beautiful saddle." A few months later, the owner claimed the saddle, and Melvin received a fifty-cent reward for his efforts ($13). The horses were a major loss, and fifty cents was a limited reward for a young man who was pasturing the horses some fifty miles north of his home. There was a goodly bit of cash value lost when the herd was rustled away: a saddle valued around $60 ($1,536), work horses around $150 ($3,839), and a good saddle horse at $200 ($5,119). What remains unknown were the number of horses in his herd. But by any calculation, this was a significant loss to the family and a traumatic experience for a young man.

At age sixteen, Melvin was finished with his schooling and "ran away from home."[21] In his writings, he gave no reason, but had just lost a valuable herd of horses to rustlers. Antipolygamy antagonism, fear, embarrassment, and tensions were high throughout the community, and Melvin was a robust, active young man confirming his independence.

---

18. "The Promontory" is a mountain in Park Valley at the northern end of the Promontory Mountain Range. Frederick M. Huchel, *A History of Box Elder County* (Salt Lake City: Utah State Historical Society, 1999), 363. It should not be confused with Promontory Point, which is at the south end of the Promontory Mountain Range extending down into the Great Salt Lake or Promontory, Utah, which was a railroad town near the point of the railways meeting, nor should it be confused with the Promontory Summit, where the first transcontinental railroad actually met 10 May 1869.

19. Huchel, *History of Box Elder County*, 363–64. Also, it is worth noting that Joseph Godfrey and Moroni Coleman were among the first landowners of Park Valley, Utah. Dryland farming and abundant springs made it ideal for summer grazing. Without much rainfall, settlers did not stay long.

20. Huchel, *History of Box Elder County*, 363.

21. "Brief History of Melvin Godfrey," 5.

Melvin's destination was Huntington, 380 miles northwest of Ogden and just across the eastern Idaho border into Oregon. Huntington was originally a small trading post until the railroads and construction stretched along the Snake River into the Northwest. Then it quickly transformed into a Union Pacific town, as it sat next to the junction of the Oregon Short Line and the Oregon Railroad, and next to the later expansion of the Northwest Railroad Company line down the Snake River. Melvin likely traveled northwest using the Oregon Short Line railway. He found work in Huntington with the railroad crews and in related building projects. It was physical, strenuous work amidst a rather crude, unruly crowd.

Melvin worked a while and "soon found out home was the best place and went back."[22] The railroads attracted a transient, rough drinking crew. These workers lived outside the gospel standards ingrained by his home and community. The work was every bit as taxing as weeding onions, and he missed his family. He returned home, and in the act of rededicating himself, he was baptized anew 28 February 1894.[23] Rebaptism was a common practice at the time, and it reflected the sixteen-year-old's renewed commitment.

**COURTSHIP**

Back in North Ogden, Melvin worked the farm until just past his twentieth birthday. Topping and bagging onions remained his primary job, second only to chasing girls around "N.O. [North Ogden] wild as a Billy goat, not mentioning some of the things I done."[24] "Chasing girls" segued into "chasing around with girls," as was natural for his age. The

---

22. "Brief History of Melvin Godfrey," 5.

23. Rebaptism was not required of the Church, but it was practiced by many Saints between 1836 and 1897, before it was halted. It was part of the Mormon Reformation. See "Rebaptism," H. Dean Garrett and Paul H. Peterson, "Reformation (LDS) of 1856–1857," in *Encyclopedia of Mormonism*, 3:1194, 1197–98. See also other rebaptisms of family in "Sketch of the Life of Richard Jones, Jr.," Floyd Godfrey Files, Cardston, Alberta, 2. Also, Edna B. Robertson [granddaughter], "Personal History: Richard Jones," Godfrey Family Papers.

24. "Brief History of Melvin Godfrey," 3, 5.

Eva Jones–Godfrey (1879–1963), with daughter Lottie and son Floyd. Courtesy of Melvin Godfrey Family.

special one in the pursuit was Eva Jones (1879–1963), daughter of Richard Jones and Elizabeth Wickham.[25] Melvin wrote that he talked Eva into marrying him. "I don't think she ever did think much of me," he said, "but I talked her into it so she did [it] to get rid of me," he joked.[26]

Marrying was not really a good way to get rid of a suitor, and Eva was, indeed, in love. She had fallen in love with Melvin at age fifteen, when her father had allowed her to attend dances: "I fell in love with Melvin Godfrey w[h]ich [whom] I married 4-years later." Melvin was ordained an elder on 3 March 1897 by his future father-in-law, Richard Jones, and Melvin and Eva were married in the Salt Lake Temple the next day 4 March 1897.[27] They were both nineteen when they married. The marriage was solemnized by John R.

---

25. Greenwell and Kump, *Our North Ogden Pioneers*, 301–2.

26. "Brief History of Melvin Godfrey," 5.

27. As a child, Melvin was blessed by his father 5 March 1878 and baptized by Newman Henry Barker 18 October 1888. See Joseph Godfrey North Ogden Ward History, 110–11. B. F. Blaylock Ward Historian, Genealogical Library, North Ogden Ward Records.

Winder and witnessed by William W. Riter and George Romney.[28] After Winder had completed the sealing, he suggested to Melvin, "Kiss the bride." Melvin later recalled, "I did not even know enough to do so."[29] They celebrated their fiftieth wedding anniversary in 1941 and lived together for fifty-nine years before Melvin passed away on 6 April 1956.

## FAMILY MIGRATION

Eva Jones was the youngest of six children born to Richard Jones and his second wife, Elizabeth Wickham, in North Ogden on 25 May 1878. She was five months Melvin Godfrey's senior, a spiritually sensitive, stern young woman. She was thin, with dark blue eyes and rich auburn hair to her waist, which she wore braided and wound in a bun on the top of her head to keep it out of the way when she worked. She was shy and conservative, but she fit in easily with everyone.

Eva's family were pioneers too. Her father, Richard Jones, was born 24 October 1824 in London, England.[30] Her mother, Elizabeth, was born 14 February 1833 in Eastwickam, England. In his youth, Richard, like Joseph Godfrey, had commenced a life on the ocean. He loved to travel.[31] He sailed the oceans and global ports of call—to Constantinople and the Isle of Patmos, through the Black Sea into Russia, and around the capes of Africa and South America. These were phenomenal experiences for a lad, even by modern standards, and significantly more so given the early 1800s. He was near the seas until his marriage on 19 November 1849 to a London orphan named Naomi Parson.[32] He

---

28. Book A, No. 1079, Godfrey Family Papers, 94. John R. Winder was second counselor to the presiding bishop of the Church, founder of the Winder Dairies in Salt Lake City. Sillitoe, *A History of Salt Lake County*, 85. Riter was Orson Pratt's missionary companion in Hungary, Douglas F. Tobler, "Europe, the Church In," in Ludlow, *Encyclopedia of Mormonism*, 2:471. George Romney was a Salt Lake City bishop and business man. Noble Warrum, *Utah Since Statehood: Historical and Biographical* (Salt Lake City: S. J. Clark Publishing, 1919): 2:46–50. Also, Joseph Godfrey, North Ogden Ward History, 111.

29. "Brief History of Melvin Godfrey," 6.

30. Greenwell and Kump, *Our North Ogden Pioneers*, 300.

31. Robertson, "Personal History: Richard Jones," 2–3, in Godfrey Family Papers.

32. Greenwell and Kump, *Our North Ogden Pioneers*, 301.

wanted to be with his new family, so he gave up his job on the seas for a management position on London's harbor loading docks.

While working the docks one day, Richard found several discarded LDS religious tracts. He was interested. He embraced the gospel and was baptized a member of the Church on 1 February 1852. He served as a missionary in London and was among the local leadership of the Church for almost a decade before he immigrated to America. With his family, he sailed from London on 4 June 1863 aboard "the splendid packet Amazon," with 895 saints aboard.[33] A packet ship was a few steps above what Joseph and Richard likely sailed in their early careers at sea. A packet vessel had a regular schedule transporting people and cargo across the Atlantic. The term "packet" originates with early mail delivery that arrived in packets. Charles Dickens visited this ship before departure and described, "These people [are] so strikingly different from all other people in like circumstances whom I have ever seen, that I wonder aloud, 'what would a stranger supposed these emigrants to be!'"[34] Richard and Naomi had six children, who all sailed to America aboard the *Amazon*.

Richard was well-to-do and paid the ship's fare for his family as well as for thirty other Saints.[35] During the journey, the Church members were organized into wards to maintain order and protocol. They held regular morning and evening prayers, conducted their regular Sabbath services, and organized a brass band. There was an abundance of speeches, socialization, and worship. In the evenings, the deck was cleared of all women at 9 p.m., and guards were posted to see that "no

---

33. Conway B. Soone, *Ships, Saints, and Mariners* (Salt Lake City: University of Utah Press, 1987), 9–10. George Q. Cannon, *Millennial Star* (Liverpool: George Q. Cannon, 1863), 395.

34. Soone, *Ships, Saints, and Mariners*, 9–10.

35. It is reported that Richard Jones earned thirty pounds per month, which translates into $150 ($3,995). See Robertson, "Personal History: Richard Jones," 3; also, Greenwell and Kump, *Our North Ogden Pioneers*, 300–302. This seems out of place. However, no additional information was available at this writing. Comparing this income to Joseph Godfrey's work evokes the question of the amount of Joseph's wealth before it was tossed overboard in a Quebec harbor.

female went up after that hour . . . and no sailor went below."[36] They encountered a few fearful high winds and blustering seas over the thirty days of their journey, but they arrived safely in New York, 18 July 1863.[37]

From New York they rode the train to St. Joseph, Missouri, where they eventually joined with the company of Thomas Ricks and a group of "light-hearted saints, bound for the promised land, now only a thousand miles away." Their only impediments were avoiding the "strife of the Civil War . . . raging in the United States."[38] The trip took four months and one day from London to Utah.

Upon arrival, Richard asked where they should settle, and Brigham Young suggested they go "north and settle near the head of a stream." Those general directions took them to North Ogden, where they arrived 10 October 1863. They settled on what became known in the family as the "cat claim." It was a location with water already used by the native Shoshone, who claimed "squatter's rights."

The cat claim story emanates from a lady who wanted to repay Richard for her passage to America. She had no personal possessions except for a "nice house cat," which Richard's children wanted, and the woman was insistent. Thus, the children acquired their first pet, taking loving care of it and playing with the cat all the way across the Plains. As it happened, in North Ogden, when Richard was negotiating with the Indians for the land, one of them spotted the cat and wanted it.

---

36. For a personalized description of the *Amazon*, see the family records of LaVern Contrell, North Ogden Museum, North Ogden, Utah. Contrell is the great-granddaughter of Richard Jones.

37. "Diary of John Watts Berrett" 4 June 1863 to 18 July 1863, FamilySearch, Mormon Immigration Index—Personal Accounts, http://mormonmigration.lib.byu.edu/Search/showDetails/db:MM_MII/t:account/id:25/keywords:John+Watts+Berrett. The journal entries of numerous passengers can be located at this site.

38. "Sketch of the Life of Richard Jones, Jr.," Godfrey Family Papers, 1–2. Note in this sketch that Jones records his "rebaptism" and that of his wife Naomi in November 1864. Also, Robertson, "Personal History: Richard Jones," 3–5. See Thomas E. Ricks Company (1863), Mormon Pioneer Overland Travel, https://history.lds.org/overlandtravels/companyDetail?companyId=253. See also Sydney E. Ahlstrom, *A Religious History of the American People* (New Haven, CT: Yale University Press, 1972).

Reluctantly, the children gave up their household pet, the land rights were exchanged for the cat, and their farm became known as the "cat claim."³⁹

In North Ogden, the Jones family at first lived primarily on sego roots as they worked clearing the fields of rock and sagebrush. They plowed and planted sugarcane and worked in a fruit orchard with raspberries. After a few years, tragedy struck. Naomi became ill and was moved one mile into town to receive better care. The children and Richard visited Naomi often. The move seemed to hurt Naomi's pride, yet she remained stalwart, serving as her health allowed, and Richard managed the two homes. Sadly, she died January 1876.⁴⁰

Richard's second wife was Elizabeth Wickham. They were married 8 February 1870. Elizabeth moved to the farm after Naomi had moved into town. She and Richard had seven children—Emma Georgina and Emiline (twins), Rosabel, Abraham (Lee), Mary Elizabeth, Joseph Edward, and Eva.⁴¹ With Elizabeth's and Naomi's children, there were fourteen in the household. They all worked, harvesting fruit from the orchard. Richard loved raspberry jam and jelly. Elizabeth was now "the Lady in his household."⁴²

They were married eleven years when calamity struck again. Elizabeth took sick at home one day when smoke began filling the house. When she opened the bedroom door, the room was ablaze. It frightened her so severely that she suffered a stroke. Little Eva, three years old, was out picking berries, and by the time she returned home, "the house had burned to the ground."⁴³ Two weeks later Elizabeth died,

---

39. Robertson, "Personal History: Richard Jones," 5.

40. Greenwell and Kump, *Our North Ogden Pioneers*, 302.

41. Floyd and Clarice Godfrey, "Book of Remembrance," Richard Jones family group sheet, Godfrey Family Papers.

42. His first wife had moved out of the house and was ill. She lived in town to be closer to the Church and to better care, but she remained a strong part of the family. Robertson, "Personal History: Richard Jones," 8. Also "Richard Jones" (life story of Jones from the LaVern Contrell Family History), 8.

43. "The Life of Eva Godfrey," Godfrey Family Papers, 9.

on 21 October 1881.[44] The home was rebuilt, but this series of events would be life changing for Eva. She never overcame her fear of fire.[45]

In December 1881, Richard married his third wife, Mary Ann Duckworth.[46] A few years later, he married again. His fourth wife was the widow Margaret Walwork. He was seventy years old, she was fifty-nine, and Eva was an impressionable teenager at age fifteen. She missed her mother terribly.[47]

Richard would have a long life, surpassing each of his wives. He was an avid reader of world and Church literature, elders quorum president, and part of the North Ogden First Ward quorum's presidency for thirty-five years. At this same time, Joseph Godfrey was a fixture in the bishopric, so they knew each other well. Their common sea adventures and gospel service likely made them devoted friends. Richard was active in building the community, constructing canyon roads, and logging the mountains for lumber to build schools, houses, and bridges. He developed irrigation throughout the area, plowing ditches and canals to divert the water to the farms and orchards. "Whatever was needed, he gladly lent a helping hand."[48] He passed away at the age of ninety on 24 September 1914.

### LOVE, GHOSTS, AND DANCING

Growing up, Eva was afraid of her stepmother Mary Ann Duckworth. She described her as "a nice lady, but real strict."[49] Eva always respectfully addressed her as "mother," likely out of fear of displeasing Mary

---

44. Robertson, "Personal History: Richard Jones," 9. See also Greenwell and Kump, *Our North Ogden Pioneers*, 302.

45. "The Life of Eva Godfrey," 9.

46. Richard and Elizabeth Jones family group sheet, prepared by Clarice Card Godfrey, Godfrey Family Papers. Eva Jones wrote she was "four" when her mother died—she was actually three. Eva was born 25 May 1878, and her mother, Elizabeth Wickham Jones, died 21 October 1881. "Eva Jones Godfrey, A Life Sketch," 21 January 1962, Godfrey Family Papers, 1.

47. "The Life of Eva Godfrey," 8–9.

48. Robertson, "Personal History: Richard Jones," 7.

49. "A Life Sketch of Eva Jones Godfrey," 1962, 1.

or her father. On one occasion when Eva was invited to go to Church general conference in Salt Lake City with her father, Eva refused to let her mother bathe her. As a result, she was not allowed to accompany him.[50]

Her father recognized his daughter's anguish following the loss of her own mother and his new marriage. He stepped in, and over the years the two developed a close relationship. He took Eva into the fields with him when she was little. She rode the plow horse while he worked—preparing, planting, and caring for the crops. She rode in the wagon, taking hay to the barn for the winter. She gathered eggs from the chicken coop and worked in the orchard, all just to be near her father and do her part as a member of the family. She took her childhood wagon into the orchard and gathered the apples fallen from the trees and fed them to the pigs. When she got older, she was allowed to go for "papa's mail." Her father was always full of praise, always loving and thanking his baby girl. "He was so kind," she wrote.[51] The affection was mutual. "How I loved my father when he came in from the fields tired and dirty. I would bathe his feet to rest him."[52]

As the years passed and her stepmother became ill, the mother-stepdaughter relationship failed to improve. Mary Ann even told Eva she would come back and haunt her after Mary died. Mary Ann Duckworth-Jones died 12 March 1894. Eva, now sixteen years old, was left in charge of the household. Her sisters were working outside of the home and had married. Eva also worked at the North Ogden Telephone Exchange to help support the family.[53] She cooked the meals and churned the cream into butter for her father and brothers, Abraham (Lee) and Joseph.

One dark evening, Eva was casually walking along the dirt road home with a friend, returning from a teenage party in town. As they strolled happily along like any two young teens, a ghost appeared in the center of the road. It was standing there like an evil spirit in the

---

50. "A Life Sketch of Eva Jones Godfrey," 1962, 1.
51. "A Life Sketch of Eva Jones Godfrey," 1962, 2, 1.
52. "A Life Sketch of Eva Jones Godfrey," 1962, 1.
53. Woodfield, *A History of North Ogden*, 349.

air above the gravel. "It stood one foot off the ground. It was white." Eva screamed to her companion, "That is my mother." The girls were so frightened they ran screeching all the way back to town. Wildly knocking on the door, a friend let them in, and they relayed the ghost story. It had stood above the road, with its white robe flowing in the wind. They were sure they had seen the ghost of Eva's stepmother. The patient friend got his dog, and, with the two girls following slowly behind, he returned to investigate. The ghost remained, floating above the road. They approached cautiously. Then the would-be ghost turned slowly around to its side and walked away. "It was my pony! She had been [walking] in the mud, so it looked like she was standing off the ground," with her white mane flowing in the wind.[54] It was a humorously sad story repeated through the generations.

Eva, now the lady of the house, was still a teenager who loved being a kid. She loved attending Church dances and parties and pulling candy. Her older stepbrother owned the hall where the dances were held, so Eva thought of herself as quite important. She attended the dances at her brother's hall and other events like the traveling Chautauqua speakers and vaudeville performances. Boys were in pursuit, but "they had to be Mormon boys." Eva's father may have held her heart in his hand, but he too was strict. He told one young man, Jessie Woodruff, that she could not go to the dance with him because he did not belong to the Church. Eva wrote that he later joined the Church and was a fine man. Her successful suitor was Melvin Godfrey. She and Melvin won a "prize *waltz*," and along with the waltz came Eva's heart.[55]

**HONEYMOON**

There was no honeymoon for the new couple. The first month and ten days of their marriage were spent working on the farm of Melvin's uncle John Price in Malad, Idaho. Malad was just south of the Utah-Idaho border. It was a Mormon-Welsh community settled by immi-

---

54. "A Life Sketch of Eva Jones Godfrey," 1962, 1–2.
55. "A Life Sketch of Eva Jones Godfrey," 1962, 2, 8.

grants from Wales, including members of both the Price and Jones families. By the late 1890s, Malad had prospered into an important stopover between Salt Lake City and Butte, Montana. The polygamists fleeing persecution stopped there as they headed north to work in the mines or railroad construction. John was the brother of Melvin's mother, Sarah Ann Price Godfrey, and he owned land in Malad. Melvin worked his uncle's farm team over the spring season, preparing the land for planting.[56] After a little more than a month, the young couple returned home. John paid them well and in kind, giving them two horses and a two-wheel cart. One of the horses, a bay, Melvin described as a fine animal, but the second, a black, "wasn't worth much." The cart held little more than the young couple and all their belongings. A single horse pulled, with the second tied to follow. The seventy-five-mile trek home took two days.

### LOSING THE NORTH OGDEN FARM

Melvin and Eva farmed Joseph's original thirty-three acres, now in the hands of his mother, Sarah, who lived in North Ogden. They did very well "raising sugar beets, onions, hay . . . , a couple of cows and four nice pigs." A baby boy joined the newlyweds. Their firstborn son, Bertrand Richard, arrived on 4 February 1898. On the family farm, Melvin thought he had the beginnings for his family. But it was going to be a difficult launch.

For some reason, his father's estate was dragging slowly through the probate courts—eighteen years after his death.[57] Joseph had left no last will and testament, so his assets were placed in probate court to administer the affairs of his estate. The probate was not filed until 9 July 1897, just after Melvin and Eva had returned and planted a crop. In 1898, creditors were invited to submit claims before the probate administrators. The probate and guardianship notices appeared in the

---

56. "Brief History of Melvin Godfrey," 6.

57. Probate courts administer the assets of a decedent, provided no last will or trust exists.

Ogden *Standard Examiner* for almost all of 1898 and a part of 1899.⁵⁸ Why probate was so long after Joseph's death remains unknown. It would be accurate to say that the farm remained active and productive. Sarah and her children lived in the home, worked the land, and rented some of it. They were making it.

Jeremiah, Melvin's older brother, was appointed the administrator of the estate along with three local appraisers. The farm and stock Joseph held in two irrigation companies were assessed at $4,543 ($123,372), along with water rights. The total value was $4,940 ($124,182).⁵⁹ There were no debtors. Jeremiah petitioned for a family allowance of $150 ($4,074) to support his mother, who was now fifty-six years old, his sister Josephine (eighteen), and Melvin, a newly married twenty-year-old with a wife and child. The petition was granted. On 26 November 1898, J. H. Lindsay objected to Sarah's rights to the homestead based on the facts that the farm was still solvent and at the time of Joseph's marriage he had another wife living with him.⁶⁰ As a result of this objection, a hearing was scheduled and creditor notices began appearing in the *Ogden Standard Examiner*.

In conclusion, there were sixteen heirs to the estate, including Sarah. The court awarded Sarah one-third of the farm, and the remaining two-thirds was divided among the children: William, George, Reuben, David, Jeremiah, Josiah, Melvin, Joseph, Josephine and John Godfrey, Mary and Martha Mecham, Sarah Jane Holmes, Jemima Campbell, and Emily Chadwick. Sarah received eleven acres, with the remaining twenty-two acres divided among the other fifteen children. It would not be enough to support a family.⁶¹

---

58. See "Probate and Guardian Notices, Estate of Joseph Godfrey, deceased," *Standard Examiner (Ogden)*, 25 January 1898, 7 through 16 March 1899.

59. No. 693, 22 January 1898, Weber Country Second District Court Probate Case Files. The name J. H. Lindsay does not appear in either of the North Ogden histories or the histories of Weber or Box Elder County.

60. Weber Country Second District Court Probate Case Files, No. 693, 26 November 1898.

61. Weber Country Second District Court Probate Case Files, No. 693, 21 March 1899.

As the youngest son, and the only one still working the farm, Melvin felt he was treated poorly, even though his brother Jeremiah was the probate administrator. Unfortunately for Melvin, who assumed he would get the farm or at least enough of it to support his new family, "the oldest of the family wanted the property sold," and Melvin's fresh crops and the animals were sold with it. "I felt very bad about that," was all he wrote of this turning point in his life. He inherited little of record.[62] This motivated a move, and it appears likely that whatever Melvin had received for his small share was used to make a new home in Wyoming, where a part of the George Coleman family had already relocated from North Ogden.

**"STARVE VALLEY"**

The result of the North Ogden farm's sale was that Melvin, his brother Josiah, and their wives were forced out. So they headed to Star Valley, Wyoming, to take up a homestead in a new locale. Melvin and Eva loaded all that they owned into the wagon—flour, fruit, two pigs—and started out. It was fall and winter was approaching, but the two brothers and their wives charged ahead. Their route took them through Mormon settlements in Cache Valley, up Logan River Canyon, past Card Canyon, the Beirdneau Mountain Peak, on to Bear Lake, then north into Star Valley, on the northwest side of the Wasatch Mountain Range.

The trek was challenging and was made even more so as winter engulfed them. The snow was heavy as they reached Bear Lake. Bear Lake sat in a beautiful valley at an elevation of 5,924 feet, straddling the Utah-Idaho border. They kept moving, making their way up the lake's west side, stopping only for assistance at the small Mormon towns established by Charles C. Rich—Paris, Bloomington, and Montpelier.[63] Rich was known for his generosity, so people passing through

---

62. "Brief History of Melvin Godfrey," 6. Also, "A Life Sketch of Eva Jones Godfrey," 1962, 2. While only two brothers are reflected in Melvin's writing, there were three brothers who all eventually went north, Melvin, Josiah, and Jeremiah.

63. Ted J. Warner, "California, Pioneer Settlements In," in Ludlow, *Encyclopedia of Mormonism*, 1:246–47.

had assistance as they traveled. The railroad had just made its way to Montpelier in 1892, and that changed the population base of that Mormon community from the original settlers to a now mixed population servicing travelers headed to Oregon and railroad workers settling the area. It had become a rail center.[64]

Melvin and Eva left the Bear Lake Valley, continuing north, ascending the mountains into Star Valley. Making life difficult, one of the horses became balky pulling the wagon in two feet of snow. The horses were cantankerous, but Melvin needed both working together to get over the mountains. The families decided to double up. Josiah's family left its wagon at the bottom of the valley and climbed into Melvin's wagon. The idea was to get one wagon to the top and then go back for the second. When they finally reached the top of the Salt River Wyoming mountain pass, they were at an elevation of 7,610 feet and freezing. They saw a house ahead, and it gave them hope. Melvin approached and knocked, and a man answered. Melvin asked if they could come in out of the snow and stay in the house. "No," the man responded; his wife did not feel well. Melvin persisted, "Can't the women come in?" he pleaded. "No" was again the stern answer. Melvin, Josiah, their wives, and young babies would have frozen that night, and Melvin knew it. So when he walked back to his family's wagons, he simply said, "*Yes*, you girls go right in." Eva and Josiah's wife, Gunda Beletta Peterson Godfrey, went straight into the stranger's home with their two babies. The occupants looked surprised to see them, "but they let us stay. She fixed us supper and we were thankful for it."[65]

The next day, the Godfrey brothers retrieved the second wagon and with their wives drove into what Eva later called "*Starve Valley*."[66] They stayed with Moroni Coleman and his son George Moroni Coleman, who had settled earlier in the valley. Joseph Godfrey was actually

---

64. Leonard J. Arrington, *History of Idaho*, vol. 1 (Moscow, ID: University of Idaho Press, 1995), 273.

65. "A Life Sketch of Eva Jones Godfrey," 1962, 3.

66. "A Life Sketch of Eva Jones Godfrey," 1962, 3.

Salt River Range, near Star Valley, Wyoming. Photo by Acroterion.

the stepfather, uncle, and brother-in-law to Moroni Coleman.[67] George had moved from North Ogden to Park Valley and was now living in Star Valley and running a small dairy.[68] They were with friends and family. George had also lost a herd of horses to rustlers in Park Valley just like Melvin. Melvin, Eva, Josiah, and his wife were now among confederates, but Star Valley would yet be difficult. Through all their trials, the Colemans and the Godfreys stayed close throughout generations.[69]

Star Valley is a beautifully demanding Rocky Mountain region running north and south along the Idaho border in western Wyoming. It sits at 6,200 feet and between the Salt River Mountain Range in Wyoming and the Webster Range in eastern Idaho. Water is plentiful. Three rivers wind their way through the area. It remains today a rich grassland with good soil and productive farming and ranching.

Mormon settlers populated Star Valley two decades earlier, in 1879, and called it the "Star of All Valleys," later shortened to Star Valley.[70] The falling snow was kinder for Melvin and Eva in 1899 than it

---

67. See "The Coleman Reeves Price Godfrey Meacham Relationships" chart, Coleman Family Papers.

68. Coleman Family Papers, 175–81.

69. Coleman Family Papers, 175–77.

70. Ted J. Warner, "Wyoming, Pioneer Settlements In," in Ludlow, *Encyclopedia of Mormonism*, 4:1598–99.

Above and right: This shepherd's wagon, circa 1900s, would have been similar to what Melvin Godfrey used in Wyoming. Replica @ Beaverhead County Museum, Dillon, Montana. Courtesy of Donald G. Godfrey.

had been ten years earlier. In 1889, forty inches covered the ground in just a few days, and the term "starve" made it descriptively into the valley's title. Melvin and Eva still competed with the winter storms and severe cold. "It was very foolish to go there for the winter," Melvin later declared.[71]

After a short time with the Colemans, Melvin and Eva rented a house about a mile away. In their first winter, Melvin had to leave to find work. Eva and Bert (who was barely two years old) were alone, but the family sorely needed an income. Melvin headed to the mountains and harvested mahogany trees. These were the curlleaf mountain mahogany, looking something like the wind-worn juniper trees of Wyoming, Idaho, and Utah. The native people used mahogany for bows and tools. The pioneers used them for construction, finer woodwork, furniture, and tools where hardwoods were advantageous. Melvin was paid $3 ($80) per cord, and it took him three days to haul a cord from the mountains.

---

71. "Brief History of Melvin Godfrey," 6.

On one occasion while Eva was alone with Bert, fixing supper and waiting for Melvin's return, "down the road came an Indian with feathers down his back and around his head." The Shoshone were drawn to the valley because deer and elk were prevalent. Eva was "hoping he would pass by, but he turned in. He was riding a pony. I picked up my Bert and went outside. He got off his horse walked past me and into the house" and said, "Meat and flour." Eva didn't have much flour, but she was "roasting some ribs for supper [and] she gave them all to him. He got on his horse and left."[72] Eva was frightened and crying. Bert was screaming. After the incident and considerable calming of nerves, Eva realized the Indian was exploring the country, as he wore a scout's head-dress. One wonders what Melvin got for supper when he returned.

The next summer, Melvin picked up whatever work he could in farm labor, mostly pitching hay and feeding the livestock for neighboring ranchers. He earned enough to homestead forty acres, acquire five head of cattle, and build a one-room log cabin. The cabin was 16 x 16 feet and had a dirt roof and factory cloth tacked to the ceiling logs. This kept the soil in the ceiling from falling into the bed or the food table.

---

72. "A Life Sketch of Eva Jones Godfrey," 1962, 3–4.

It also helped keep the mice and rats out of the cabin.[73] Eva wrote that they did "very well in three years."[74]

The next winter, in 1900, Melvin again left Eva and Bert, heading east, this time herding sheep. It was the only work he could get, and it paid $40 ($1,023) per month. He drove a sheepherder's wagon and rode with a dog and provisions. The two horses led the wagon at a walking pace. The wagon was perhaps ten to fifteen feet long. The main door was in the back. A window was in the front behind the driver's seat, all covered in canvas. Inside was a one-man bed, a small cook stove, an ice box, and a tiny kitchen cupboard. Storage and shelves occupied any empty space. More storage was available in boxes hung outside the wagon. The sheepdog was an important companion and excellent at protecting and herding the sheep. The shepherd, once the sheep were settled for grazing, strung another canvas five feet high around the outside of the wagon, where the dog stayed, protected from the wind. When the sheep depleted the grass in one area, they packed up and moved to another pasture.

Melvin roamed a range he called "the Red Deseret [Desert]" that ran as far east as Cheyenne, Wyoming, and south to Greeley, Colorado. The Red Desert was a high-altitude expanse in south-central Wyoming. Both the Oregon and Mormon Trails ran through the area. Melvin herded the sheep through the grasslands of this winter range and fed "the woolleys" corn and beet pulp. He was alone in the hills with two good sheep dogs herding "two or three thousand sheep. . . . He slept and ate in the wagon. When he came [home] for provisions he would ride one horse and tied the pack horse to his horse's tail."[75] He wasn't happy leaving his family each winter, and he "finally quit sheep."[76]

---

73. The factory cloth was likely a type of burlap. Eva records the dimensions of the cabin as 12 x 14. "A Life Sketch of Eva Jones Godfrey," 1962, 4. See Kathleen Godfrey Watts, "Life of Bertrand Richard Godfrey," 3 February 1980, Godfrey Family Papers, 1.

74. "A Life Sketch of Eva Jones Godfrey," 1962, 2. The 1962 story indicates five cows; the 1960 version says four.

75. "A Life Sketch of Eva Jones Godfrey," 1962, 4.

76. Melvin Godfrey, "Brief History of Melvin Godfrey," 7.

Amidst life in Star Valley, their second son, Parley Melvin, was born on Christmas Eve, 1901, in Smoot, Wyoming.[77] Life was a physically severe struggle in "Starve Valley," where neither Melvin nor Eva liked being alone. The family was growing, and Melvin heard reports of opportunities in Canada. After almost four years in Star Valley, on 1 March 1903, Melvin sold his Wyoming land and headed for southern Alberta, Canada.[78]

**NORTH TO CANADA**

Melvin and Eva made the move from Smoot, Wyoming, to Magrath, Alberta, by train rather than trek. They sold their Wyoming homestead, making sufficient cash for their travel. It took planning and approximately two weeks in route. Even though their household belongings were to be shipped by train, they packed the wagons for the ride so that way their belongings could be loaded and unloaded in bulk at different railroad transfer points. The railroad cars in 1903 were approximately nine feet wide and about forty feet in length.[79] If Josiah or the Colemans had traveled with them, it would have taken more than an entire railroad car. Livestock was generally placed in one train car, with freight and family in the other.

From the Afton area in Wyoming, they had two choices to get to a railroad center: south to Montpelier or west to Idaho Falls. It is uncertain which route they chose. Montpelier, south, was familiar territory. Idaho Falls, to the northwest, was on the Union Pacific route. The northern route crossed into the Snake River area of what is Yellowstone and reportedly some rugged territory toward Idaho Falls. Melvin's son Mervin writes that as "they were going along the Snake River,

---

77. Melvin Godfrey Family Group Sheet. Genealogical data comes from the records of Floyd and Clarice Godfrey, Godfrey Family Papers. The information is also available on FamilySearch.org, although this is not always a consistent source.

78. Melvin gives this exact date for the beginning of the move. See "Brief History of Melvin Godfrey," 7. Eva indicated it was fall. See "A Life Sketch of Eva Jones Godfrey," 1962, 4.

79. George W. Hilton, *American Narrow Gauge Railroads* (Stanford: Stanford University Press, 1990), 436–37.

they just about ended up in the river as the sleigh slipped off the road" and almost ditched them.⁸⁰ This suggests that they took the northwest route. But later it appears the southerly route was the choice, as "they hauled all their stuff to Montpelier, Idaho," on a well-traveled pioneer route, which would have taken then by wagon south to the more active railroad center to catch the train.⁸¹

The route from Montpelier would have taken them to Pocatello, then to Idaho Falls, north to Butte, Montana, all on the Union Pacific and its subsidiaries. In Butte, the cars would have been transferred to the Chicago Burlington & Quincy Railroad (CB&Q) with the Burlington Route and its associated line through the West and on to the Canadian border. The final leg of the route took them through Helena, Great Falls, and directly north to Shelby. They crossed the US-Canadian border at Sweet Grass, then to Stirling, Alberta, Canada, where they disembarked.

The Godfreys joined many other Mormons in western Canada. The Mormons started settling southern Alberta, creating a community at Cardston in 1887. The Moroni Coleman family had moved to Canada a year before Melvin, in 1902.⁸² So once again, they were among family, friends, and people of a common faith.

By the turn of the century, the Mormons in southern Alberta were farming and with their experience had teamed with Elliot Galt to develop irrigation systems throughout southwestern Alberta.⁸³ The rumors of cheap land and land in exchange for work on the canal spread throughout the Mormon colonies in Wyoming and Utah. Charles Ora Card wrote in the *Deseret News*, "We invite . . . all trades to make our towns and hamlets a success . . . and grow up within an enterprising and healthy country. Don't forget to secure good farm land adjacent

---

80. Mervin Godfrey, oral history, interview by Floyd Godfrey, 25 March 1982, Godfrey Family Papers, 1.

81. Mervin Godfrey, oral history, 1.

82. The Coleman Family Papers, 175–76.

83. Howard Palmer, "Polygamy and Progress: The Reaction to Mormons in Canada, 1887–1923," in *The Mormon Presence in Canada*, ed. Brigham Y. Card, Hebert C. Northcott, John E. Forster, Howard Palmer, and George K. Jarvis (Logan: Utah State University Press, 1990), 118–19.

to one of the grandest irrigation systems of *modern* times."[84] Southern Alberta was painted by Card poetically as possessing a variety of grasslands, grass reaching a horse's belly, migratory bird routes, birds that serenade the forests, fragrancy exhaled from plants in full bloom, mellow sunlight, and the grasses taking on a new life.[85] Immigration and travel into Canada were improving at the same time. Short narrow-gauge railway lines provided north–south and local travel. These expansions were facilitated by increased mining and agricultural development. By 1889, Lethbridge, Alberta, and Great Falls, Montana, were connected by the Great Falls and Canadian Railway. In 1900, a route from Stirling, Alberta, to Cardston was developed through the towns of Magrath and Riley by the Galt Alberta Railway and Coal Company. Roads were dirt wagon and horse trails. There were steam automobiles appearing in the industrial East, but it is highly unlikely that any in this rural family migration had yet seen one. Trains had become the means of mass transportation and industry.[86]

The train ride to southern Alberta would have seemed luxurious compared to the covered wagon move from North Ogden to Star Valley. However, they would once again arrive in a snowstorm. They arrived at Stirling, Alberta, Canada, during "a terrible storm and couldn't leave the station." The snow was blinding; they could not see. They waited outside the railroad station, sitting on the northeast station benches, protected somewhat from the wind, until the next morning produced a beautiful sunshiny day. The ground was covered in deep white snow, the sky was clear blue, and it was cold.[87] Even so, immediate preparations were made to head to Magrath on horseback. Eva and Bert rode one horse, and Melvin and Parley were together on the other. The snow was so deep it came up to the horses' bellies. The horses did not walk through the snow as much as they lunged their way through it. It was a

---

84. See C. O. Card, "Letter to the Editor," *Deseret News*, 16 April 1898, 6.

85. For descriptions of the time, see C. M. MacInnes, *In the Shadow of the Rockies* (London: Rivingtons, 1930), 299–315.

86. Hilton, *American Narrow Gauge Railroads*, 436–37.

87. "A Life Sketch of Eva Jones Godfrey," 1962, 4.

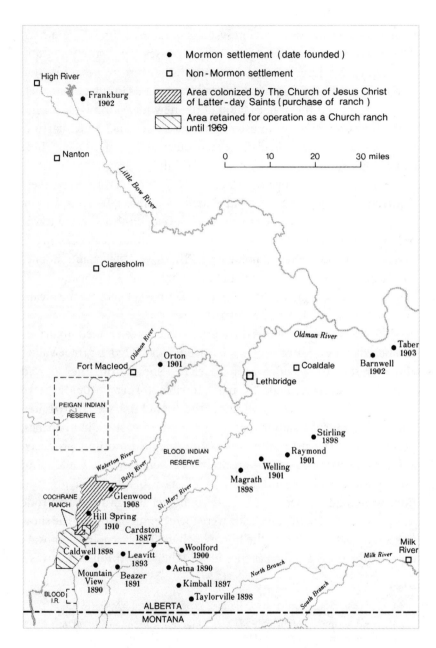

Early LDS Communities Scattered across Southern Alberta. Courtesy of Michael Fisher, Cartographer, University of Alberta.

rough ride. "How frightened I was," Eva wrote describing the journey.[88] When they arrived, they stayed with Sarah Ann Jones, Eva's aunt, for a few days until the train brought their provisions to Magrath.

Magrath, known as the Garden City of southern Alberta, was first settled in 1899 by Mormon settlers coming from Utah, Idaho, and Wyoming.[89] It was a small village, young and growing, incorporated in 1901.[90] Their new hometown of Magrath was a farming town. Many of the settlers were attracted by the glowing descriptions they had heard from Charles Ora Card and earlier settlers via letters and the newspaper. By the time Melvin and Eva settled, Alexander and Elliot Galt of Lethbridge had already developed the Lethbridge coal mines and wanted to establish irrigation in the region east of the Blood Indian Reserve and south from Lethbridge to the US border.[91] Galt and Card teamed with the Mormon immigrants developing the region for farming. The Godfreys and Colemans expected plenty of work, but it was not as advertised. By 1900, the first canal had already been completed. In 1902, it rained for two weeks straight, and a severe flood took out the head gates on Magrath's Pothole Creek and threatened the community.[92] The flood created more work, but in 1903, when Melvin, Josiah, and the Colemans arrived, work seemed scarce.

Once again Melvin and Josiah were forced into traveling. This time Oregon seemed in need of carpenters and construction workers. The brothers left their wives in Magrath for a brief time. They likely caught the Great Northern Railroad out of Shelby, Montana. But finding work in Oregon was just as difficult, especially when the Oregon settlers discovered that the Godfrey brothers were Mormon and refused to hire

---

88. "A Life Sketch of Eva Jones Godfrey," 1962, 5.

89. "Magrath, The Garden City of Southern Alberta," *Deseret News*, 14 December 1907, 51. Also "Early Settlers," *Immigration Builders*, 90–92.

90. Gary Harker and Kathy Bly, *Power of a Dream* (Magrath: Keyline Communications, 1999), 29.

91. For a map of the Galt land, see Harker and Bly, *Power of the Dream*, 12.

92. Harker and Bly, *Power of the Dream*, 59.

Southern Alberta irrigation canal laborers with their teams. Courtesy of Magrath Museum.

them.[93] After a few months with no success, they returned to their families.

Eva, Bert, and Parley were alone in a tent while Melvin was in Oregon. They were dependent upon the love and generosity of their extended family, neighbors, and friends. More than food, it was their faith and love that sustained them. After they had just arrived, 6 May 1903 brought a brutal late spring blizzard. "It snowed and the wind blew for two days and nights," as Eva remembered.[94] There were no fences on these open prairies, so hundreds of cattle from the nearby ranches stampeded toward the settler's homes for protection from the blowing snows. Men scared them away from the scattered barns, homes, and tents as best they could. Eva was afraid the cows would run over her tent. One evening during the storm, she and her young children, now

---

93. See "Brief History of Melvin Godfrey," 6–7.

94. "A Life Sketch of Eva Jones Godfrey," 1962, 5. Also, "Life of Bertrand Richard Godfrey," 1–2.

five and two years old, were huddled together. They had run out of coal. As a blizzard howled, they were hunkered down trying to keep warm and hoping for the passage of a storm that seemed endless. Eva turned to Bert and said, "Bert, we've got to pray!"[95] Together this young mother and her sons knelt in the dirt of their tent floor and prayed to their Father in Heaven for help. Outside the tent, the cold north wind swirled the snows, shaking their only shelter with every biting gust of horizontal snow. They did not know from where help might come or when. But they had the simple faith that "the Lord would provide." It wasn't but a few minutes after they had risen from their knees when someone outside called through the wind and snow, "Sister Godfrey, Sister Godfrey." It was brother David Bingham, who lived down the road.[96] He knew of their circumstances. He knew they were alone. He carried half a sack of coal over his shoulder. "I thought you might need this," he said as he handed the coal to Eva.[97] Then he pulled the wagon and buggy closer to her tent and tightened the ropes so that the cattle would not knock over Eva's only protection.[98] He likely saved their lives. After the storm subsided and people emerged from their dwellings, there were dead cattle everywhere. "The men skinned them for their hides."[99] Nothing went to waste.

Shortly after the storm, Melvin returned. Downtrodden and discouraged, he was yet determined and still seeking work. His first job in Magrath was breaking sod, which meant plowing virgin soil. The pioneers created fields for raising crops by breaking sod, and it was also a part of the expanding canal construction. Horses were hooked in teams, sometimes up to six animals pulling a single plow through

---

95. "Life of Bertrand Richard Godfrey," 1–2.
96. This is likely David H. Bingham, who arrived in Magrath about the same time as Melvin and Eva. See *Irrigation Builders*, 414–16.
97. Eva writes that Brother Bingham brought the coal. Bert remembers it a little differently as a child. He later wrote, "When we got up in the morning and opened up the door and pushed the snow out, there was a tub of coal." See "Life of Bertrand Richard Godfrey," 1.
98. Floyd Godfrey oral history, 20 March 1982.
99. "A Life Sketch of Eva Jones Godfrey," 1962, 5.

centuries of hardened soil. Eva cooked for crews as well as cared for her family.

After breaking sod for a time, Melvin started working as a carpenter building houses. He moved his family from the tent they had brought from Wyoming into a lean-to, a dugout he constructed on the south bank of Pothole Creek. It was again a one-room shack. Their only possessions were a few clothes and their horses. This was the birthplace of their first daughter, Lottie, born 12 December 1903; and their third son, Floyd, born 7 April 1906. Eva was twenty-seven years old.

The winters in Magrath were harsh and unforgiving. The blizzards always came directly from the North. In one storm, the cattle from a neighboring ranch huddled near Melvin's haystack for protection, and by the end of the storm they had devoured the entire stack in one night. It could be so cold, Melvin's son Bert recalls, "I have seen cattle freeze to death standing up."[100]

Then, as Eva described it, they had "a streak of good luck."[101] Melvin was appointed the "town Marshal." This provided security and a small but steady income for the family. "We moved out of the shack, uptown to be with the populace," Bert wrote.[102] It was the beginning of a new era for their family. They built a one-room home on Second Street East, one block north of the Fletcher's home on the corner and across the street from a steep drop to Pot Hole Creek.[103] "Two rooms were [later] added to their little home and we were happy."[104] They were stable and growing as four more boys joined the family: Mervin "J" was born 21 April 1909; Joseph arrived 20 February 1911; Norris, 9 March 1913; and Douglas, 12 July 1918.[105]

---

100. "Life of Bertrand Richard Godfrey," 4.

101. "A Life Sketch of Eva Jones Godfrey," 1962, 6.

102. Bert Godfrey oral history, 3 February 1980, Godfrey Family Papers.

103. The Willard T. Fletcher family moved from Salt Lake City in 1889. See *Irrigation Builders*, 448–50.

104. "A Life Sketch of Eva Jones Godfrey," 1962, 6.

105. Family Records of Melvin and Eva Godfrey, Floyd Godfrey Family Papers. See also, https://familysearch.org/tree#view=ancestor&person=KWCJ-GYD&section=details.

Eva had just given birth to Mervin and was in fact still in bed with him when his older brother Parley caught scarlet fever. Today this infection would be easily treated with antibiotics. In 1909, it was especially deadly for children. "He took fits for six days. They would wrap him in hot sheets; that would settle him down . . . [but Eva] was in bed with Mervin only a few days old." Parley was eight and suffering. Bert was twelve; Lottie, six; and Floyd, only three; and all waited helplessly. Parley called to his mother over and over for days, "Mama, Mama." Melvin never left his son's side. Eva could hear him, but the doctor would not allow her out of bed. New mothers were not allowed out of bed for days after birth in those days. "We thought if we got out of bed or bathed we would surely die." Eva remained in her bed even when Parley passed away and his body was taken to the church for preparation, services, and burial. "Sister [Allie Rogers] Jensen stayed with me and held my hands as we prayed. I was surely blessed and was as calm as could be. I was thankful he [Parley] was released of his suffering."[106]

---

106. "A Life Sketch of Eva Jones Godfrey" (1962), 6. It was likely Allie Rogers Jensen, who stayed with Eva during these difficult hours. See *Immigration Builders*, 484. Interestingly, Eva's grandson Ririe Melvin Godfrey would later marry Allie's granddaughter Crystal Diana Robinson.

# INTO THE CANADIAN WEST

CHAPTER 3

In the 1800s, southern Alberta, Canada, was wide-open grassland crisscrossed by rivers, dotted with lakes, and covered with rolling foothills leading west to the Canadian Rocky Mountains. The First Nations people moved about following their food supply—the buffalo. By the time Charles Ora Card arrived in 1886, the land was owned mostly by the Galt Alberta Railway and Irrigation Company and the Blood Indian Reservation.[1] The company land was part of the coal mining rights established by Alexander Galt and his son Elliot. They lived in Lethbridge, just twenty miles northeast of what is now Magrath, Alberta. Charles Alexander Magrath worked for the Galts as their corporate officer in charge of land development and sales. He was instrumental in establishing the town that today bears his name. Later, he became the mayor of Lethbridge, the speaker of the Northwest Territorial Legislature, and a member of the Dominion (Canadian) Parliament. The tribal

---

1. Lowry Nelson, *The Mormon Village: A Pattern and Technique of Land Settlement* (Salt Lake City: University of Utah Press, 1952), 216, figure 16.

reserve was land set aside for the First Nations people, assuring its preservation and protecting it from the growing western immigrations.[2]

## MCINTYRE RANCH

In 1887, the Mormons arrived and acquired land for settlement immediately south of the Blood Indian Reserve. In 1894, the Galts sold a large tract of land south of Magrath to Utah rancher William McIntyre.[3] Known as the McIntyre Ranch and operated by William and his son William Jr., it became a huge operation, running six thousand to nine thousand head of cattle. The ranch covered approximately "160,000 acres, with six sets of ranch and farming buildings" for housing family and the cowboys working the cattle and maintenance sheds. The McIntyres branded "2,000 calves per year and annually marketed about that same number."[4] The herds had the freedom of the prairies. Cowboys in their saddles, with guns and rifles at their sides, protected them day and night from the roaming buffalo and the wolves. They all shared the open plains. The First Nations people were given forty to fifty head each year, which helped keep the peace. Stampeding buffalo created havoc and the several wolves that inhabited the area were hungry for easy prey, so cowboys were kept busy.

The McIntyre Ranch was centered at the edge of the western Canadian prairies in the foothills of the Rocky Mountains near the US border at Del Bonita. The land was largely unsettled until the Mormon pioneers arrived in Cardston, twenty miles west. The only city of any

---

2. Alex Johnson and Andy A. den Otter, *Lethbridge: A Centennial History*. City of Lethbridge and the Fort Whoop-up Country Chapter, Historical Society of Alberta, 1985. See also Howard Palmer, "Polygamy and Progress: The Reaction to the Mormons in Canada, 1887–1923," in Brigham Y. Card et al., *The Mormon Presence in Canada* (Edmonton: University of Alberta Press, 1990), 117–19. And Nelson, *The Mormon Village*, 239–48.

3. William H. McIntyre Jr., "A Brief History of the McIntyre Ranch" (Lethbridge, 1947). A local history published by the ranch. See also Magrath and District History Association (hereafter cited as MDHA), *Irrigation Builders* (Lethbridge: Southern Printing, 1974), 41–44.

4. McIntyre, "A Brief History," 31.

size was Lethbridge, twenty miles north of the ranch. Mormon settlers had come to Cardston seven years earlier, in 1887, under the leadership of Charles Ora Card, the first LDS pioneer in southern Alberta. They set their hopes on religious freedom, ranching, and farming opportunities.

### FINANCING IRRIGATION

During the 1890s, southern Alberta was in the throes of an economic depression which dampened the spirit of bankable growth envisioned by the Galts. Future development required water, financing, and people. Irrigation was required to stimulate economic growth and diversification. The trio of the first irrigation builders were Galt, Magrath, and Card. Galt and Magrath recognized the feasibility of irrigation in southern Alberta as a means of expanding the potential of the land. Magrath, who was in charge of planning under Galt, was impressed with Card, who had irrigation experience from Cache Valley, Utah. Card extolled the southern Alberta potential of the rivers providing an abundance of water for both farming in the prairies and ranching in the foothills. Basically, the Galts provided the financing, Magrath provided the planning through his surveying and land development expertise, and Card provided the personnel to make it happen.

By 1891, Charles Ora Card and John W. Taylor (son of the LDS Church President John Taylor) had convinced Church authorities of the Canadian potential and, with Galt, they signed a contract for a purchase of 720,000 acres.[5] On this land the towns of Magrath, Stirling, Welling, Raymond, and other small settlements emerged. Settlers provided the labor for building a canal system in exchange for money and land. The Godfrey, Card, and Coleman families, along with many others from Utah and Wyoming, were part of this northward Mormon migration.

---

5. MDHA, *Irrigation Builders*, 41–45; see also Cary Harker and Kathy Bly, *Power of a Dream* (Magrath: Keyline Communications, 1999), 10–15; and Howard Palmer, "Canada, LDS Pioneer Settlements In," in *Encyclopedia of Mormonism*, 1:252–54.

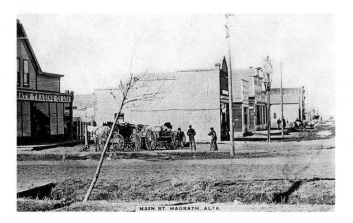

Downtown pioneer Magrath, Alberta. Courtesy of Glenbow Museum.

### TOWN OF MAGRATH

The first settlers arrived along Pothole Creek (Magrath) in 1899, but it was not until 1901 that the settlement had progressed into what could be called a village by the Northwest Territorial Legislature. It was named "Magrath" in honor of Charles Alexander Magrath. Within six years, on 24 July 1907, it was incorporated as a town. The first election created a mayor and council: Levi Harker (mayor), Andrew Hudson, Dr. Charles Sanders, Orson A. Woolsey, J. J. Head, J. B. Ririe, and Anthony Rasmussen (counselors). Two months after incorporation, the town council appointed the first town constable, Melvin Godfrey.[6] This was the "stroke of luck" of which Eva had spoken earlier. Melvin's salary was eighty dollars ($1,941) a month.

Melvin's work with the town gave his family a foundation. In addition to his role as marshal, he was also appointed secretary-treasurer of the town council, "to look after all of the affairs of the town business." That meant he was the town's "secretary, assessor, road master, water master, and trouble man in general,"[7] as well as the town foreman, pounds keeper, and bookkeeper. Shortly after his appointment,

---

6. Minutes of the Town Council Meetings of Magrath, 16 September 1906, 22, Magrath Historical Museum, Magrath, Alberta, Canada.

7. "Melvin Godfrey," 2. Autobiographical two-page document written in first person, Godfrey Family Papers. See also Magrath Historical Museum Family Papers. "Melvin Godfrey," in MDHA, *Irrigation Builders*, 459.

Lethbridge High Level Bridge, 1909. Courtesy of Galt Museum.

the council thought the marshal should have a phone in his home, so they installed one and they paid half the bill.[8] The council meetings were first held in the LDS Church tithing office, later in an assembly hall constructed by Hyrum Taylor (another son of Church President John Taylor), and then in 1910 officially at the first Magrath Town Hall. As constable, Melvin worked and served at the bidding of the councils through the mayoral terms of Levi Harker, James B. Ririe, Chris Jensen, and Ernest Bennion.

Melvin was an enthusiastic supporter of his town. As a member of the Magrath Board of Trade and the Agricultural Society, he helped organize community activities and supported improvements as the town expanded. The town was an important part of his life, pride, and service. He represented Magrath when the high-level Canadian Pacific

---

8. Minutes of the Town Council Meetings of Magrath, 2 December 1907, 37, Magrath Historical Museum.

Railway bridge, located in Lethbridge, was opened in 1909. He was with the first group to ride across the bridge. This massive steel structure over the Old Man River remains the largest railway structure in Canada even today. By 1914, Melvin was the city clerk.[9] He accompanied Mayor Bennion to Calgary, securing the first electric lights for Magrath.[10] The electrical system they created was later purchased by Calgary Power, which was then supplying efficient reliable energy and signing franchises with smaller towns throughout the province.[11]

Melvin remained a dedicated town servant throughout the years of Magrath's expansion. He served during council debates regarding the evils of the pool hall, and on one occasion the council directed him to remove all tobacco products from the shelves of his own grocery store. He complied. When the town temporarily closed his theater for back taxes between 15 and 29 March 1919, he came after the council for the $372 ($5,162) loss incurred. His petition was denied.[12] He caught up on his taxes and moved forward positively, never again faltering on them. He served on the Sports Committee, the Board of Education, and the Board of Health Committees. The minutes of the town council meetings reflect that Melvin supported those who sought tax relief during difficult times.

During the Great Depression of the 1930s, everyone in Magrath struggled financially and citizens were all behind in their taxes, including Melvin. He advised patience and lower taxes. "We have a nice little town as could be found in the province," he commented. "The idea was to work cooperatively and pull together for the good of the community and we could pull out of this difficulty all right."[13] His motto was one of

---

9. "Province of Alberta," *The Canadian Almanac and Miscellaneous Directory* (Toronto: Copp, Clark, 1913): 439.

10. "Magrath Town Council Minutes," 26 January 1917.

11. Max Foran, *Calgary Canada's Frontier Metropolis: An Illustrated History* (Windsor, Ontario: Windsor Publications, 1982), 76.

12. "Magrath Town Council Minutes," 7 May 1919. We get an interesting glimpse of the Empress Theatre profits in this exchange and it would be important to recognize that this was the time of the Spanish Flu pandemic.

13. Comment of Melvin Godfrey before the Magrath Town Council, Minutes of 14 March 1934.

service and commitment: "Magrath first, and everybody work to make Magrath the best place to live."[14]

## "MEAN" TOWN MARSHAL

Melvin held a variety of legal responsibilities in the growing town of Magrath. In 1912, and again in 1917, he became a justice of the peace, a position he retained into the late 1940s.[15] In 1915, Melvin was appointed as a bailiff.[16] His responsibilities kept him in close contact with the town council and the citizens.

Being the town marshal had its dramatic moments. One such experience was when Melvin was the officer in charge of the search for John Taylor, son of Hyrum and Louisa Taylor. The boy went missing from the farm near Welling, six miles northeast of Magrath.[17] Because nothing was more important than family to these pioneers, Melvin easily recruited the entire town to volunteer to find the lost child, and they did.[18]

In the summers, Melvin organized and recruited firefighters to battle the prairie wildfires that occurred regularly just southeast of Magrath. One fire burned almost two square miles before it was extinguished. The prairie fires were annual events sparked by the lightning and thunderheads blowing across the plains. The fires usually burned themselves out or were stopped by a natural barrier or a creek.

---

14. "Melvin Godfrey," 2.

15. "Magrath Town Council Minutes," 3 July 1912. Also, Melvin's biographical document mentions he was justice of the peace at the time as well as on his fiftieth wedding anniversary, which was in 1947. It is therefore assumed this document was typewritten in the late 1940s and early 1950s. The last entry in his journal, "Court Cases Held by Melvin Godfrey, 1946," was written on 5 March 1947. For "passing another vehicle on a hill," the fine was $2.50 ($27), court costs $4.50 ($48).

16. Bailiff is the British term for a sheriff. Although utilizing different terms, Melvin was the only law in the town. It would appear that these were responsibilities for which payment was rendered for services performed, but not full-time employment positions as considered in the modern day. Dates of appointments overlap considerably. Magrath was a small, growing town, with expanding municipal and business ventures.

17. "Hyrum Ririe," in MDHA, *Irrigation Builders*, 513–14, 527.

18. This was likely Hyde Taylor. See MDHA, *Irrigation Builders*, 527.

However, those threatening life or a farmer's crops were fought by community volunteers working together.

Perhaps Melvin's less dramatic—but certainly emotionally charged—experiences were just the regular passions that accompanied the job as a "cop [dealing] with drunks, kidnappers, and the such."[19] As a judge, he later tried many such cases and some people went to jail, while others paid fines.[20]

Marshal Godfrey worked hard as a law officer and a father. He taught his children the meaning of work. Bert, Floyd, Mervin, and Joseph were recruited to recover stray cattle that had broken out of their corrals and wandered the public streets and into neighborhood gardens. Gardens in the early 1900s were important assets, unlike the modern-day ornamental hobby they are today. Building lots accommodated the need for large gardens. Magrath lots averaged at least an acre apiece and included space for the house, a barn, perhaps a pig pen and chicken coop, and gardens. The gardens were a means of year-round food. A stray cow in the summer garden meant less food on the winter table, so the Godfrey boys' responsibility was herding the stray cattle into the town corral, an impound lot where the owner could retrieve the cattle after paying a fine. It cost fifty cents ($11) for the owner to free the cow from the pound, and the boys were paid twenty-five cents ($5.50) per head. Thus, the streets of the town were kept free of cattle, gardens grew, and Melvin taught his boys to work.[21]

Within a few years, Melvin purchased a horse and saddle for herding the strays. The horse was a French coach buck with long legs named "Old Baldy," but he was more than a buggy horse. The horse knew more about rounding up cattle than the kids. Occasionally, when chasing the cows, which naturally did not want to be in the pound because of its lack of food, the boys led the horse one direction, but Old Baldy turned another. Old Baldy was better at anticipating the move-

---

19. Melvin Godfrey, "Brief History of Melvin Godfrey," 7–9.

20. "Court Cases Held By Melvin Godfrey, 1946." Original handwritten journal in Godfrey Family Papers, copy placed with the Magrath Museum.

21. Floyd Godfrey, oral history, conducted by the author, 1972, Godfrey Family Papers.

Magrath's First Elementary School House. Courtesy of Magrath Museum.

ment of the cows than his riders, who with his quick turns were often launched into the air, landing them right in the irrigation ditch.[22] There was a rumor that the boys were earning a little extra cash by sometimes letting the cows out of their pens in the first place, but no charges were ever pressed or proven.

With a father as the town marshal, Melvin's boys were exposed to unique experiences. When they were small, they accompanied Melvin into the bell tower of the old school to announce the evening curfew. The three-story school stood in the middle of town, just two blocks from main street, and it welcomed students from first grade through eleventh grade. To a child, it seemed like a monstrous brick building. In the dark of night, while fighting off the pigeons and sometimes catching them, Melvin and his children rang the nightly curfew. The curfew signified that people were to clear the streets at an appointed hour. For Melvin, ringing the bell was a responsibility as bailiff, but for his sons and daughter it was an adventure. They climbed the rickety stairs, making their way through the dark halls, going forbidden places other students—their friends—had never seen. They carefully made their way up three floors to the tower, edging closer to where the rope

---

22. "Life of Bertrand Richard Godfrey," recorded by Kathleen Godfrey-Watts, 3 February 1980, 2, Magrath Museum. See also Floyd Godfrey, *Just Mine: Poetic Philosophy* (Mesa, AZ: Chrisdon Communications, 1996), 36.

of the bell hung.²³ At the top they grabbed the rope and pulled. It rang at 10:00 p.m., calling young and old home for the night.

As the law officer and an officer of the courts, Melvin visited the school often to engage the youth.²⁴ But being marshal at times made him unpopular. One gentleman, who had three or four cows in the pound, "slipped over at night and slashed the tires of Melvin's Model T Ford."²⁵ The vandalism was vengeful and hurt Melvin because he loved his cars. He even collected license plates on the wall inside his garage.

Melvin's nerves were not easily rattled. When a Royal Canadian Mounted Police officer kidnapped his own daughter, Melvin was called by the officer's family to bring her back. The Mountie had married a Magrath girl, they had a child, and then they divorced. His wife raised their child—a girl—for the next two or three years after they had separated, but after that, the ex-husband wanted his little girl back. Melvin was simply a town marshal and was about to confront a Royal Canadian Mounted Police officer as he waited at the train station on the north end of town. While standing on the station platform, he was the target of a group of rebellious teens being daringly boisterous, who threw raw eggs at him and ran. Luckily for them, he was more concerned about the child and the Mountie than being covered with raw eggs. Melvin found the Mountie on the train with the little girl, and other than being egged, tragedy was averted.²⁶

Melvin was especially unpopular with the rowdy teenagers of the town, who he called "a gang full of mischief." Sometimes their consequences were jail or fines, and other times their consequences were natural. One evening, this gang of mischiefs was tipping over the outside biffies (toilets) when one of them fell into the hole up to his knees

---

23. Arlene Janet Payne-Godfrey, "Magrath School Bell Memories," September 1993, 1–2, transcript in Godfrey Family Papers.

24. "Hither and Yon," *Magrath Store News*, 10 November 1933, 3. "Hither and Yon" appears to be a school edition of the *Magrath Store News*.

25. Bert records that this incident occurred when he was thirteen or fourteen years old, which would make the year 1911 or 1912. The Model T's Fords were manufactured 1908–27. See "Life of Bertrand Richard Godfrey," 2.

26. Floyd Godfrey, oral history, 1972.

in raw sewage. The incident was reported to Melvin, who simply let the natural consequence play out.[27] Not only was it awkward to lift a companion from the sewer hole, but one had to wash off in the cold irrigation ditch before returning home wet and smelly. Melvin's work with these mischief-makers was double-barreled. When teenagers were in trouble with the law, they knew Marshal Godfrey was a direct pipeline to their parents, and that too was a natural consequence because that meant the trouble multiplied when they returned home.

One summer day, Melvin confronted two boys for allegedly stealing a chicken. They wanted candy and the confectionary on main street was giving it away for the simple exchange of a chicken. The boys were carrying a fresh hen toward the store when Melvin approached. They told him the bird had come from their own chicken coop. They pleaded their innocence, but unfortunately at some point tried to run and hide, which weakened their case. They got off that time with only a disciplining action from their own father. However, the same two boys, along with a friend, were later caught trying to sneak into the evening movie theater without a ticket and "in walked old Man Godfrey the town cop." This time Melvin took them all to jail and locked up the three frightened friends. The jail was a "cold cell with no lights whatever," they whimpered. A few hours later he returned, jangling his keys to warn them of his approach. He released two at midnight and the third at 3:00 a.m. "He was really an old devil, that old man Godfrey."[28] Melvin knew the boys' families and made sure the youngsters would have to explain their actions and return home late to their parents. In this small community, such things seldom escaped the marshal's knowledge. Melvin was easygoing on a first offense, but afterward he became increasingly stern.[29] Melvin was tall, a little over six feet. In his younger years he was slim with black hair and a mustache. His demeanor was imposing even to his own family. "A stern look was all he used to discipline" his children as well as the first warning to others

---

27. "Life of Bertrand Richard Godfrey," 3.

28. "Our Pioneer Heritage: The Charles Heber Dudley Family" (n.p., 2008), 267–68, Magrath Museum.

29. MDHA, *Irrigation Builders*, 442–45.

who might be just testing the limits of the law. He never swore, but when he looked at his daughter Lottie, she knew "he meant get up and do the dishes."[30]

Melvin's most quietly compassionate service came as he cared for the aging and those who died, meaning that when anyone passed away, he got the first call. He was once summoned to the basement of a grain elevator where a man's clothing caught in one of the fly wheels of the machine moving the grain. The wheel had quite literally whipped him around and around, beating the man to death. Melvin prepared the man's body with the same care as others. He dressed it in clothing for the funeral and burial. This combined both civil and sacred religious service he performed as marshal and as a member of the high priests group of the Magrath First Ward.[31]

### MAGRATH'S BASEBALL TRIO

The history of Magrath and the story of the Godfrey family into the twentieth century would be incomplete without noting their love for baseball and competitive sports. "Pothole Against the World," was the Magrath slogan in sports of every kind.[32] Pothole Creek was a stream running through the town and the town's first name was Pothole. Melvin was on every Magrath celebration planning committee, and baseball was as much a part of the festivities as the parades, community picnics, and fireworks. Every celebration began early in the morning with a cannon fired from the back of a flatbed, which was heard all over town. Afterward, the band roamed the town streets performing familiar tunes and marching songs, waking everyone for the celebration and the parades, which started at 10:00 a.m. Sometimes the band gave a concert in the assembly hall. There were races and activities of all kinds for all ages—the rooster chase, the three-legged race, novelty

---

30. Douglas Godfrey, "Memories of My Father, 1818–1957" (6 December 2011), 1; see also "Memoirs of Lottie Harker," 5.

31. "Ordination Certificate," Floyd Godfrey Family Papers.

32. Harker and Bly, *Power of the Dream*, 71–73. MDHA, *Irrigation Builders*, 388–91, 394.

pony races for the older children, and tug-of-war contests for the town masses. Softball at noon pitted the single women against the married women. Men's baseball was the early evening highlight, followed by feasts and dancing at the pavilion.[33]

Southern Alberta intercommunity sports competition had its roots in those games. Each town fielded a team and competition was aggressive. They played against every settlement in the vicinity, creating the foundations of fierce but friendly contests. The tradition continues even now throughout southern Alberta.

Melvin and his two brothers, Josiah and Jeremiah (Jerry), were an integral part of early Magrath baseball. They were a mean trio, and baseball was one of their favorite pastimes. Melvin was the catcher, and "with his bulk, no backstop was required."[34] Josiah was the pitcher, with Jerry at first base. Because these brothers were so close, they knew one another's expressions, movements, and characteristics well. They also anticipated the opposition on the field, making it difficult for the opposing team to get anything past them. When Melvin got too old to play, he umpired. His youngest son, Douglas, remembered the "little ivory colored hand device that recorded the strikes and foul balls."[35] Baseball continued as family lore and recreation through the decades. It was a favorite relaxation from the rigors of marshaling the town.

### SILENT MOVIES AND THE EMPRESS

Melvin was an entrepreneur as well as a marshal and a baseball player. He was a vigorous business man with a lot of ideas, always alert for ways to improve the town and the family income.[36] His employment with the town provided stability but little promise for advancement or increased income. So while he continued with his responsibili-

---

33. "Celebrate July 24th Magrath," *Magrath Store News*, July 1934, Magrath Museum. The *Magrath Store News* was a mimeographed publication of the Magrath Trading Company, Ltd.
34. MDHA, *Irrigation Builders*, 459.
35. Douglas Godfrey, Letter, 2 January 2013.
36. MDHA, *Irrigation Builders*, 157.

ties as Magrath's law officer, he also branched out.³⁷ He constructed a three-section brick building downtown and rented out each unit: one for a barber shop, another for a Chinese restaurant, and the last for a grocery store, which he operated and called the Gusts Grocery. He paid his children one dollar a day ($18) for an 8 a.m. to 6 p.m. workday at Gusts.³⁸

The Empress Theatre was the most significant of Melvin's commercial entrepreneurial ventures. The motion picture business at that time was new and innovative. There were no movie theaters in Hollywood let alone Magrath in these days. It was after the turn of a new century, around 1910, that independent producers began producing films and, along with traveling performers, lecturers, actors, and actresses, moved in theatrical circuits with the early movies. Radio broadcast demonstrations were even a part of the attractions. Melvin exhibited the pioneering films as well as hosted the live performances. He pioneered film and its new culture in Magrath. Melvin ran the family theater business from 1915 to 1945, first in Magrath and then in Picture Butte, just north of Lethbridge, Alberta.³⁹ He was synonymous with Magrath's first movie theater.

---

37. MDHA, *Irrigation Builders*, 157.

38. Douglas Godfrey, "Memories of My Father . . . ," 2. See also Mervin Godfrey, "I Remember an Autobiography," 8.

39. Douglas Godfrey, 7 October 2014. "Autobiography of Douglas Godfrey" (22 November 2009), 8, Godfrey Family Papers. There is a discrepancy in dates reported as to when the Empress was sold to the Brewerton Brothers. Douglas Godfrey reports 1945. One Magrath Museum document, titled "Empress Theatre," by Nyal Fletcher, indicates that the Empress was sold to the Brewerton brothers in 1930. Furthermore, both "Lee Brewerton & Moving Picture History of Brewerton Family" and "Empress Theatre" by Steele Brewerton report it being sold in 1930. These articles are from the Steele Brewerton Family Files. However, "Park Theatre Magrath," from the Steele Brewerton Family Files, indicates floor plans and that the construction of the Magrath Park Theatre was to be done between 1947 and 1948. These are all secondary sources and primary documentation is not available. Thus, both dates are possible. A convincing argument for 1945 is the substantial history on the "potato" movies featured by the Godfreys during the Great Depression as well as the Park Theatre construction permits of 1947.

John H. Bennett actually owned the first Magrath film theater, called "The Electric."[40] Bennett's theater doubled as a roller-skating rink when it was not exhibiting films. He sold it to the partnership of George Coleman and Melvin Godfrey and they changed the name to "The Movie Theater."[41] The theater was just off Main Street near Earl Tanner's lumber yard, the Pioneer Lumber Company.[42] Unfortunately, the Movie Theater burned to the ground in 1915.[43] Although what started the fire remains unknown, it is a fact that the first films were highly combustible.[44]

After the Movie Theater fire, it was rumored that the Colemans would rebuild, but they were concerned and cautious. Melvin, however, was unafraid and marched forward. In 1915, he bought out the Colemans and sought permission from the town to build the Empress Theatre.[45] This theater was on Main Street, just south of the Town Hall, across the street from Magrath's primary place of business, the Magrath Trading Company.

The Empress was a small, wood building perhaps fifty feet wide and one hundred feet long. It featured a projection booth and a stage. The main floor sloped slightly toward the front screen and seated 375 people on long, heavy, wooden benches. There were no individual seats. The audience sat on two sides of the auditorium in rows, extending fifteen feet long. The screen, twelve feet by twelve feet, was behind

---

40. MDHA, *Irrigation Builders*, 154–55.

41. MDHA, *Irrigation Builders*, 155. See also Tandy Stringam, "Nyal Fletcher: Memories of Magrath's Movie Theater," Magrath Museum. Fletcher's memories do not always correlate with other accounts. It is unknown as to when they were written. Fletcher was a boyhood friend of Douglas Godfrey, the youngest of the Godfrey boys.

42. Floyd Godfrey, oral history, March 1982, in Godfrey Family Papers. Earl Pingree Tanner Sr. had come to Magrath in 1903 from Afton, Wyoming. MDHA, *Irrigation Builders*, 525. See also *Power of the Dream*, 57, 150.

43. "Magrath to Get a Fine New Picture House," clipping from an unidentified Raymond, Alberta, newspaper, 16 April 1915, from personal files of Steele C. Brewerton, Cardston, Alberta.

44. Musser, *Emergence of the Cinema*, 443–44.

45. "Magrath Town Council Minutes," 6 May 1915. See also Floyd Godfrey, oral history, March 1982, Godfrey Family Papers.

Empress Movie Theatre, 1926. Courtesy of Marilyn Ockey-Pitcher.

the stage on the front wall. The stage was about four feet high and stood below the screen. Live traveling vaudeville acts performed here. Once, a child named Orin Harker was injured when he fell off the stage while playfully jumping. He reached out to stabilize himself, grabbing the door to ease himself down, but his ring caught on the top of the door and cut off his finger as he fell.[46] Children didn't jump around much on the stage afterward.

When needed, the theater was heated by a large, potbellied, coal-burning stove in one corner. This wasn't a perfect system because people close to the stove were too warm, while those far away from it were too cold. In the corner opposite the stove sat the piano, with which a pianist would provide the sound accompaniment for the movie.

There was no concession stand in the theater, so the first audiences brought their own refreshments or purchased food from the Chinese restaurant across the street. Their favorite treats were bottles of orange soda, popcorn, candy, and peanuts. Theatergoers ate bushels of peanuts, eating the shells and dropping them on the floor. By the end of the show, the old wooden floor was littered with peanut husks. Also, because families had come by horse and wagon straight from the farms, the floor was covered with manure from the boots of the farmers. Furthermore, the roads were dirt or gravel, so in wet weather,

---

46. Floyd Godfrey, oral history, 1972. See also MDHA, *Irrigation Builders*, 466–67.

audiences would also track mud into the Empress. At the end of the day, the mud, manure, and peanut shells were swept up, burned, and hauled out with the ashes.

In its day, the Empress rode the first wave of cinematic and theatrical pop culture. Families watched Charlie Chaplin, Mae West, Douglas Fairbanks, and D. W. Griffith, as well as the Tom Mix westerns. They also watched the Canadian-born Mary Pickford, one of the founders of United Artists.[47] Films they saw included *Million Dollar Mystery*, *Birth of a Nation*, *Ben Hur*, *Girl of the Golden West*, *Poor Little Rich Girl*, and *Girl of the Game*, which featured Pearl White.[48]

The earliest films were hand cranked and silent. At the Empress, this assignment went to Melvin's sons. If one of these projectionists had invited a date up into the projection booth, then the film was cranked a little faster than it should have been. There was no sound to these movies other than that produced by a live pianist. Vera Babcock, Wanda Gibb-Coleman, Zelpha Harris-Dow, "the two Ririe Sisters," and Lyal Fletcher all played piano accompaniment for the Empress.[49] These local musicians never needed sheet music. During a romantic scene, they played tender love songs and during the battles they played up-tempo marching music, which fit right into the theme of the film.[50]

In 1927, the music of Al Jolson's *Jazz Singer* delivered the first sound-on-film to viewers. Technology and the industry were progressing rapidly.[51] The Academy Awards gave their first Oscar to a movie called *Wings*, starring Buddy Rodgers, Richard Arlene, and Gary Cooper. Melvin advertised this film with a World War I model biplane hanging outside of the theater. It was made of balsa wood by young

---

47. Richard Koszarski, *An Evening's Entertainment: The Age of Silent Feature Film* (Berkeley: University of California Press, 1995), 263–71, 288–91.

48. Koszarski, *An Evening's Entertainment*, 259.

49. MDHA, *Irrigation Builders*, 157. See also Tandy Stringham, "Nyal Fletcher: Memories of Magrath's Movie Theater," Magrath Museum; Floyd Godfrey, oral history, 1972.

50. Mervin Godfrey, oral history, 7. See also "Life of Joseph Godfrey," 22; and Floyd Godfrey, oral history, 1972.

51. Koszarski, *An Evening's Entertainment*, 90. For technological advances, see 139–61.

Rulon Bingham, and it had a two- to three-foot wingspan to attract attention to the upcoming feature. Years after the show, Eva found the plane and returned it to Rulon.[52]

Melvin used all kinds of activities to promote the movies. Posters and banners in front of the theater pitched both current as well as coming attractions. If the posters were not required to be returned to the distributor, they became wallpaper for his grandchildren. Occasionally, he advertised in the *Magrath Store News*, and other times, on the evening of the movie, the whole town could hear his electric generator start up and see the beam of the arc light circling around in the sky.[53]

An evening of entertainment at the Empress consisted of a newsreel; a reel of comedy, cartoons, or vaudeville; a serial film; and, finally, the feature film. Movie serials were popular and sometimes continued for fifteen weeks. The last act of these short films always left the hero or heroine in some precarious cliffhanging situation, resolved miraculously in the next week's episode. All told, the evening lasted two hours.

Not all cliffhangers were due to film creations. If the film broke, there was a delay, and the evening lasted for a bit longer. Electricity ushered in significant change; however, in rural theaters, electrical power came not from the urban street lines, but rather from a gasoline-driven electric generator. If the generator faded out in the middle of the movie, as it often did at the Empress, it sent Melvin, his boys, and all the males in the audience outside to grab the engine handle and hand-crank the heavy flywheel, thus restarting the engine. Once restarted, they returned to enjoy the end of the show.[54]

Melvin and the Empress Theatre were keeping up with changing technology and multitasking. When the generator was not being used for powering a projector, a conveyor belt converted it into a machine

---

52. MDHA, *Irrigation Builders*, 415–16; see also "Information from Jack Harker, December 7, 1986," from the Steele Brewerton Files. Copies in Godfrey Family Papers.

53. *Magrath Store News*, 28 November 1934. This paper advertised *The Parole Girl*, starring Mae Clark and Ralph Bellamy, and *Soldiers of the Storm*, starring Reg Toomey and Anita Page.

54. Bessie Godfrey, "Life of Joseph Godfrey," February 1979, 23. Bessie was the wife of Joseph, the son of Melvin.

for chopping farmers' grain. Then, in the evening, the belt was removed and the whole town again heard the series of explosions as the machine started up for theatergoers. When it did, "the light burst forth on a pole above the theater. It was time to go to the show."[55] Melvin guided the bright beam of light from the projector's carbon arc up and down the street, alerting the town that the movie was about to begin. He estimated the crowd size for an evening's entertainment by climbing to the roof of the theater and scanning around to see how many wagons or cars were heading for town. At times, people lined up for three hundred yards waiting to get their tickets. Depending on the movie or performance, tickets sold between ten cents ($1.11) for children and twenty-five cents ($1.66) for adults.

During the Great Depression when money was scarce, tickets were bartered for some potatoes, eggs, or produce to feed the family. For the price of three potatoes, families were admitted to the movie. At one point, Melvin offered a prize for the best potatoes. This promotion sent children scouring their parents' root cellars searching for their best ones. Eva and her daughter Lottie worked the ticket booth and during the Depression, and while they did, there were piles of potatoes in the corner. Later, the egg shows produced so many eggs, it was more than the family could eat.

Following a full workday at home, Eva went to the theater every night without complaint.[56] One evening, she found a good deal of money on the floor—375 dollars, or what is now worth a little more than 4,000 dollars. She put a slide up on the screen for a while, but no one claimed it. She kept advertising and finally someone came, properly identified the amount, and she returned it. He gave her a five-dollar ($56) reward.[57]

---

55. Floyd Godfrey, oral history, March 1982. See also MDHA, *Irrigation Builders*, 154.

56. Melvin Godfrey, oral history, interview by Floyd Godfrey, 25 March 1982, 5. See also Godfrey Family Papers, "Life of Joseph Godfrey," 23.

57. Douglas Godfrey, "Memories of My Father Melvin Godfrey, 1918–1957," 6. See also Floyd Godfrey, oral history, 1972, Godfrey Family Papers.

The Godfrey boys—Bert, Floyd, and later Joseph—were the projectionists, licensed by the Province of Alberta. The tiny projection room was at the back of the theater, up the ladder five steps to the second floor, and through a narrow door. This dark, mysterious little room was off limits to most. Floyd and Joseph were the primary projectionists, since Bert, the oldest, had married and was out on his own. Douglas, the youngest, was always sent to the Chinese restaurant for sodas. But the brothers all crowded in together, often making so much noise that Melvin had to scold them.

The first projectors used a carbon lamp for the light. These lamps were white-hot and dangerous. The projection room in the Empress was unfurnished. Opposite the projector was a bench for handling and rewinding the film. At first, when the theater had only the one projector, the audience waited while each finished reel was unloaded and the next film reel was loaded and restarted. There was a small window where the projectionist watched the screen and looked down at the audience. Floyd recalled, "I had to stop the show every 1000 feet of film and change the reels I had to be fast or the crowd became uneasy and started to shout and applaud."[58] It was not long before the Empress added a second projector, which required Melvin to cut a hole in the wall for the second and another to the outside through which he shone the light into the street, thus gathering a crowd. The Empress exhibited films, but the enterprising Melvin rented the theater for vaudeville events, which featured speakers, traveling stage entertainers, and demonstrations. Films were brokered through the Motion Picture Exhibitors Association out of Calgary. Melvin, accompanied by two of his sons, Floyd and Joseph, attended the National Committee meetings in Calgary to book upcoming events.[59]

---

58. Handwritten note from Floyd Godfrey to his son Kenneth, n.d. Reproduced by Lorin Godfrey for the 2008 Godfrey Family Reunion, Godfrey Family Papers. See also Floyd Godfrey, oral history, 1972.

59. Joseph Godfrey would later become one of the directors of the association. See "Theater Convention at Calgary," 15 September 1957, clipping from an unidentified newspaper; Bessie Godfrey, "The Life of Joseph Godfrey," 54.

The first live entertainers at the Empress Theatre were varied. There was a phrenologist who placed his hands on Douglas's head, feeling for bumps and claiming that would predict his future. Though not technically an entertainer, a doctor from another part of the province gave lectures on sex to the young people in the eighth through eleventh grades. One circuit entertainer introduced the newest in radio technology at the Empress. Another demonstrated the building of a crystal radio set, "so simple even a youngster could listen to the radio." Even sounds of static excited the audience.

Radio was a novelty. There were probably no more than two receivers in Magrath, but a demonstrator from Calgary gladly set up his radio antenna outside the Empress, advertising for three or four weeks to draw a crowd. On the evening of the event, the radio set was carefully placed in front of the audience on a platform so everyone could see. The loudspeaker was likely akin to the RCA Radiola horn, popular in the day. The radio master searched the air for a station. The radio squealed and squawked and nothing materialized. Just once, he caught a station from San Francisco, just over 1,300 miles away. The audience cheered so loud at the sound that "no one could hear even if the radio had been on loud." The evening ended, and with the radio and antenna disassembled, the audience went home content with the miracle of listening to a voice from San Francisco on this new "thing called the radio."[60]

The Empress participated in a historic radio demonstration on 2 July 1921. It was a US national radio broadcast of the infamous Jack Dempsey–George Carpentier boxing match. Producers of the event promoted and linked the broadcast to radio stations and theaters across the United States and Canada. They generated significant profits, filling theater seats and launching the newest medium of radio. It resulted in the largest mass radio audience at that point in history.[61]

---

60. Floyd Godfrey, oral history, March 1982.

61. Douglas Gomery, *A History of Broadcasting in the United States* (Malden, MA: Blackwell Publishing, 2008), 1–7.

The Empress brought this radio demonstration to Magrath with record crowds attending.⁶²

During these kinds of demonstrations and performances, hawkers walked up and down the aisles carrying a tray attached to a strap hung around their neck, and selling candy. "Every box contained a valuable prize, such as watches, rings . . . all for only 25 cents. Usually, the prize was a metal tin frog clicker."⁶³ These profits went to the event organizers.

The Empress existed on the exhibition of films, vaudeville shows, magicians, actors, jugglers, and dancers. This was a family business, as Eva proudly declared, "We ran it without hiring."⁶⁴ At the end of the movie or any event, the boys cleaned the floors. They pushed the long, wooden benches toward the front of the theater and swept the peanut shells toward the rear. Afterward, it was family time, and back at home around the kitchen table they tallied the income from the tickets while dining on oyster soup. One night after the show, Douglas slipped a fake pearl into the can of soup and made a "big production out of finding a real pearl in his supper."⁶⁵ The family laughed and went right on eating.

In 1935, the middle of the Great Depression, Melvin branched out and opened a second theater in Picture Butte, Alberta. Picture Butte was a small town seventeen miles north of Lethbridge. Picture Butte had begun growing in 1923 with the construction of the Lethbridge Northern Irrigation System and the Canadian Pacific Rail Line passing through. Two years later, the town had been chosen as the site for the Canadian Sugar Factory. Thus, Melvin reasoned that the community had potential, and more motivation was the fact that his older brother Jeremiah lived there. So they moved to Picture Butte and started working at the theater. The new Picture Butte theater was managed by Joseph, who had segued into the position of projectionist at the Empress after his brother Floyd married and moved to Cardston in 1937. Joseph was the only son to continue his father's film legacy.

---

62. Handwritten note from Floyd Godfrey to his son Kenneth, n.d. Reproduced by Lorin Godfrey for the 2008 Godfrey Family Reunion, Godfrey Family Papers.
63. Floyd Godfrey, oral history, March 1982.
64. Eva Godfrey, "A Life Sketch," 6, Magrath Museum.
65. Douglas Godfrey, "Memories of My Father Melvin Godfrey, 1918–1957," 8.

The Picture Butte operation was called Melody Theatre. It offered a small room on the south side of the building that served as an office or living quarters for Melvin and Joseph while both Magrath and Picture Butte theaters were operating. It was Joseph's first home when he married and took over the business.[66] There were two beds, a chesterfield sofa, a kitchenette table, and a few chairs. Visiting grandchildren stayed in this room with their grandfather and uncle.[67] On opening night, Melvin took free tickets to Jeremiah's family. His nieces and nephews were mesmerized and happy that they got to see a free movie. If they were old enough, they helped with cleaning and taking tickets.

The Melody Theatre was constructed with a small concession stand selling popcorn and candy to the audience. It was a new theatrical profit center. Saloon-like swinging doors separated the concession area from the theater auditorium. In the auditorium, people took their popcorn and sat on either side of two aisles, separating the audience into thirds. At the end of the movie, they exited two doors toward the front and on both sides of the building. At this point, World War II was coming to an end, and the motion picture industry was growing with the rest of the nation's economy.

Melvin kept his boys busy with work, who supported themselves with the little they earned while their father encouraged them as they grew. Working with their father and their mother at the theater and at home was just a part of growing up and life training.

### EVA'S HOUSEHOLD ROUTINES AND HEARTACHE

Life in these early years of the twentieth century offered little leisure time. It came with challenge and tragedy. Eva worked at Melvin's side in the theater and held down the home as his responsibilities grew in town and business. Their fifth son, Joseph, was born on 29 February 1911. Their sixth son, Norris, was born on 9 March 1913, just two years later. One day, Eva and Melvin had gone to work at the movie theater

---

66. Bessie Godfrey, "Life of Joseph Godfrey," 34.
67. Lorin Godfrey, "Grandpa Melvin Godfrey," 4 December 2012, Godfrey Family Papers.

and left fifteen-year-old Bert in charge when Norris became ill. The six-month-old baby was choking, and they were called home along with the doctor. Baby Norris's lungs had filled with fluid and he passed away. People poured into the Godfrey home to pay their respects. "Horses and buggies were tied up in front of our home and across the street."[68] As Eva wrote of this tragedy years later, her last lines reflected her heart and her attitude: "I am thankful for my lovely children that never caused me to worry over them."[69] As she aged, she retained her "sweet, kind and gentle soul . . . she dealt with her children without anger, only kindness and love."[70]

Eva maintained all types of homes: tents, dugouts, log cabins, wooden shacks, and finally, a beautiful brick home on Magrath's main street. Her earliest homes lacked modern conveniences such as electricity, running water, refrigerators, or indoor bathrooms. Instead, they hauled water in buckets one at a time from an outside spring or a well, and they collected soft rain water in barrels at the eaves of the house. Eva liked the soft water to wash her hair. The well water was outside the house, about ten feet deep and away from the outhouse.[71] The outhouse was the bathroom, simply built over a hole in the ground with two holes in the bench and an old Eaton's catalog as the only toilet paper.[72] There may have been a chamber pot under the bed if it were winter and too cold to run outside. However, a boy's quick outside run assured there was little constipation within the children.

Their first Magrath home had no insulation. The children slept three to a bed, and in winter, they huddled deep under many covers. In the morning, the water reservoir in the side of the stove and the bucket

---

68. Bessie Godfrey, "Life of Joseph Godfrey," 11, Godfrey Family Papers.

69. Eva Godfrey, "Eva Jones Godfrey, A Life Sketch," 7.

70. Douglas Godfrey, "Memories of My Mother: Eva Jones Godfrey, 1918–1963," (1 July 2012), 1–3.

71. Mervin Godfrey, "I Remember and Autobiography," 2.

72. The Eaton Company of Canada was a major retail store. The Eaton's mail order catalog was published from 1884 through 1976. These catalogs sold merchandise of all kinds throughout the rural populations of Canada.

in the house were frozen.[73] A coal-burning stove was their only heat, meaning that most of the house was bitterly cold on winter nights. The children undressed and dressed in the kitchen, sat on the oven doors for warmth, and then ran for the quilt covers of their beds.

The Saturday-evening bath was an interesting ritual requiring significant preparation. Children bathed once a week in a large, round wash tub. They hauled water from the well or melted snow. In the winter, the parents sent the boys out to the yard for a "tub full of snow," which they put on the stove to melt. As snow levels decreased, they went back out to "roll up a good size snowball," about two feet in diameter, and it was added to the tub. As it filled and heated, Eva would skim the leaves and grass from atop of the water. The youngest bathed first, then the rest, all using the same water, perhaps "freshened" with warmer water as each took their turn. The older brothers always protested at being last, claiming the brother just before them had peed in the tub, and that "this didn't freshen it up much."[74]

In the summer mornings, thousands of flies covered the ceilings in the house. It was an astonishing sight. Melvin got the kitchen broom and swept them off, shaking the broom into the burning stove. The boys helped, using dish towels and whirling them around their heads to "herd-and-drive" the flies out the screen door. Just three or four such fly drives would clear most of the house.[75]

Monday was wash day. Laundry water too was heated on the stove and then poured into the hand-cranked washing machine. Clothes were then rolled through a wringer to remove excess water, after which they were hung outside on the clothesline for drying. In the winter, long underwear froze instantly and looked like ghosts swinging in the wind. Mysteriously, when brought back into the house, they were dry. The family would then iron the laundry in the kitchen using a heavy black iron, heated and reheated on top of the cook stove as the full day's work progressed.

---

73. Mervin Godfrey, "I Remember and Autobiography," 1.
74. Mervin Godfrey, oral history, 1–2.
75. Douglas Godfrey, "Memories of My Mother: Eva Jones Godfrey, 1918–1963." See also Floyd Godfrey, oral history, March 1982.

Eva was a great cook. The family all ate together around a table in the kitchen. Every meal was preceded with a prayer blessing the food. Breakfast was oatmeal—"mush," as it was called—pancakes, eggs, ham, and buttered toast. Dinner, the noon meal, included fresh summer vegetables grown in the garden or stored in the basement from summer harvest. Eva canned the vegetables, dried the corn, bottled the fruits, and churned her own butter from the cream from the milk cows. Also, the smell of homemade bread filled the house and brought everyone together. Finally, the evening meal was supper.[76] Melvin's favorite dish for this meal was mutton stew. And every Saturday night after the movies, supper was oyster soup. Desserts included freshly baked apples, a wild berry or rhubarb pie, and raspberries with cream or homemade ice cream.

Eva was a dedicated service worker for the LDS Church in addition to her duties to her family and to the Empress. She worked in the children's Primary organization and the women's Relief Society for many years.[77] While she was in the Primary Presidency, she tried to teach her boys to stay out of the pool hall, telling them that "you learn no good there." She also instructed her boys to stay clear of face cards, as they were "the work of the devil."[78] In the Relief Society, she was a dedicated class instructor and visiting teacher. She and Henrietta Crookston traveled by horse and buggy to complete their visiting teaching. Some women on the route were ten miles out of town and it took most of the day fulfilling their monthly visits. Visits focused on performing service to the aging, giving individual attention to those they visited, and lightening spirits along the way. Eva was in the Relief Society presidency for eight years, and she always loved the gospel and the women she served.

---

76. Breakfast, dinner, then supper was the British connotation and order. Lunch was something packed in the morning and taken to school or out into the field for a work lunch.

77. Douglas Godfrey, "Memoirs of Lottie Harker" (taken from notes and interviews, 1999–2001), 3–4, Magrath Museum.

78. "Memoirs of Lottie Harker," 4.

Eva was an active member of the Magrath women's organizations that were not a part of the LDS Church. In town, she was among the organizers of "the club." This was a group of ladies who regularly gathered in one another's homes to visit, sew, do handwork, do needlework, and just enjoy one another's company. After these visits, they had a "lovely lunch." There were almost twenty women in Eva's Magrath circle.[79]

The life of a pioneer meant work at every turn, and the Godfreys did this as they moved from North Ogden, Utah, into Magrath, Alberta. As they traveled, they witnessed a few new conveniences appearing much later in their lives such as automobiles, washing machines, and indoor plumbing and water. Melvin drove one of the first cars in Magrath and enjoyed trips to Waterton Park and Lethbridge. For the most part, they were really just an average family, like everyone else in Magrath, establishing themselves and their faith in a new community, in a new land.

---

79. "Eva Jones Godfrey, A Life Sketch," 9.

Part 2

# TRAVELERS IN THE AMERICAN & CANADIAN WEST

1839–1906

# ON THE WESTERN FRONTIER

Chapter 4

It had been the hope of the earliest English settlers in New England that they could establish "a virtual theocratic state, governed by a Calvinist clergy."[1] This idea of an absolute religious theocracy was hotly contested by those with a more liberal interpretation of doctrine whose ideas allowed complete freedom of religion. It was within this atmosphere, "a cauldron of religious excitement," that Mormonism and the Card families fostered their American beginnings.[2] For generations, the Card ancestors lived in New England. They were among the English settlers who had arrived in the New World during the early 1600s. They were spirited independents, farmers, and crafts people. These were challenging and changing times. William Card (1722–85) served in the Continental Army. The family experienced the onslaught of the wars and the turmoil that created a nation as they raised their families. Elisha Card

---

1. Wrage and Baskerville, *American Forum*, 75.

2. Leonard J. Arrington and Davis Bitton, *The Mormon Experience: A History of the Latter-day Saints* (Urbana: University of Illinois Press, 1992), 3–19.

(1738–90) was a Revolutionary War veteran.[3] William Fuller Card (1787–1846) served the American Armed Forces in the War of 1812 as a lieutenant in "Captain Bell's [Campbell] Company of the New York Militia." Cyrus William Card's (1814–1900) family coped with the conflicts that would lead to the American Civil War (1861–65). William, and his wife Sarah Sabin Card (1793–1864), along with Cyrus W. and his wife Sarah Ann, were the first Cards to join the LDS Church.[4] In the South, slavery provided the labor force for the flourishing cotton industry. The debate over slavery was intense and would eventually result in the Civil War. At the same time, the Mormons were pouring into the Great Salt Lake Basin. Most of them were Northerners, including the Cards, who advocated for an end to slavery. Charles Ora Card (1839–1906) was yet in his youth.

The Card ancestors were among those common pioneers who forged the nation. They experienced economic and cultural revolutions that engulfed the United States. Following the Civil War, they witnessed the Industrial Revolution of the 1800s which fostered new factories in the East, increasing employment and urbanization. Railroads were just beginning to interconnect the eastern seaboard cities to coal, lumber, mining, and industrial interests. Individuals, families, and groups began migrating in great distances and numbers. News of the times came to rural America and Canada from travelers, touring politicians, preachers, and performers who traveled the Chautauqua circuits. The traveling speakers spoke at community congregations and gatherings, sharing stories about religious revivals, philosophy, and politics. Sometimes their speeches were simply a form of entertainment. Many travelers' names are known today: Ralph Waldo Emerson, William Ellery Channing, Lyman Beecher, John Calhoun, and Daniel Webster. They spoke of ideological disputations and strug-

---

3. "The Story of Charles Ora Card," handwritten notebook by Clarice Card Godfrey, Godfrey Family Papers. See also "Charles Ora Card," Pearl Card Sloan Family Papers, BYU Archive (hereafter referred to as the Sloan Papers). In these two references, "Campbell" is also simply referred to as "Bell."

4. Notes from the family history files of Clarice Card Godfrey, reproduced in *The Floyd Godfrey Family Organization News* 1, no. 5 (May 1979), insert 10.

gles that when resolved formed the fundamentals of our nation. The frontier newspapers often published letters from travelers. The idea of professional journalists was still on the horizon. On 13 July 1859, a young New York 97 reporter Horace Greeley was granted a two-hour interview with Brigham Young.[5] The article appeared 20 August 1859 and was simply an abbreviated transcript of the interview.[6] Some forty years later, colonizer Charles Ora Card used the frontier newspapers to recruit settlers to Canada. In the newspapers, readers generally learned about distant places simply from people who were writing home.[7]

**EARLY WHEELMEN**

Cyrus William Card was born at Painted Post, Steuben County, New York, about seventy-five miles south of Rochester and Palmyra, and just under three hundred miles northwest of New York City. This is where his son, Charles, spent his earliest years. The family home was in Ossian, where the Canaseraga and Sugar Creeks converged. It was a mostly rural countryside, with picturesque rolling green hills and forests at the edge of the Allegheny Mountains just north of the Pennsylvania line. It was a rich agricultural land. The Cards were fairly affluent settlers, skilled craftsman, and well-educated people for their day. Cyrus spent eight to ten years of his young adult life learning the trades of a wheelwright. A wheelwright was a skilled craftsman who specialized in wagon wheels. He built several wood mills within the Caesarea and Sugar Creek areas. This eventually led him into the lumber industry.

In adulthood, Cyrus was a man on the go. He believed that order was the first law of heaven and the home. His tool sheds, home, and even outhouse were so clean and well organized that "he could find anything in the dark," because he knew where it was, and he expected

---

5. Louis L. Snyder and Richard B. Morris, *A Treasury of Great Reporting* (New York: Simon and Schuster, 1962), 106–9.

6. Snyder and Morris, *A Treasury of Great Reporting*, 107–9.

7. Edwin Emery, *The Press and America: An Interpretative History of Journalism* (Englewood Cliffs, NJ: Prentice-Hall, 1962), 213–44.

the same of his family. His neighbors brought wagons of all kinds to his workbench, including "a little red wagon," sleds, and carriages, because they knew they could find the missing part and get things fixed.[8] Women brought him milk pans to solder, wooden barrels rims to tighten, and barrels to convert to water troughs for the animals. Cyrus never left home without taking a shovel. He wanted to be prepared, if needed, to fill a chuckhole in the road or repair an irrigation ditch that might be flooded. His garden and their small farm supplemented his wheelwright services and provided food for his family.

Cyrus and his wife, Sarah Tuttle (1819–94), were married in 1837. They had five children: Abigail Jane, who lived only a few short years (1837–41); Charles Ora, the second child and first son (1839–1906); Polly Caroline (1841–56), who would die while crossing the Plains; Matilda Francis (1852–75); and Sarah Angeline (1854–71). Sarah Tuttle complemented her husband's work ethic and generosity. She was the "typical New England mother. . . . Their home was almost like a hotel."[9] People coming and going were always welcome and well fed. To her school children, she was known as "auntie." Her cookie jar was always full.

The family was baptized into the LDS Church on 12 April 1843 by William Hyde in Canaseraga Creek, near Whitney's Crossing in the township of Burnes, Allegheny County, New York. Charles was baptized by his uncle Joseph Francis. They became part of the New York Ossian East Branch of the Mormon Church.[10] Cyrus's father, William Fuller Card, died three years later. Even before his death, William and his wife, Sarah Ann Sabin, had buried five of their eleven children and four more would eventually die, leaving only Cyrus and his younger sister Sarah. Cyrus moved his family to Park Center, Mich-

---

8. "Charles Ora Card," Sloan Papers.

9. "Charles Ora Card," Sloan Papers.

10. William Hyde, in Davie Bitton, *Guide to Mormon Diaries and Autobiographies* (Provo, UT: Brigham Young University Press, 1977), 170. Also, Andrew Jenson, "Charles Ora Card," *LDS Biographical Encyclopedia* (Salt Lake City: Jenson Historical Company, 1901), 1:297. The records do not indicate how the Cards came in contact with a Mormon missionary.

igan, where they cared for his mother and several younger children who were seriously ill. He was there to arrange his father's affairs. The sadness, depression, and agony were likely challenging. Cyrus's family were in Michigan for five years, 1847–51, during which young Charles attended school.[11] They returned to New York to recuperate and make preparations for the long journey to the Salt Lake Valley to be with the Saints who gathered there.

Back in New York, the family settled at Whitney's Crossing in the township of Burnes, close to their first home. Charles and his younger sister Polly continued in school until April 1856. Finally, preparations were complete and they started for the Salt Lake Valley. Within days of Charles's baptism, they were on their way.[12]

### LIFE AND DEATH TREKKING WEST

It was at this time that the first handcarts were authorized by Brigham Young as a new and improved means of moving people across the country. The handcarts were an inexpensive solution compared to the more expensive oxen-drawn covered wagons. The handcarts were intended for traveling light and increasing the flow of people. They were fashioned after the fruit and vegetable peddlers' wagons common in larger eastern cities, designed to be pulled from location to location without the need for livestock. Each cart carried minimal provisions for about four to five people.[13] One wagon per twenty handcarts was assigned to carry heavier provisions. Each person was allowed seventeen pounds of belongings. This included cooking utensils, bedding, and personal items such as clothing. If the carts were overweight or people had additional luggage, it went into a wagon, and they were charged extra. If the traveler could not afford the extra freight charges, their materials were

---

11. 19 January 1872, entry in *The Diaries of Charles Ora Card: The Utah Years, 1871–1886*, ed. Donald G. Godfrey and Kenneth W. Godfrey (Provo: Religious Studies Center, 2006), 19 January 1872. Card was in Michigan on a mission at the time of this entry.

12. Jenson, "Charles Ora Card," 297.

13. Arrington and Bitton, *The Mormon Experience*, 133–34.

abandoned. The handcart pioneers all walked across the plains pulling their carts loaded with whatever they could afford.[14]

The Cyrus Card family traveled with the Edmund L. Ellsworth company. Their little group included Cyrus (42), Sarah (37), and children Charles (16), Polly (14), Matilda (3), and Sarah (2), along with Grandmother Sarah Ann Tuttle Card and uncle Joseph Francis.[15] By 15 April 1856, the family took the first steps of their journey. The first leg was via train from New York State to Iowa City, Iowa, where they joined others in the main group of their handcart company. The Cards enjoyed two advantages: Cyrus's wheelwright experience and their two wagons.[16]

The company set out 9 June 1856. There were 52 wagons and 275 people. Progress crept forward slowly and was filled with individual challenge. Handcarts and wagons were in constant need of repair. One can safely assume that Cyrus was at the center of those repairs. Finding drinking water was tricky and at times water they could find was unpleasant to swallow. Rain captured in prairie buffalo wallows provided some welcomed yet nasty relief.[17] At one point, Cyrus was so desperate that he dug out a spring to reach fresh water. The company stopped routinely at a stream at least every ten days to fill their water barrels.

Young Charles took his turn in adult chores. If wood was unavailable for the evening fires, he gathered buffalo chips. The dried buffalo dung might have smelled a bit, but it was fuel sufficient for cooking. He stood guard at night. He joined the hunters who scouted for buffalo herds. Hunting was the major food source. Apparently, a few of the

---

14. Arrington, *Great Basin Kingdom*, 156–60.

15. Cyrus's younger sister Sarah Lavantia Card was not listed with the traveling group, but she did make the trek at some time as she died and was buried in Logan.

16. Cyrus left New York mid-April and would have arrived in Iowa within a few days. It is uncertain as to where they caught the train to Iowa. The handcart company did not leave Iowa until a month and a half later, 9 June. One wonders if Cyrus constructed the wagons for his family or if he had the finances to buy them from inheritance or his trade.

17. A wallow was a naturally occurring shallow water hole found on the prairies. The water was often stagnant and filled with animal hair, skin oils, and debris.

trek leaders were unkind to the foreigners from Italy. These new folks were unfamiliar with the herding of the domestic animals, hunting, and the ways of the West. As a consequence, they were blamed for slow progress and forced to walk more than others. Charles quietly smuggled women and children who were weak and tired aboard his father's wagons to rest for a few miles. Crossing the strong rivers and gentle streams, Charles carried the women and children one at a time on his back. As one of the travelers wrote, "The captain was not too kind, but that Charles O. Card was a kind boy. . . . God bless that man. I love him for his kindness and I hope I will never forget his name."[18] When Cyrus and Charles's uncle took sick, it fell to Charles to care for their wagons and four yoke of oxen, as well as all the travel and camping chores. He was forced to grow up quickly.

One stormy night in July, almost two months into the journey, Charles's sister Polly became ill. She had a fever, developed a bloody cough, and turned very pale. It was consumption.[19] She was only fourteen and died along the trail. Archer Walter, a traveler in the company, crafted a coffin for Polly. Cyrus paid him 50 cents ($13). Her "burrying [sic] ground [was] at the Town of Linden (I think)."[20] The family was distraught, but they carried on.

On 11 September, the company was surprised by a chance meeting with Apostle Parley P. Pratt and seventeen missionaries headed east for missions in Great Britain. Elder Pratt tried to address the travelers, but "observing that this was a new era in American as well as Church history . . . my utterance was choked, and I had to make a third try before I could overcome my emotions." What Pratt saw was a crowd a few weeks away from their destination. "Their faces were sunburnt and

---

18. Notes from the family history files of Clarice Card Godfrey. Reproduced in *The Floyd Godfrey Family Organization News* 1, no. 5 (May 1979), 10.

19. Diary of Ann Han Hickenlooper, 29 July 1856, https://history.lds.org/overlandtravels/trailExcerptMulti?lang=eng&pioneerId=18430&sourceId=89829. Consumption was a form of tuberculosis in which the body seemed to waste away from within.

20. Journal of John Oakley, journal excerpt 1856, June–August, https://history.lds.org/overlandtravels/trailExcerptMulti?lang=eng&pioneerId=18406sourceId=2872. The brackets in this quote are from the diaries.

lips parched; but cheerfulness reigned in every heart, and joy seemed to beam on every countenance."[21] The chance meeting produced a joyous celebration, and the next day both groups continued on their way.

Eight miles east of Salt Lake, President Brigham Young and the Nauvoo Brass Band met the Ellsworth company. President Young rose to offer his welcome, but when he saw the hunger in the little ones' faces, he simply said, "Come, let's serve the food; speeches can wait."[22] They ate and then were addressed by President Young and Ellsworth. "Never has a company been so highly honored . . . since Israel has arrived in these mountains, as the Pioneer handcart companies."[23] They had walked 1,300 rugged miles.

### MISSIONS AND THE MAN

Within a week, the families were attending the October general conference, where for the first time they listened to the authorities of the Church. It was a climactic celebration, after months of travel hardships, when they heard Brigham Young's call for volunteers to travel back to Wyoming to assist the Willie and Martin Handcart Companies, which had set off late in the season and were tragically trapped in a severe winter snowstorm.[24]

Cyrus and his family first lived for three years in Farmington, a hamlet twelve miles north of Salt Lake City. In 1858 Charles was ordained to the office of a Seventy in the Church lay priesthood. He was now nineteen years old. He held that office for the next nineteen years.

---

21. Parley P. Pratt, *Autobiography of Parley Parker Pratt* (Salt Lake City: Deseret Book, 1950), 434–35. Newell R. Walker, "They Walked 1,300 Miles," *Ensign*, 44–49. Walker has this meeting on 18 September. Pratt records it as 11 September.

22. Walker, "They Walked 1,300 Miles," 48.

23. Walker, "They Walked 1,300 Miles," 49. The Cards are not listed in the newspaper as arriving with the immigrants. One record indicates they may have left the company at Fort Bridger. It is also possible that only the handcart pioneers were listed.

24. Howard A. Christy, "Weather, Disaster and Responsibility: An Essay on the Willie and Martin Handcart Story," *BYU Studies* 37, no. 1 (1997–98), 6–74.

In 1859, Cache Valley was being settled. Crops reported by the earliest pioneers had been plentiful, and President Young sent Apostles Orson Hyde and Ezra T. Benson to organize several communities. James Henry Martineau, a convert and surveyor, was creating city blocks with lots at 1.35 acres.[25] Cyrus and his son, Charles, traveled to Logan to stake out a homesite. Cyrus left Charles in Logan to build their first cabin. It would be a one-room structure among a small group of houses arranged like a fort for protection from the Shoshone natives and any interference from the federal government.[26] Within a year, Cyrus moved the whole family to the new settlement of Logan. There were soon one hundred homes in the rapidly growing Cache Valley.[27]

Cyrus sustained the family with a new business, the Card & Son Sawmill, Lath, and Shingle Mill. Cyrus and Charles were business partners. Logan and the lumber business did well. Their sawmill was essential to the valley's homesteaders and the town. Between 1862 and 1880, Charles calculated he and his father had paid $2,480.90 or $137.82 per year tithing ($58,137 or $3,234).[28] Over this same time they purchased four three-quarter-acre building lots in the city and a thirty-five-acre farm.[29] They were not farmers as much as businessmen, but crops were planted, and gardens provided food for their families. This is how everyone was fed. The Cards acquired their raw lumber from the Green and Logan Canyons, although the Logan Canyon road extended only

---

25. F. Ross Peterson, *A History of Cache Country* (Salt Lake City: Utah State Historical Society, 1997), 35–37. Also, Godfrey and McCarty, *An Uncommon Common Pioneer*, 148. Martineau's surveys spanned several decades reaching from Logan and south to the Mexican Mormon colonies.

26. See Chapter 15, "The 'Invasion' of Utah," and Chapter 16, "Babylon Wars: Zion Grows," in Leonard J. Arrington, *Brigham Young: American Moses* (Urbana: University of Illinois Press, 1986), 251–302.

27. Joel E. Ricks, "The First Settlements," in *History of a Valley*, ed. Joel E. Ricks and Averett L. Cooley (Logan, UT: Deseret News Press, 1956), 43–47.

28. Godfrey and Godfrey, *The Diaries of Charles Ora Card: The Utah Years, 1871–1886*, 17 April 1880.

29. James A. Hudson, *Charles Ora Card: Pioneer and Colonizer* (Cardston, AB, Canada: Hudson, 1963), 164.

a few miles into the mountains.³⁰ Trees were harvested in early fall or late winter. The light snows made it easier for the teams to drag out the logs. They hauled them to the mill for sawing in preparation for construction and sale. Until 1875, their sawmill faced only one competitor, the F. N. Peterson & Sons Planing Mill.

In 1875, Cyrus and Charles supported the establishment of the United Order in Logan. The Card & Son Sawmill, Lath, and Shingle Mill and the P. N. Petersen & Sons Planing Mill merged under the new United Order Manufacturing and Building Company of the Logan Second Ward.³¹ One year later it opened for business "with a paid-up capital of $10,410" ($221,368).³² No matter how these finances were divided, the sum was significant.

The United Orders were established in Mormon communities from Utah to Mexico during the late 1800s. These cooperative enterprises were originally regarded as ideal for the development of individual independence while eliminating poverty. This was to be accomplished by having everyone deed all their personal property to the Church for redistribution according to individual stewards. The system was short-lived, but it did aid colonizers. It promoted self-sufficiency as everyone was expected to work and contribute. Most importantly, the United Order symbolized a more perfect society in which everyone worked supporting each other.³³ Cyrus and Charles were leaders in the Logan United Order. Charles became a member of the governing board. After the Card Sawmill went to the Order, Cyrus managed the mill that pro-

---

30. Ricks and Cooley, *History of a Valley*, 161.

31. The LDS Church is organized geographically and by population within specific areas. A ward or branch consists of members living within a geographically defined area. A stake is the combination of multiple wards. In this way, the larger organization kept the emphasis on the local service as opposed to the megachurch concept.

32. Leonard J. Arrington, Feramorz Y. Fox, and Dean L. May, *Building The City of God: Community & Cooperation Among the Mormons* (Urbana: University of Illinois Press, 1992), 223. Also Ricks and Cooley, *History of a Valley*, 198.

33. Leonard J. Arrington, *Great Basin Kingdom: An Economic History of the Latter-Day Saints, 1830–1900*, 330–33. See also L. Dwight Israelson, "United Orders," in *Encyclopedia of Mormonism*, 4:1493–95; Ricks and Cooley, *History of a Valley*, 198–99.

vided lumber for the town as well as the construction of the Logan Tabernacle and the temple.

Charles was a part of a loving family and had a deep respect for his father and his father's families.[34] Cyrus instilled a desire for education, a respect for order, and a love for the Church. Cyrus died 4 September 1900, having nurtured his son's deep-rooted foundation of faith.

**CACHE VALLEY LEADERSHIP**

In maturity, Charles emerged as a prominent leader in Cache Valley. He was elected to the first Logan City Council (1866), at age twenty-seven, and served as a city councilman for sixteen years. As a member of the Logan City Council, he served on a special committee organized to curb the consumption of alcohol.[35] They were unsuccessful, but it was a colorful point of contention between members of the Church who wanted to be left alone and nonmembers who too had recognized the farming and business potential in the valley. Charles was appointed to the Board of Teacher Examiners and the Logan School Board. He worked as director of the Logan Irrigation Canal Company and was a road commissioner for almost three decades. This experience was invaluable when he later helped develop Alberta irrigation. In Logan, he was elected a county selectman with the assignment of regulating timber and water privileges. When the Logan Board of Education was created in 1872, he was elected to it and chosen as the chairman of the board of trustees for two years. In 1877, when Brigham Young College

---

34. Godfrey and Godfrey, *The Diaries of Charles Ora Card: The Utah Years, 1871–1886*, 273f28. Also James A. Hudson, *Charles Ora Card: Pioneer and Colonizer* (Cardston: Hudson, 1963), 176–77. Cyrus entered into two polygamous marriages with sisters Emma Booth (in 1859) and Ann Booth (in 1861). The family records of Jo Anne Sloan Rogers and Marilyn Godfrey Ockey Pitcher all confirm the Tuttle and Booth marriages. Internet sources add a Nancy Campbell (1862) and a Sarabette Stone (1857), thus bringing Cyrus's possible total number of wives to five. The sealing dates of the latter were 2003 and 1994 respectively. The Internet data on these last two wives are conflicting and undocumented.

35. See Godfrey and Godfrey, *The Diaries of Charles Ora Card: The Utah Years, 1871–1886*, 1 March 1883, also 10 July 1883 for activities.

was founded, Charles was appointed to its board of trustees, in which he served for another twelve years.[36]

Charles was a strong proponent of education. He had attended schools in New York and Michigan. He attended business school in Ogden and taught school in Logan.[37] As a community and church leader, he spoke relentlessly, encouraging "the schooling of our children," praising their capability for the "highest attainments."[38] Charles taught school in the Logan First Ward meetinghouse. One of his pupils was his future wife, Sarah Jane Painter. One day, Sarah and her friends were tardy because they had been out picking wildflowers. The penalty was each one taking turns "standing on the block." Sarah left for home after school crying, "I am never going back to that old Charley Card's school anymore." She apparently had forgotten the incident when they married nine years later.[39]

Charles's daily life was an interwoven pattern of activities dedicated to his family, community, and religious service. He worked on any project he thought would improve his community. When the Church proceeded with construction of the Logan Tabernacle in 1873, he was asked to act as the building superintendent. In 1877, he was transferred from this project to a still more imposing religious edifice, the Logan Temple.[40] The cornerstone was laid 17 September 1877.[41] These building assignments involved establishing specialized mills, factories, rock quarries, and kilns along with roads to get the materials to the building sites. He solicited donations for buildings and main-

---

36. "Charles Ora Card Activities Timeline," in *The Diaries of Charles Ora Card: The Canadian Years, 1886–1903*, ed. Donald G. Godfrey and Brigham Y. Card (Salt Lake City: University of Utah Press, 1993), xxxix.

37. Hudson, *Charles Ora Card*, 297.

38. Godfrey and Godfrey, *The Diaries of Charles Ora Card: The Utah Years, 1871–1886*, 17 April and 2 May 1881.

39. "The Story of Charles Ora Card," Godfrey Family Papers.

40. Correspondence from John Taylor to Charles O. Card, 19 October 1877, CR 1 20, John Taylor Papers, Church History Library. Kenneth W. Godfrey, *Logan, Utah: A One Hundred Fifty Year History* (Logan, UT: Exemplar Press, 2010), 28.

41. Godfrey and Godfrey, *The Diaries of Charles Ora Card: The Utah Years, 1871–1886*, 17 September 1877.

tained the accounting records along with recruiting and supervising workers and volunteer laborers.

The most important agricultural industry experience Charles drew from Cache Valley was irrigation, which he would use in Canada. Like Cache Valley—southern Alberta, Canada, was semiarid. Farming success was dependent upon drawing and controlling water from the mountains. In Utah, the Hyde Park, Smithfield, and Richmond canals were an immense complex, channeling water into Cache Valley through about thirty-two miles of ditches dug by hand and horse-drawn machinery. The water irrigated eleven thousand acres of farmland.[42] Card's greatest accomplishment in Canada "was to oversee the construction of the Kimball-Lethbridge Canal [in southern Alberta]. . . . This canal had 65 miles of channels, besides the natural waterways, irrigating about 200,000 acres of land."[43] It brought homesteaders to southern Alberta—providing sustaining work, establishing settlements, and stimulating economic growth.

### NEW ENGLAND MISSION

Like most Church leaders, Charles was called to serve a mission.[44] His New England Mission was comparatively brief. He was called and directed to revisit the states of his youth. He departed Saturday, 9 December 1871, taking with him a list of family and friends' names as he headed out on foot.[45] His companion was William Hyde Jr., the son of the missionary who had converted the Cards. For four months, Charles and William traversed Wisconsin, Michigan, and New York. They walked the distance with food and rest provided by friends and

---

42. Peterson, "History of Cache County," 58–61. Also, Hudson, *Charles Ora Card*, 21.

43. Hudson, *Charles Ora Card*, 21.

44. The LDS Church has no paid ministry in missionary, local, and stake organizations. The work of the Church is accomplished through volunteer service. "Callings" or assignments come from Church leaders. Ludlow, 248–50.

45. See Godfrey and Godfrey, *The Diaries of Charles Ora Card: The Utah Years, 1871–1886*, 9 April 1872, 9 December 1891.

people along the way. Anti-Mormon literature and polygamy issues preceded them. More than teaching converts, they "had the privilege of defending the cause of Celestial Marriage [polygamy]. . . and met with a little abuse."[46] They were treated warmly when they introduced themselves as missionaries to a Baptist minister who immediately turned cold when he realized they were Latter-day Saints. Charles reported that generally, "religion was at a very low ebb in these parts, the majority of the people seeking after quick fortunes and it seems to the passer that everyone is trying to see who can make the most with the least labor and many don't mind grinding the faces of the poor."[47] This was a commentary both on conditions, as he saw them, as well as revealing his own work ethic.

Perhaps the most significant experience of Charles's mission was his incidental meeting with a former non-Mormon neighbor of the Prophet Joseph Smith. It was in the midst of the anti-Mormon publishers and authors, such as Eber D. Howe's *Mormonism Unvailed* (1834), attempting to tarnish the reputation of the Church and character of Joseph Smith, calling the members a lazy, shiftless, and poor people. Amidst the criticism, it is revealing that Card and Hyde encountered Mrs. Canfield Dickenson, who offered her own assessment. She "lived about two miles from the Smith family," and she "gave us a very favorable account of Joseph Smith and his parents," describing them as "farmers and industrious and neat and tidy about their house."[48]

As the companions headed home in the green mountains of "old Mass," Charles was walking among the laurel bushes where he selected a walking cane "as a natural curiosity to cary [sic] home to our distant Utah."[49] He and his companion stripped the bark from the canes,

---

46. See Godfrey and Godfrey, *The Diaries of Charles Ora Card: The Utah Years, 1871–1886*, 25 February 1872.

47. "Correspondence: Whitney's Cross, Allegheny Country, N. Y. February 3, 1872," *Deseret News*, 6 March 1872, 50.

48. See Godfrey and Godfrey, *The Diaries of Charles Ora Card: The Utah Years, 1871–1886*, 30 December 1871. The complete name and circumstance of Mrs. Dickenson is unknown in this writing.

49. See Godfrey and Godfrey, *The Diaries of Charles Ora Card: The Utah Years, 1871–1886*, 28 February 1872. A laurel is an aromatic evergreen shrub. The leaves are

varnished them, and carried them home.[50] Over time, the cane has become a priceless antique.

## "QUORUM OF WIVES"

Charles's community and church responsibilities increased with his age and service. "He seemed to know the hearts of men and have a persuasive technique to draw the potential abilities from others."[51] His service was continuous throughout his life, as was his service to his four wives and fifteen children. With the exception of his first wife, the remaining three worked together, loved one another, supported each other in their trials, and enjoyed a flow of communication among them. In August 1923, they were all seated together for Heber J. Grant's dedication of the first Canadian temple.[52]

### Sarah Jane Birdneau (1850–1926)

At age 28, on 17 October 1867, Charles married his first wife Sarah "Sallie" Jane Birdneau.[53] Sallie was the daughter of Nehemiah Birdneau, who was among the Cache Valley pioneers. Charles was already a partner in his sawmill business, a teacher, and a member of what would become the Logan School Board. The newlyweds' first home was a one-room log cabin with a dirt floor, located right next door to his father's residence. Four years later, their first child, a daughter, Sarah Jane Card, was born (1870–1930). She was affectionately called

---

used in seasoning and the oil from them can be made into a salve for healing open wounds.

50. This cane was handed down from Clarice Card Godfrey to her son Kenneth Floyd Godfrey, then to Donald G. Godfrey.

51. Hudson, *Charles Ora Card*, 47.

52. The best description of each wife is found in Brigham Y. Card, "Life Histories of the Wives of Charles Ora Card," M270 L 7225, Church History Library. The life of Zina is detailed in Donald G. Godfrey, "Zina Presendia Young Williams Card: Brigham's Daughter, Cardston's First Lady," *Journal of Mormon History* 23, no. 2 (Fall 1997), 107–27. Also, Bradley and Woodward, *Four Zinas*.

53. The name Birdneau comes with several different spellings in history: Beirdneau, Birdeneau, and Birdno all refer to the same person or family. In this writing, the author selected the first spelling, as this is how it appears throughout Card's diaries.

"Jennie." She was eight months old when Charles was called to serve a mission in the eastern states. It might have seemed difficult, yet he and Sallie corresponded regularly, exchanging photographs and many letters during his mission.[54] Charles Ora Card Jr. was born six years later (1873–1930).

Over the next ten years, Charles built Sallie a frame home with wooden floors. As he evolved into an influential church and community leader, he was often called upon to defend the ideals of polygamy. At first Sarah shared the beliefs. In 1882, when she fell ill, he cleared his schedule for six days, never leaving her side. There was a love and caring "shown during these hectic . . . years."[55] Sallie and children, Jennie and Charles Jr., traveled with him to his various business and Church assignments, but there was also mounting tension.

Unfortunately, Sallie was finding herself stretched between different worlds.[56] On 14 April 1879, while Charles was away, his father and her father entered her home and ejected a male visitor. The affair left Charles devastated with deep "feelings of anguish . . . seemingly more than I could bear."[57] His heart would survive this first affair, but not the second, this time with one of Charles's construction workers on the temple, Benjamin Ramsel. Ramsel had been Charles's companion on numerous chores in temple construction. Charles had admired him for his outdoor skills. He had visited Charles's home often—apparently too often. Charles felt betrayed. Defending herself in the affairs, Sallie became increasingly antagonistic, living in and out of Church norms. After the affair with Ramsel, she finally requested a divorce. Charles did not want a divorce. Sallie counseled with her father and Charles.

---

54. Card, "Life Histories of the Wives of Charles Ora Card," 2.

55. Godfrey and Godfrey, *The Diaries of Charles Ora Card: The Utah Years, 1871–1886*, 17 February and 5 June 1878. The diaries of this time are replete with these family outings and birthday celebrations. See Card, "Life Histories of the Wives of Charles Ora Card," 3.

56. See Godfrey and Godfrey, *The Diaries of Charles Ora Card: The Utah Years, 1871–1886*, 17 June 1878.

57. See Godfrey and Godfrey, *The Diaries of Charles Ora Card: The Utah Years, 1871–1886*, 14 April 1879. Also, "The Story of Sarah Jane Beirdneau," in Brigham Y. Card, "Life Histories of the Wives of Charles Ora Card," 4.

She struggled with the implications of plural marriage. Sallie would repent, continue in the affair, get counseling, and repent again. It was a cycle that ended in heartache. Finally, the divorce was granted. Charles wrote, "I desire not a separation, but desire peace."[58]

After the divorce, Charles built a separate residence for Sallie in Logan, but the custody of the children was given to Charles. Sallie would eventually marry Ramsel, and while Charles was in hiding from federal authorities, she persuaded the children to leave the Church and follow her ways. The two who suffered most from the divorce were the children. They would eventually move to Baker, Oregon, where they spent the rest of their lives.[59]

*Sarah Jane Painter (1839–1936)*

On 17 October 1876, Charles wed his second wife, Sarah Jane Painter. This was his first polygamous union. They would have six children: Matilda Francis (1878–79), George Cyrus (1880–1958), Lavantia Painter (1881–1937), Pearl Painter (1884–1965), Abigale Jane (1886–1939), and Franklin Almon (1892–1972). Sarah was eight years younger than Sallie, yet it was Sarah to whom Sallie went for counsel during her own conflicts with Charles.

Sarah Jane was the daughter of George Painter and Jane Herbert, long-time residents of Logan.[60] She was born 15 March 1858 in Bountiful, Utah, and passed away 9 February 1936. Her parents were a hardworking, no frills, traditional English family. George Painter supported this family by making brooms and selling them from his home along with managing a small coal business. As with all the pioneers, a modest farm kept the family fed. George taught his children a rigorous work ethic as they toiled at his side. Jane dried apples and made apple cider. The cider was often fermented to make a cider vinegar. All three products were used in the family and sold to neighbors. Sarah was a profi-

---

58. Godfrey and Godfrey, *The Diaries of Charles Ora Card: The Utah Years, 1871–1886*, 18–21 March 1884.

59. Sarah was buried in Baker, Oregon, in 1930, and Charles Jr. in Portland, Oregon, also 1930.

60. "Sarah Jane Painter," *Life Histories of the Wives of Charles Ora Card*, n. p.

cient bookkeeper. She managed the accounts of the family businesses, skills she would use in her own family. She attended the Logan First Ward School located on First North and Main Street where Charles Ora Card was her teacher. She remembered him in that role as a strict, "rather interesting gentleman."[61]

Sarah would translate her English customs, skills, and heritage into her family with Charles. She managed their Logan farms and their own home while Charles was in exile and hiding from the marshals, then again while he was in Canada for sixteen years. She never spoke negatively about polygamy and in fact tried to encourage Sallie, who would have been considered the senior wife, to stay the course, repent, and hold true to the gospel.

Charles and Sarah's home was a humble one, but it was always full of the smells of good cooking—such as homemade bread, red potatoes, and peas dipped in melted butter. "Well, it isn't very much," she would say, as family, visitors, and Church dignitaries surrounded her table, "but you are surely welcome." Her English upbringing was apparent in her table manners, as she could eat her peas with even a knife without dropping a single one. After dinner, the children helped clear the table and clean the kitchen. Then they gathered around to listen as she told stories of pioneering and Indians. These stories were laden with gospel principles and her testimony.[62]

Sarah's position was significant in the Card family. She became the de facto senior wife as she attempted to pull Sallie back into the fold. Her life revolved around her family and service. During Charles's mission in Canada, she was alone. Persecution weighed on her, but she was faithful.[63] The wives were scattered. She remained in Logan, managing family and business affairs. She participated in the dedication of the Logan Temple and served as the Logan Relief Society president for decades. Following Charles's death, Sarah would live the next thirty-six years as a widow with her five children.

---

61. "Sarah Jane Painter," *Life Histories of the Wives of Charles Ora Card*, n. p. Also, Kenneth W. Godfrey, *Logan, Utah: One Hundred Fifty Year History*, 44.

62. "Sarah Jane Painter," *Life Histories of the Wives of Charles Ora Card*, n. p.

63. "Sarah Jane Painter," *Life Histories of the Wives of Charles Ora Card*, n. p.

*Zina Young Williams (1850–1931)*

Charles's third wife, Zina Young Williams Card, was the daughter of Brigham Young and Zina Diantha Huntington. Charles and Zina were married 17 June 1884. They would have three children: Joseph Young Card (1885–1956), Zina Young (1888–1975), and Orson Rega Card (1891–1984). Their daughter Zina would later marry Hugh B. Brown. Their son Orson was the grandfather of Orson Scott Card, the famous science fiction writer. Their family was one of distinction.

Zina Young was an extraordinary woman. She was one of the eldest daughters of Brigham Young, a position which gave her prominence within the Church, as well as in Utah and later southern Alberta societies. She was among the earliest leaders of the Young Women's Mutual Improvement Association and the first "Ladies Matron" at what would become Brigham Young University. It was at Brigham Young Academy that she met Charles. He had enrolled Charles Jr. and Jennie in the academy, and he had arranged visiting and counseling for them with Zina, the school's matron, as they struggled with the divorce of their parents.[64]

Zina, who was not yet thirty, was one of the first women from the state of Utah working in the suffrage movement. This assignment gave her national recognition. She toured the eastern United States as an ambassador, meeting with President Rutherford B. Hayes, speaking before the United States Senate, and even interviewing with Senator George Franklin Edmunds, a sponsor of the antipolygamy legislation known as the Edmunds Act and Edmunds-Tucker Act.[65] In her day, she was an outspoken feminist and a spokesperson for her beliefs. As a part of the Mormon immigration into Alberta, she hosted a parade of curious Canadian dignitaries in her home.

---

64. At this time, Charles was in hiding, and in his forced absence, Sallie's influence increased over her children. They would eventually leave the Brigham Young Academy in Provo and enroll in the Logan Protestant School. They then followed Sallie and her new husband to Oregon.

65. Godfrey, "Zina Presendia Young Williams Card: Brigham's Daughter, Cardston's First Lady," 114–15. Also, Bradley and Woodward, *A Story of Mothers and Daughters on the Mormon Frontier*, 349.

Pioneer home of Charles and Zina Card, 1887. Courtesy of Marilyn Ockey-Pitcher.

Zina was forced from the comfort of her Utah home in 1887 to escape the persecution she and Charles endured at the hands of the US marshals during the days of polygamy. They were forced into the Mormon Underground to avoid the US marshals.[66] Zina was among the first women to settle in southern Alberta. Apostle John Taylor singled out Zina as a major influence in the Canadian settlement: "Zina had a mission here [in Canada]." In southern Alberta literature, Charles is credited as founding the town of Cardston; and Zina was the settlement's first lady.[67]

*Lavinia Clark Rigby (1839–1960)*

Lavinia Card married Charles on 2 December 1885.[68] She was his fourth wife. They had five children: Mary (born 1887), Lavinia (1890),

---

66. Godfrey, "Zina Presendia Young Williams Card: Brigham's Daughter, Cardston's First Lady," 118–21.

67. Godfrey, "Zina Presendia Young Williams Card: Brigham's Daughter, Cardston's First Lady," 124–27.

68. There are two spellings for the name Lavinia in the family papers: Lavinia and LaVinia. Both are the same individual. See "History of Lavinia C. Card," *Life Histories*

Brick home of Charles and Zina Card, circa 1903. Courtesy of Marilyn Ockey-Pitcher.

Charles (1896), Sterling (1899), and William (1904).[69] She was the sixth daughter of William F. Rigby and Mary Clark Rigby, who would become pioneers in southern Idaho.

Lavinia lived and grew up in the Cache Valley. Her parents lived in their covered wagon as they moved about finally settling in Clarkston, where her father constructed a one-room log cabin with an attic. It was cold and cramped, but roomier and warmer than the wagon. In nearby Newton, their next home was to be a six-room log cabin. However, before they could occupy it, one of the workmen kicked wood shavings into the fireplace, and the house caught fire. Their entire home, furniture, and all personal belongings were reduced to ashes. William's next home was larger than any in the vicinity, and here he often hosted local meetings and dances.

---

*of the Wives of Charles Ora Card*, n. p.

69. Death dates of Livinia Card's children were footnotes in Brigham Y. Card's, "Life Histories of the Wives of Charles Ora Card." Alternate sources give conflicting dates.

Lavinia wrote that her childhood days were happy. Entertainment meant making popcorn or molasses candy. The molasses was made from sugar cane raised on the farm. William read the scriptures to his children in a loud and spirited voice and laced his other stories with gospel principles. He had a good sense of humor. One day he gave the children the task of harvesting the peas in the field. When he returned, he asked how many they had picked. The dutiful children reported that they had "stepped it off" and found "all twelve acres were pulled." This surprised their father because he had planted only one acre of peas. The children were caught in their ways and thereafter whenever William told his evening stories with hyperbole, he would end with "now that is ten acres of peas."[70] The children got the message. After his stories, the evenings closed with a song. This nightly event took place in many pioneering homes after all the chores were done. It was their form of entertainment and social communication.

In 1879, when Lavinia was twelve, she was hired on as a cook for the loggers in Beaver Canyon. Beaver Canyon was east of Logan, into the mountains up Logan Canyon between Logan and Bear Lake.[71] She was taking on adult responsibilities. As she grew into teenage and dating years, she accompanied her father, who had the lumber contracts in the area, and for the next two years she helped support the family. They worked harvesting trees from the mountains and crops on the farm. They fought off the grasshoppers by digging a large hole in the field and covering it with a green cloth. The children then took long sticks and herded the hoppers onto the cloth. Then they dumped the critters into the hole and covered it with dirt. It taught the children good work habits, but the grasshoppers likely won the battle.[72]

With each year, Lavinia grew in her responsibilities, and she attended school. She was counselor in the Mutual Improvement Organization and taught a Sunday School class. At eighteen, she moved to

---

70. "History of Lavinia C. Rigby Card," *Life Histories of the Wives of Charles Ora Card*, 3.

71. Today Beaver Canyon is a ski resort. Peterson, *History of Cache Country*, 273.

72. Lavinia Rigby Card, "Ingredients of the Happy Home Life of the Rigby Family," Godfrey Family Papers. See also box 186, William F. Rigby Collection.

Logan and entered the Brigham Young College. It was in 1885 that Charles proposed marriage. Lavinia was nineteen and Charles was forty-six. She had known Charles all of her life, and she was active and dating when Charles approached her. His proposal was a surprise. She counseled with her father and family who advised her to do what she thought was the right thing. She accepted. Zina helped make her wedding dress. Lavinia and Charles were married 2 December 1885.[73]

This marriage was a little different, as the federal marshals were now aggressively hunting for Charles.[74] In a letter to President John Taylor, Card notes, "They watch me so closely I have retired for the present to the mountains where I am writing this. They have spotters and detectives to work watching my houses as well as streets and roads."[75] One of his secret hiding places was the Rigby home attic. Because of these conditions, Lavinia and Charles had a quiet temple wedding with a family gathering afterward for supper and celebration. Even moving around the valley with his new bride and meeting his other families invited disaster. Traveling must have been a frightening experience for young Lavinia. Charles often took other leaders with him and they hid out together. The persecution was increasingly severe. Lavinia hid in the woods alone, away from the marshals when they came looking. They wanted her to testify against Charles. Eventually, Charles purchased a home for her near Rexburg, and she lived there with their children away from the prowling federal authorities.[76]

---

73. "History of Lavinia C. Rigby Card," *Life Histories of the Wives of Charles Ora Card*, 3–5.

74. Godfrey and Godfrey, *The Diaries of Charles Ora Card: The Utah Years, 1871–1886*, 565.

75. Letter from Charles Ora Card to John Taylor, 15 August 1886. Reproduced in Godfrey and Godfrey, *The Diaries of Charles Ora Card: The Utah Years, 1871–1886*, 570.

76. "History of Lavinia C. Rigby Card," *Life Histories of the Wives of Charles Ora Card*, 7.

## POLYGAMY, PERSECUTION, AND STRENGTH

Charles's life was increasingly complex. In 1879, he became a member of the Logan Stake presidency, serving with Marriner W. Merrill as counselors to William B. Preston. He was still the superintendent of construction on the Logan Temple, along with all his other city and county offices. His diaries reflect extensive travels throughout the region from Bear Lake to Salt Lake, which must have felt like continual weeks of service. In 1884, William B. Preston was called to be the presiding bishop of the Church, and Charles was called as the new president of the Cache Valley Stake. This made him the presiding Church officer of the region. Again it increased his responsibilities, and this time it placed him higher on the list of primary targets in the eyes of the marshals.[77]

The passing of the Edmunds Act and Edmunds-Tucker Act disenfranchised Charles. Now, he was no longer allowed to vote, hold a public office, or serve on a jury. He was legally stripped of all his civic titles and responsibilities, which were given to the minority non-Mormons. Yet, the majority of the population, the Mormons, still depended on his leadership in every aspect of their lives. The acts aimed at eradicating polygamy sought to punish those engaging in "cohabitation." It was directed specifically at the Mormon population and its leadership who engaged in the practice. Charles was among this group. He supported three wives. Following passage of these laws, Charles and many other Church leaders struggled in the conflicts over families, polygamy, and power that effectively divided Mormons and non-Mormons ("gentiles"), polarizing the territory. Families were forcibly divided. Charles's own home was unsafe. The US Marshals wanted to put him on trial. As a result, he stayed with friends and relatives in what has been called the Mormon Underground. He hid in the attic of the Tabernacle and various rooms in the temple as well in Logan Canyon brush and timber. Yet, he still was concerned and responsible for the administration of Church-owned assets, now being transferred to local entities to avoid

---

77. Godfrey and Godfrey, *The Diaries of Charles Ora Card: The Utah Years, 1871–1886*, notes found on inside the cover of the diaries, 570, 8 October, 1900.

financial loss and federal takeovers.⁷⁸ He was constantly dealing with disruptions in local Church leadership, families, and his work. It was the increasing pressure of the 1882 and 1887 acts that forced Charles's departure from Logan without even enough time to organize for his traveling.

**CAPTURED AND ESCAPED**

Persecution increased to the point that Charles and other Church leaders were afraid to go to their homes. They were afraid for their families. They administered their Church responsibilities as best as they could while in hiding. Charles was forced to move his wives and families. Families struggling to make a living were physically separated, and they scattered across the West. Some headed north to Montana to work in the mines and on the railroad. Others went to southern Arizona and the colonies of Mexico. Wives were alone. Single-parent family responsibilities were forced upon them. Husbands disappeared, then visited when they could and tried to provide some sustenance and support. Such was the environment in which Charles found himself. Something had to be done. Charles planned his escape. Sarah was to stay in Logan and manage his properties there, Zina would head into the Mormon Underground, and Lavinia was to move with Charles to Arizona. It was as good a plan as any. However, it was not to be.⁷⁹

By midsummer 1886, Charles went into the Mormon Underground, which basically meant "keeping out of the way of the U.S. Deputy Marshals." He knew they were watching for both him and Apostle Moses Thatcher, who also lived in Logan.⁸⁰ Charles was conducting the

---

78. Arrington, *Great Basin Kingdom*, 362–63.

79. See *The Diaries of Charles Ora Card: The Utah Years, 1871–1886*, 14 and 25 September 1886.

80. Moses Thatcher was a leading businessman and Cache Valley Stake president from 1871 to 1879 when he was called to be a member of the Quorum of the Twelve Apostles. See *Deseret News 1989–90 Church Almanac*, 50. Also Ricks and Cooley, *History of a Valley*, 278–81.

family business, mostly left to his father, and Church business as best he could.

Hiding out with a relative, he woke in the morning and was invited to breakfast, but he declined, preferring to be home with his wife Sarah Jane. So he went home, finding that breakfast had already been served. Even though Sarah had not been expecting him, she went about preparing an additional "cozy meal" while Charles went to the stable, greased his buggy, hitched up the horse, and drove to the front gate. He watched his stepson Sterling Williams pulling a load of hay from the field. Seeing his father, Sterling announced that they needed a pitch fork. So Charles drove into town, purchased a fork, and returned with it for his boys to unload the hay. He did not know if the marshals had seen him in town, so he took the extra precaution not to tie his horse.

He was half finished with his breakfast when Ben Garr and US Marshall E. W. Exum were at his back door.[81] As Charles walked toward them he was "impressed not to run." The marshal drew his revolver and commanded Charles to stop. Charles "instantaneously almost and intuitively . . . reached for one I had in my hip pocket. . . . I did no more than place my hand upon my pocket, as we both knew the consequence." Mr. Exum drew out a warrant from his pocket, and Charles was arrested.[82] He was taken to town, where he telegraphed Church headquarters to secure a bondsman. As the group moved about the community conducting business, Charles engaged his captors in conversation as to their unjust persecution against the polygamists. They went to dinner at the hotel and granted Charles his request to visit the bank, the telegraph office, and even accompanied him home to say goodbye to his wife Sarah.

Word had spread through town that morning and when the Charles and the marshals arrived at the train depot for the afternoon

---

81. Ben Garr was a former member of the Church but was now part of the group hunting the Church leadership. The Garrs came to Cache Valley among the herders working some three thousand head of cattle and horses, of which two thousand head belonged to the Mormon Church. William Garr had been a town selectman in 1856. See Ricks and Cooley, *History of a Valley*, 29–31, 90.

82. See Godfrey and Card, *Diaries of Charles Ora Card: The Canadian Years, 1886–1903*, 24 July 1886.

train, there was quite a crowd gathering about. Charles shook hands with everyone while the marshal obtained the tickets. As the party boarded the train with other passengers, the marshal and Charles got separated. The train started slowly, and Charles saw his escape opportunity. He jumped off the train to the ground looking for a horse or buggy. As it happened, a "young powerful horse" was on the east side of the street and Charles jumped on. The previous rider, however, was long legged, and Charles's feet could not reach the stirrups. As a result he was bounced around in with one of the "roughest [rides] of his life."[83]

Reportedly, the marshal demanded the train be stopped, but the conductor refused.[84] Charles hid out in the bushes and spent the night with friends. It was a dramatic experience.[85] It was a time that made it difficult to hold families and Church organizations together. Fathers and leaders were scattered. Charles was assisted by his counselor, Elder Orson Smith, in the stake presidency, and when Smith was targeted, he headed north and worked in building railroads in Montana.[86]

---

83. The horse belonged to Logan's mayor Aaron Farr, who was arrested for leaving the horse at the depot. Card wrote the *Utah Journal*, denying any prearrangement with Farr and recounting again his impromptu decision to escape. The letter was also reprinted in the *Deseret News*, Wednesday, 17 November 1886. See Hudson, "Charles Ora Card: Pioneer and Colonizer," 80–81.

84. When Card learned that the conductor refused to stop the train is not known, except it must have been before 14 September 1886. The conductor himself recounted his refusal to stop the train as recorded in Card's diary for 14 February 1890.

85. Up to 14 September 1886, there were four arrests in Cache County according to the compilation of Professor Lowell Ben Bennion from Andrew Jenson's *Church Chronology* (Salt Lake City: Deseret News, 1914). Apparently the two Wellsville arrests were not known to Andrew Jenson, whose record of arrests by years is 1884: 2; 1885: 2; 1886: 5 (or 7), C. O. Card's being the first for that year; 1887: 15; 1888: 17; 1889: 6; 1890: 3; 1891: 4; and 1893: 1; all in Cache County—a total of 55 to 57 arrests.

86. See Godfrey and Card, *Diaries of Charles Ora Card: The Canadian Years, 1886–1903*, 6 August 1886. For the detailed story of his escape see *Diaries of Charles Ora Card*, 25 July–7 August 1886.

From a community, church, and family perspective, Cache Valley was a very successful settlement endeavor. It had achieved a blend of private and cooperative enterprise, educational institutions, varied agricultural operations, numerous local industries, and it had produced local leaders called to Church-wide positions. The *Utah Journal* noted that "no other Utah city matched the percentage of growth—24%." This was Charles's experience and his legacy until persecution intensified.[87]

Early in 1886, Charles met with the president of the Mormon Church, John Taylor. Knowing it would be a long time before he would be able to appear again publicly in Logan, Charles asked permission to leave Cache Valley with his family and migrate to Mexico. A number of other Mormons including Apostle Moses Thatcher, all in similar circumstances, were already making this trek. John Taylor surprised Charles, asking that he not go south but north to explore the British territory. Exploration and preparation for migration to Canada began 14 September 1886. Lavinia would move to her exiled father's home in Idaho, away from the marshals, and Zina would go with Charles to Canada.[88]

---

87. *The Utah Journal*, 3 October 1888. See also Godfrey, *Logan, Utah: A One Hundred Fifty Year History*, 49–77.

88. For correspondence from Charles Ora Card to John Taylor, see John Taylor Papers and the John Taylor Letterpress Copybooks, Church History Library.

# MORMONS MOVING INTO SOUTHERN ALBERTA

### Chapter 5

The state of Utah and the Cache Valley were settled mostly by the Mormons, who were united in their religious, civic, economic, and cultural values. They were the majority. In contrast, the Mormons heading into Canada found a land far different in culture and people. Nineteenth-century Alberta featured a diverse people with a lively array of multicultural political characteristics. The Mormons would have to learn about them and adjust to their role as citizens in a new land.[1] The first permanent Mormon settlement in Canada would be called Card's Town, after its founder.

**CANADIAN NORTHWEST SETTING**

Canada's Northwest Territories made up a vast region stretching from the Hudson Bay through Manitoba, Saskatchewan, and

---

1. A. A. den Otter, "A Congenial Environment: Southern Alberta on the Arrival of the Mormons," in Card et al., *The Mormon Presence in Canada*, 53–74.

Alberta.[2] It was a wilderness filled with thousands of lakes dotting the Canadian Shield. It featured the waving grassland of rolling prairies and the wind-blown foothills of the Canadian Rocky Mountains. Its resources seemed inexhaustible. The first whites in the territory were French-Canadian trappers. The Hudson's Bay Company, chartered in Great Britain in 1670, gave these trappers exclusive trading rights to all the rivers of the West, which drained into the Hudson Bay. In this region, the company systematically directed fur trading operations for two hundred years. By 1870, the company had transferred the land to the Dominion of Canada, which had been formed in 1867. Twelve years later, the parliament of Canada had divided the Northwest Territories into the districts (later the provinces) of Alberta, Saskatchewan, and Manitoba.[3]

An Order in Council of 1881, issued from the House of Commons, provided more incentives for western Canadian settlement. It allowed for land leases up to one hundred thousand acres for twenty-one years at a rental fee of one cent ($0.23) per acre.[4] Canadian Senator Matthew H. Cochrane took advantage. He acquired two ranches in Alberta and a third in British Columbia. In Alberta, his ranches were along the Belly River in Southern Alberta, where he would meet Charles Ora Card. His third ranch was near Calgary, in what is now the town of Cochrane.[5] In 1885, Alberta was given one seat in the Canadian House of Commons.[6] Sixteen years before Charles Ora Card's first trip reached the Rockies, ranchers were already working the land in British Columbia and central Alberta. Farming and agriculture had blossomed on the prairies. By 1886, the railways ferried more immigrants to the area.

---

2. The terms "North-West" and "Northwest" are both correct. The former refers to British colonial times and the latter to any time after 1912.

3. Anthony W. Rasporich, "Early Mormon Settlement in Western Canada," in Card et al., *The Mormon Presence in Canada*, 136–49.

4. Alex Johnson and M. Joan MacKinnon, "Alberta's Ranching Heritage," *Rangelands* 4, no. 3 (June 1982), 99.

5. Johnson and MacKinnon, "Alberta's Ranching Heritage," 99.

6. Provinces in Canada are the equivalent of states in the US. The House of Commons is a legislative body of the Canadian national government, somewhat equivalent to the US House of Representatives but with more power.

This railroad construction reached coast-to-coast and funneled more people West.[7] All of these elements caused the Dominion of Canada to rapidly expand. The Order in Council was an aggressively open policy, encouraging settlers into the West. It was into this setting that the new Mormon immigrants came into southern Alberta.

The Northwest Territories were originally populated by the First Nations people of the plains. They knew no borders, following the buffalo herds for their survival. The coming of the fur traders, explorers, whisky traders, and missionaries of all types radically changed their lives,[8] as they were exploited and threatened with extinction. They were denigrated particularly by the white traders from the United States, who came to the area and killed buffalo and sold alcohol. The tribes had always depended on the wildlife for their sustenance, and with the arrival of the trappers and traders, those resources were disappearing.[9] The Canadian government recognized the need to protect the native people, and as a result, they stationed the Northwest Mounted Police in the area.[10] In 1874, small detachments were scattered along the border between Canada and the United States, with headquarters at Fort Macleod, Alberta.

The Canadian Pacific Railway played a vital role in western settlement, moving people east to west just as the Union Pacific in the United States. The first train excursion across Canada occurred in 1886, just months before Charles Card's first exploration through British Columbia. Growing rail lines attracted contractors and provided jobs for people, including the Mormons, who were hired from both sides of the border to build spur lines. These narrow gauge lines created a web of transportation routes throughout the western regions of

---

7. Doug Owram, *Promise of Eden: The Canadian Expansion Movement and the Idea of the West, 1856–1900* (University of Toronto Press, 1980), 79–100.

8. Hugh A. Dempsey, *Indian Tribes of Alberta* (Calgary: Glenbow Museum, 1997), 26–33.

9. Owram, *Promise of Eden*, 1–3. See also W. Keith Regular, *Neighbors and Networks: The Blood Tribe in the Southern Alberta Economy, 1884–1939* (Calgary: University of Calgary Press, 2009), 35–69.

10. Donald Ward, *The People: A Historical Guide to the First Nations of Alberta, Saskatchewan, and Manitoba* (Markhan, Ontario: Fifth House, 1995), 25–26; 42–44.

both nations. Branch lines from Calgary and Lethbridge would connect the transcontinental United States and Canadian lines. They connected communities throughout southern Alberta and down to Shelby and Great Falls, Montana. By the standards of the 1880s and 1890s, this little corner of the West was changing. It was not a stop on the transcontinental routes, but neither was it totally isolated.[11]

### SETTLING SOUTHERN ALBERTA

Charles Ora Card moved quickly to mix with the already established influential classes of southern Alberta. It was a small group of ideological leaders whose thoughts and ideas Charles sought out as his colonies evolved. This group included the Chief Red Crow, Frederick Haultain, William Pearce, Elliot T. Galt, and Charles A. Magrath.

Chief Red Crow was the leader of the Blood Indian Tribe. He was the political statesman for his people when in 1877, under Treaty Number 7, the tribe took possession of the large Blood Reserve in southern Alberta.[12] In 1883, the land area was expanded to today's borders, which include 352,000 acres between the Belly and St. Mary Rivers.[13] Red Crow was the leader who took them from being a nomadic tribe of hunters into an agricultural tribe. He was a warrior who had survived the tribal wars and led his people through conflict and plague. He had survived the effects of small pox and measles that had ravaged his and other tribes.[14] He had traveled across Canada at the invitation of the Canadian government to observe Mohawk progress in education and industry.[15] Before Red Crow met Charles in 1886–87, he had a dream of his people meeting those encroaching from the civilization

---

11. A. A. den Otter, 161–2; 110–11; 183–87. See also R. F. Bowman, *Railways in Southern Alberta* (Lethbridge: Lethbridge Historical Society, 2002), 7–8; Map, 36.

12. Mike Mountain Horse, *My People the Bloods* (Calgary: Glenbow-Alberta Institute and Blood Tribal Council, 1989), 1–3, 105.

13. Dempsey, *Indian Tribes of Alberta*, 27–28.

14. Hugh A. Dempsey, *Red Crow: Warrior Chief* (Saskatoon, Saskatchewan: Fifth House, 1995), 15–17, 75–77.

15. Dempsey, *Red Crow*, 197–99.

with dignity and equality through their own industry, education, and strict preservation of reserve lands.[16] While this vision is most likely associated with the overall wave of western migration, it could also apply more specifically to the coming of the Mormons. Charles Card saw the native people and saw a great missionary opportunity, since he felt he had a common biblical heritage. Furthermore, they had been denigrated by the unscrupulous white traders from the US, and in his mind, Charles believed that he and Red Crow would become friends, working for the common good of their people.[17]

Frederick Haultain was a Fort Macleod lawyer from whom Charles and the Mormons would seek advice and counsel. He was a member of the Canadian Territorial Assembly in 1886 when Charles first met him and in 1897 became Alberta's Premier.[18] Haultain's view of liquor laws, politics, and new settlements complemented Card's ideology.[19]

William Pearce was the Northwest Territories superintendent of mines and chief federal officer in the region. He was a strong advocate of irrigation. Even before the Mormon immigrants entered southern Alberta, Pearce had already conducted a field study of irrigation practices, including those in Utah, and he was convinced that the Alberta mountain rivers could be used to water the semi-arid land of the plains. With the expected new immigrants, Card and Pearce drafted the Northwest Irrigation Act of 1894, thus giving Pearce the title "The father of irrigation in Alberta." However, it would take both the Mormons

---

16. Dempsey, *Red Crow*, 159–61, 183–89.

17. W. Keith Regular perpetuates the rumor that the Mormons acquired the land for settlement by "getting Red Crow drunk." He offered no substantiation for the charge. In fact, the evidence provided through Charles Card's diaries more accurately suggests that Card had nothing but respect for the First Nations people. He continually described them positively but was not so kind in his descriptions of the white whisky smugglers. See Keith Regular, *Neighbors and Networks: The Blood Tribe in Southern Alberta Economy, 1884–1939* (Calgary: University of Calgary Press, 2009), 26. For an example of Card's descriptions of the First Nations people, see Godfrey and Card, *The Diaries of Charles Ora Card: The Canadian Years*, 24 October 1886.

18. A provincial premier is the equivalent of a US state governor.

19. For those interested in reading more about Haultain, see Grant MacEvan, *Frederick Haultain: Frontier Statesman of the Canadian Northwest* (Saskatoon, Saskatchewan: Western Produce Prairie Books, 1985).

and the Galts in Lethbridge to actually introduce the first fully operational system into the region.[20]

Elliot T. Galt was the son of Sir Alexander T. Galt, one of the fathers of the Canadian Confederation, and the founder of the city of Lethbridge, Alberta. This father-and-son team developed the coal industry of Lethbridge and the two men were major landowners. The younger Galt reflected his father's vision of western prosperity in terms of his organizational ability and economics.[21]

Charles A. Magrath was a land surveyor who worked for the Galts. In 1885, he was the land officer for their Northwest Coal and Navigation Company. He managed company affairs and was active in social and political circles. He and the Galts understood the need for employment to attract new settlers. The southern Alberta irrigation project succeeded in providing water and crops and generating jobs under the combined leadership of Magrath, Galt, and Card.[22]

Charles Card led the workforce of Mormons into Canada in 1887. It was not by choice that the Mormons were moving from their Utah homes—it was by design to avoid the US government's Edmunds-Tucker Act of 1887, which defined marriage as being between one man and one woman. Plural marriage had started among the Mormon leadership almost forty-five years earlier in the early 1840s. It was ceased by a Manifesto issued by Wilford Woodruff, the President of the Church, on 6 October 1890.[23] During the time of the most severe persecution, the US government sought to confiscate LDS Church property and strip community leaders of their elected offices. Individuals practicing polygamy were tracked down, taken to court, fined, and served jail time. Plural marriage became a rallying point for anti-Mormons, and the resulting persecution scattered the Mormons through-

---

20. E. Alyn Mitchner, "William Pearce: Father of Alberta Irrigation" (unpublished master's thesis, University of Alberta, 1966), 3, 33, 48–40.

21. den Otter, *Civilizing the West*, 92–93, 203–6.

22. den Otter, *Civilizing the West*, 165–66, 206–11.

23. Leonard J. Arrington and Davis Bitton, *The Mormon Experience: A History of the Latter-day Saints* (Urbana: University of Illinois Press, 1992), 183–4.

out the West.[24] They fled as far west as Hawaii, as far south as Mexico, and as far north as Canada to escape persecution.[25] Although the official practice of polygamy ended, the movement of people fleeing Utah had established migrations from which opportunities and settlements grew. It is from this hostile environment that opportunities arose in which new Mormon colonies could be created and the Mormons could live in peace.

## EXITING A HOSTILE ENVIRONMENT

By summer 1886, Charles's work in Cache Valley, Utah, was considerably inhibited. If caught and prosecuted, his fine would have been $300, or what today would be worth about $7,549 today. In addition to this, he could face six months in jail for each charge. Charles had three wives, meaning there would be a minimum of three charges that could be filed against him. Considering these personal costs became unimaginable. In Logan, the new temple and Church-owned properties were deeded to an independent association in order to legally sidestep federal government takeover of LDS properties.[26] The local and national Church leaders were in hiding to protect themselves, their families, and the Church. Governance, as the Mormon majority had known it, was now almost untenable. Their meetings were in secret, taking place behind locked doors in ever-changing hiding places, which made communication difficult. Charles often used aliases to prevent intercepted mail from giving away his location or plans. Correspondence signed as Cy Williams, Jessie Tuttle, and Zimri Jorgenson were all

---

24. Arrington and Bitton, *Mormon Experience*, 69, 183–85.

25. See Brigham Y. Card et al., eds., *The Mormon Presence in Canada* (Edmonton: University of Alberta Press, 1990). See also Nelson, *Mormon Village*, 219–20; Thomas Cottam Romney, *The Mormon Colonies in Mexico* (Salt Lake City: University of Utah Press, 2005); and Grant Underwood, ed., *Voyages of Faith: Explorations in Mormon Pacific History* (Provo, UT: Brigham Young University Press, 2000).

26. John Taylor to Charles O. Card, 10 July 1885, CR 1 10, Historical Department Church, Archived Division, Church History Library of The Church of Jesus Christ of Latter-day Saints, Salt Lake City, Utah, hereafter referred to as CHL. The government eventually returned the property it had taken over, but with an added cost.

Logan Temple, with shed in the foreground, 1884. Courtesy of Merrill-Cazier Library, Special Collections and Archives, Utah State University.

fictitious names he used during his time in the underground and while traveling to and from Canada. Ever the optimist, Charles continued his community, family, business, and Church responsibilities, even under these persecutions. It was barely workable, and it had to change.

In mid-July 1886, Charles had been captured, but he then escaped from the marshals (see chapter 4). He wrote to John Taylor, President of the LDS Church, asking about relocating to Mexico to avoid being captured again and being imprisoned. In northeastern Mexico and in the far corner of southeastern Arizona, polygamous families already found a temporary, somewhat safer haven.²⁷ Charles reasoned that he might be released from his calling as Cache Valley Stake president and that he could purchase a tract of land in Chihuahua, Mexico, or Thatcher, Arizona.²⁸ In fact, he was already planning on taking Lavinia (one of his wives) and his children, and he was literally preparing his wagon for the trek. Responding to Charles's request, President Taylor joked about his escape, which appeared in the Logan newspaper: "We heard the horse ran away with you, but this is better than to have your enemies run away with you." Taylor's directives to Charles were shared in underground meetings and reported in a few surviving letters. Taylor surprised Charles, asking him to explore the land above the Washington Territory.²⁹ Charles summarized the directives much later, noting that President Taylor asked him "to go into the Dominion of Canada and British Columbia and explore the British Domains to find a place of refuge for the much persecuted Latter-day Saint."³⁰ Sterling Williams, Charles's stepson with Zina, reported that Charles was directed "to go north and seek a place of refuge for the Saints upon British Soil." Bates records Taylor saying, "I am impressed to tell you to go to the British North West, for I have always found justice under the British Flag."³¹ Taylor's own Canadian heritage gave him hope for

---

27. Charles Ora Card to John Taylor, 15 August 1886, John Taylor Papers, CR 1 180, CHL.

28. For the contrasting experience of those who left Cache Valley for Mexico and Arizona, see Thomas Cottam Romney, *The Mormon Colonies in Mexico* (Salt Lake City: University of Utah Press, 2005); and James H. McClintock, *Mormon Settlement in Arizona: A Record of Peaceful Conquest of the Desert* (Phoenix: Manufacturing Stationers, 1921).

29. John Taylor to Charles O. Card, 19 August 1996, John Taylor Papers, CR 1 20 DKS, CHL. Letters are reproduced in Godfrey and Godfrey, *The Diaries of Charles Ora Card*, 566–69.

30. Charles Ora Card to John W. Taylor, 8 September 1902. John Taylor Papers, CR 1 20 DKS CHL.

31. The Sterling Williams manuscript is quoted in Hudson, *Charles Ora Card*, 83. See also Jane Eliza Woolf Bates and Zina Alberta Woolf Hickman, *Founding of Cardston and Vicinity—Pioneer Problems* (Cardston: William L. Woolf, 1960), 1. Bates and Hickman blend Card's diaries with their own records of historical events in the manuscript that was edited and published by her sister Zina. The Woolf family was among the first to follow Card into Canada.

opportunities in his old homeland as an alternative to those who were hesitant to go to Mexico.[32] They charted a new direction, and the history of the Mormons in Canada, along with the families of Card and Godfrey, would take root and new communities would grow.

## A BRITISH CANADIAN LAND

As Mormon exploration of the British Territory began, the British Hudson's Bay Company had just transferred the land to the Dominion of Canada. British Columbia, not wanting to be annexed by the United States, linked itself to the Dominion with the completion of the Canadian Pacific Railway. The Canadian federal government's willingness to assume the provincial colonial period debts cemented the decision. Mining, forestry, and agriculture encouraged pioneers to find a home in the western provinces, particularly the coast and central Okanagan Valley where the temperatures were mild. Similarly, the resources in southern Alberta were based in agriculture and coal mining.

This was the landscape into which Charles would lead the colonists. Mountain peaks reached the sky and deep canyons directed swift waters to the Pacific or the Hudson Bay, depending upon where the travelers were located in regard to the Continental and Hudson Bay Divides. The prairies were wide open, rolling hills of grass, free of any fences. There were no roads, though perhaps there were a few trails followed by animals and the native people. The Canadian Blood Indian Reserve had just been established. Since there were no roads, there were also no bridges to cross the large Columbia river in Washington or the small Lee's Creek in Alberta. Years later, pioneers that moved to the area would call it the best land on the continent.

The first exploration was launched from the home of James Z. Stewart in Logan, Utah, on 10 September 1886. Charles and John W. Hendricks were called and set apart for their callings with a blessing

---

32. John Taylor has British roots. His family had emigrated to Canada from Britain in 1830. By 1839, they were living in Toronto, and a missionary, Parley P. Pratt, baptized the family. See Paul Thomas Smith, "John Taylor," in Leonard J. Arrington, ed. *The Presidents of the Church* (Salt Lake City: Deseret Book, 1986), 75–114.

by Apostle Francis M. Lyman. Their mission was to explore the British Northwest Territories above the Washington State line, the 49th parallel, for a place of refuge. This was the official start and the charge for their mission: explore and find a land for settlement.[33]

Four days later, on Tuesday, 14 September 1886, Charles Ora Card spent the evening visiting his wives and his oldest children, giving them each a father's blessing and saying goodbye to his parents. His son George, who would later join him in Alberta, was six years old. Charles left his family and friends that evening under the cover of midnight darkness. He reported having $750 ($18,873) in his pocket, two horses, and a wagon. The following people helped raise expenses for the exploration: John Taylor, as Trustee in Trust, raised $300 ($7,549); C. O. Card raised $100 ($2,516); M. W. Merrill raised $100; William D. Hendricks raised $50 ($1,258); P. G. Taylor raised $20 ($503); Henry Hughes raised $20; Ralph Smith raised $2; and the Cache Stake Defense Fund raised $178 ($4,479). This brought the total to $770, or what would today be worth around $19,376.[34]

The objective of the first leg of travel was to make it to the British Territories unscathed and without arrest. Card was to be accompanied by Hendricks and David E. Zundell. Hendricks was an experienced pioneer who lived in Richmond, Utah, near Logan. Zundell was a missionary to the First Nations people, Shoshone, and Bannock Tribes in northern Utah and southern Idaho. He spoke the native languages and

---

33. Francis M. Lyman was a member of the Quorum of Twelve Apostles. Stewart was President of Brigham Young College and a friend. See Godfrey and Card, *The Diaries of Charles Ora Card: The Canadian Years, 1886–1903*, 14 September 1886. See also Charles Ora Card to John Taylor, 8 September 1902.

34. Charles Ora Card to John Taylor, 2 November 1886; and 27 January 1887, John Taylor Papers, CR 1 180, CHL. In the 2 November correspondence, he indicates that he had $750, and on 28 January, he reports that the total was $770. George's daughter Clarice would later connect with the Godfreys. "Trustee" refers to the President of the Church as a corporation. "Trusts" refers to accounts the president administers and to which he has free access. A Trustee in Trusts provides a manner in which religious corporations can conduct business transactions. Arrington, *The Great Basin Kingdom*, 431.

served as the first bishop over a Native American ward in Washakie, Utah.³⁵

Card and Hendricks were leaving Logan together and planned to pick Zundell up along the way. They were accompanied by Charles's brother-in-law William F. Hyde as they left Logan that night. Hyde was to take them as far as American Falls, Idaho, in his democrat wagon, where they would connect with the Oregon Short Line train, upon which he would return to Logan. This first wagon ride was nothing like the sturdy covered variety commonly associated with western migrations. A democrat wagon was a simple, framed, flatbed wagon fitted with temporary seats for the passengers. It was inexpensive, lightweight, and only sometimes had cover. This was basic, even rough transportation. The group drove through the night arriving at Washakie, named in honor of a Shoshone chief, located just south of Portage and the Idaho border.³⁶

Zundell was not at the rendezvous spot to meet them, but a native, James Brown, agreed to help them search. He took the two across the Idaho state line to Samaria, where they spent two days searching for him. They finally found Zundell just north of the Snake River, and with him joining the group, the exploration party was now fully assembled. They gave Brown two blankets for his scouting services and thanked the Lord in prayer for locating Zundell.³⁷ "The Lord is always on our side," Card wrote, "when we trust in Him, for surely we did, for not a person in Washakie knew of B. Zs [Bishop Zundell] whereabouts." The confusion they experienced here may have sprung from the reality that Zundell likely knew little or nothing about the call he was about to receive.³⁸ As the three prepared to depart, they exchanged food with

---

35. Zundell assisted the First Nations people in digging a canal from Samaria to Washakie. He also taught in the Portage Branch. See Gale Willing, *Fielding: The People and Events That Affected Their Lives* (Logan, UT: Herff Jones, 1992), 14–15, 173, 209.

36. Jenson, *Encyclopedic History of The Church of Jesus Christ of Latter-day Saints*, 1312.

37. Godfrey and Card, *The Diaries of Charles Ora Card: The Canadian Years, 1886–1903*, 14–17 September 1886.

38. There was no evidence to tell whether or not Zundell knew he was about to be a part of this exploration party. It would appear he did not know. However, his

the locals, giving them apples for hay. The locals accepted the exchange in kind and let them off without a cash payment, "because we were his Mormon brethren all of which we appreciated."[39] The trio drove their wagon to the Oregon Short Line train depot in American Falls and caught the train to Spokane, Washington. "We were watched closely by the conductors and others as much so as if we were desperados," but no one said a word.[40]

Card, Henderson, and Zundell rode the train northwest from American Falls, Idaho, through Huntington, Oregon, where they switched to the Oregon Navigation Company Railroad and continued on to Pendleton, Oregon. They crossed over the Columbia River to Pasco, Washington, finally arriving at Spokane, early in the morning of 20 September, six days after they had left their homes. They had come almost 880 miles by wagon, horseback, and train. They needed rest but felt uneasy about stopping. Instead, the day was spent readying for more travel, and they purchased three saddles and seven horses, two of which were used as pack horses.

Early that afternoon they retired to the Spokane Keystone Hotel and rented an upstairs room in the southeast corner of the building, just above the saloon.[41] For protection and to save money, all three stayed in a single room. Card and Hendricks were soon asleep from exhaustion and jangled nerves. Zundell took the first watch, staying alert to any potential dangers. At one o'clock in the morning, Zundell heard a threatening conversation growing in intensity among the men from the bar below, "these Mormons are here and I am after them."[42] The would-be captors crept quietly upstairs, and within moments they

---

services were indispensable because he knew the native peoples and their languages. Card writes on 10 October 1886 that they each wrote in their journals, but the journals of Hendricks and Zundell were not located at the time this book was written.

39. Godfrey and Card, *The Diaries of Charles Ora Card: The Canadian Years, 1886–1903*, 16 September 1886.

40. Godfrey and Card, *The Diaries of Charles Ora Card: The Canadian Years, 1886–1903*, 17–18 September 1886.

41. The Keystone area was in northern Spokane along the Spokane River.

42. Charles Ora Card to John Taylor, 8 September 1902.

were only a few feet from the door. Zundell woke his companions, and after listening to the men outside their door and discussing their options briefly, Card and Hendricks went back to sleep, leaving Zundell wide awake. He heard the intruders again shouting at the hotel keeper about the "renegade Mormons and demanded admittance into our room," but the keeper refused.[43] Zundell again woke his companions, they listened to the threats outside their door but now could hear only whispers. Contemplating the possibilities of a second arrest, this time so far away from home, Card "asked the Lord to cause the [threatening] party . . . to sleep long enough for us to pack up and get out of the way. We all exercised our faith in this direction . . . [then] got up one at a time, went downstairs, passing their snoozing opposition. They met on the banks of the Spokane River, packed their horses and by 9:20 A.M. rode out of harms way."[44] They did not get much rest, but they were safe.

The tension of constant danger was unsettling, but at the same time, it motivated them to move forward. They put the danger aside and focused on their mission. As they traveled, they visited the locals, who did not know them. They asked directions and marked their travels. North of Spokane, they happened upon more Native Americans, Chinese, and Caucasians, all of whom were mining. They were often unintentionally misdirected and took several wrong turns. But even these exchanges were seen positively as giving them the opportunity to learn more of the countryside, trails and wagon roads. In this rugged mountain terrain, they met generous people who assisted them with food, information, and feed for their horses.

The explorers stopped at one mine when Zundell was sick, and the miners offered him medicine, suggesting that he had been "with too many women the night before," prostitution being common in these

---

43. Godfrey and Card, *The Diaries of Charles Ora Card: The Canadian Years, 1886–1903*, 21 September 1886.

44. Godfrey and Card, *The Diaries of Charles Ora Card: The Canadian Years, 1886–1903*, 21 September 1886.

parts.⁴⁵ Not wanting to give away his identity, Zundell played along with the group and avoided their medicine. The next day, as he was recovering, the miners gave them directions which once again proved incorrect. By 26 September, they had reached the banks of the northern Columbia River and were in search of a ferry to get them across. It took two days to find a ferry, but once they did, they paid $7 ($176) to cross.

On the north side of the Columbia, they met a party of Native Americans from Colville who were headed to a powwow at the Okanagan Lake, where they "were going to dance, run horses and have a good time."⁴⁶ They were cheerful and friendly, so Card and his party rode along with them.

### "IN COLLUMBIA WE ARE FREE"

Wednesday, 29 September 1886 was a historic day in the history of Canadian Mormonism. Card, Hendricks, and Zundell broke camp south of the Canadian border, headed north, and at 9:35 a.m., they crossed the 49th parallel onto British soil. There was a unanimous sigh of relief. They felt they were out of danger and had reached the land they were sent to explore. Charles took off his hat, swung it into the air round his head and shouted, "in Collumbia We are free."⁴⁷ At this point, the serious search for settlement land began.

Charles met with John C. Haynes, who was a collector of customs, a justice of the peace, and an owner of a small ranch in the Okanagan Valley.⁴⁸ Charles took time with him to learn of the regulations relative to immigration. He got the impression that the British and American

---

45. Godfrey and Card, *The Diaries of Charles Ora Card: The Canadian Years, 1886–1903*, 21 September 1886.

46. Godfrey and Card, *The Diaries of Charles Ora Card: The Canadian Years, 1886–1903*, 21 September 1886.

47. Godfrey and Card, *The Diaries of Charles Ora Card: The Canadian Years, 1886–1903*, 29 September 1886.

48. Card indicates that he met on 29 September with a "Mr. Jones," who was a customs officer, and again with Haynes three days later. Godfrey and Card, *The Diaries of Charles Ora Card*, 29 September 1886.

customs officers were "not on the most friendly terms," likely lessening his own anxiety and making the group feel safe.⁴⁹ Their intention then was finding a location within British Columbia and returning to Utah via the same route that brought them this far. They registered their horses to avoid paying import duty when they returned to the United States. They also paid an incoming duty of $28 ($705) for their belongings, and then they rode up the Osoyoos Lake a few miles away, camping with the First Nations people.

The first LDS sacrament meeting conducted on western Canadian soil under the authority of the Melchizedek Priesthood occurred on Sunday, 3 October 1886. Only the three men attended, and they met at 1 p.m. They rested and prayed, and Card preached, blessed the land, and asked the Lord to direct them in their explorations to find the right place. They blessed and passed the sacrament, and then each declared their testimonies of the gospel, declaring that they had "never felt better in their lives." The meeting ended, and they went down to Osoyoos Lake, bathed, and retired for the evening early. Truly, this was "a day long to be remembered by our little party."⁵⁰

### EXPLORATION OF ALBERTA

The Okanagan Valley was a beautiful region of southern British Columbia, right on the border between British Columbia and Washington state. It was defined by the Okanagan Lake and its tributaries, and it was a land with a moderate climate, rich in water, minerals, and timber. Card's exploration party zigzagged along the terrain as they worked their way northward.⁵¹ They stopped at the home of Michael Keogan, who was among the first settlers in the valley. He gave them

---

49. Godfrey and Card, *The Diaries of Charles Ora Card: The Canadian Years, 1886–1903*, 3 October 1886. Prior meetings were held in eastern Canada. See Pratt, *Autobiography of Parley Parker Pratt*, 133–42.

50. Godfrey and Card, *The Diaries of Charles Ora Card: The Canadian Years, 1886–1903*, 21 September 1886.

51. See Paul M. Koroscil, *The British Garden of Eden: Settlement History of the Okanagan Valley, British Columbia* (Burnaby, British Columbia: Simon Fraser University, 2003).

information and a parting gift of fresh fruit.⁵² As the three men continued traveling, they were keenly alert to the natural resources of the land and the people. The Natives were the farmers and whites the ranchers, the opposite of Charles's experience in Cache Valley. Stock cattle cost between $28 and $30 and milk cows $45 ($705–755 and $1,132).⁵³ Though the land was rich for farming, the best land was already occupied. They traveled up the Okanagan River to Penticton, which Charles described as a "small Indian Village."⁵⁴ They explored Mission Valley, west of Kelowna. Mission Creek was the main source of water running into the Okanagan Lake and of special interest to Card, but despite all this, the most farmable land was already taken.

Traveling was uncomfortable. In some areas, there were no roads or even trails. Instead, the three men were high on rocky ridges, low in deep ravines, and surrounded by dense forests, all of which they crossed on horseback. However rough the trip, they were treated warmly by those whom they met. For example, people gave them fruit all along their journey. Card watched the natives fish for salmon in the river. Zundell shot a deer and they ate well, but because Card did not eat a lot of meat, they gave it to the natives.⁵⁵

It was at the northern end of the Okanagan Valley near Mission Valley where the explorers met an old mountaineer, Duncan McDonald. Duncan was a British trader, who in 1871 worked the Hudson's Bay Company Flathead Post at Fort Connah.⁵⁶ McDonald was the son

---

52. Godfrey and Card, *The Diaries of Charles Ora Card: The Canadian Years, 1886–1903*, 5 October 1886. A part of Koegan's log cabin is still intact today. See John Moorhouse, "Chimney Link to the Past," *Penticton Herald*, Thursday, 25 September 2014: A3.

53. Godfrey and Card, *The Diaries of Charles Ora Card: The Canadian Years, 1886–1903*, 2 October 1886.

54. Godfrey and Card, *The Diaries of Charles Ora Card: The Canadian Years, 1886–1903*, 5 October 1886.

55. Godfrey and Card, *The Diaries of Charles Ora Card: The Canadian Years, 1886–1903*, 6 October 1886.

56. Kate Hammond Fogarty, *The History of Montana* (New York: A. S. Barnes, 1916), 84–87. See also Steve A. Anderson, *Angus McDonald of the Great Divide: The Uncommon Life of a Fur Trader, 1816–1889* (Coeur D'Alene, ID: Museum of North Idaho Press, 2011).

of the Canadian Hudson Bay Company trader Angus McDonald. As a young man, Duncan hauled freight—likely beaver and trapped fur—for the Hudson Bay Company from the Flathead Lake Reservation in Montana into Alberta. On these trips, he had passed through the mountains of what today is the Waterton-Glacier International Peace Park in northern Montana and Southern Alberta. Lake McDonald bears his name.[57] He knew the area well, so when McDonald gave Card information, it changed their direction and ultimately led to a settlement in southern Alberta. He told them about a sparsely settled land on the eastern side of the Rockies. Charles felt this information came "as we needed and we all feel to acknowledge the hand of the Lord in it."[58]

They then were heading as quickly as they could to Kamloops, where they would catch a Canadian Pacific Railway east to Calgary, Alberta. They were approaching Priest's Valley at the head of Okanagan Lake when they were forced to seek shelter from an autumn deluge. They stayed with a rancher just in time to save his life. The man's wife had deserted him and when Card's party arrived, he was in the middle of a "drunken spree and sought to nearly" commit suicide. The group counseled the distraught rancher, "talked with him, quieted him, [and] gave him good moral advice."[59] They had saved his life, at least for a time. They stayed the night and left in the morning.

Three days after receiving McDonald's directions into southern Alberta, they crossed the Salmon River, and then reached the Thompson River. All through British Columbia they consistently noted the best land was still inhabited by the monopoly of the larger ranchers who had arrived earlier and already homesteaded. Eighteen miles east of Kamloops, they came across a stagecoach station. Charles boarded the coach arriving ahead of Hendricks and Zundell so that he could make arrangements for train tickets as well as report to Church head-

---

57. Graham A. MacDonald, *Where the Mountains Meet the Prairies: A History of Waterton Country* (Calgary: University of Calgary Press, 2003): 9, 30.

58. Godfrey and Card, *The Diaries of Charles Ora Card: The Canadian Years, 1886–1903*, 6 October 1886.

59. Godfrey and Card, *The Diaries of Charles Ora Card: The Canadian Years, 1886–1903*, 8 October 1886.

quarters. He reported to President Taylor that they were unsuccessful in British Columbia because "the laws of this land are so liberal that a few cattle kings hold all the country, especially the desirable portions. ... We have learned of a fine and extensive tract of prairie land situated on the east side of the Rocky Mountains .... [with] much easier access to our people through Montana."[60]

Kamloops was a bustling railroad town and had just celebrated the first train excursion across Canada, which had passed through only four months earlier, in June 1886.[61] Hendricks and Zundell followed along the Thompson River and arrived shortly after Charles. It took a few days to sell their horses, and they kept their saddles, satchels, bedding, and purchased train tickets for Calgary. The fares were $26.10 each ($657), plus freight costs for their saddles and belongings. Total costs were $87.50 ($2,204). They boarded the train at 2:00 a.m. and rode through the Canadian Rockies. "We rode all day through mountains, gorges, and around sharp curves and over high trestle bridges across ... dry ravines all wending our way to the Territories of the North West." They arrived in Calgary at 3:00 a.m. on 15 October.[62] Away from home for more than a month, they traveled by every conceivable means of the time.

The explorers found Calgary different from the warmer valleys of the Okanagan Valley. It was a rapidly growing rail and cattle town on the Bow River with some 1,300 inhabitants.[63] Originally, the Bow River land was occupied by the Blackfoot, Blood, and Psuu Tina tribes. The Hudson's Bay Company traders had begun camping along the Bow, and by the mid-1880s, farmers were moving onto the plains. By 1883, the Canadian Pacific Railway had reached Calgary, Alberta.

---

60. Charles Ora Card to John Taylor, 13 October 1886, John Taylor Letterpress books, CR 1 180, CHL.

61. For a history of the Canadian Pacific Railroad, see Pierre Burton, *The National Dream: The Great Railway, 1871–1881* (Toronto: McClelland and Stewart, 1970).

62. Godfrey and Card, *The Diaries of Charles Ora Card: The Canadian Years, 1886–1903*, 14 October 1886.

63. Calgary was incorporated as a town just two years earlier, in 1886, with 500 people. In the 1891 census it had grown to 3,976. See "Calgary," *Encyclopedia Canadiana*, vol. 22 (Ottawa: Canadiana, 1958), 167.

Charles and his companions were hesitant, because when they exited the train in Calgary, they had arrived in the middle of a blizzard. It lasted all day, so they were not too impressed with the frigid weather. However, their spirits remained buoyed by the descriptions McDonald had shared and they decided against their urge to "take the next train for a warmer clime."[64] They needed horses again, but their funds were low and prices were much higher in Calgary. They visited the stables, looking for the best deal, and with their budget of $180 ($4,529), they purchased two horses and a wagon. They settled on a rather wild team of broncos they dubbed "Brit" and "Bert" in honor of British Columbia and Alberta. The horses were nearly uncontrollable, jumping, jostling around, and charging in every direction. Zundell got kicked in the leg, which left him limping for a few days. One horse, while the men tried to harness the team, "threw himself under the tongue of the wagon." Unfortunately, this was the best team available, despite considerable shopping.[65] They stayed a second night at the Calgary Royal Hotel. The next morning, they paid their bill and hitched their team to their wagon.

On the first travel day south, they covered just eight miles. They crossed the beautiful well-watered prairie with its rich black loam soil, and they noted unlimited timber resources in the mountains just to the west. Fort Macleod was a "little warmer" and not so frostbitten as Calgary. Established in 1874, Macleod was a Northwest Mounted Police Post, and by 1886, it had become a trading and administrative center of several hundred people.[66]

They stayed a night in Fort Macleod, camping along the Old Man River and learning what they could from the Mounties. The next day, they traveled to the junction of the Kootenay and Belly Rivers. Today, the Kootenay River and the Kootenay Lakes are the Waterton River

---

64. Godfrey and Card, *The Diaries of Charles Ora Card: The Canadian Years, 1886–1903*, 15 October 1886.

65. Godfrey and Card, *The Diaries of Charles Ora Card: The Canadian Years, 1886–1903*, 16 October 1886.

66. In 1901, Fort Macleod's population was 790. See Franklin J. Junkunis, "Urban Development in Southern Alberta," in *Southern Alberta: A Regional Perspective*, ed. Franklin J. Junkunis (Lethbridge: University of Lethbridge Press, 1972), 76–77.

and the Waterton Lakes. Here they observed the least signs of frost and that "good land and water, the two essentials for farmers and husbandman" were abundant. They further noted that there were coal miners east in Lethbridge. Settlers reported that the "winters [were] very light here."[67]

## LOCATING THE SETTLEMENT SITE

Card and his companions were in the heart of the Blackfoot Confederacy with the Blood and Piegan First Nations people. Card thought that "this would be a good place to establish a mission . . . [the people] are intelligent . . . although degraded by the many low lived white men that allure them to whoring" and alcohol.[68] They stayed a few days at Standoff, Alberta, a name given the area by the Natives who had stood off US whiskey traders attempting to sell alcohol. Card was resting the horses over the weekend, one of which had gone lame. They searched for another horse but without success. On Sunday, he and Zundell hiked west along the Waterton River, two miles from Standoff, where they knelt down and "dedicated the land to the Lord for the benefit of Israel both red and white."[69]

After this, they set out to locate the settlement site. There are three stories as to how the Cardston town site was selected. The first has roots from the meeting with Duncan McDonald in British Columbia. Some suggest that McDonald gave them more than a description. He related "a grass-covered buffalo plains where the country could be plowed for miles," and which Charles later declared, "where the buffalo can live, the Mormon can live."[70] Charles's wife Zina records, "Card gathered

---

67. Godfrey and Card, *The Diaries of Charles Ora Card: The Canadian Years, 1886–1903*, 20–23 October 1886.

68. Godfrey and Card, *The Diaries of Charles Ora Card: The Canadian Years, 1886–1903*, 22–23 October 1886.

69. Godfrey and Card, *The Diaries of Charles Ora Card: The Canadian Years, 1886–1903*, 24 October 1886.

70. Bates, *Founding of Cardston and Vicinity—Pioneer Problems*, 2. Hudson mentions Zina Young Williams Card as quoting an unpublished manuscript from

them [Zundell and Hendricks] close and with their arms around each other's shoulders said, Brethren, I have an inspiration that Buffalo Plains is where we want to go."⁷¹

The second is an apocryphal story of one night in 1886 when they were camping at the junction of Lee's Creek and the St. Mary's River. The trio had pitched their tent and had retired for the night. The wind was blowing and snow covered the ground. Charles was pondering the location for settlement, his mission, and what would come of it. As he lay in thought, he sensed "someone in the tent with him." He looked up and an angel appeared. He was dressed in the tradition of the First Nations people, "immaculately clean." The angel introduced himself as Rega, an ancient Native who had once lived on the land. The two talked through much of the night about what was ahead for the country and the new colony Charles was sent to establish. He supposedly told Charles that the place for the Mormon settlement was there along Lee's Creek, and then the angel disappeared as suddenly as he had appeared. Charles got up, questioning what had just happened, went to the door of his tent, and looked out over the land. There were no tracks in the recent light snow, which someone one would have made had they walked into and out of Charles's tent. He was certain he had seen the vision and was equally bewildered.⁷²

The third version of the location decision is most likely accurate. On the first 1886 exploration trip, there was no specific settlement site selected. However, the explorers camped in the vicinity of the St. Mary's River and Lee's Creek and explored the area thoroughly. They rode along Lee's Creek to the Mounted Police Outpost, toward today's Bea-

---

J. Y. Card, titled "An Incident in the Settling of Canada." See Hudson, *Charles Ora Card*, 90n1.

71. Hudson, *Charles Ora Card*, 90n1. Primary evidence of this conversation has not yet been found.

72. Lowry Nelson, *The Mormon Village: A Pattern and Technique of Land Settlement* (Salt Lake City: University of Utah Press, 1952): 265–66. There is currently no primary documentation to verify this story. The author was told the story by Hudson, who first indicated that it was "in Charles's diaries." It is not. In the Nelson version of this event it is implied that the Native was one of the Three Nephites. See 3 Nephi 28:1–28.

zer town site, where the officers gave them hay for their team and possibly more directions. They camped the night and headed southeast toward the North Milk River. They were within a few miles of the US border, traveling east along Boundary Creek toward today's Del Bonita and Whiskey Gap areas. Finding no wood for their own fire, they cooked their supper over a fire of dry buffalo chips, "a rather smokey uphill business."[73]

The exploration was complete. They were on their way back to Utah. They had a regional destination and a recommendation for President Taylor, but the exact location was undetermined until spring 1887.

### EXPLORERS PART WAYS

Card, Hendricks, and Zundell had completed their exploratory mission, and they were in a hurry to return home. Yet even in these homeward travels, Charles remained focused. Now he was creating a route for future settlers who would migrate to Canada.

On 1 November 1886, they camped in Prickly Pear Canyon south of Great Falls, near Wolf Creek, Montana. Here, they unintentionally met some Cache Valley friends who had been working on the Canadian Pacific Railway near Medicine Hat, one of whom was Charles's counselor in the Cache Stake presidency, Orson Smith. It was a joyous occasion. Simeon Allen collected $75 ($1,887) to help Hendricks and Zundell complete their return home, no doubt understanding the financial needs of the exploration team.[74] The team drafted a report to President Taylor in final preparations for leaving.

The report was written by Card and signed by all three: Card, Zundell, and Hendricks. They described what they had learned from the old settlers, mountaineers, the Natives, and their own experiences. They liked the Kootenay and Belly River area of southwestern Alberta

---

73. Godfrey and Card, *The Diaries of Charles Ora Card: The Canadian Years, 1886–1903*, 25 October 1886.

74. Allen was from Cache Valley. He had a rock and grading crew that worked the railroads. See Godfrey and Card, *The Diaries of Charles Ora Card: The Canadian Years, 1886–1903*, xxiii.

because they were less frostbitten than the other locations they scouted and the grass was plentiful. The land between Red Deer and Calgary, Alberta, was better for farmland. Good coal was abundant and the industry was growing, as were the spur rail lines that served southern Alberta and northern Montana. As proof of successful farming, Card carried home samples of oat, barley, potato, and wheat crops raised by the Blood Tribe. He noted both ranching and farming success without irrigation, but suggested irrigation would be needed south of Macleod. He wrote appreciatively of the information he received from the people of the Blood Tribe. He noted their location near Standoff, and he again commented disgustedly on the "degrading influence of the unprincipled white man." He closed his report with a note comparing the southern Alberta climate with that of Bear Lake Valley, in northeast Utah. "The snows are melted earlier and oftener by the south west winds (chinook) is the only advantage I can see or learn at present [different from Bear Lake]. Southern Alberta had been a grazing ground of the buffalo, but now only their bleaching bones mark their last resting place."[75] After signing the report, "I bade Bros. Zundell and Hendricks goodbye and had become so much attached to them I could not refrain from tears." The original Canadian Mormon explorers' work was complete and they parted company, acknowledging "the Hand of the Lord" in all things.[76] Charles was alone, and he filled the day writing to his family, doing laundry, and resting. He celebrated his forty-seventh birthday writing in his journal and expressing love for his mother.

Charles was anxious to hear about his next assignment and whether he would be sent to the north or to the south. "I am setting alone . . . my thoughts turn homeward to my wives, children, parents and many friends . . . who risk their own liberty for the servants of God. . . . I would enjoy the caresses of my wives and children, could we be free from the hand of tyrants that lust after our homes and property. Free

---

75. Charles Ora Card to John Taylor, 1 November 1886. CR 1 180 John Taylor Papers, CHL.

76. Godfrey and Card, *The Diaries of Charles Ora Card: The Canadian Years, 1886–1903*, 2 November 1886.

from those that demoralized our community. Free from those that would debauch our son and daughters... of their virtue. Sometimes we feel to say, 'Oh Lord how long . . .'"[77] On 12 November a letter arrived from President Taylor thanking Charles for his service and directing him to return to Cache Valley.

### HOMEWARD IN DISGUISE

Charles was anxious to return to his family and at the same time was nervous about returning to the United States, but he prepared his wagon and left immediately. Heading for Dillon, Montana, he passed through Helena and Boulder City. He slept under his wagon as the snows increased, alert to the fact that he was an outlaw. As he approached Dillon, where he could catch the train, he donned a disguise. As part of this disguise, he shaved his beard. It was the first time in fifteen years he had shaved it off. He then dressed in a "greasy canvas coat and blue jeans." He boarded the train, saw both people he knew and people who opposed him, but he went about undetected by both. "One young man was so taken up with his sweetheart so much that he did not recognize me with my beard off."[78] Those who knew Charles and recognized him said nothing.[79] Those who could have arrested him must have regarded him as a mountain man working for the railroads. He passed safely, getting off at Preston, Idaho, just north of the Utah border. He stayed with friends and met with William C. Parkinson, bishop of the Preston Ward. Parkinson took him into his own home where Charles caught up on some sleep and ate before the last few miles of his journey. Parkinson had already organized confidential communications for getting Charles back to Logan. In an ironic twist, as Parkinson was making arrangements for Charles, he himself was

---

77. Godfrey and Card, *The Diaries of Charles Ora Card: The Canadian Years, 1886–1903*, 7 November 1886.

78. Godfrey and Card, *The Diaries of Charles Ora Card: The Canadian Years, 1886–1903*, 15–17 November 1886.

79. Godfrey and Card, *The Diaries of Charles Ora Card: The Canadian Years, 1886–1903*, 16 November 1886.

preparing for his incarceration because of polygamy. That very evening, his children were gathered around him saying their good-byes. The scene drew tears from Charles.[80] The next day, Charles had arrived safely back at home.

### RECRUITING SETTLERS

Charles's exploration travels had ended. The larger task before him was now recruiting settlers for a new colony. Working from exile while simultaneously organizing an immigration movement was a challenge. The Edmunds-Tucker Act was passed on 19 February 1887, just four months after Charles's return. This new act increased the pace of persecution and confusion, as well as the intensity of the rhetoric on both sides. On one side, the anti-Mormons pushed to rid the nation of polygamy. On the other, the Church was in a scrambling, moving assets away from possible government takeovers. The new law put into effect greater persecuting, fining, and jailing of polygamists, and marshals had become increasingly aggressive. This was the atmosphere in which Charles was expected to recruit.

Charles again hid among family, friends, and in the wilds of Logan Canyon. He so wanted to be with his wives and family where he was freed of his loneliness, but he felt unsafe, knowing the marshals were already watching his houses. He maintained his beardless disguise and remained in hiding, even scaring a few friends who thought he had been called away on a mission to England. His anonymity allowed a little flexibility to recruit reluctant volunteers for the expedition to Alberta in the spring. People were afraid because without financial assistance, which the Church could no longer provide, and no calling to go from President Taylor, it seemed that no one could afford the move. Some just thought it wiser to take their chances, remaining hidden in Logan.[81] In short, Charles was not having a lot of success.

---

80. Card and Godfrey, *The Diaries of Charles Ora Card: The Canadian Years, 1886–1903*, 17 November 1886.

81. Godfrey and Card, *The Diaries of Charles Ora Card: The Canadian Years, 1886–1903*, 30 January 1887.

Card met with Apostle Franklin D. Richards on Friday, 4 March 1887, for four hours. At this time, he received directions and his calling. He was feeling "nearly alone to go to Alberta [but at the same time] . . . expected to go." He persuaded a few recruits but not many. He poured out his lonely soul to his friend and leader, and Richards replied only encouragingly to Card, telling him, "If I went I would be the founder of a city and do a good work as a pioneer in a new country and should be known for my good works."[82] He gave Card a blessing and sent him on his way. The meeting boosted Card's spirit and determination. Soon after, he was preparing for his second trip to Alberta. He counseled with his wives, particularly Lavinia, who originally was to accompany him to Mexico, and Zina, who would now accompany him to his "northern mission." He received Lavinia's blessing, which she freely gave and wished him a safe journey free from the "vengeance of [his] enemies." Card was touched. "When a man has a quorum of wives that pray as faithful for my safety, he is much inspired . . . God Bless the faithful wives of all the undergrounds. Also, those of the Imprisoned and exiled."[83]

**CANADIAN MISSION**

Card visited family and friends over the several days before again departing for Alberta. He stayed with Lavinia, and her youthful spirit buoyed his own. He would have preferred staying home with his wives if he could just be left alone to care for them—but it was not to be. At 8:00 p.m. on Wednesday, 23 March 1887, he started north again. This time his disguise had a few refinements. Besides being clean shaven, he sported a new mustache, a heavy cane, and a pipe, even though he had "not learned that filthy habit." William Rigby again provided transportation to the train depot in Idaho. However, before they barely made it out of Logan, he accidentally drove the wagon over an embankment

---

82. Godfrey and Card, *The Diaries of Charles Ora Card: The Canadian Years, 1886–1903*, 4 March 1887. Hudson reports this meeting as 10 March, which is incorrect. See Hudson, *Charles Ora Card*, 100.

83. Godfrey and Card, *The Diaries of Charles Ora Card: The Canadian Years, 1886–1903*, 6 March 1887.

and into a river. Charles and William were soaked in the cold mountain runoff and their possessions were swept downstream. In all the commotion, a group of marshals who were camping across the stream hurried to investigate. Charles spoke to them in a heavy "Irish Brogue" explaining the situation. They did not recognize him, and they headed back to their camp.[84] Charles and William changed their clothes, did a little repair on the buggy, and were quickly off again. Charles felt the accident was the hand of Providence, for had they not fallen into the creek, they would have driven directly into the camp and the hands of the law.

The remainder of the trip was solemn and uneventful. Charles caught the train at Marsh Center, south of Pocatello, and two days later arrived in Helena where he met his friends Simeon F. Allen, Joseph Ricks, Michael Johnson, and Niels Monson, who were working on the railroads.[85] He waited with them for the arrival of Thomas E. Ricks, who he expected would join him.[86] Card did not like waiting, but he passed the time writing, reading, attending Catholic services, and shopping for farm tools. He also attended a dramatic production of "Over the Wall," performed by the George S. Knight Comedy Company, which displeased him.[87] He lamented missing the birthday of his oldest daughter, Sarah, with the feelings of a helpless father. He had given her a blessing a few days earlier, but he was anxious about the reappearance of her mother, Sallie, who had divorced him, and he was

---

84. Godfrey and Card, *The Diaries of Charles Ora Card: The Canadian Years, 1886–1903*, 23 March 1887.

85. Joseph Ricks would move to Alberta in early winter 1887, Michael Johnson was a Cache Valley farmer, and Niels Monson is likely Niels Hanson, who was a bishop.

86. Thomas E. Ricks had worked on the Logan City Council with Charles and was active in irrigation development. He was at one time a member of the Cache Valley Stake high council.

87. This was likely "Over the Garden Wall," by Scott Marble. Card did not indicate in his journals just why he was displeased, but it probably didn't appeal to his sense of humor.

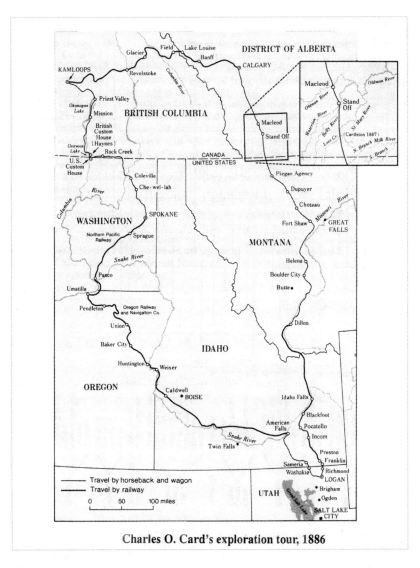

First immigration route, 1887. Courtesy of Michael Fisher, cartographer, University of Alberta.

afraid that her anti-Mormon beliefs would influence their daughter, who he sensed was vulnerable without a father's influence.[88]

By 2 April, Card could wait no longer. He said his goodbyes and left with Thomas X. Smith and Henry Morrison, who was driving the wagon.[89] Thomas Ricks finally caught up with the group west of Great Falls, near Flat Creek in Choteau country.[90] Charles knew these men from Church and community endeavors. They were trusted friends, and several were in the same predicament, running from the marshals. He called his friends the "exiled band."[91]

Attempting to recruit immigrants, Card called on people even while he traveled. He must have been somewhat nervous when the sheriff of Choteau warned him about a group of threatening Natives roaming the area. However, his small band of brethren "rode the ranges [and] were heavily armed as a rule."[92] They always took precautions, tethering their horses at night to prevent theft. The group was always friendly with the local natives while on this trip and purchased their hay for their horses.

Once Card arrived in southwestern Alberta, he and his companions immediately began scouting for a specific settlement site. They met with Canadian senator Matthew H. Cochrane.[93] Taking advantage of settlement laws, Senator Cochrane owned a one-hundred-thousand-acre lease on the property along the Waterton River in southwest

---

88. Godfrey and Card, *The Diaries of Charles Ora Card: The Canadian Years, 1886–1903*, 2 April 1887.

89. Smith was the treasurer of the United Order and the first bishop of the Logan Fourth Ward.

90. Choteau in 1890 was an expansive First Nations people territory in northwestern Montana. The town of Choteau had a post office, established in 1875, and was a stopover point for Charles. The town of Choteau was not incorporated until 1913.

91. Godfrey and Card, *The Diaries of Charles Ora Card: The Canadian Years, 1886–1903*, 7 April 1887.

92. Godfrey and Card, *The Diaries of Charles Ora Card: The Canadian Years, 1886–1903*, 13–14 April 1887.

93. Charles Ora Card, Letter to John W. Taylor, 8 September 1902. This letter indicated that Charles was in Fort Macleod and sent Ricks, Smith, and Monson to the area of the Cochrane Ranch, and they reported it to be under lease and unavailable.

Alberta. This interested Card, but Cochrane told them he had no authority to lease the land to them.[94] Ironically, this very Cochrane Ranch operation went out of business in 1903 and was sold to the LDS Church for $3,128,000 ($78,705,000).[95] The locals would later call it "the Church Ranch" until 1968 when it was sold.[96]

Charles was unsuccessful in purchasing the land from Cochrane, so he headed to the Belly River. As he traveled, he communicated with Thomas White, the Canadian secretary of the interior, as well as Elliot Galt, asking for information on leasing land for a settlement. He checked in with the Fort Macleod Customs at this same time.[97] Then, finally, he wrote President Taylor and suggested the lands be purchased south of the Blood Reserve. On Monday, 25 April 1887 at 8:00 a.m., he and his companions traveled up Lee's Creek, passing a coal prospect, finding plentiful grasslands and several unoccupied flats of land. They returned at 7:00 p.m., hunted and ate prairie chicken for supper, and then retired for the night.[98]

The next day, they headed back to the St. Mary's River and Lee's Creek junction. They traveled upstream to the Mounted Police post for dinner, after which Charles and Smith again went up the river another five miles exploring. "River bottoms were gravelly, good [farm] land being vastly in the minority, however it will all afford good pasture, but the best soil is not so good as on the bench of the plateau on the south side of Lee's Creek." That night they fished and had three rainbow trout for supper, "their first from Canadian waters." It was a windy but

---

94. The 1881 Order-in-Council had provided for leases not to exceed one hundred thousand acres for twenty-one years at a fee of one cent ($0.23) per acre. The law created a farming and ranching bonanza and helped settle western Canada. Johnson and MacKinnon, "Alberta's Ranching Heritage," 99.

95. Johnson and MacKinnon, "Alberta's Ranching Heritage," 100.

96. Byron C. Palmer and Craig J. Palmer, "Mormons in Western Canadian Agriculture from Irrigation to Agribusiness," in Brigham Y. Card et al., *The Mormon Presence in Canada*, 234–59.

97. Thomas White was minister of the Interior and superintendent general of Indian Affairs, 1885–88.

98. Godfrey and Card, *The Diaries of Charles Ora Card: The Canadian Years, 1886–1903*, 25 April 1887.

pleasant evening. "This evening we voted unanimously that Lee's Creek was the best location at present and decided to plant our colony thereon."[99] Card felt this was a place from which they could grow, and the North West Coal and Navigation Company, owned by the Galts, purchased the land.[100]

On Sunday, 1 May 1887, the first settlers arrived: Andrew L. Allen and Warner H. Allen, from Logan. They cheered Card's heart.[101] Within days they had begun plowing and planting. Shortly after, twelve families would arrive, including Card's third wife, Zina, whom he met on route near Helena. It was a small beginning, but the settlement would grow. Charles's labors in Canada extended over sixteen years, starting with the exploration in 1886 and ending with his release as the Alberta Stake president in 1902.

### LEGACIES OF THE MAN

It would be easy to write about the towns and pioneering legacies that Charles left behind. He and his father owned the Cache Valley Lumber Mills of the Card and Son Company, and they worked together for the Central Mills under the United Order. He was on the Board of Trade in the Order and was the superintendent of the construction of both the Tabernacle and the Logan Temple. He was experienced in construction, which included building his own homes. In irrigation development, he was instrumental in three Logan systems: Logan and Hyde Park, Logan and Richmond, and the Logan and Smithfield.

---

99. Godfrey and Card, *The Diaries of Charles Ora Card: The Canadian Years, 1886–1903*, 26 April 1887. Charles Ora Card, Letter to John W. Taylor, 8 September 1902. This correspondence indicated the date was 17 April and that Cardston was "Section Nine (9), Township Three (3), Range Twenty-Five (25) west of the Fourth Meridian."

100. Lethbridge, Alberta, Canada, "Agriculture," https://familysearch.org/learn/wiki/en/Lethbridge_Alberta_Canada. See also Donald G. Wetherell and Irene R. A. Kmet, *Town Life: Main Street and the Evolution of Small Town Alberta, 1880–1947* (Edmonton: University of Alberta Press, 1995), 3–4. There is no specific dollar figure mentioned in either the papers of Charles Ora Card or John Taylor.

101. Godfrey and Card, *The Diaries of Charles Ora Card: The Canadian Years, 1886–1903*, 1 May 1887.

He brought this experience into Alberta. Irrigation fostered farming throughout southern Alberta, and it invited Mormon settlers to the area, who could be paid in land and dollars for their labors. In Cache Valley, he was a teacher and was on the Logan School Board and the Brigham College Board. In civic activities he was a Logan city councilman, a road commissioner, a justice of the peace, and a selectman and coroner. His Church callings in Cache Valley included being a Sunday School teacher, Sunday School superintendent, counselor in his high priests group, counselor in the Cache Valley Stake presidency, and finally stake president. His stake at one time included Rexburg, Idaho, and stretched all the way into Canada.

Apostle Franklin D. Richards told Charles that if he went to Canada he would be the "founder of a city, . . . a pioneer in a new country and known for his good works." That blessing clearly came to pass. He conducted the first Latter-day Saint exploration of western Canada, scouting south-central British Columbia and southern Alberta for settlement land. He led the first Mormon immigrants into Alberta and established the settlement. He networked with the influential people of Canada, and with them, he developed irrigation through the area. Many of the southern Alberta towns and irrigations systems had their foundations in his leadership. These accomplishments reflect his success, but they also reveal something about the spirit and the heart of the inner man.

Charles was in Logan for only a few months recruiting settlers and then was on the road again. Lavinia and Sarah were the wives he sorrowfully left behind. Zina would meet Charles in Canada.

### A TENDER HEART

There is ample evidence to trust that Charles had a tender heart. His diaries and letters exhibit several undeniable examples that reflect the love of a husband and father. His work ethic and commitment to church assignments were balanced with a tender heart, supportive wives, and an infallible faith in the gospel of Jesus Christ.

His teenage heart reflected tenderness even along the Mormon Trail as he crossed the plains with the first handcart company. He was sixteen and assisted his father and uncle as they buried his little sister Polly. Charles felt sorry for the European immigrants who were treated unkindly by the trek leaders because they were unfamiliar with cattle, horses, and the oxen, thus causing too many delays. They were forced to walk more than others. Charles quietly snuck them into his wagons as the company progressed and he let them ride and rest.

He loved his parents and conveyed a deep respect for them. He was a business partner with his father, and his mother was the first president of the Logan Second Ward Relief Society. Charles lived with them until he was twenty-eight, when he was first married. On his forty-seventh birthday he paid tribute to his mother, saying, "The lucky boy [I was] to be given a mother . . . an excellent faithful one."[102] His parents taught him honesty, hard work, faith, and constant service to the Lord. While visiting from Canada in 1889, he saw his mother, who was then seventy years old. Her body was "broken with toil," and he did not know how much longer she was going to live. When they met, "she clasped my hands kissed me then embraced me and we wept together."[103]

A most loving tribute to his mother came a year later when Card visited his wife Sarah. His mother brought him a piece of her pie, which caused him to write that "every time she comes she brings me some little nicknack. A kinder hearted mother never lived. She is always kind to everybody."[104] Within five years, he would return for his mother's funeral, where he was to have paid his last tribute "to a mother that has been very dear to me and always faithful to her trust as ever valiant in the testimony of Jesus Christ." Sarah, Lavinia, and their children attended the funeral, but Card did not. Washed out roads and flooding

---

102. Godfrey and Card, *The Diaries of Charles Ora Card: The Canadian Years, 1886–1903*, 5 November 1886.

103. Godfrey and Card, *The Diaries of Charles Ora Card: The Canadian Years, 1886–1903*, 17 April 1889.

104. Godfrey and Card, *The Diaries of Charles Ora Card: The Canadian Years, 1886–1903*, 24 February 1890.

delayed his arrival until after the funeral and after his mother's burial. His heart was broken as he could only visit her grave. He was buoyed by the knowledge that he would be with her in the eternities: "She had died faithful. Now it is left with me to follow and if I am faithful it will sur[e]ly come to pass."[105] His father died a short time later on 8 September 1900, and Charles attended the funeral in the Logan Tabernacle, "a grand edifice that I superintended . . . at a cost of about $80,000 ($1,699,724). Father and I tried to do our part in this."[106]

### A CARING FATHER

Charles and his second wife, Sarah Jane Painter, lost their first daughter, Matilda, to death. On Saturday, 13 December 1879, after a series of church meetings, he returned to find Matilda Francis critically ill. She was just twenty months old. Over the next eight days, as he went about his duties, his mind was filled with dread. On Sunday, 21 December, she was worse. He called Elders Charles W. Nibley and William Apperly to administer to her, after which Charles laid his hands on her head and gave her a father's blessing. She ended up passing away. Four days later, it was Christmas. He was happy to spend time and eat dinner with his family, but he declared, "I feel more to sorrow than joy."[107]

This experience repeated itself on 17 November 1894, when Zina's son, Orson Rega, fell sick with life-threatening fever. Charles left his home quietly, remembering a promise made at the dedication of the Salt Lake Temple that if anybody desired a blessing, he or she should take it to the temple and ask the Lord. He went to the temple at 9:00 p.m. Secretly, while sitting alone in the sitting room of the Logan Temple, he poured his soul to his Father in Heaven. He pleaded with the Lord to "spare our son, to relieve him of the raging fever and give

---

105. Godfrey and Card, *The Diaries of Charles Ora Card: The Canadian Years, 1886–1903*, 11–21 May 1884.

106. Godfrey and Card, *The Diaries of Charles Ora Card: The Canadian Years, 1886–1903*, 9–11 September 1900.

107. Godfrey and Card, *The Diaries of Charles Ora Card: The Canadian Years, 1886–1903*, 25 December 1879.

him rest." He returned home and his son's recovery was so sudden that it startled both him and Zina. Two days later their hearts were filled "with gratitude toward our God and deliverer."[108]

One day, four-year-old George and his three-year-old sister Lavantia (son and daughter of Sarah Jane Painter) were entertaining themselves in the parlor of the home. Their mother was down the block helping a neighbor and left the children for a few minutes in the care of an elderly gentleman. Charles, their father, was in Ogden attending to Logan Temple construction business when he felt impressed to take an early train home. He arrived, visited with an aging brother, and, determining all was well, he relaxed by reading the newspaper as his children played. Suddenly, there was a "peal of laughter followed by screams." He ran to the door and saw his daughter on the floor, looking up at the lace curtains blazing with fire almost as high as the ceiling above her head. She just sat watching the fire and smiling as though it were entertainment. He moved with the speed only a parent can muster, rushing into the room, pulling the curtains down, and smothering the flames. The older gentleman was hard of hearing and never sensed the danger. Charles, however, immediately realized why he had been prompted to take the earlier train. His children were safe and disaster was averted.[109]

By 17 April 1889, Charles had been on the road for almost three years, exploring and creating the settlement and that would continue for more than a decade. To stay away from the marshals, he could visit only briefly and write under a pen name. During this time, he visited the children at home when he could. One evening when Sarah had brought supper and their children, Charles realized that he did not recognize two of his youngest, Pearl and Abbie. They were three and one years old when he had left for Canada, and now five and three respectively. "But the trial came . . . when I drew each one to my bosom and

---

108. Godfrey and Card, *The Diaries of Charles Ora Card: The Canadian Years, 1886–1903*, 17–18 November 1894.

109. Godfrey and Card, *The Diaries of Charles Ora Card: The Canadian Years, 1886–1903*, 8 January 1884. See also Clarice Card Godfrey, "The Story of Charles Ora Card," handwritten notebook story.

kissed them was more than I could do without bursting into tears. Who would not weep for their own flesh and blood when forced from them by the power of an unrighteous government?" He was always delightfully pleased to know his children were well and especially enjoyed the photos, "just lovely and much appreciated by their exiled father I can assure you," which he underlined for emphasis. "Tell Georgie [George Cyrus Card] it pleased papa much to hear he can cut wood for ma . . . I hope to hear he takes good care of the garden and is a good boy in school."[110] As George grew into teenage responsibilities, his work was much more in the garden and on the farm.

Charles wrote and praised each child. He loved the letters he received, and although Sarah wondered if he could read the children's writing, he responded "those loving letters of Pearl's and Abbies, why papa can read them like a book and knows every letter and mark came just from their dear little hearts. God bless you my sweet little daughters. I love you and return you a kinder kiss each and so many for Georgie."[111]

**FAMILY TRAVELING TOGETHER**

Charles had a special affection for his wives, who he called his quorum of good, faithful wives.[112] He married four times, and he spent as much time as possible with his wives and families. They were all together when they could be and met individually when circumstances would otherwise allow. During the years prior to persecution, he often took them on his travels throughout the stake. He established each of them in different locations during the years of persecution, removing them

---

110. Charles Ora Card to Sarah Jane Painter, 19 May 1887, Godfrey Family Papers.

111. Charles Ora Card, Letter to Sarah J. Card, 25 February 1891, Godfrey Family Papers.

112. Godfrey and Card, *The Diaries of Charles Ora Card: The Canadian Years, 1886–1903*, 22 November 1886. See also Bradley and Woodward, *Four Zinas*, 278; and Shane LeGrande Whelan, *More Than One* (Lehi, UT: Zion Publishers, 2014), chapter 1, epigram header.

from danger and incarceration. During the years in Canada, he visited them each at least once or twice a year.

On 6 February 1887, he had just returned from his first exploratory trip into Canada. Keeping out of the way back in Logan, he described as "pleasant to meet one's family in these precarious times and when man is deprived of these things they seem nearer when they come. Thank God I have wives that love me for I know I have the ones I implored the Lord for and I pray ever they may keep the faith and rear their children of my loins in fear of God and not of man." Just a few days later he was hiding behind a door listening in on a testimony meeting at his home. It filled his heart. Zina and Sarah both spoke expressing their spirit, "which was a great satisfaction to a husband that so much desires their children behold an example of faith."[113]

### EMOTIONAL TRIALS

In 1887 while in Canada, Zina would serve as the private secretary to her mother, Zina D. H. Young, who had been called as the president of the Relief Society of the Church. Charles's response was both humorous and reflective of his person. "While it will leave me wifeless in this land, I have never refused to comply with the wishes of my [church] leaders and always desire to act in concert with the prophets of God."[114] On 4 November, a dozen years since his first trip to Canada, Charles wrote to Zina in Salt Lake, "I have no greater interest in heaven than my wives and children and some of them have been a sore trial to me, ... yet I have done my duty by them."[115]

There were several emotional trials in Charles's life that spanned the spectrum of life's challenges: illness and death, capture and escape from the US marshals, leadership in exile, exile from home because of

---

113. Charles Ora Card, Letter to Sarah J. Card, 25 February 1891, Godfrey Family Papers.

114. Charles Ora Card, Letter to Zina Card, 16 June 1897, MS 784, CHL.

115. Charles Ora Card, Letter to Zina Card, 3 November 1898, Godfrey Family Papers.

vigilant marshals, children without a father, wives without a husband, and, unfortunately, unwanted divorce.

One of his wives, Sallie, had what Charles saw as a negative influence on their children during his exile, and this influence drew them away from him. Charles had done everything within his power to avert the divorce, which dragged out over almost seven years. He had counseled Sallie. He admonished her to repent from her promiscuity but all to no avail. She would promise to be faithful and then recant. "Many is the day I [Charles] have tried to drown those affiliations with hard labor and seeking the Lord for consolation and aid, which I have received and thus far have been able to carry the burden."[116] The burden was growing with each passing year. "How sad to contemplate such a thing as the parting of a man and wife, a circumstance, I have always abhorred from my youth, but when a wife or husband ceases to love the truth there is no knowing what length they will go."[117] He learned, on 24 March 1889, that Sallie had enrolled their oldest son, Charles Jr., in the Episcopal School in Logan. This was painful to a father who wanted his children "to walk in the light of truth." Despite his aching heart, his letters to his eldest daughter, Jennie, and Charles Jr. reflect only love and concern. He was never negative in his writing about their mother or the divorce.

### PROTECTING HER IN DIVORCE

One wonders how far Sallie would go in this divorce and how Charles would handle the emotions of her attacks in addition to his own trial for polygamy. She filed a lawsuit against him in 1886.

He was in Canada in 1890 when his feelings of frustration and isolation climaxed to the point that he visited with his lawyers, Charles C. Richard, Henry H. Rolapp, and a Mr. Barton. After that meeting he

---

116. Godfrey and Card, *The Diaries of Charles Ora Card: The Canadian Years, 1886–1903*, 23 September 1883.

117. Godfrey and Card, *The Diaries of Charles Ora Card: The Canadian Years, 1886–1903*, 24 March 1889. Hudson incorrectly has this entry as 23 September 1883. See Hudson, *Charles Ora Card*, 160.

decided to take his chances in the US courts, so he returned to Logan. He was going to fight for his freedom. His own father was so concerned that he "came stalking to my bedside" one morning and he asked why Charles had come, to which he responded that it was for "liberty."[118] He laid out his defense for his father, wives, family friends, and church leaders, and with their approval, he voluntarily surrendered to the marshals at 2:00 p.m. on Wednesday, 23 July 1890. He took the train with his captors to Ogden, where he was arraigned, posted a $1,500 bond ($37,745), and was set free to await trial. He retired late that evening to "enjoy my first nights repose of freedom for 4 years. Thus, the Lord opens the way. He opened my way of escape 4 years ago and now has opened my way for liberty with less sacrifice."[119] The lawsuit indictment carried no gains for Sallie, other than spite, but she was the prosecution's chief witness. The charge was that Charles "did unlawfully, live and cohabit with more than one woman as his wives," contrary to the laws of the United States.[120]

It would be nearly Christmas before Charles would have his day in court on Monday, 22 December 1890 at 10:10 a.m. Sarah Jane and Sallie were called as witnesses, but they were late. Sarah's train had delayed her arrival by twenty minutes, but Sallie did not appear until 11:00 a.m.—a move that worried the prosecution and irritated the judge. Sarah was the first witness. She was nervous and apprehensive, but Charles had faith in a blessing he had given her earlier comforting her that she could endure the ordeal. "She was put on the stand and nagged for 1/2 hour," but the Lord protected her. Sallie was the next witness. She was "pale and when she spoke her lips quivered."[121] The attorneys questioned Sallie about Zina, but as that marriage had

---

118. Godfrey and Card, *The Diaries of Charles Ora Card: The Canadian Years, 1886–1903*, 22 July 1890.

119. Godfrey and Card, *The Diaries of Charles Ora Card: The Canadian Years, 1886–1903*, 23 July 1890.

120. The indictments are reproduced in Godfrey and Card, *The Diaries of Charles Ora Card: The Canadian Years, 1886–1903*, 18 October 1890 entry.

121. Godfrey and Card, *The Diaries of Charles Ora Card: The Canadian Years, 1886–1903*, 22 December 1890.

occurred after her divorce from Charles, she knew nothing of it. The prosecuting attorneys then attacked Charles and Sallie's divorce, which questions the judge allowed despite defense attorney objections.

Even under these pressures, Charles protected his ex-wife, Sallie. His attorneys had obtained a marriage certificate documenting her marriage to Benjamin Ramsel. They turned to Charles asking excitedly, "Shall I fire that in now?" Charles declined to use the evidence against Sallie, including the marriage certificate and testimony of three other known affairs in which she had engaged during her marriage to Charles. When asked the reason for the divorce, Sallie responded, "We did not agree upon religious principles." Charles sat quietly, said nothing, but wrote, "She was correct, for she desired a plurality of men and I practiced only with my wives that I had taken by the Laws of God." The last witnesses were Mark Fletcher, whom Charles called "his avowed enemy" and N. W. Crookston, a former Logan marshal but a friend to Charles. The two witnesses contradicted each other in their answers, and in answer to Charles's prayer, the prosecution rested. And Charles was acquitted. The case had "insufficient evidence."[122]

Even in this emotionally charged court environment, Charles's heart and faith led him to a higher ground. He did not defame Sallie. In fact, he protected her from public humiliation. In a literal sense, the case against Charles was true, according to the laws of the land. The evidence against Sallie was also true but would have embarrassed and crushed her and his children Charles Jr. and Jennie, as well as the Birdneau family, who were among his friends in Logan. Charles had always counseled against the spirit of contention in anyone, urging humility and faith, and seeking the Lord in prayer.[123]

---

122. These legal challenges are narrated in Godfrey and Card, *The Diaries of Charles Ora Card: The Canadian Years, 1886–1903*, 139–41, 152–64.

123. Charles Ora Card to Joel Ricks Jr., 12 January 1884 [or 1904]. Godfrey Family Papers. The year is likely 1884, but the date was simply unclear on the original.

## 170 TEMPLES IN CARD'S LIFE

The work and dedication of the Logan Temple in May 1884 reflect Charles's heart in unique ways. It was through his pioneering legacy as superintendent of construction that the fourth temple was built by the Church. His leadership brought him into contact with multitudes of people whom he asked to dedicate their time and talents to complete the work. The temple was a spiritual experience in solemn, symbolic learning in which his heart and soul were touched.

During construction, parents and leaders urged small children to save their nickels and donate them to the temple fund. One day, a small child showed up at the construction site and climbed up on the construction walls. He wanted to see where his nickel was going. Thinking of the child's safety, a worker turned the child away sorrowfully. Charles saw the interaction and the disappointment in the boy's eyes, and he took the youngster on a private tour.[124]

After the dedication of the Logan Temple, one might expect that the superintendent would want to be among the first to receive the blessing of the temple, but Charles did not. Perhaps he sought to put others before himself. He witnessed the three dedicatory services of the temple and watched as the blessings were bestowed upon others. He had opened the way for the Lord to confirm the blessings. "While sitting there [in the temple] nearly noon Pres[ident] George G. Cannon bade me to go and get myself and wife ready to receive our 2nd anointing." Charles and Sarah Jane Painter were "the first to receive their 2nd anointings in the house of the Lord." He returned home in "joy." It had been seven years since Brigham Young had called Charles as superintendent, so when the temple had been finished and dedicated, Charles declared, "Great is my joy and satisfaction in beholding its completion."[125]

---

124. Hudson, *Charles Ora Card*, 72.

125. Godfrey and Godfrey, *The Diaries of Charles Ora Card: The Utah Years, 1871–1886*, 16 May 1884. The dedication of a temple is a sacred occasion of celebration. See Ludlow, *Encyclopedia of Mormonism*, 2:659, 4:1455–56. Second anointing refers to a special ceremony reserved for those who were called by the President of the Church.

The Logan Temple was one of the most significant achievements of Charles's life. However, it would not overshadow eighteen years of service in Canada where again friends and family were relocated in protection from persecution. There, he established the foundations for new communities, regional irrigation, and another temple, the first built outside of the United States. His wives would attend that dedication in 1923, but Charles would not. He passed away on 9 September 1906.[126]

### UNCEASING DILIGENCE

On 12 September 1902, Charles was released from his Canadian Mission, which had started in 1886. He presided over the Cache Valley Stake from 1883 to 1890 and over the Canadian Mission, including the Alberta Stake, from 1886 to 1902. The Canadian Mission during the early settlement period was actually considered a part of the Cache Valley Stake. He was praised for his unceasing diligence. The *Deseret Evening News* noted, "His name will never be forgotten, but upon history's pages we shall find him chronicled as the 'Pioneer of Southern Alberta and the Father of Cardston.'"[127]

Charles's work ethic and his determination, as well as the unusual pressures of persecution and travel, eventually wore him down, causing his health to deteriorate. In 1903, he and Zina were living in their new two-story brick home in Cardston, but they did not enjoy it long.[128] In December, Charles turned his business affairs over to his son Joseph and left Cardston for Cache Valley on a stretcher. He was

---

See David Duerger, *The Mysteries of Godliness: A History of Mormon Temple Worship* (San Francisco: Smith Research Associates, 1994), 87–88.

126. Godfrey and Card, *The Diaries of Charles Ora Card: The Canadian Years, 1886–1903*, 643.

127. News Stake Presidency," *Deseret Evening News*, 18 September 1902, 7. Two other publication have this date listed as 5 September, which is an error. The *Deseret Evening News* of 18 September can be retrieved from the Library of Congress, Historic American Newspapers.

128. In Hudson, *Charles Ora Card*, 163, he indicated the value of the home was $6,500 ($163,550).

critically ill. He had never slowed long enough to rest and recuperate before he was up and back at it. For almost sixteen years he had been on the rough roads of southern Alberta and Cache Valley, Utah. After he was released from his Canadian mission, he made the decision to return to Logan, where in August 1903, he retired. He occasionally attended the temple. He also had been ordained a patriarch and spent much of his time blessing others. He lived primarily with Zina and Lavinia, who cared for him until his death on 9 September 1906. It would be his Canadian family who would remain and carry on his legacy and assure his name continued in history.[129]

---

129. Joseph Young Card would carry on Charles's businesses and was a Cardston entrepreneur in his own right. Brigham Young Card, a grandson with a Stanford PhD, authored many journal articles and books on the southern Alberta Mormons.

# FAMILIES FOLLOW TO ALBERTA

Chapter 6

**A QUIET, LOVING SON**

George Cyrus Card was the eldest son of Charles and Sarah Jane, born in Bountiful, Utah, on Monday, 26 January 1880, at 9:00 p.m. George took the name of his grandfather. It was a snowy winter evening, and the snowdrifts delayed the trains, making Charles late getting home from a church assignment at the Oxford Branch. He made it just in time to take care of some temple business and then be with his wife at George's birth.[1] Within a few months, on Thursday, 6 May, George was given his name and a blessing by Henry W. Ballard. By the afternoon, Charles was back to work on the temple with Benjamin Ramsel.[2]

During the early 1880s, Cache Valley was expanding west as settlers formed new communities, thus causing business and industry to grow. "The city boomed with lawyers, doctors, and men of various processions, some not desirable," wrote Joel E.

---

1. Godfrey and Godfrey, *The Diaries of Charles Ora Card: The Utah Years: 1871–1886*, 26 January 1880.

2. After Charles's first wife, Sallie, divorced him, Ramsel became her husband.

Ricks.³ People who were not Mormons saw the opportunities of the valley and that the population was growing. There were not adequate farmlands around the city, so communities around the valley sprang up. The Utah State Agricultural College was established in 1888 and was "a great prize for the region."⁴ Agriculture and its related industry were becoming well established. Government, education, and financial institutions were moving into the valley.⁵

George grew as most Cache Valley pioneer children did. He worked around the home with his mother, helped her in the gardens, helped on the farm, and attended school. However, unlike most other pioneer children, he received two patriarchal blessings instead of just one. The first was administered by John Smith on 10 September 1884, when George was only four years old. He was told that "the angel that was given to thee at thy birth shall watch over thee by day and night, direct thy course, give thee counsel in time of need and power over evil and unclean spirits." The second blessing was administered by Henry L. Hinman on 19 August 1895, when George was fifteen years old. The persecution of his father, mother, and family no doubt frightened and unsettled him. The blessing reconfirmed the earlier promises and focused on spiritual admonitions. Be "respectful of thy parents and to the priesthood of God; . . . be prayerful; . . . be humble; . . . seek your wife in prayer. . . . I say unto thee strike against all weaknesses, even the weakness of the flesh that thy body may be strong." George's final blessing was given by his father as a newly ordained patriarch on 25 September 1902. George was twenty-two and living in Canada.⁶

George had lived in a peaceful, loving atmosphere—until the antipolygamy laws were passed in Congress and persecution began. He was an impressionable youngster. He was likely close by the house the day it was surrounded by the US marshals who arrested his father and

---

3. Ricks and Cooley, *The History of a Valley*, 63.

4. Peterson, *A History of Cache County*, 151.

5. Peterson, *A History of Cache County*, 185.

6. The first blessing by John Smith and the second by Henry L. Hinman are in Godfrey Family Papers. The third is mentioned in Hudson, *Charles Ora Card*, 151, but there is currently no transcription.

led him away. No doubt he was scared for his life, as well as those of his father, mother, and little sister.

It was his mother's influence that taught him the daily values of work and faith. However, the letters between him and his father during these years reflect lessons of life and love. Charles was always "papa," Sarah Jane was always "mama," and love was a constant. Charles cherished these while he was in exile, as George was the only one "old enough to bless me [and] that has the disposition to do so." Charles always responded with love, teaching, and compliments. He told George his writing was of the quality that before long he could write for a newspaper and directed his son as to the proper use of a full signature in legal documents.[7] In a letter addressed to George from "Card on Lees Creek, N.W.T. Canada," Charles encouraged and praised George in school progress, reminding him that his father and mother never had such formal opportunities.[8]

George's writing would indeed improve and he would even try his hand at poetry. To his sister Pearl, at Christmas 1902, he wrote:

> Our lives are albums written through
> With good or ill, with false or true.
> And as blessed angels turn
> The prayers of our years
> God grant they read the good with the smiles
> And blot the ill with tears.[9]

### TEMPTATIONS AND TRIALS OF YOUTH

At seventeen years of age, George decided he had enough schooling. Charles was visiting Logan at the time and put him to work plowing the west field of the family farm. He purchased a horse and wagon for his son, helping him get started in a life on the farm. By 1898, George was engaged to Rose Elizabeth Plant, an aspiring teacher. She wanted

---

7. Charles Ora Card to George Card, 3 January 1893, Godfrey Family Papers.
8. Charles Ora Card to George Card, undated, Godfrey Family Papers.
9. George Card to Pearl Card, 25 December 1902, MS 8735, reel 5, CHL.

to complete her schooling, and soon after the engagement they left Logan to complete her education.

Rose traveled almost three hundred miles north by train to Dillon, Montana, to attend the new Montana State Normal School. The school was established in 1893 to train teachers. Rose lived at the Hotel Metlen, where she also worked as a waitress to support herself and her goal of an education.[10] One of Rose's small notebooks indicates that she took courses from a Professor Cooper in language, symbols of thought, grammar, literature, biology, science, religious truth, economic truth, and teaching. Her turn-of-the-century education came just before the Industrial Revolution and Gilded Age, giving speculative substance and debate to the subjects taught. Oil had just been discovered in Texas, and Rose studied how oil was affected by the weather. The science of weather on plants and people was critical for future farming. Her notes cover a spectrum of learning and continued faith in what she had been taught at home. She kept several recipes, among which are the following: gunsy gargle, which included a mixture of borax, potash, camphor gum, and a pint of brandy (likely Guernsey gargle used for throat relief); and black salve, which was a paste applied to the skin for cancer and skin ailments. Her other recipes were probably tastier, such as those for Christmas pudding, carrot pudding, mint jelly, cocoa fudge, and peanut brittle. Rose loved to cook, and her grandchildren would later attest to the smell of date cookies whenever they entered her home.

While Rose was at school, George began dating Alice Louise Jones. They began a relationship and had a son, Edgar George Card, born on 2 March 1899, at which time he was given a name and a blessing by his grandfather Charles. George and Alice were married on 30 March 1899. Charles counseled George to hold onto the marriage with his new wife and son. Charles had learned the difficult life lesson and devastation of losing a wife and child through divorce. Nevertheless, the young couple eventually separated. Alice was given custody of their son, Edgar, and moved to Salt Lake City, where she married David

---

10. Clarice Card Godfrey, "Family Stories," spiral notebook in Godfrey Family Papers.

University of Montana Normal School. Rose Elizabeth Plant Card attended, 1897–99. Courtesy of University of Montana Western.

Franklin Shelton.[11] These events were catalysts that drove George north to Canada and on an inward journey.

Rose was no doubt heartbroken and upset that George chose not to wait for her. But despite all this, she forged forward with her life. After acquiring her teacher certification, she accepted a position at the College Ward School.[12] College Ward was a small town at the southern end of Cache Valley, west of Millville, just five miles south of Logan. It had a one-room schoolhouse that doubled for church services. Rose taught grades one through eleven, and she loved learning. George and Rose were likely in contact, as she was still friends with his sister, Lavantia; but their relationship as a couple had obviously stalled.

Immediately after his divorce, George worked temporarily at a mining camp, but he soon decided it was not to his liking and moved to Canada to work with his father. He lived with Charles and Zina

---

11. Clarice Card Godfrey, "Family Stories." See also Godfrey and Card, "Editor's Notes," *The Diaries of Charles Ora Card: The Canadian Years, 1886–1903*, 474–75; and Maxine Smith, "Life Story of Edgar George Shelton," Godfrey Family Papers, Maxine Smith was Edgar's daughter.

12. John A. Hansen, "The History of College and Young Wards, Cache County, Utah" (master's thesis, Utah State University, 1968), 66. A listing of the early school teachers includes Rose Plant.

for two or three years in the log cabin that still stands in Cardston. He worked construction, shingled his father's new brick home, and labored in an old meat market. "He was making a pretty good fist of the business, . . . a fair way to getting steady employment with the builders here."[13] He sought other employment, reaching out beyond his father. The telephone was arriving in southern Alberta, and he helped build and repair the lines that were bringing electronic communication into the world.[14] Eventually, George acquired a job with the North West Irrigation Company. This would change his life. He was one of the workers who dug the canal from the St. Mary's River to Magrath, carrying water from the mountain river to the fertile lands of the prairie farms. About five miles north of the border between the US and Canada, workers constructed a diversion dam on the St. Mary River, directing water toward the settlements of Kimball, Spring Coulee, and Magrath. Charles had plowed the first furrow of the canal in 1898.

George was a part of a $100,000 ($271,623,385) project "to make homes for and gain grown for a portion of the Kingdom of God."[15] The canal was thirty feet wide at the top and twenty feet at the bottom, and when completed, it carried five feet of water. At Spring Coulee, a natural ravine carried the water along to Pothole Creek and Magrath. George drove his father's horse team, plowing and dredging the canal. He was paid in cash and received 160 acres of farmland near Magrath. It was a quarter section and included mineral rights. He deeded a portion of the land to his father for use of the team and plow, but the land was later combined under George's ownership. The land was comparatively inexpensive at the time and cash was extremely rare. This was George's southern Alberta foundation and would continue in the family for better than a century.

---

13. Charles Ora Card to daughter Pearl Card, 11 June 1902, Godfrey Family Papers.

14. Godfrey and Card, *The Diaries of Charles Ora Card: The Canadian Years, 1886–1903*, 26 June 1899.

15. Godfrey and Card, *The Diaries of Charles Ora Card: The Canadian Years, 1886–1903*, 26 August 1899. Underlining is C. O. Card's.

College Ward, Cache County, Utah, schoolhouse and class, 1899–1901. Teacher Rose Plant, standing with her class at far right. Courtesy of Marilyn Ockey-Pitcher.

## A TEACHER IN THE FAMILY

Rose Elizabeth Plant eventually married George in Canada. She was the youngest daughter of Henry Plant and Sarah Harris Plant, who lived in Cache Valley's town of Richmond. She was born on 11 March 1879 and had five older sisters and three brothers. Her hair was wavy, and she had a small mole on her nose.

The Plant family had its roots in Cadeby, Leicester, England, where they owned a stocking factory. Henry, Sarah, and their first five children, along with Sarah's sister, joined the Church and saved for years to make the journey to Salt Lake City. On 24 June 1868, they boarded the ship the *Constitution* for New York with some 457 other Church members. Forty-two days later, they arrived at New York.[16] As they disembarked, they met a man who claimed to be a representative of the Church sent to help them. In good faith, Henry gave the man all the money he had with him, holding back only sufficient to pay for the remainder of the travel. The family became a part of John Gillespie's company that consisted of about five hundred people and fifty-four wagons. They traveled by train and wagon, arriving in Utah on 15 September. They had depleted their resources and went looking for the man to whom they had trusted their cash while in New York, who supposedly had taken it to make preparations for their arrival in Salt Lake. The man was nowhere to be found.[17]

It was difficult in a new land, but they established themselves in Richmond, Cache Valley County, north of Logan. They farmed, and during the times of persecution, their home was a safe haven for Church leaders, who hid in the attic when the marshals came around.

Rose was the youngest of nine. The Plants were a family who believed in hard work. Her father felt going to school was unnecessary for farm workers. However, her mother was a strong advocate of education. Rose's mother and older sisters taught her numbers and the alphabet. Years later, she could still recite the alphabet backwards just as fast as she could forwards, without missing a letter. Rose had an express desire to learn. She worked hard and learned quickly. Her father died when she was just ten, and four years later, her mother passed away. This left Rose in the care of her older sisters. Her family was large, and all the children were expected to work. She completed her elementary and high school in Cache Valley and, in 1896, earned her common school diploma.[18] She worked in the summers, living with her sister in Blackfoot, Idaho, where she saved money so she could

---

16. Conway B. Sonne, *Ships, Saints and Mariners: A Maritime Encyclopedia of Mormon Migration, 1830–1890* (Salt Lake City: University of Utah Press, 1987), 54–55.

17. Clarice Card Godfrey, "Family Stories," spiral notebook.

18. Rose's common school diploma states the following: "Rose Plant of Richmond Cache County, has satisfactorily completed the Common School Course of Study prescribed by the laws to be taught in the Public Schools of the State of Idaho. Logan, Utah 12 June 1896." Her teacher was S. W. Hendricks, and superintendent of the

Metlen Hotel, Dillon, Montana, 1897, the building still stands. Rose Plant boarded and worked here while attending school. Photo by Donald G. Godfrey.

attend school in the winter. She was determined to be a schoolteacher, and it was at this time she attended the new Montana State Normal School in Dillon. She lived and worked at the Metlen Hotel just west across the street from the train station.[19] When she completed school, she moved back to Logan, where she took a position in the College Ward School, 1899–1901.

Little is written about George's first marriage, but it is reasonable to assume that Rose must have been disappointed with George, and it must have taken more than a little persuasion before he finally convinced her to marry him and move with him to Canada.[20] Rose

schools was Samuel Oldham. Certificate in possession of Marilyn Rose Godfrey Ockey Pitcher.

19. The Metlen Hotel still stands in Dillon, Montana.

20. "Story of the Plant Family," transcribed by Clarice Card Godfrey, Godfrey Family Papers. Arlene Godfrey Payne has a small notebook Rose used during her school years. Writing on the back of the photo of Rose Card indicates the class and the years. Notebook in possession of Marilyn Rose Godfrey Ockey Pitcher.

Elizabeth Plant and George Cyrus Card were married on 14 October 1902. The newlyweds lived with Charles and Zina in Canada until they had acquired the farmland just outside of Magrath. George hauled the logs to the farm using a team of horses and a wagon, and with those logs, he built a cabin. A few years later, George hired a Magrath carpenter named Melvin Godfrey to build a small two-room home. The home stands today, but with some additions. This was where George and Rose's children were born: Leland Plant Card (1904–16); Clarice Card Godfrey (1907–80); Cyrus Henry (1909–87); Glen Charles Card (1911–90); and Melva Rose Card Witbeck (1925–2011).

**PIONEERING FARMERS**

George plowed the first furrow of his land and seeded it with the help of a friend, fellow canal worker Zebulon W. Jacobs. Jacobs owned the land just east of George's plot, so they planted their crops together.[21] Wheat was their first crop. In these days, the seed was broadcast, meaning it was scattered across the furrows, cast by hand as the farmer walked the fields. It was then cultivated into the soil with a disk harrow pulled by horses. George worked with a shovel in his hands and gumboots on his feet. He worked hard to keep the weeds under control and the crops watered. The first crop was successful. George and Zebulon harvested the crops, hooked up a team of four horses to the wagon, and hauled the wheat to Lethbridge, where they sold it. This farming brought neighbors together in work and friendship. There were cows, chickens, and pigs on the farm. George corralled his pigs in the mud, and he was stern with any child or grandchild who approached the pen to gawk at the sow and her piglets.[22]

George was a loving father and a thoughtful, caring, and charitable friend. He and Rose eventually moved into the town of Magrath in 1918 so that their children would be closer to the schools. Many times,

---

21. Reminiscences of Cyrus H. Card, circa 1980. See also Clarice Card Godfrey, "Family Stories," spiral notebook; and MDHA, *Irrigation Builders*, 482.

22. Floyd and Clarice Godfrey, joint oral history interview, 8 May 1977, Godfrey Family Papers.

family and friends in need lived in their little home. Sometimes it was two entire families. If the husband was ill and the wife alone, George invited the wife and their children to live with them while their father recuperated in the hospital. When the husband died, George shared their sorrow and the family remained in his home with his support. Once, they took in a young girl whose father was abusive, and she lived with them for two years. When their son Cy's first wife, Leta Cook, died, their children came to live with their grandparents.

There were also times when George could be too generous. He once tried to help a friend establish a business by loaning him money. When the friend indulged in too much alcohol, George was forced to take over the business. Then the Great Depression plunged him and the business deeply into debt.[23]

**COMMUNITY AFFAIRS**

George was easy to get along with and always willing to accept a service assignment from his ward and town leaders. He and Rose were both active supporters working for the Red Cross during World War II. George worked as a member of the "Old Folks Committee" of the town and church. He was always reaching out, organizing parties, and providing activities for the elderly. "He really liked to work with people and he was good with people," especially those in need.[24] He was an active member and chair of the school board. In retirement, George enjoyed life working his gardens, visiting with friends and being with his grandchildren.[25] He was not one driven by the clock. "If he worried about anything, he did not show it." He loved people, always lending a helping hand, and people loved him in return. In 1952, at George's retirement from the farm, his eldest son, Cyrus, commented, "in our

23. Reminiscences of Cyrus Henry Card, circa 1980, 3, Godfrey Family Papers. Cyrus was the son of George and Rose. Nothing was written about the type of business venture it was.

24. Clarice Card Godfrey transcription, Godfrey Family Papers.

25. Reminiscence of Cyrus Card. See also unidentified newspaper obituary, "Southern Alberta Pioneer, George Cyrus Card, Magrath, Dies at 78 After Long Illness," Magrath Museum and Godfrey Family Papers.

22 years of farming together, we never had one serious disagreement; . . . he was honest . . . trustworthy" and never critical of anyone.[26]

George's grandchildren described him as gentle and kindhearted. They all thought they were his favorites until they talked to one another and the secret was discovered: he cared for them all. One summer evening, Rose was out of town visiting their children, Glen and Helen, who lived in British Columbia. George's granddaughter Arlene Godfrey had come to stay with him. She had gone to a movie with a friend when a fierce hailstorm struck. The wind took the power out, the show was cut short, huge trees were toppled, and gardens were left without a leaf blossom. Arlene walked to George's home with a friend, but when she could not find him, she was scared. Too frightened to stay alone, she went to her friend's home. Meanwhile, George was out looking for her. He found her the next morning after he had searched all night.[27]

George passed away on 4 September 1958, after an extended battle with Alzheimer's disease.

Rose was a hard worker. On their Magrath farm, Rose raised a flock of chickens and turkeys that the family ate, and they sold the surplus of those that were not eaten. Only when a badger burrowed his way up through the dirt floor of the chicken coop did George get involved. The badger killed thirty-five chickens and stored them in his hole. The loss of that many chickens was significant for any pioneer farmer. Taking action to fight this, George flooded the hole, forcing the angry badger to the surface, at which point he shot it. There were also beehives on the farm to pollinate the crops and provide the family honey. It was bottled, stored, and used by the family, and the excess honey was sold.

George and Rose's farm home had none of the conveniences of modern day. Oil lamps and candles furnished the only light until the 1950s. Coal stoves were the only heat for warmth and cooking. The

---

26. "Reminiscences of Cyrus Henry Card," circa 1980, 3, Godfrey Family Papers. See also unidentified newspaper obituary, "Southern Alberta Pioneer, George Cyrus Card, Magrath, Dies at 78 After Long Illness," Magrath Museum and Godfrey Family Papers.

27. Arlene Janet Godfrey Payne, "My Memories of George Cyrus Card and Rose Elizabeth Card: My Grandparents," 3 March 1980, Godfrey Family Papers.

George and Rose Card with children Clarice and Leland, circa 1912. Courtesy of Marilyn Ockey-Pitcher.

townspeople would haul coal from the mines in Lethbridge, or they could dig a cheap, soft coal from the banks of Pothole Creek. Horses were the means of transportation and energy necessary to pull the plow and haul coal, lumber, and the harvest. They would pump water from a hand-dug well. Furthermore, multiple children slept in the same room and in the same bed.

There was also a form of refrigeration. People would cut large chunks of ice from Pothole Creek in the winter and preserve them in the summer with sawdust and gunnysacks. Fresh milk came straight from their cattle, and if the milk sat in the bucket or a bowl, by morning the cream would have risen to the top. George paid his grandchildren one penny per tail for each mouse or gopher they caught around the farm or the house. He worked for his father, installing the phone lines and helping in irrigation construction, but his own home had no phone or running water. The children walked to school in town even when they lived on the farm.

Rose and George were different in many ways. While George never worried, Rose worried about everything. She seemed to worry persistently, while George either did not notice or just did not say anything. She wanted things done right and according to schedule. She was perky and less than five feet tall. George was laid back and medium height. When she went to town or anywhere in public, she dressed formally, with her black hat sitting atop her head, a net draped over her eyes, and a black purse hanging on her arm. George was casual either in town or on the farm. Rose did her share of farm work, but with four little ones under her feet, there was a great deal to be done. She experienced the loss of her first son, Leland, when he mistook a bottle of poison in the cupboard for a bottle of wild berry juice and passed away on 22 June 1916. It was a devastating loss for George, Rose, and his younger sister, Clarice.[28]

Rose served in the Church, teaching in both the Primary and the Relief Society. For more than a half dozen years, she was a counselor

---

28. Clarice Card Godfrey, oral history, April 1977. An unidentified family group sheet notes that the death of Leland was due to "heart failure following measles." Both records in Godfrey Family Papers.

to Mary Watson, who served as Primary president. In the community, she was the director of the Women's Agriculture Fair competition. People from the town would bring their vegetables, flowers, and such to the fair to be judged. She and George loved their flower and vegetable garden. There were paths in the garden which allowed for grandchildren to pick bouquets for the table. Rose taught her grandchildren to make doll dresses from hollyhock blossoms and colored dye from the blossoms. Her home always smelled like date cookies whenever her grandchildren were visiting. She passed away on 6 May 1959, a little more than one year after George.

Rose and George had worked together on the farm. When they moved into town, they worked their huge garden together, harvesting and sharing with family, friends, and neighbors. They were supportive of one another in their service to others. However, Rose never let George forget his first marriage. She could not forget the hurt she felt, so there were differences between them, challenges to overcome, and stress in the marriage. However, they held it together, raising a successful family and providing a foundational heritage.

PART 3

# BRIDGING THE WESTERN FRONTIER & THE MODERN WEST

1887–1980

# FRONTIERS COMING TOGETHER

### Chapter 7

Bridging decades of frontiers can appear as rapid transitions if people simply look back. In reality, those bridges come one day at a time, with significant physical labor, trials, and a hope for the future. Pioneer life revolved around the essentials of shelter, food, and clothing. It was an agrarian farm and ranch lifestyle, at the start, often isolated from the big city and national business centers. Homes were constructed with the available local materials surrounding the farm. This is why Charles Ora Card, as he explored British Columbia and Alberta, was always alert for land with timber and water resources. As settlers moved into the West, they organized local communities, churches, schools, and governments. People worked together, particularly in small villages. Working together meant clearing the land, building homes, and practicing a cooperative enterprise. A quilting bee brought women of the neighborhoods together to sew quilts. Similarly, barns were raised, and crops were planted, harvested, and preserved.

It was the Union Pacific Railroad and the Canadian Pacific Railroad that brought the East to the West in both nations. It happened just before Card's exploration. Distances once traversed slowly by horse, covered wagon, and foot were now comparatively quickly. The first Mormon settlers into southern Alberta came in wagons and later by the rails. The trains of Alberta linked the US and Canadian railways.[1] By 1899 the first pioneers were arriving at Stirling, Alberta, on the Alberta Railway and Coal Company (AR&CC) trains. By 1900 the St. Mary's River Railway Company (SMRRC) connected Stirling with Magrath and Spring Coolee. Between 1902 and 1905, the lines were extended to Cardston, Raley, Woolford, and Kimball, Alberta.[2] All interlinked to the rail centers in Lethbridge and Calgary. These lines moved people and freight in unprecedented numbers.

At the turn of the century, other modes of transportation and communication were evolving. The steam-driven automobiles were first called the horseless carriage. The first US patent for the gasoline engine was actually filed in 1885. The Stanley Steamer was in production in 1896. By 1899 there were eighty-four automobile manufacturers in the United States, all of which were in the New England states. In Canada, the first automobile plant was near Windsor, Ontario, in 1904. The steam engines burned kerosene, also used in home oil lamps. The burner heated the water, creating steam pressure to push the crankshaft driving the engine. The electric cars were quieter, but the batteries were too heavy, and the drivers had to stop often and recharge. The gasoline-powered engine would take over the market simply because an abundance of oil had just been discovered in Texas and Alberta. By the 1920s, automobiles were becoming the primary means of transportation.[3] Distances were closing. Along with automobile travel, the Industrial Age ushered in mechanical farm machinery and a host of new technology, including film and radio.[4]

---

1. Claude Wiatrowski, *Railroads across North America* (New York: Crestline, 2012), 12–13. Also, Pierre Berton, *The Last Spike: The Great Railroad 1881–1885* (Toronto: McClelland and Steward, 1971).

2. R. F. Bowman, *Railways in Southern Alberta* (Lethbridge, Alberta: Lethbridge Historical Society, 2002), 36, 38.

3. Godfrey, "The Jenkins Horseless Carriages," in *C. Francis Jenkins: Pioneer of Film and Television*, 78.

4. David E. Kyvig, *Daily Life in the United States, 1920–1940* (Chicago: Ivan R. Dee, 2002), 71–90; 91–105.

At the same time transportation was growing and countries were expanding, territorial issues of imperialism ideology were debated. Card was not the only individual who saw missionary opportunities among the First Nations peoples. Josiah Strong, an American Protestant clergyman, argued that it was the mission of America to "carry the blessing of spiritual Christianity, to the backward areas if the earth."[5] Missionaries of all faiths were reaching out around the globe to convert and educate native peoples to the new ways of Christianity. It was a national debate, and the approach was not always gentle.[6]

At almost the beginning of the twentieth century, illness, war, frivolity, and depression seemed to come in rapid progression: World War I, the 1918–20 Spanish Flu, the Roaring Twenties, and Great Depression of the 1930s. World War I broke out in 1914, and the armistice was signed 11 November 1918. Children in elementary schools were taught the exercises of war, and boys were taught how to handle a rifle. It was 1917 when the United States ultimately declared war on Germany. "It is a fearful thing to lead this great peaceful people into war," Woodrow Wilson declared. He was thinking of a time when "a concert of free people" could eliminate the necessity of war.[7] The end of WWI was followed by a flu epidemic that killed millions. The flu touched every community and almost every household in North America and the globe.[8] The Roaring Twenties followed, with the Charleston on the dance floor. It was a short decade of social revolution, economic prosperity, cultural development, new freedoms, and a revolution in morals and manners. Darwin's *Origin of the Species* introduced the idea of evolution into the religious debates. Freud brought forward the open discussions of sex. It was a comparatively footloose and free decade

---

5. Josiah Strong, *Our Country: Its Possible Future and Its Present Crisis* (New York: The American Home Missionary Society, 1885), 159–61, 165, 170, 178–80.

6. Ernest J. Wrage and Barnet Baskerville, *American Forum: Speeches on Historic Issues, 1788–1900* (Seattle: University of Washington Press), 343–68.

7. Kyvig, *Daily Life*, 209–30; also Wrage and Baskerville, *American Forum*, 51–52, 76–86.

8. Mark Osborne Humphries, "Paths of Infection: The First World War and the Origins of the 1918 Influenza Pandemic," *War in History* 21, no. 1 (2014): 55–81.

of history. It ended abruptly on 29 October 1929, often referred to as Black Tuesday. The stock market suddenly crashed, and the Great Depression would last more than a decade.⁹

**FAMILIES ON THE FRONTIERS**

The histories of the western frontier and the modern West were bridged by families. During frontier times, the Cards led the Mormon migration into Canada (see chapter 5). Charles Ora Card established "Card's town," along with multiple LDS settlements throughout southern Alberta. He organized, directed, and worked to construct the irrigation systems that opened a new land for farming and ranching. He promoted the Canadian Mormon immigration through the *Deseret News*, calling for "200 Men With Teams Wanted, who will become actual settlers in Southern Alberta, Canada."¹⁰ It offered Latter-day Saints "a grand opportunity to accumulate means to pay for [homes and farms] without incurring the bondage of debt." Twelve years after the first LDS settlers arrived, the town had "a newspaper, a cheese factory, a gristmill, two blacksmith shops, two carpenter shops, one tin shop, a shoe shop and a meat market. Taxes? We have none except those we impose on ourselves."¹¹ Card's town was incorporated 29 December 1898 and became Cardston. In 1904 the Alberta Railway and Irrigation Company connected Cardston with Lethbridge, the major city of the area. The settlements of Magrath, Raymond, Mountain View, and others were just beginning to dot the district.¹²

A decade after the establishment of Cardston, the Godfreys, who had been living in Star Valley, Wyoming, packed their horses, car-

---

9. Kyvig, *Daily Life*, 257–300.

10. Godfrey and Card, *The Diaries of Charles Ora Card: The Canadian Years, 1886–1903*, 11–12 January 1886.

11. Godfrey and Card, *The Diaries of Charles Ora Card: The Canadian Years, 1886–1903*, 12 January 1899. This was a circular to be published in the *Deseret News*, 12 January 1899. See the actual flyer at https://www.collectionscanada.gc.ca/obj/021017/f1/nlc010647-v6.jpg.

12. "Survey of Cardston," August 1963, Industrial Development Branch, Department of Industry and Development, Government of the Province of Alberta, 3.

riages, and belongings into a train car and headed for Stirling, Alberta. Their destination was Magrath, twenty miles west of Stirling and east of Cardston. They arrived in Stirling in the middle of a late spring blizzard. They were venturing into the new land, following the first pioneers, all of whom labored with a vision of hope and opportunity. When their train arrived at the Stirling Station, the snow was so deep the horses could not even walk through the wind-packed drifts to Magrath. The train track had not yet reached Magrath, so each step was a forward lunge. This made progress excruciatingly slow and created significant stress on horses and riders. Riders felt like they were sitting atop a bucking bronco in a freezing winter rodeo, but there were no spectators or cheering crowds.

The family struggled reestablishing themselves. Melvin settled into a routine of working a handful of construction jobs, all the time looking for permanent work. He served as a carpenter, as town marshal, as a judge, and later as the owner of several small businesses. He would become heavily involved in public projects, working with Levi Harker and others, creating the framework for success in agriculture, electricity, roads, churches, schools, local businesses, and town government. The town boasted a growing complement of Main Street enterprises and by 1906 offered a post office and general store, the Magrath Trading Company, Christensen's Blacksmith Shop, and the Tanner Lumber Yard to serve the continual flow of settlers still arriving from Utah.[13] Magrath would eventually be on the railway line between Cardston and Lethbridge. Available land, successful farms, irrigation, and transportation encouraged newcomers. Magrath farmers were shipping fifteen to twenty tons of sugar beets per acre to the Raymond Sugar Factory, twelve miles east.

Charles Ora Card had broken the first ground for planting in southern Alberta. He even had a handy grocery store in his Cardston log-cabin home. His son George followed his father's entrepreneurial footsteps, working on the vital irrigation canals—earning both salary and land in Magrath for his labors. Settlers were coming, going, and

---

13. *Magrath's Golden Jubilee: Commemorating 50 Years of Irrigation* (Magrath, Alberta: n.p., 1949), 121–43.

growing with an abundance of available opportunities. Religious freedom, land, and employment opportunities were catalysts for growth. But it took hard work and ingenuity of the pioneering kind to succeed.

The Godfrey and Card families were poor, but like most pioneers they were determined. They were adventurous agrarians and were bold in new business undertakings. There was little difference between the "haves" and "have nots." Most had very little of anything, but they were a bit daring and certainly industrious.

Melvin Godfrey arrived at the turn of the century. He eventually became the town marshal and constructed a three-unit business building. Gust's Grocery was in the third unit, and Melvin owned and operated the store. He rented space for Long Jim's Chinese Restaurant. The third unit was rented to a barber and periodically a dentist. It was the Godfrey children's job to work the grocery store, and the youngest, Douglas, was in charge of keeping the new sidewalk clear of snow.[14] Melvin introduced the first silent movies to Magrath when he purchased the Electric Theater and Skating Rink. His Empress Theater took viewers from the silent screen into the age of sound and color. All the early settlers supported growing families taking advantage of every opportunity to prosper in peace.

**CHILDHOOD ON THE FRONTIER**

Magrath was a western frontier town. Cattle ranges were wide open, barbed wire fences only just beginning to appear. The McIntyre Ranch was the largest in the region. It was just south of Magrath and north of the US border. Each fall and spring they shipped and received hundreds of cattle from the Magrath train station. The station was at the north end of Main Street. Herds were driven from the ranch right through the town center by real cowboys, much to the excitement of

---

14. Douglas Godfrey to Donald G. Godfrey, 26 September 2014, Godfrey Family Papers.

the youthful wannabe cowboys who lined the dirt road, cheering the parade. Youngsters ran alongside the galloping cattle, at times grabbing the tails of the calves and hanging on for dear life. Laughter rang out as they were pulled along and splatted with fresh, wet cow dung, before falling into the irrigation ditch to clean off their bib overalls. Local branding and dehorning of the cattle kept the boys entertained almost as much as the cattle drives or watching the local blacksmith.[15] Every household had a barn and large gardens, so there was always plenty of work to do.

Melvin and Eva Godfrey's children were Bert, Parley, Lottie, Floyd, Mervin, Joseph, Norris, and Douglas. Parley and Norris both passed away as children, leaving six in the growing family. Lottie was the only sister. The children were robust, playful, fun loving, full of themselves, and pranksters. They were outgoing, and, being a little rough around the edges, they liked a good boxing match. They could be mischievous, but they were easily loved. Bert and Floyd were perhaps a little shyer and more conservative than their younger brothers, Mervin and Joseph. Douglas bore the brunt of friendly teasing. Harassing the littlest was a favorite pastime of the elder brothers. Joe and Mervin once convinced their kid brother that "Watkins Salve" would remove his freckles. The salve was an ointment used to soften a cow's chapped nipples before daily milking, with no effect on freckles.[16] Playing on the hay ropes hanging in his father's barn, Floyd once fell and bit a hole right through his tongue. He later liked to pull out his tongue with his thumb and forefingers, grossing out his children and grandchildren as the story grew with each telling.[17]

One of the Godfrey boys' favorite pranks happened at the Magrath Agricultural Fairs when they were ribbon winners. Everyone brought his or her best chickens, horses, cows, homemade pies, and alfalfa to be judged. Floyd and his brothers were winners for their alfalfa crop entries. The local farmers never figured out how Melvin Godfrey's

---

15. Gary Harper and Kathy Bly, *Power of the Dream*, 104–5.
16. Autobiography of Douglas Godfrey, 4, Godfrey Family Papers.
17. Floyd Godfrey, oral history, 20 March 1982, Godfrey Family Papers.

Melvin and Eva Godfrey's second home. Courtesy of Godfrey Family Organization.

town boys were raising such good alfalfa. It was full and sometimes five feet tall. What the farmers didn't know was that, although Melvin's sons had no alfalfa field, they had an irrigation ditch where wild alfalfa flourished. Floyd and his brother would gather a large bundle, cut and tie it together with one of their mother's sewing ribbons, and take it to the fair. They won first prize every year.[18]

The irrigation ditches that wove throughout the town were a popular place for children to play. The water flowed toward the east and the north, with larger lateral ditches feeding smaller yards. These water funnels fed gardens throughout the town and neighboring farms, and they were summer swimming holes and bathing troughs for the young at heart. If a serious farmer diverted water to his field and bypassed the children's favorite swimming spots, it was not beyond the rabbles

---

18. Floyd Godfrey, oral history, January 1977, Godfrey Family Papers, 6.

to redirect the fun back where they wanted it. The farmer patrolled the length of the dig ditch, checking to see that no one used the water out of turn. When the farmer rode by, the boys hid in the barn until he had passed. Then the mischievous children ran to the head gates and switched gates so water would flow down the ditch where they played. Later, they'd run back to the barns and watch for the farmer to return, fuming and scolding as he closed the gates again. It was a game played between the working granger and the neighborhood children. Although no fun for the farmer, it would become a tale told often by the ruffians.[19] Such was the life of rambunctious frontier children.

### HUMBLE, HUMBLE HOMES

Melvin and Eva's Magrath homes were modest. The very first, where Floyd was born, was a lean-to dugout built into the south banks of Pothole Creek near the north end of the Magrath Cemetery. These structures were temporary homes used often by the pioneers. They were sometimes called pit houses or mud huts.[20] They were just shelters for families and often their animals. Melvin simply excavated the ground from the side of the hill facing the creek and built a lean-to cutting into the bank. The sides of the structure were wood, and the roof was loose lumber covered with sod. This was how many western pioneers started what they called home.

Godfrey's second Magrath home was one house north of the Cards on 2nd Street. Melvin dismantled the old lean-to and with a team of horses dragged the lumber up to the meadow and used it to build his second home. This more than doubled their living space. There were originally two rooms, but more were added as Mervin, Joseph, Norris, and Douglas came into the family. The walls and roof were wood framed. The outside wall was covered with chicken wire, stuccoed with mud, then painted. There were two small enclosed entries on the south

---

19. Floyd Godfrey, "The Irrigation Ditch and Children," in "Life Stories," a file of undated handwritten stories from the life of Floyd Godfrey, Godfrey Family Papers.

20. See Cass G. Barns, *The Sod House* (Lincoln: University of Nebraska Press, 1930).

and east sides. Dirty gum boots and overshoes were stored here in these entryways, with parkas hung against the wall.

Wooden shingles covered the roof. They were soaked in thick red lead paint and nailed to the double-pitched roof. The roof was held in position by skeleton-like walls erected from the foundation. There was no insulation in the walls. In the winter, ice built up inside the room on the northwest corner of the house, just below the children's bed, due to poor air circulation. The structure itself was the only protection against the elements. Water in the tea kettle on the old coal stove froze at night. Winters were stinging cold.[21]

Outside and just west of the house was the all-important coal and wood shed. These 8 x 10–foot structures kept the coal and wood dry and usable in the winter, and they were close enough to haul a heavy bucket in the cold. The fire was stoked early each morning with the wood over any burning embers from overnight. Once a good fire was burning steady, mother cooked breakfast as the children gathered around the stove to get warm. In the summer, the woodshed was a secret retreat—a place to play out childhood dreams and cool down from the summer sun.

The outhouse was the coldest place in the winter world. "You didn't stay long out there."[22] The Godfrey's outhouse was a "two holer," a little bigger than usual.[23]

A water well was dug outside and away from the outhouse. It provided the water for cooking, drinking, and bathing. It was hauled indoors by the bucket full. The well was more than a fresh water source. It served as a summer refrigerator, a place for keeping butter and meat. Perishable foods were packed in a sack and lowered down the well on a rope close to the cold water. Eventually, Melvin installed a water pump in the kitchen, replacing the outside well. Running water in the house was a luxury, even though it still required being drawn up by hand

---

21. Floyd Godfrey, oral history, 20 March 1982, 26.

22. Floyd Godfrey, oral history, January 1977, 18.

23. See Bob Jackpine Cary, *The All-American Outhouse: Stories, Design & Construction* (Cambridge, MN: Adventure Publications, 2003).

with a pump. An ice box would eventually replace the well to keep things cool. This was indoor progress in small doses.

A root cellar was dug between the house and the barn. It was a hole about six feet deep, six feet wide, and twelve feet long with a door at one end. An A-frame roof covered the hole, and soil was spread over it for insulation. Inside, vegetable bins were dug deeper into the earth. These bins were for food storage. Shelves jutted from the dirt walls. The harvest from the gardens yielded potatoes, carrots, beets, parsnips, and turnips, hence the name root cellar. The bins were covered with a layer of dirt, and square lids were placed over the holes. This was sufficient insulation against the winter freeze and offered access when a child was sent for food.

A root cellar was not without its unexpected dangers. When Floyd was a young boy, his mother went into the cellar, filled her bucket, and was returning when she spotted a rattlesnake under the first step up to the door. She put down her bucket and made a run for it, jumping over the reptile onto the steps. The snake was hibernating, but she hurried inside, leaving Melvin to take care of the snake.[24]

After Floyd and Clarice were married and took over the old Godfrey home, young Kenneth went missing one summer day. Parents and grandparents engaged in a prayerful search. After a time, Clarice's father thought, "Look in the root cellar." There was Ken. He'd been playing in the yard, gone into the cellar for a carrot, and fallen asleep on the cool soil atop the vegetable bin.

The barn was farther back from the root cellar and woodshed. Their barn housed the family's milk cow, pigs, chickens, and horses, which they used for transportation. A buggy shed on the south side of the barn was just a large lean-to structure. It faced east. It was large enough for two or three wagons, but Melvin owned just one buggy. It had the luxury of a cover that made it a more expensive model, $87.50 ($1,957). Around 1914, after he purchased his first Model T Ford, the shed was converted into a garage.[25]

---

24. Journal of Floyd Godfrey, 5 February 1986, Godfrey Family Papers.

25. The Model T Ford was produced from 1908 to 1927. See Floyd Clymer, *Floyd Henry's Wonderful Model T, 1908–1927* (New York: McGraw-Hill, 1955).

Melvin was proud of his car. His first had headlights, a taillight, and two wide lamps operated with coal oil on each side of the windshield. There was a running board along the sides, allowing passengers to step up into the vehicle. On the driver's side, there was a toolbox with pliers, a screwdriver, a tire-patching kit, a jack, and tire tools. The gas tank and spare tire were mounted on back. The front radiator was gleaming polished brass, and a hand crank in front got the engine fired, often more difficult to use than perceived. Many a broken bone was created when the cold engine backfired, spinning the crank back and smacking the driver's arm. The car's canopy was heavy leather; the windows were isinglass that flapped in Alberta's west winds.[26] The morning after buying the car, Melvin showed it off to the family. He cranked it up and the engine started with a bang. The family all jumped in. Melvin released the brake, stepped on the gas, and "went right through the back of the buggy shed."[27] A second version of this tale has Floyd's brother Bert coming home late from a dance, and he drove the car through the back of the shed, "pushing the wall into the air." Both stories were memorable family firsts. While he was a policeman, Melvin even tried his hand as a car salesman, but being an officer and running the Empress Theater took his time. Car sales proved one job too many.

The family garden filled the largest section of the yard, perhaps a half acre. Every spring their horse, "Old Baldy," was hooked to the plow to prepare and plant the garden. The Alberta growing season was short—June through September, if the weather cooperated. Golden Bantam sweet corn, head lettuce, potatoes, peas, carrots, and all kinds of vegetables ripened in the summer sun. Old Baldy plowed the garden for Melvin, but the kids thought the horse was for their entertainment. After working all day, Old Baldy did not always agree. He was smarter than the boys who wanted to ride him and act like cowboys. If they approached with a bridle, even when it was held behind their backs, he could see it. He turned and ran, playing his own game of "catch me

---

26. Isinglass, also called mica, is a transparent silicate that hardens into a clear sheet akin to today's clear plastics.

27. Floyd Godfrey, "The Buggy Shed," in "Life Stories," file of undated handwritten stories from the life of Floyd Godfrey, Godfrey Family Papers.

if you can." Melvin taught his boys a better way to bridle Old Baldy. First, put some oats in the feed boxes. This attracted their horse, and the bridling became easy. They would say, "Old Baldy trained everyone well."[28]

## CHILDHOOD IN MAGRATH

The childhood house for Floyd was Melvin and Eva's second home at 155 1st Street West. Only Mervin, Joseph, and Douglas spent any time in the new brick home constructed later on Main Street. Floyd was close to his brothers, but around others he felt insecure and somewhat shy. He saw himself as "An Unkempt Lad."[29] His bib overalls, which he did not like, were worn. He went barefoot for play and wore gum boots for work, and his shoes were half-soled with slick rubber his father cut to shape from an old piece of boot or a tire. He was embarrassed to wear his short knee pants because they were baggy. When he stood straight, his more formal bloomers looked like a "girl's skirt." After much pleading, his mother bought him long pants and a suit. He proudly headed to church in his new outfit, when a neighbor saw him cutting through the yard and teasingly commented, "Well look at the little girl." Floyd ran home crying. His mother hugged him, "telling [him] not to pay attention" to that old man but to just go to Sunday School. However, Floyd never wore the suit again. Years later there were rumors that this man's cow kept ending up in the town corral on the weekends. The boys always pleaded their innocence.

The Godfrey boys played with the other neighborhood kids, the Andersons, Jensens, Colemans, Schaffers, Merkleys, Cards, and Fletchers.[30] The Fletchers' home, immediately south of the Godfreys', became the Cards' new place when George and Rose moved their family into town. In the Fletchers' attic one day, after parents warned them they

---

28. Floyd Godfrey, "Old Baldy," in *Just Mine* (Mesa, AZ: Chrisdon Communication, 1996), 36.

29. Godfrey, *Just Mine*, 24.

30. Floyd Godfrey, "Our Neighbors," in "Life Stories," file of undated handwritten stories from the life of Floyd Godfrey, Godfrey Family Papers.

were "not to go up there," Lottie lost an expensive watch while playing "dress-up" and posing behind empty picture frames. Her younger brother Floyd, their friends Howard and Gail Fletcher, and Lottie all went outside and knelt down around a bush. They prayed, "and when we got up there was the watch in the bush." It was the beginning of their faith in prayer.[31] As the only girl in the family, "Lottie was spoiled," her brothers said, which she denied, but "they were good to [her] sometimes taking the blame for what [she] had done."[32]

There were friendly and not-so-friendly boxing matches in the house to settle childhood disagreements. Floyd seemed to be on the losing end of the matches, so his father bought two pairs of boxing gloves and taught Floyd some moves. At the next bout, the boys put on the gloves and went at it, but Floyd landed a few blows with his newly acquired skills, and the disagreements ended.

The Godfrey family may never have had much, but their needs were always met as family and community worked together. Harvesting ice in the winter was one such collaborative effort. There was no refrigeration, but there was a deep, muddy slough along the creek, south of the Card and Godfrey homes. It was the place where the community cut ice for preserving summer vegetables in their root cellars and ice boxes. The blocks of ice were perhaps eighteen inches square and three or four feet long, cut straight out of the creek, winched up to the ground with a team of horses, and hauled home. The ice blocks were placed in the cellars and covered with sawdust to prolong their shelf life. When needed, pieces were sawed for the ice box in the house.

One winter day, wearing his father's awkward-fitting gum boots, Floyd went down to the creek to watch the workers cut the ice. It was slippery and wet. The adults tried to shoo children away from the icy creek, but as Floyd stood to move, his boots slipped out from under him and he skidded into the water. One of the workers, Alva Merkley, grabbed him at the back by his overcoat. He pulled him out of the creek, took off his boots, drained the icy water and gave him "a kick in

---

31. "Memoirs of Lottie Harker," Family Files, Magrath Museum, 5.
32. "Memoirs of Lottie Harker," 11.

the pants" to encourage him to leave. Floyd really didn't need a lot of encouragement. He was freezing as he ran up the hill and back home.[33]

In the summer, the creek provided a place to swim. Pothole Creek was filled with adventure. It was a boy's wilderness paradise. At first, Floyd just wandered down to the canal and watched the older boys. He was timid. Bravery came slowly and with experience. He started to swim with his clothes on. He learned a lot faster when one of the older boys, Red Stoddard, picked him up and threw him off the bridge into the middle of the swimming hole. Floyd "dog-paddled" to shore and afterward took a liking to the sport. He eventually had his own circle of swimming buddies and a secret swimming spot called "the old whirlpool." It was not a well-kept secret. After school, in the warmth of spring, even with the water still cold, it was a popular place to go. In the summer, the boys lay in the warmth of the sand and tanned in the sun. No girls allowed! The boys were skinny-dipping.[34]

Guns were in every home as a necessity, not recreation. Fathers and sons hunted for food, and serious respect for weapons was paramount. Melvin instructed his boys to especially leave the shotgun alone. Floyd, at age eleven, thought he was old enough to hike down by the creek and get a prairie chicken or partridge for supper. Despite his father's warnings, he took the shotgun and walked toward the stream. As he approached, he sat on the ground to look around, watching for any movement of the birds in the grass. He laid the gun down beside him, and the trigger caught on a sturdy dry weed, and it went off. The recoil from the shot spun the gun around and a second shot went off as the barrel struck Floyd in the leg like a swinging baseball bat. The incident scared Floyd, and he went directly home. It was a situation that could have ended in tragedy, but it reinforced his father's admonitions, leaving Floyd with a lifetime respect for firearms.

Floyd was around twelve years old when he decided to run away from home since "no body loved me." His father, at age eighteen, tried

---

33. Alva Marion and his wife Jehzell Gibb Merkley moved to Magrath just a few years prior to the arrival of Melvin and Eva Godfrey. See Magrath and District History Association, *Irrigation Builders*, 492.

34. Floyd Godfrey, "The Whirlpool," in *Just Mine*, 37.

the same thing in his own North Ogden youth and knew what would result. Eva asked Floyd where he planned on going. He didn't know, but he figured he could live with friends. "Just let him go," Melvin told Eva. His father rolled up an old blanket with some of Floyd's belongings and put a rope around it. The plan was that after school Floyd could take his things and leave to live with his childhood allies. Later that day he left home, heading south around the block, but he didn't get far. He sat down on the hill overlooking the creek and cried. He gazed at the old creamery where the farmers sold their milk for butter and home delivery. He thought of the crystal-like garnet pitcher his mother filled with buttermilk from the creamery for hot breakfast pancakes. The recollections sent him home. When he walked back in the house, his mother and father there waiting for him. "I love you," Floyd said. He did not want to live with a friend, "I want to stay here."[35] Years later, Floyd would teach a similar lesson to one of his own sons.

### LEARNING RESPONSIBILITY

Melvin was strict with his boys. Floyd learned to work while he was a youngster. He and his brothers worked around the home, doing their part as members of the family, whether milking or helping their mother in the garden. Like all boys, they preferred fun over work.

Daily milking was required if you wanted the cow to produce milk for the family. In preparation, Floyd led the cow out of the barn each morning and down to the creek for water. He liked to jump up on her back and ride to and from the stream. One day, Howard Fletcher wanted to ride with him. Unfortunately, someone kicked the cow, and she ran under the fence. The fall cut Howard up a bit. He ran to his mother for help, and Floyd ended up in trouble.[36]

Floyd has a haunting memory of when he was twelve and failed to help his mother when she was pregnant with Douglas. Melvin pitched a tent outside for Floyd and Mervin so Eva would have privacy. The two

---

35. Floyd Godfrey, oral history, February 1977, Godfrey Family Papers.
36. Floyd Godfrey, oral history, January 1977, Godfrey Family Papers, 5–6.

boys were out there for a few weeks, thrilled that they were camping. One morning, Eva called Floyd, asking him to pick some peas from the garden for supper. Floyd knew what he was supposed to do, but the temptation of friends who were headed down to the swimming hole was too much. Fun won out that day, but not without consequence. When Floyd returned from swimming, his mother was feeling worse because she had strained herself picking the peas. She was in labor, and Douglas was on his way. That night Floyd's father, Melvin, took his son to the woodshed. Many a time the boys received a thrashing with a willow from the yard for their misbehavior. "I can still feel it to this day around my legs."[37] The next morning, Floyd and Mervin went into the house and met their new baby brother.

When Melvin started the movie theater, Floyd was expected to deliver the movie films. The train station was about a mile north of their home, and the multiple film reels were heavy. Melvin devised a two-wheeled cart that he hitched to their pony so he and his brothers could easily pick up and return the films sent from Calgary to Magrath by rail. If they missed the deadline, a fee was assessed, so punctuality was a part of the lesson. Generally, the conductor waited patiently, and when he saw them coming, he teasingly scolded, "You Godfrey kids have got to hurry up. I can't hold this train just for you."[38] In his late teens and into his early marriage, Floyd progressed from film delivery to projectionist and earned his Third Class Projectionists' License.

Washing the clothes was a rigorous Monday affair that required help from the whole family. The boys were expected to gather their own clothes and help wash all of the laundry. In the days before electricity, the clothes-washing machine featured a large wheel or lever on one side. The Godfreys' had a wheel model. Two boys took turns keeping that wheel spinning so the machine could agitate the clothes in the tub and clean them. This was tiring physical labor. Each took ten minutes at the wheel while the others rested. They kept up this rotation until all of the clothes were clean and hung on the outside line to dry.

---

37. Floyd Godfrey, oral history, February 1977, Godfrey Family Papers, 11–12.
38. Floyd Godfrey, oral history, February 1977, 11–12.

Clothes washing was different after their dad purchased his Model T Ford. The boys and their father dreamed up a washing machine idea that proved to be a labor-saving one. With their father's help, they backed the car up to the washing machine, hooked a wide, heavy leather belt around the car's back tire and placed the other end of the belt around the wheel of the washer. "You've never seen a washing machine move so fast in your life. I think it about shook the machine to pieces." But it worked. "That was the first power washer" in the Godfrey family.[39]

As teenagers, Melvin pushed his boys to find full-time summer work during the farm harvests. A successful harvest was critical to the Canadian farmer. Grain crops, wheat oats, and barley required a lot of work to harvest. The fields were worked largely by hand. Like all farm workers, Floyd and Mervin cut and then bunched the grain into bundlers. The bundles were then stooked, or set up in groups for drying, and then taken to the thrasher.[40] "A boy is not worth his salt if he doesn't know how to work," Melvin said, and work the boys did.[41] Their goal was to earn a little winter spending money and buy their own clothes. Floyd was fifteen years old when he traveled with his brother Bert and later Mervin. They worked on farms in Raymond and in the foothills west of Cardston. The ranch of Richard Bradshaw was among the first that provided work. The Bradshaws had moved from Magrath to Cardston and purchased a part of Charles Brewer Ockey's ranch.[42] They harvested hay for winter feed, and the farmers sold grain to the elevator operators, who shipped it across the country. Harvesting took

---

39. Floyd Godfrey, oral history, February 1977, 11–12.

40. For Alberta farming history, see Howard Palm and Tamara Jeppson Palmyer, *Alberta: A New History* (Edmonton: Hurtig Publishers, 1990).

41. Floyd Godfrey, "Large Bundles," in "Life Stories," file of undated handwritten stories from the life of Floyd Godfrey, Godfrey Family Papers.

42. On the road from Cardston to Beazer, Alberta, turning south to the Badger Valley Ranch, it was these fields seen from that turn where Floyd and Mervin worked during their teenager years. Keith Shaw, ed., *Chief Mountain Country: A History of Cardston and District* (Cardston, Alberta: Cardston and District Historical Society, 1978), 258–59. The southern portion of the Ockey homestead remains in the family today, with Rod and Joan Shaw as the owners.

teams consisting of laborers, horses pulling the cutters, and the hay wagons. A cutter mowed the hay, creating wind rows. After it dried, farm workers such as Floyd and one of his brothers walked on each side of the wagon and used pitch forks to toss the dried hay up into the hayrack. There were no bailing machines, and there was no stopping to rest for a drink. There was a water jug sitting in the sun at the end of a line that was sometimes a half mile long. It was appealing to the boys, who were always thirsty from the workout in the summer heat. The hay was either loaded in the wagons and driven to a nearby haystack for storage or to the barn for immediate use. During the winter, the hay was loaded back into a wagon, driven over the frozen pastures, and scattered for the animals.

Harvesting grain was a little more challenging than harvesting hay for the animals. The work was defined by the size of the field and the yield of whatever crops were harvested. The grain was first cut and bound by hand or a mechanical grain binder and then laid in wind rows across the field. The job was to create a stook, seven to ten bundles together in a sheave; it got its name because it looked something like miniature teepee-shaped bouquets called stooks. The bouquet shape made the grain dry quicker. If a thresher was unavailable, the workers cut the grain with a scythe, a long sword with the blade forged into a C shape. The swing of the farm worker's arm cut the grain and helped gather the stalks together. The stalks were long and heavy. The stooks were tied together by hand with binder twine just above the center of the straw below the grain. The first stooks stood exactly vertical. Then others were placed around them, leaning into each other. This was stooking the grain. It was not casual nor unskilled labor. Stooking the grain was dirty, hard, and long work. Each bundle weighed perhaps thirty to forty pounds, and by evening the workers' hands were cramped from picking up and tying so many bundles. One thousand acres would produce hundreds of stooks. Proper stooking protected the harvest from rain while the grain dried and finished ripening prior to further harvest.

Once dry, the granulated seed was extracted from the straw and husk with a new separator machine. These early mechanical separators were about thirty-five feet long, five feet wide, and six to ten feet high. The whole rig was drawn by a team of horses. This involved Floyd, Bert, and Mervin tossing the bundles of stooks up onto the separator belt that fed them into the thresher, where it removed the dust and shook the grain stalks violently, separating the seed from the husk and the stalk.[43] Floyd enjoyed this dusty, heavy work. Working with his brothers created lifelong memories and strong relationships between them.[44]

On the Lockmans' farm, Floyd was assigned to the threshing crew. The crew pitched the sheaves of grain on a bundle rack moving up and down the fields by a team of horses. When the rack was full, the sheaves were hauled to the separator and fed along the belt through the machine. If the crew was in a hurry, then too many bundles would overload the machine, stopping the engine. Then one of the men in charge, the threshing operator, would dig out the jammed straw and restart the engine. It was a good way to get ten or fifteen minutes' rest before they could go again. Floyd's reward for the backbreaking work was one cent per harvested bushel ($0.13).[45]

Good cookhouse meals were provided for the hungry crew. They included steaks, vegetables aplenty, cold milk, and pies of every kind: "You name it, our cook could prepare it," Floyd reported.[46]

Within a few years, Floyd was promoted to handyman on the harvesting crews, more commonly known as a roustabout. Floyd was paid $7.50 ($97) per day, and he thought he was rich. He did whatever the boss wanted done. He went to town for groceries, transported the boss to the next farm to secure the next job, got repairs done, posted the mail, took the men to and from the fields for their 3:00 p.m. lunch break, and helped the supervisor and the engine man on the thresher.

---

43. Seager Wheeler, *Seager Wheeler's Book on Profitable Grain Growing* (Winnipeg: Grain Growers' Guide, 1919), 175–77.

44. Floyd Godfrey, oral history, 1988, Godfrey Family Papers, *Seeds, Faith and Family History*, 4, 18.

45. A bushel is a dry volume equivalent of just over 9.1 US liquid gallons.

46. Floyd Godfrey, "Large Bundles," Godfrey Family Papers.

The job and the harvest were intense and lasted only for a month or two at summer's end. Then it was back home and to school.

Floyd learned the meaning of work early in life. He earned his longtime job at the Magrath Trading Company as a result of his reputation for honesty and hard work. At the trading company he started as a delivery boy and worked as hardware clerk. He did this ten years into his marriage, through to the mid-1930s and into the Great Depression.

**LOVING DISCIPLINARIAN**

Floyd admired his father's courage and work ethic. The two had a good relationship. Melvin was energetic and at times also "very emotional . . . and had a tender heart."[47] He taught work by example and discipline. Coming home from Calgary after municipal meetings, Melvin asked for little Floyd to meet him at the train station. They had one of the few telephones in town because Melvin was the marshal. Floyd was not yet in school and was unsure what to expect. Melvin told him to go and look in the baggage car, "There is something for you." Floyd ran excitedly down the station's wooden platform. In the baggage car he found an iron-wheeled red tricycle with his name on it. He was thrilled. Melvin likely thought the gift was to share with Floyd and his younger brothers, Mervin and Joseph, but "my name was on it," and he felt like one special little boy.[48]

Melvin created memories for his boys even when it would have been easier to work alone. He took Floyd out for a day on a forty-acre plot he thought he might buy near the Magrath graveyard. Floyd took a sack lunch, and they went together. Worried about the gophers getting his lunch, Floyd placed it on the fence post for safe keeping while they were working. He didn't notice until it was too late, but a wild donkey had come along and eaten his whole lunch, bag and all. So his father shared his lunch with him.

---

47. Floyd Godfrey, oral history, 1982, 15; also oral history, January 1977, 5–6.
48. Floyd Godfrey, oral history, January 1977, 10.

As the town police officer, Melvin created unique teaching moments with his children, whether it was ringing the curfew bell or just riding along with their father. On a legal outing, Floyd went to Spring Coulee to repossess a sewing machine. Floyd was an impressionable seven-year-old. As they approached the home, the owner stepped out of the house, striding toward the gate with a shotgun in his hand. "Godfrey, I know what you want and you're not going to get it. I'll blow your head off if you come any closer." Floyd was petrified, but Melvin never slowed his pace, "Now . . . you wouldn't do that. . . . I'm here for the company. . . . I know you're having a hard time." After a few minutes of conversation, the stand-off ended and the man put down his gun. "Hell Melvin, come in and get the darn thing."[49]

On a later trip to Spring Coulee, Melvin drove with Floyd in his Model T Ford. The road was rough, and they sheared off the axle, forcing the father-and-son team to walk down the railroad track back eleven miles to Magrath where they could get help to retrieve and repair the car. Floyd wrote of that experience, "Dad and son were never closer."[50]

Melvin wielded a great influence on Floyd. He molded him from a shy boy into a confident young man unafraid to reach out. His often-repeated line was "You can, if you try hard enough." He instilled enthusiasm in his son and the significance of bringing a project to a successful conclusion. His acts of bravery were indelibly impressed on Floyd's young mind.

Some would not describe Melvin as a religious man, but he had a love for the gospel. He was in the elders quorum presidency in his ward. He had the solemn responsibility of caring for the dead and preparing them for their funeral and burial. He was always there when family needed him, leading, directing—sometimes rather firmly—and he was outspoken in his beliefs.[51] Everyone knew where Melvin stood

---

49. Floyd Godfrey, oral history, February 1977. Also, Floyd Godfrey, "Great Events in My Life." in "Life Stories," file of undated handwritten stories from the life of Floyd Godfrey.

50. Floyd Godfrey, "Great Events in My Life."

51. Floyd Godfrey, oral history, February 1977.

on any issue. He was a fair man in all his endeavors as a police officer, a judge, a theater owner, and a grocer.

There was never a doubt that Melvin loved his family. He twice sacrificed his own safety saving Floyd's life. The first lifesaving incident occurred in Magrath when Floyd was small. Melvin had picked up extra work putting up hay for the Eldridge Cattle Company. There were severe storms in the area that spring. Heavy rains and melting snow filled the coulees, canals, and streams. Melvin was concerned that the hay he had recently cut would rot on the wet ground, so he headed to the Bradshaw siding to check the field. On his way, he crossed a small ravine that usually held only a trickle of water. However, this time it was a raging river. Melvin's horses hesitated until he gave them a crack with the reins. They moved forward and disappeared into the water. Midstream, the horses' heads were all that could be seen. Then the buoyant wooden wagon box came loose from the wagon frame and began to float downstream in the swift current. Melvin was holding the horses while his sons, Bert and Floyd, floated away in the wagon box. Without hesitation, Melvin dropped the reins and swam with the current, catching the box and its terrified passengers. He took Floyd, then Bert, and literally flung them out of the wagon onto the soft wet bank. Then he fought his own way to the edge of the ravine to recover the horses. They had escaped and were waiting for Melvin to come and find them. It was a dramatic rescue.[52]

A second rescue occurred in the summer of 1919, when Melvin and Eva took the family to Waterton for a week. Waterton-Glacier was described by George Bird Grinnell as "The Crown of the Continent," with watersheds feeding the Atlantic, the Pacific, and Hudson's Bay.[53]

---

52. Bertrand Richard Godfrey, oral history, 3 February 1980. Also, Floyd Godfrey, oral history interview, February 1977, Magrath Museum.

53. George B. Grinnell, "The Crown of the Continent," in *Century Magazine*, September 1901, 660–71. A forest reserve was established around Waterton Lakes in 1895. It was the rich timber, and later oil that promoted its value. Then in 1927, the Prince of Wales Hotel held out the promise of tourism. The National Parks Act of 1930 established the tone for park and land use. Graham A MacDonald, *Where the Mountains Meet the Prairies: A History of Waterton Country* (Calgary: University of Calgary Press, 2003), 1, 106.

Floyd, now thirteen, had heard about the wonders and the beauty of this spot, where mountains supposedly reached into the sky. It was hard to imagine, so he was anxious. And Melvin wanted to show off his new Model T Ford.

Melvin left his two oldest, Bert and Lottie, in charge of the theater. He then took Floyd with his two younger brothers, Mervin and Joseph, packed groceries, frying pans, and everything else into a large wooden box and loaded it into the car along with quilts, pillows, clean clothing, a shovel, and bamboo fishing poles. Melvin cranked and cranked. The engine sputtered to a start, and they were off. The car was running, but the boys had to wait while their mother checked the stove one last time and instructed Lottie on the danger of fire.

Heading west, the roads were rough and dusty but graveled. They were used mainly by farmers, lumber wagons, and oil entrepreneurs hauling building supplies, equipment, and pipe into the mountains near Cameron Lake. There were no bridges, and the family crossed the St. Mary's and Belly Rivers where they could find shallow rapids. Reaching their halfway point, Cardston, the rear wheel of the car collapsed under the extra weight. The wooden spokes and the wheel rim broke. They hiked to the nearest farm house and found a telephone, and soon Mr. Low came with a new wheel and got them on their way.[54]

As the family left Cardston, they got their first glimpse of the mountains. Chief Mountain stood out, invitingly majestic. They kept moving and finally camped at the park entrance and registered at the office. The hills were green, the water clear and refreshing. Exploring everywhere, they hiked from their camp on Crooked Creek. The fish were so plentiful they actually shoveled the white fish out of the water. At night, the boys spread their bedding and quilts. Melvin and Eva sat by the campfire, just talking and laughing. Every day was an adventure for Floyd and his brothers as they trekked down the paths left by the deer and mountain animals. One day they had hiked quite a distance from the camp and stopped for supper. Melvin cleaned the fish and was preparing supper when he could not find the frying pan. He

---

54. This is likely Sterling Oliver Low, who was employed at Cardston Motors. Shaw, *Chief Mountain Country*, 392–93.

improvised. Using a short-handled shovel, he cleaned it in the sand, washed it off in the creek, greased it up, and soon the fish were sizzling in the shovel over the fire. They returned to camp tired but well fed. Building a raft and heading out to the end of Waterton Lake was the plan for the next day. That idea was vetoed by Eva: "In no way are my sons going on that water." The plan was revised to a hiking excursion to Cameron Falls, which was equally exciting.[55] The boys pleaded with their father to go the next day.

They slept quietly under their denim quilt with mom and dad close by, only the food box separating boys and parents. They were sound asleep and woke immediately as a bear searching for food began tossing knives, forks, and plates across the camp. Two stunned parents with three scared boys sat straight upright from their deep sleep and in unison let out a loud scream. Their scream startled the bear, and all that the boys could see peeking out from under the covers was the bear's retreat. For an excited and still-shaken group of children, the sun rose slowly as they anticipated the hike to the falls the next morning.[56]

Melvin explained that the unique geography of the falls was formed by a steep cliff and rocks plunging deep into the earth. The falls were actually created by older layers of rock, which over the centuries were displaced by the pressure of upper layers of new rock, giving it a dramatic angular presentation of water and rock.[57]

Breakfast that morning was hotcakes and eggs. "We'll wash the dishes when we get back," they told their mother. Eva made jelly sandwiches, with carrots to chew on the hike. The kids stuffed their pockets full of cookies and picked out a walking stick to fight off any wild bears encountered on the seven-mile hike. They marched up the

---

55. Floyd Godfrey, "Cameron Falls," in "Life Stories," file of undated handwritten stories from the life of Floyd Godfrey. Also, Keystone Steno Book, Godfrey Family Papers. These comparative reports indicate ages eight and thirteen for this event. Crooked Creek is aptly named. Its headwaters start in the mountains just west of the Blood Timber Reserve, and it flows north near today's park entrance where it turns south and empties into the Lower Waterton River.

56. See Keystone Steno Book version, Godfrey Family Papers.

57. This geological wonder is called the Lewis Overthrust. See MacDonald, *Where the Mountains Meet the Prairies: A History of Waterton Country*, 58–59.

hills and forged the Waterton River and Blackston Creek. It seemed like a long hike. They had heard so much about the falls that when they arrived it was "almost, to we boys, like one of the seven wonders of the world. . . . The falls were massive. The huge cliffs rose [and] excited the opportunity to climb." They cooled their feet in the pool at the base of the falls as they watched the waterfall. But they were not content to sit too long. They coaxed their reluctant father into going with them to climb the face of the cliff at the top of the falls. He agreed so long as they followed in his footsteps.

They made it to the top but needed to descend downward just a little to reach a lookout point above the falls. When they reached the point, they were again delighted at their view as the water thundered over arms of the very rocks on which they were standing. They sat and stared into the deep pool carved by the falls below. They inched a little farther along a large, flat stone outcropping where they could get an even better view. "Floyd, Mervin, Joe . . . come away from that edge," Melvin instructed. The rock at this spot was slanting down at about a thirty-degree angle. There were small slivers of water dripping over the stone face right where they stood. They were too close to the edge, but it was spectacular. Floyd was trying to discover the source of the water noise when his feet slipped from under him and he began sliding toward the falls. He was going down. Melvin had been watching about ten feet away and immediately plunged forward prostrate on the west rock in front of Floyd, just as Floyd slid straight into his dad "with a thump." They both stopped at the very edge of the roaring falls. "Take off your shoes, son," Melvin directed, "and creep to that trail above." With hearts racing, they dragged themselves back to the dry rock. Melvin was frightened, Floyd was shaking, and his brothers had already scampered back down to the creek below. Not a word was said between the two as they climbed down the fall's cliff and hiked back to camp. Melvin reported to Eva, "The boys enjoyed themselves." She did not find out until later what had actually happened.[58] In writing about this event, Floyd commented, "I have never thanked him [for saving

---

58. Floyd Godfrey, "Cameron Falls." Also, Floyd Godfrey, oral history, February 1977; Keystone Steno Book, Godfrey Family Papers; and *Seeds, Faith and Family His-*

Cameron Falls, circa 1925. Courtesy of Cardston Court House Museum Archives, Wolsey Collection.

my life]. I would like to do it now, but he is long gone. When I see him over there, I'll do this thing and I supposed he will laugh about it."[59]

## CHURCH AND FAMILY

Eva always threw her arms around her children, hugging them and teaching them to love and pray. She had a firm testimony of the gospel. She was as firm as she could be with eight children. If a child was too slow at following Mother's directions, it was Melvin who applied the motivation and the rescue. Eva pushed them to attend their Church meetings and involved them with learning and activities that taught them spirituality. Bert would serve a mission in the eastern states, spending most of his time in Vermont. Floyd would remain home to work in the theater.[60] Eva reinforced the principles of honesty and hard

---

*tory*, 15–16. The Keystone report places Eva at the scene of the falls. The oral histories indicate she was back at the camp and did not hear about the incident until later.

59. Floyd Godfrey, "Men of Greatest Influence," in "Life Stories," file of undated handwritten stories from the life of Floyd Godfrey, Godfrey Family Papers.

60. Bertrand Richard Godfrey, oral history, 3 February 1980.

work that Melvin taught and that they both had learned in their youth and from pioneering parents.

It was a bright sunshiny day on 7 June 1914, a day Floyd had been anticipating for a long time. The chapel had no baptismal font, so the ordinance took place in Pothole Creek, near today's Magrath Park. It was two months after his eighth birthday. His mother had scrubbed him clean for the event. He was not sure why, because he was a boy of eight who swam twice a day in the creek and did not see the need for all the scrubbing. The air was cool, so his mother put him in a pair of fleece-lined underwear, a clean pair of overalls, and a clean shirt. He and his dad hitched Old Kate to the single-horse buggy, and they all rode to the creek. Floyd waited his turn and walked down into the water with his father. It was summer, but still cold, and when he came out of the water he was almost stiff because the clothing his mother had him wear was now soaked. She took him and wrapped him in a blanket, and he stood while Bishop Harker confirmed him.[61] Afterward, the family hurried home. His mom, who feared he would get pneumonia, changed him into dry clothes. "She was a wonderful mother."[62]

It was a proud day for the eight-year-old. He was proud to be a member of the Church; "I feel (really) this was the beginning of church activity in my life." He was now expected to live, serve, and help more in Church activities. He had always had something to do, but he now felt the duty.[63]

### THE CHILDREN'S PRIMARY

Eva took Floyd and all her children to Primary when they were young. Idell Jane Toomer was an influential Primary teacher in Floyd's pursuit of those things sacred.[64] "A little smart for his britches," one day he ran

---

61. Certificate of Ordination, book 2, no. 477, Magrath Ward Records of Ordinations. See also Floyd Godfrey, oral history, February 1977, Godfrey Family Papers.

62. Floyd Godfrey, "Baptism," in "Life Stories," file of undated handwritten stories from the life of Floyd Godfrey.

63. Floyd Godfrey, "Baptism."

64. Magrath and District History Association, *Irrigation Builders*, 531.

into the church classroom, stepped on the bench, and jumped up into the window sill to sit and listen to the lesson. He was at the center of attention, but it was a different lesson that day. Sister Toomer saw him sitting in the windowsill, grabbed hold of his feet, pulled him out of the window and sat him down so hard the bench broke. Afterward, Floyd was the ideal of reverence and remembered Miss Toomer as "the best teacher ever."[65] She disciplined him "very harshly, which I needed, but I loved her."[66]

Elmer Ririe was the Magrath First Ward bishop during Floyd's growing years.[67] Louisa Alston was Floyd's Scoutmaster.[68] Although Scouting was not as prevalent in the LDS Church during the early 1900s as it is today, it was a social experience. Floyd was a patrol leader in his troop when Mrs. Alston planned a special outing for the children to see Lord Beaverbrook, who was coming to Lethbridge. William Aitken Beaverbrook was a famous Canadian and British author, businessman, and politician.[69] The Scouts went to Lethbridge on the train. It was snowing and cold the night before the dignified British lord was to arrive. It was still snowing the next morning. Nevertheless, the Magrath Scout Troop stood in full dress uniform (short pants and bare legs), with their Scout staves, standing at attention on the train station platform as the lord stuck his head out the train window for a minute, waved a celebrity "hello and goodbye," and that was it. Though it was only for a few seconds, the Scouts enjoyed being that close to such a celebrity.[70]

---

65. Floyd Godfrey, oral history, February 1977.

66. Floyd Godfrey, "School Teachers in My Life," in "Life Stories," file of undated handwritten stories from the life of Floyd Godfrey.

67. Magrath and District History Association, *Irrigation Builders*, 354.

68. Magrath and District History Association, *Irrigation Builders*, 406.

69. See Ann Chisholm and Michael Davie, *Lord Beaverbrook: A Life* (New York: Knopf, 1993).

70. Floyd Godfrey, oral history, February 1977, 21–22.

Floyd Godfrey, at Pot Hole Creek, where he was baptized in 1914. Courtesy of Donald G. Godfrey.

## LEARNING HONESTY

Honesty was a characteristic that paid dividends, as Floyd learned from both his mother and father. The dividends for his honesty were realized quickly when he was digging a trench for Richard Bradshaw. They had agreed on a specific price for the work, and when the job was completed, Bradshaw wrote a check for more than the agreed amount. When Floyd pointed out the error, Bradshaw gave him a corrected check. He was out at his front fence making this exchange when Alfred Ririe, owner of the Magrath Trading Company, happened to be passing by, and Bradshaw hollered at him, "Alf if you want a good man to work for you, here is a real honest fellow." Ririe hired Floyd that same week, and he worked for the Magrath Trading Company for the next ten years.[71]

Floyd was fifteen when he started working a weekend job at the Magrath Trading Company. His first responsibilities were assisting the man who delivered the groceries and dry goods to local customers in his horse-drawn wagon. One Saturday, Floyd was cleaning and closing the store. He was working behind the counter. This was a long cupboard-style counter where parcels were wrapped and groceries bagged for delivery. Inside the counter drawers were bulk products: rice, raisins, current berries, coffee, and dry products. The customers made their selections, and workers scooped out the order into a paper bag and weighed it. On one evening, at the end of a busy day, the floor behind the counter was particularly messy. Spills from the scoops, labels, old paper bags, and a mess of scrap paper covered the aisle. Floyd's job was to sweep, clean, and separate all the paper into the burn box. As he swept, he found a $20 ($254) bill on the floor behind the cash register near the telephone. A thrill shot through his body. He hesitated, then hastily picked it up and put it into his pocket, wondering if anyone had noticed. It was late at night. He finished cleaning the store, closed shop for the night, and hurried home to tell his mother of

---

71. Floyd Godfrey, "Honesty," in "Life Stories," file of undated handwritten stories from the life of Floyd Godfrey; also, Floyd Godfrey, oral history, February 1977; and, Magrath and District History Association, *Irrigation Builders*, 418–20.

the treasure he'd found and all the things he could now buy for himself, along with a present for his mother, of course.[72]

Floyd waited until he could talk alone with her and then told her of his good fortune. She listened quietly and asked, "Do you really think that is your money?" In his excitement, that question had barely registered with him. He thought about it, and he realized she was right. Eva paused for the right words to teach honesty and the Golden Rule, "Floyd it is not yours, it belongs to the store." After a few tears of disappointment, he knew what he must do. The next day was Sunday, but early that Sabbath he was at the door of Ben Hood, who was in charge of balancing the cash register receipts at the store.[73] Floyd was nervous as Hood answered his door, but he did as his mother directed. Hood questioned him about the find. Truth be known, Floyd was proud to be honest. Hood explained that he had been unable to balance the books that evening, he was $20 off and preparing to make up the difference out of his own pocket. He was grateful that Floyd had returned the cash, advising him, "Always listen to your mother."[74]

Eva loved the gospel and planted it in Floyd's heart. He attended his Primary, Mutual Improvement Association, Sunday School, sacrament, and priesthood meetings as expected. He was the deacons and teachers quorum president. He would marry in the temple. Eva and Melvin instilled the lifelong regard for ethics, honesty, and hard labor into their boys. These were the never-ending lessons of their lifetime, passed from generation to generation.

**FRONTIER PUBLIC SCHOOLS**

At age seven, in the fall of 1913, Floyd started elementary school. The school was a four-room, two-story, square wooden structure that faced south, with a belfry dominating the front of the building. The school was in the center of town about two blocks from Main Street and a

---

72. Floyd Godfrey, "Honesty," in "Life Stories," file of undated handwritten stories from the life of Floyd Godfrey.

73. Magrath and District History Association, *Irrigation Builders*, 144.

74. Floyd Godfrey, "Honesty."

block and a half from Floyd's home. There were two classrooms on each floor and two windows on the east and west sides of the building.[75] Two outhouses were behind the school and just beyond a small barn housing the horses students rode from nearby farms into school. The blackboards at the front of the room were small, and the pupils sat two to a desk. There was a two-inch hole drilled through the center top of the desk for an inkwell, which held a small glass bottle of black ink. A young lady sitting in front of a spirited young male might get her braids dunked into an open inkwell. Pencils and straight pens were stored in grooves cut on each side of the inkwell. Books were stowed under the desktop.

Within a few years, a second, much larger brick building was constructed under the supervision of Daniel T. Fowler, with the assistance of Melvin Godfrey.[76] The old wooden schoolhouse was abandoned, and "it became the local ghost haunt."[77] The new structure had sixteen rooms and until 1930 served for both the elementary and high school students.[78] The curfew bell was retained from the old school and placed atop the new structure. It was here that Floyd climbed the stairs with his father to ring the nightly curfew. The bell could be "heard for miles, especially in cold weather."[79]

Floyd's education took place in both of these school buildings. In the old school hall he would often sneak into the attic at night, nervous but determined to catch a pigeon from the flock that nested in the

---

75. Floyd Godfrey, oral history, February 1977.

76. B. W. Dow, "Our Elementary School," in Magrath and District History Association, *Irrigation Builders*, 332–36, 452.

77. Floyd Godfrey, "The Old School House," in "Life Stories," file of undated handwritten stories from the life of Floyd Godfrey.

78. The dates of the construction related to the two schoolhouses conflict. Floyd describes attending the old four-room schoolhouse, but his first attendance would have been 1913–14. Dow reports this structure was "abandoned in 1909 and torn down in 1917." Dow, "Our Elementary School," 332–33. Harket and Bly, "School Days," in *Power of the Dream*, 53–65, indicates the first schoolhouse was constructed in 1902.

79. See "Why Does Sound Sometimes Seem to Travel Farther on Cold Days?," *New York Times*, 10 March 1981, http://www.nytimes.com/1981/03/10/science/q-why-does-sound-sometimes-seem-to-travel-farther-on-cold-days.html.

rafters. He climbed to the top and crawled his way through the trusses, feeling his way to where the pigeons nested. The pigeons couldn't see the boys, and the boys couldn't see the pigeons. It was too dark, but the boys heard the cooing. They followed the sound and the birds were easily caught. They would crawl in, reach out, grab one, and carefully cross the wings so that in the struggle the birds were unhurt. Then they would place them in a gunny sack and head home. Floyd fed and watered his captive in a box he kept in his father's barn. Within a few weeks, they were his pet pigeons. "I remember I had so many in the top of our barn, they were spoiling the hay. Dad was not too happy." He seemed pleased when one night some boys from across town snuck in and stole most of them.[80]

### ELEMENTARY SCHOOL AND WAR

Elementary school between 1914 and 1918 was about reading, writing, and arithmetic, along with military training. World War I began 4 August 1914, when Britain declared war on Germany, and Canadians of British ancestry supported the war.[81] War was frightening even for those not on the front lines. In addition to scholastics, the boys at the Magrath schools were marched to the north side of the building, where in the park they trained using wooden guns to be the soldiers of the future. This was World War I preparation for service and possible attack. Floyd and his classmates were taught how to lay prone, run, drop, and shoot in one motion. After the outside exercises, they went to the school basement for target practice with 22-caliber rifles. The Canadian Army almost immediately began recruiting. Floyd was eight, obviously too young, but he felt the strain. Farmers were in the middle of their harvest. "Men from 19-40 Your King and Country Needs You," the posters advertised.[82] Patriotism was strong among the Mormons, no matter which side of the border they settled.

---

80. Floyd Godfrey, "The Old School House."

81. See Tim Cook, *No Place to Run: The Canadian Corps and Gas Warfare in the First World War* (Vancouver: University of British Columbia Press, 1999).

82. See poster photo in Magrath and District History Association, *Power of the Dream*, 77.

Magrath High School. Courtesy of Magrath Museum.

Prior to the war, a recognized LDS southern Albertan, Hugh B. Brown, had handpicked men to serve with him in the "C" Squadron 13th Mounted Rifles of the Canadian Overseas Expedition Force, the "COEF" of Calgary.[83] Eventually, sixty-six soldiers from Magrath served in World War I. Six were killed in action. The town's population would have been around nine hundred people.[84] Emotions were high everywhere, and Magrath was no exception. German Kaiser Wilhelm II, blamed for starting the war, was depicted as a straw man, like a scarecrow standing in the fields. The town built a mock scaffolding

---

83. Eugene Campbell and Richard D. Poll, *Hugh B. Brown: His Life and Thought* (Salt Lake City: Bookcraft, 1975), 52–77.

84. Magrath and District History Association, *Irrigation Builders*, 279–84. Also, Harker and Bly, *Power of a Dream*, 75–79; Floyd Godfrey, oral history interview, February 1977, transcript and certificate in Godfrey Family Papers. The Magrath population in 1916 was 938.

from which they hung the straw man, set the hay on fire, and burned him in effigy. It was a patriotic action repeated across nations.⁸⁵

Floyd was blessed to miss both wars. He was too young for World War I and too old for World War II.

### HIGH SCHOOL IN THE ROARING TWENTIES

World War I ended and history moved into the Roaring Twenties as Floyd reached high school age. US President Woodrow Wilson characterized the 1920s as moving from war "Back to Normalcy."⁸⁶ Canadian author Pierre Berton implied that as a result of their success in WWI, the "Canadians were a cocky lot in the twenties."⁸⁷ They kicked up their heals dancing the Charleston, and the morals and manner changed in the decade.⁸⁸ There was no such thing as cinema. Early film was experimental, moving into the '20s with silent film entertainment.⁸⁹ "There was no such thing as radio broadcasting."⁹⁰ Stations were experimental, and technology was just developing before the radio boom.⁹¹ This was the environment of Floyd's teenage growing years.

High school changed Floyd's life. He broke free of his boyhood shell. He started noticing girls. Following the encouragement of his father, he went to work outside the family, earning his own money.

---

85. Floyd Godfrey, oral history, 20 March 1982, 25.

86. Ernest J. Wrage and Barnett Baskerville, *Contemporary Forum* (Seattle: University of Washington Press, 1962), 51–60.

87. Pierre Berton, *The Great Depression, 1929–1930* (Toronto: McClelland & Stewart, 1990), 25, 68.

88. Wrage and Baskerville, *American Forum*, 87–98.

89. Terry Ramsaye, *A Million and One Nights: A History of Motion Picture*, 3rd ed. (New York: Simon and Schuster, 1964), 308–33. Also, Charles Musser, *The Emergence of Cinema: The History of Motion Picture to 1907* (Berkeley: University of California Press, 1994), 109. Also see Donald G. Godfrey, *C. Francis Jenkins: Pioneer or Film and Television* (Urbanna: University of Illinois Press, 2014).

90. Frederick Lewis Allen, *Only Yesterday: An Informal History of the 1920's* (New York: Harper and Row, 1964), 11.

91. Christopher H. Sterling and John Michael Kittross, *Stay Tuned: A History of American Broadcasting* (Mahwah, NJ: Lawrence Erlbaum Associates, 2002), 63–74.

He worked harder and grew respectful and "more considerate of his mother and father." If Floyd asked his dad for a little cash for a weekend date, he knew the answer before he asked: "How do you suppose I got mine?" Melvin responded.[92] Melvin's boys got what they needed in terms of home, food, and shelter, but they had to earn their own spending money and pay for school clothing.

Floyd remembers his instructors fondly and fell in love with the beauty of his first grade teacher, Miss Parish. Floyd appreciated all of his teachers, including Miss Sutherland in grade four; Drew Clark, grade five; Ammon Mercer, grade eight; Drew Clark and Nephi Head, grade nine; Mr. Pharis and Miss Redd, grade ten; and Golden Woolf, grade eleven.[93] His high school teacher Golden Woolf survived Floyd's pranks and instilled in him the idea that he could accomplish something if he would apply himself.[94] In high school, a group of friends in his science class decided to play a trick on Mr. Woolf involving chemistry and electricity, which they were studying. From inside the classroom they created a battery and connected it to the doorknob. As Mr. Woolf approached, the boys poured water under the door. Of course, when Woolf grabbed the doorknob he was shocked and could not let go. Several students, including Floyd, were temporarily expelled. Ironically, Mr. Woolf, who later became the principle, reached out when Floyd was in the eleventh grade, giving him the responsibility to monitor the twelfth-grade chemistry class. Woolf's assignments and mentoring gave Floyd confidence to be trusted, and the prank was forgiven.

Floyd competed in debate and won several awards. One judge thought he might have even been more effective if he had only stopped pacing back and forth behind the podium during his speech. "Well

---

92. Mervin J. Godfrey, oral history, 25 March 1982, Magrath Museum.

93. His 1977 oral history names his teachers: Miss Parish, Miss Sutherland, Levi Head, Ammon Mercer, Mr. Ferris, Miss Read, Golden Woolf, and Willard Keith. Only Keith, Mercer and Woolf appear in Magrath and District History Association, *Irrigation Builders*, 333–35, 490. Some teachers were called by the Church to teach, and they took a Canadian preparatory normal school course in Calgary to prepare for the assignment, Magrath and District History Association, *Irrigation Builders*, 335.

94. Floyd Godfrey, "School Teachers in My Life," and "The Band Wagons," in "Life Stories," file of undated handwritten stories from the life of Floyd Godfrey.

done, now young Godfrey, had a good talk if he'd just stand still."[95] Floyd's favorite subjects were geography, math, chemistry, and the study of foreign countries. He did not care for English or grammar.

Floyd played the clarinet in the high school band. "My dad wasted a lot of money on me playing the clarinet," Floyd said. He "hated every minute of it," but his mother was persistent.[96] The day his band leader tuned all of the instruments to Floyd's clarinet's middle C bolstered his confidence, and he continued with the instrument several years. The Magrath Band performed around the town for the 1 July "Dominion Day" parades and celebrations. Dominion Day was created to celebrate Canadian independence, 1 July 1867. It was changed to Canada Day 27 October 1982.[97] Band members were up at 4 a.m. A loud cannon announced the beginning of the day, and the sixteen-member band rode round town in a hay wagon decorated in red, white, and blue, along with the Union Jack (Canadian flag at the time). All climbed aboard the wagon with their instruments and kitchen chairs borrowed from their mothers' tables. The wagon was drawn by four beautiful Clydesdale horses, a powerful breed used to pull heavy loads. They stopped at the corners of the town blocks. Sleepy people emerged out of their houses for the national anthem, "O Canada," or a rousing march. Spectators sometimes brought the musicians a cake, which delayed their progress as they ate. It was a morning revelry lasting until 6:30 or 7:00 a.m., after which the band left to prepare for the big town parade down Main Street, and the townspeople readied themselves for the celebrations.

Floyd might have thought the clarinet was a waste, but the band added to his self-confidence and gave him an appreciation for John Philip Sousa and good music that he carried all his life. As an adult, he loved the town celebrations, rodeos, and parades. He sang in the ward

---

95. Floyd Godfrey, oral history, February 1977.

96. Floyd Godfrey, "The Band Wagons."

97. Journal of Floyd Godfrey, 1 July 1982. Godfrey Family Papers. Dominion Day was created to celebrate Canadian independence, 1 July 1867. It was changed to Canada Day on 27 October 1982. Also, Floyd Godfrey, oral history, 1982.

choirs and around the house. If he knew the melody but had forgotten the words to the song, he would just invent them and keep right on singing.

## DATING, DANCING, AND SCHOOL

Teenage Floyd was initially a reluctant dancer. His mother had tried to encourage him during a community-wide assembly hall dance, but he clung onto the post of the balcony for dear life as she pulled him onto the floor. Drucilla Passey, a young girl his own age, was a little more persuasive.[98] He didn't like it at first, but he warmed to the notion as he began paying attention to possible dance partners.

It was about this time he started noticing the girl across the south fence from his home—Clarice Card. As teenagers, she and her girlfriends generally attended the dances alone, but as they matured, a boy would escort them home. Floyd saw Rose Bennett, May Sabey, and Clarice home from various dances. Sometimes they all came home in a group. Occasionally, Clarice was escorted by Reed Bennett (Rose's brother) and Floyd.[99]

Dancing with Floyd was quite the Charleston experience. He was always into the swing of the music, carefree and fun. Chaperoning adults sat on the sides of the dance floor and watched with a careful eye. These new freestyle dances were far different from those of their parents, which were more rigid.[100] Floyd and Rose were dancing one evening when her petticoat suddenly fell to the floor. Rose was faster than the eyes of the chaperones. She leaned over, quickly pocketing her undergarment, without missing a step.

Floyd was a cutup. He loved a teenage good time. After a dance or a movie, revelers all headed uptown to the Jones Bakery, where ice cream and pie topped off the night. The dances were, of course, all

---

98. Magrath and District History Association, *Irrigation Builders*, 503.

99. Rose Hudson, "Our Early Friendships." Letter from Rose Hudson to Floyd Godfrey, 7 April 1982, Godfrey Family Papers. Reed and Rose Bennett were the son and daughter of Austin R. and Alice Emily Harding. Magrath and District History Association, *Irrigation Builders*, 411–12, 481. Rose would eventually marry Eldred "Dad" Hudson.

100. Kyvig, *Daily Life*, 205–6.

chaperoned by the mothers of the community, who positioned themselves on the stage where they could watch and make sure their teenagers behaved. After a dance one evening, Floyd's father asked if he had been drinking alcohol at the dance. "No, I have never drank in my life," Floyd responded. "Well," his father replied, "somebody said you were cutting-up at the dance last night." Floyd had indeed led a chain of dancers, holding on at each other's waists in the bunny-hop fashion all around the dance floor while chanting to the music. "There must have been 150 of them following me," Floyd recalled.[101] Floyd's teenage memories of fun and frolicking stayed with him as he enjoyed life.

As president of the student organization, Floyd was at the forefront of those organizing the parties and dances throughout the year. They relied on lots of teenage creativity generating their own entertainment. One Halloween night, Floyd and fellow students constructed a tall water slide where students slid down and landed in an old sofa at the bottom. It was fun until one of the girls broke her leg. Every event featured the Magrath High School song. There were no radio stations and few record players, so the dance bands were local and live. Their only entertainment beyond Floyd's father's Empress Theater were dances, school, church, and community socials.

In the late 1920s few students finished high school. Most completed the eighth grade and headed for the real-world work opportunities. A small group graduated, but most were unable to afford university studies. Floyd finished the eleventh grade. His high school experience in leadership and academics had helped him out of his shell. He was a member of the student body leadership. He mixed with the girls and worked summers in the harvests. He was evolving into an adult with a new respect for the wisdom of his parents.

**FRONTIER HOLIDAY CELEBRATIONS**

In pioneering days, holidays were comparatively few and all locally organized. Even then there were chores to be done, cows to milk,

---

101. Floyd Godfrey, oral history, February 1977.

and animals to feed before the fun began. The national holidays were Dominion Day, Easter, and Christmas.

Dominion Day, 1 July, is the celebration of Canadian independence from Great Britain in 1867. Magrath's commemoration started at sunrise with the firing of the cannon, followed by the band touring the town, the parade, and the evening baseball game and feasting. The parade floats were farm wagons decorated with Canadian flags and red, white, and, blue crepe paper. They were organized by local groups and included a few of the businesses.

Baseball games featured regional competition. In the Godfrey tradition, Floyd was the catcher for the team, as his father had been earlier. Once he caught the ball on the end of his fingers and split them, after which he was not too fussy about being the catcher. Games were mostly a social event and were played in every community. The teams piled into a wagon or the car as they rode into neighboring towns to play ball. The evening concluded with more food, more dancing, and the singing of "Oh Canada." Dominion Day was a highlight of the year.

Easter and Christmas were more family celebrations. School was dismissed for only Good Friday and Easter Monday. Hiding and finding Easter eggs was unique to a child's memories of these days. Floyd, with his brothers and sister, checked the chicken coop and selected one or two eggs each day. They hid them in the barn until Easter, and by then they might have a dozen eggs each. Eva hard-boiled the eggs and colored them with food dye for her children. For the finale, they walked to the coulee hill, just a half block south of their house, and rolled them down toward the stream.[102] The prankster in Floyd appeared one year when he found a fresh egg and slipped it into the pocket of one of his sister Lottie's friends. He thought it was a big joke when he kicked her pocket. However, the joke was on him! As she reached into her coat, retrieving what she could of the broken egg, she threw it right in his face.[103]

Christmas was the most exciting children's holiday of the year. Eva decorated the house with brightly colored green and red crepe paper.

---

102. Floyd Godfrey, oral history, January 1977, 11–12.
103. Floyd Godfrey, oral history, February 1977, 11–12.

The children cut paper into strips and created paper chains that hung from the ceiling. The chains were draped from the corners of the room to the center where Eva placed a large decorative Christmas bell. Eva and Lottie did most of the decorating. The family popped corn on the stove in a wire basket. Shaking the basket over the top of the red-hot coal was intriguing, as the kernels of corn exploded. After it cooled, the children took a needle and thread and crafted long strings of popcorn cascading around the tree. These were family activities as well as holiday preparations. The tree was likely acquired from the Magrath Trading Company or a local entrepreneur who had a license to cut trees and had ventured into the foothills to Pole Haven or Dug Way on Lee's Creek near Cardston. They were scrawny trees compared to the lush trees harvested today for the holiday, but in the eyes of the children they were a wonder as they stood in the northeast corner of the front room.[104] There were no lights on the Christmas tree, as there was no electricity. Eva and Lottie cautiously placed and lit the candles on the branches. Eva's memories of the fire in her childhood home kept her fearful even as an adult. The candles were lit only briefly and not too often. They were placed in a small cup to capture the melting wax and held the flame steady on the branch. There was a large stove with windows on three sides. As the fire burned, it would cast flickering light across the festive decorations and the tree.

Christmas was simple and exciting. On Christmas Eve a small wooden box of Japanese oranges (imported tangerines) appeared. The Godfrey family sat around the stove and ate them all. Often on Christmas Eve the children had to wait for their father, who was patrolling the streets. It was his job to see that the people and cattle were home at night. It was always snowy and cold, but they waited patiently for their father.

One Christmas the snow was twelve inches deep. Sleigh bells rang passed their home. There was a long expectant pause as Melvin dramatically threw open the door, covered with snow, and hollered, "Santa just drove by and may not come back if there are any lights still

---

104. Floyd Godfrey, "Christmas," Floyd Godfrey Life Stories.

on, so you guys better get to bed." The children were already tired but too excited to sleep. They scrambled for their beds. Bert, the oldest, pretended to sleep for a few hours. It was more than he could take. He slid from under the covers and crept "very quietly, into the front room, found his long black stocking" and scurried back to bed. He hid under the covers, took out one orange and one apple, and down in the toe of his sock he found Santa's present. He had left Bert with his "own cherished dollar watch."[105]

Christmas mornings the children were allowed to light the candles on the tree. Gifts were simple. Santa brought each child a gift or two: perhaps a pocket knife, a new flashlight, and a doll for Lottie. Eva got Lily of the Valley perfume every year from her son Douglas. Cast iron toy cars came from Santa.[106] Gifts such as a sleigh or a wagon were often shared with one another. Each child had their own stocking hanging on a chair with their name on it. The stockings were filled with apples, oranges, peanuts, homemade candy, and sometimes a package of the new sweet chewing gum. Gifts of clothing were always needed and received. "We didn't have to have much, but we were happy with what we had."[107]

Christmas dinner was turkey, dressing, potatoes, carrots, and gravy. Plum pudding, apple pie, and homemade ice cream were dessert. Eva cooked the plum pudding in a cloth and a pot of boiling water. It was a traditional Christmas treat and often called Christmas pudding. It had no plums but was a mixture of dried fruits, hard beef or mutton fat, molasses, and spices—such as ginger, cloves, nutmeg, or cinnamon—providing a fragrance throughout the house for several weeks as Christmas approached and their mother prepared.

---

105. Bert Godfrey, "Canadian Christmas," December 1980, Family Files, Magrath Museum.

106. Today these cast iron toys are highly collectible. Douglas Godfrey's grandson Mason now has the toy Douglas received from Santa as a child.

107. Floyd Godfrey, "Christmas," in "Life Stories," file of undated handwritten stories from the life of Floyd Godfrey. Also, Douglas Godfrey to Donald G. Godfrey, 18 February 2014; Floyd Godfrey, oral history, February 1977.

All holidays were a delightful respite from the physical demands of work, but there were always chores and the cows to be milked both morning and night. They were heartfelt celebrations and a day or two to relax and socialize. They came too slowly and left too quickly in the pioneer lives. Soon the holiday was over and done, and it was back to work meeting the challenges of keeping food on the table.

**FRONTIER MEDICINES AT HOME**

Pioneers relied on their own knowledge when it came to medicine, and it was no different for the people of Magrath. Healthcare came in the form of herbal remedies passed from previous generations. Accidents and illnesses were treated with a poultice, a tonic, and a prayer. There were no ambulances or emergency rooms. Medical doctors were just beginning to appear in the local communities, and they drove to the homes of their patients to administer their services. Until 1938, child birth generally took place at home with assistance from female relatives, a midwife, or a local physician.[108] For those living in Magrath, if the patient did not get well, the Lethbridge hospital was two hours away by horse and buggy, assuming the family had a fast horse and the patient was well enough to make the journey. Dr. C. W. Sanders was the first doctor in Magrath. He visited the homes of his patients.[109]

The mustard plaster was one such natural cure applied to Floyd's legs and feet when he "got the itch." His feet and legs below his knees were covered with welts. When he sat on the lawn scratching his legs, they bled and he cried. A midwife was called, and she applied the mustard plaster. A typical treatment plaster included mustard powder and flour with water or egg whites mixed into a paste. This was applied to a cotton cloth and placed on the infected areas. The paste never came in contact with the body, as it would burn the skin, but it was believed to have the capacity to reduce inflammation. Eva held Floyd tightly as she tried to prevent him from scratching while the mixture was applied.

---

108. Kyvig, *Daily Life*, 141–42.
109. Magrath and District History Association, *Irrigation Builders*, 365–67.

How he contracted the infection they did not know, but it was common for kids to go barefoot, and as an adult Floyd speculated that this was how he had caught the disease.[110]

Mervin caught diphtheria when he was small. This was an acute, often fatal disease at the time, often a major cause of death among children. It was an upper respiratory infection growing in the throat of the patient, producing a thick coating on the back of the throat, which could be caught simply by touching.[111] Eva was ill, and she was down in bed. The family was frightened. Floyd particularly so, as Mervin was his best buddy and only three years Floyd's junior. Melvin sent for the doctor from Lethbridge. The doctor came and examined Mervin, and Floyd overheard the conversation. "Melvin, that boy [Mervin] won't live until morning. You had better go in and tell your wife." Fear shot through Floyd. He knelt that night, praying like he had never prayed before. "I knelt down on my knees and prayed hard for my brother, and the next morning he was well. Our Heavenly Father blessed him." The doctor had stayed the night to help Eva, and when he saw Mervin the next morning, he could not understand: "All that puss and stuff in his nose and throat was just gone, I can't understand it." But Floyd knew the Lord had answered his prayer.[112]

Floyd always had problems with his teeth. In the early twentieth century, dentistry was in its infancy. There was no thought to brushing one's teeth or even a toothpick to remove food from between the teeth. When the cavities grew, the pliers from the toolbox were the answer. Floyd lost several teeth that way, with his father on the other end of the tool. Sometimes Melvin got creative and tied one end of a linen thread around the troublesome tooth and the other end to a doorknob. Whoever came through the door next then extracted the patient's tooth. Floyd never forgot how his father had pulled his aching teeth.[113]

---

110. Floyd Godfrey, oral history, February 1977 and 1982.

111. See "Glossary of Medical Terms Used in the 18th and 19th Centuries," http://www.thornber.net/medicine/html/medgloss.html.

112. Floyd Godfrey, oral history, February 1977, 23.

113. Floyd Godfrey, oral history, 20 March 1982, 24.

In his teenage years, while working in the fields, Floyd got a severe toothache. His brother Mervin, working at his side, told Floyd to just toughen up and take it. One of the workmen provided Floyd with a little paste he indicated would take away the pain. Just put a little in the mouth and "don't swallow it, but keep it in your cheek, your mouth will be moist and you'll be all right." It was chewing tobacco. Rather than relieving the toothache, the nicotine made Floyd very sick. He was driving the team and had to stop the horses. He laid down in the hay for several hours and missed dinner before his boss found him. After learning what had happened, he took Floyd to the barn a mile away where Floyd slept. Then the boss went off to take care of the boys who had given him the tobacco.[114]

In 1919 the most serious health issue of the era arose after World War I—the Spanish flu pandemic ravaged the world. It killed more people than World War I and was remembered as one of the most devastating epidemics in world history. Almost every family in Magrath lost someone or knew friends who lost a loved one. Businesses, churches, and schools were closed. Infected homes were quarantined. In southern Alberta, it had also been a year of drought. Tumbleweeds followed the wind across dry farm fields, and dust storms blew in from the north. In the Magrath Godfrey family, no one contracted the disease.[115] Melvin struggled getting permission to open the Empress Theater just once a week, and everyone was required to wear a mask. Selling tickets at the theater frightened both Eva and Lottie, so they wore masks to ward off infection. "It was a sight I won't forget, to see people with this white cloth over their nose and mouth" filling the theater.[116] Eventually, everything, including the theater, was closed by government order.[117]

---

114. Floyd Godfrey, oral history, 20 March 1982, 22.

115. Floyd Godfrey, "The 'Flu' of 1918–19," in "Life Stories," file of undated handwritten stories from the life of Floyd Godfrey. Also, recorded in a Keystone Steno Book.

116. Floyd Godfrey, "The 'Flu' of 1918–19," in "Life Stories," file of undated handwritten stories from the life of Floyd Godfrey, Godfrey Family Papers.

117. Floyd Godfrey, oral histories, February 1977, March 1982.

Third home of Melvin and Eva Godfrey. Courtesy of Godfrey Family Files.

## THE GREAT DEPRESSION

The Great Depression hit the world, including Canada and Magrath. People lost their jobs, unemployment relief was scant, and a steady job was the supreme goal as people huddled around the new technology of radio, listening with hope to government leaders. The old adage of "rugged individualism and minimal government was obsolete," replaced with "the new conception [that] government had a positive responsibility for social and economic welfare."[118]

Two years before the Depression started, Melvin built his third and final home, a new brick house at 125 1st Street, and they moved uptown. Mervin, Joe, and Douglas were the only children living in this home. The older brothers, Bert and Floyd, along with their sister Lottie, had married and moved on. The new home was modern. There were two bedrooms, a kitchen, a living room, and an indoor bathroom on the main floor. Upstairs in rooms with sloping ceilings were two more bedrooms where the children slept. Downstairs, the basement had a coal bin and a cistern for collecting water.

The Great Depression of the 1930s hit like a financial landslide. In Magrath it was no different. People incurred debt just trying to keep ahead. There was no cash, so "in-kind" payments were common. This meant goods were exchanged for services rendered and the like. Those attending the Empress Theater brought potatoes, eggs, and produce in exchange for admission.[119] Families struggled to pay taxes and put food on the table. Their gardens were their main source of sustenance. Magrath was a little farm town, and people never had the best of riches. They had their challenges in life, but whatever the challenges, they kept the family and community pulling together. The Depression and poverty failed to dampen their spirits. The Magrath Trading Company, a food and hardware store, accepted a farmer's credit until the harvest, when bills could be paid. Mothers improvised. They could take a fifty-pound flour sack, wash it, sew it, and create clothing or simple dish cloths. Coal was dug from the creek bank. Ice for refrigerators was cut in the winter from the stream. People moved, searching for employment. Melvin's sons Bert and Mervin left for Cardston and Lethbridge in the middle of the Depression. Bert would later encourage Floyd and his young family to join him.

---

118. Wrage and Baskerville, *Contemporary Forum*, 143. Also, Pierre Berton, *The Great Depression, 1929–1939*, 11–15.

119. Magrath and District History Association, *Irrigation Builders*, 157. Also, Harker and Bly, *Power of a Dream*, 101–11.

From the broadest perspective, the Depression affected the farmers of the world, including those of Magrath, differently than people in the cities. There were few soup lines in farm towns, but the farmers had the ability to grow their own food. They had been independent from the beginning of the settlement years. They traded in kind. However, some farms were lost. George Card was behind in his taxes and was asking for relief.[120] Homes were lost, including Floyd and Clarice's second home, which was under construction. Taxes were in the arrears. Everyone was suffering. The stress of the Depression was balanced by family, friendships, and the Church. Continuing Church socials and dances provided an escape. During the Christmas season, dances were nightly.[121] Summers were still full of baseball, Church activities, and even the occasional vacations to Waterton Lakes.

### FAMILIES COMING TOGETHER

Clarice Card Godfrey was the oldest daughter of George Card and Elizabeth Rose Plant. She was born 30 March 1907 on the Magrath farm, which was located two and a half miles west of the town. Her father had earned the farm working on the Kimball-to-Magrath irrigation canal. This is where Clarice spent most of her childhood. She and her older brother, Leland, helped their parents with the chores. They entertained themselves with things surrounding them. The new railroad tracks ran by at the eastern end of their sugar beet field. The trains mesmerized the children as they passed, heading west to Cardston or east to Raymond, Stirling, and Lethbridge. When children heard the train whistle, they carefully placed pins, pennies, tacks, and nails on the rails and watched the train flatten them. After the train passed, the children ran to the tracks to check their railroad crafts. Two nails crossed, one lying over the other, resembled a pair of miniature

---

120. Minutes of the Magrath Town Council, 20 May 1931, Magrath Museum.
121. Harker and Bly, *Power of the Dream,* 108–12. "Magrath Store News," in-house newsletter of the Magrath Trading Company, 7 September 1934. Magrath Museum.

scissors after the heavy train bound them together. Pennies were smashed beyond recognition.[122]

An irrigation ditch flowed on the north side of the Cards' farm, providing water for growing crops and a summer swimming hole for Clarice and her friends. Clarice's father placed wooden planks in the ditch to hold back the water and channel it into the field when needed. It also made a good swimming hole and even a stage for putting on a water show for an audience of parents or friends. Clarice never owned a swimming suit, but she was modest and wore her dress whether playing or swimming. In the summer, she picked bouquets of the sweet-smelling Alberta wild roses that grew wild along the ditch. She gave them to her mother—a rose for a Rose.

As a child, Clarice raced with the geese her father raised on the farm. On one occasion the gander thought she was getting too close to its little ones, and he turned the tables, chasing her. Frightened by the suddenly aggressive bird, she ran, fell, and hit her hand on an open-end gate lying on the ground. The force of the fall closed the gate on her left hand and crushed her little finger. The doctor was called, but Clarice was uneasy about him touching her. When she saw Doctor Norman T. Beeman approaching in his horse and buggy, she hid under her bed.[123] There was no antiseptic or dulling of the pain when the country doctor worked on a patient. Clarice carried the scar for her lifetime.[124]

George Card's farm was next to the William Sabey farm. The Sabey family had big hearts and were generous with their neighbors. After each harvest, William loaded his wagon with produce and drove into town sharing what he had with the needy.[125] The Cards were alone in Alberta for a while. George's father, Charles Ora Card, had become ill and moved back to Logan, Utah, and the larger Sabey family had children Clarice's age. As a result, the Magrath Cards were taken into the Sabey family circle, and lifelong friendships evolved. They helped

---

122. Floyd and Clarice Godfrey, joint oral history, 8 May 1977.

123. Normon Thomas Beeman was a physician and surgeon. See http://canadiangreatwarproject.com/searches/soldierDetail.asp?ID=108190.

124. Clarice Card Godfrey, handwritten story in Godfrey Family Papers.

125. Magrath and District History Association, *Irrigation Builders*, 514–15.

George and Rose Card farm home, circa 1977. Courtesy of Donald G. Godfrey.

one another in planting and harvesting. They were friends, babysitters, party companions, and fellow church-goers. At the Card and Sabey family gatherings, the adults always ate before the children. This was the family order of things during the early 1900s. Clarice, her brother Leland, three years her senior, and the Sabey children all congregated near the kitchen door, fearing there would not be enough food left to eat after the adults, "who were sure eating a lot and taking a lot of time," Clarice remembered. Of course, there was always plenty for everyone.[126]

---

126. Floyd and Clarice Godfrey, joint oral history, 8 May 1977.

Once all stomachs were full, the hour was generally late. The bedroom floors of the host's home were covered with quilts as the children curled up to sleep. The adults spent the rest of the evening playing "Hi Five."[127] As the late night approached, fathers prepared to return to their own homes, while mothers helped with the cleaning and restoring of the host home to normal. Dads placed large rocks in the wagon. These stones were between the size of a fist and a small boulder and were heated in the kitchen stove then placed in the back of the buggy. A quilt covered the warm rocks. Sleeping children were placed into the back of the wagon, with a second quilt covering them. The children traveled in the warmth of an open buggy in what felt like loving luxury.[128]

### RIDING THE HORSE TO SCHOOL

Farm life was not limited to work, play, and parties. Education for their children was important to both George and Rose. George served on the Magrath school board, and Rose was a former school teacher.[129] They saw to it that Clarice, Leland, and all of their children attended school in town.

Clarice's first school year began in 1914.[130] In grade one, her teacher, A. I. Wall, graded her reading and arithmetic as "excellent." Her conduct and writing were "good," but her report card showed she missed twenty days of school that year.[131] As an elementary school child, Clarice had more than her share of ailments, including earaches and sore throats.

---

127. Clarice Card Godfrey, story in Godfrey Family Papers. "Hi Five" was a popular card game of the twentieth century. Often called "Pedro," there were four adults to a table, two partnerships, and multiple tables rotated throughout an evening's entertainment. A little like "Rook," the high trump card was a five.

128. This was a common method of keeping warm while traveling short distances.

129. Minutes of the Court of Revisions in School Land, 10 July 1916, Magrath Museum.

130. Clarice indicates in her history that she was past eight years old when she went to school. She was born 30 March 1907, and her first report card is dated 1914–15, which would make her seven, almost eight. See "Clarice Card Godfrey," story in Godfrey Family Papers.

131. The scale at the bottom of the report card was as follows: Excellent, 99–100; Commendable, 80–90; Good, 70–80; Fair, 60–70; Unsatisfactory, 50–60; and Poor, below 50. Clarice Card Godfrey, story in Godfrey Family Papers.

Her legs ached painfully, emanating from the bones into the muscles. Her mother heated bags of salt and placed them around Clarice's legs. The salt retained the heat and soothed the pain. The school absences were likely related to these ailments. There were no cars or school buses for transporting the farm children. When she was feeling well, her father took her and her brother in the buggy, or Clarice simply rode the horse with Leland. At school there was a barn for stabling the children's horses. In the spring and early autumn, they sometimes just walked. It took them two or three hours to get from the school back to the farm.

Clarice's first grade class was released out of school an hour earlier than the other classes. This made it sometimes hard for a little sister to wait a whole hour for her big brother. One day Clarice decided to start walking home without him, likely figuring he would catch up to her on the horse. But as children do, she wandered and lost track of time. Leland hunted for her but finally went home. Clarice stopped to play at the home of Sarah Poulsen.[132] As the sun started setting, Sarah sent Clarice on her way and notified her parents. It was the only time Clarice received a spanking.[133]

Corporal punishment was rare in the Card home. If the children were misbehaving, they were sent into the garden to fetch a good switch, a "swishy limb of the currant bush."[134] At times, a child was sent back, making several trips to the garden, assuring that their pick suited their father. It was never used, but George placed it behind the mirror over the wash basin and left it there for the child to see. Selecting then displaying the right switch was enough to reinforce appropriate behavior.[135]

---

132. There were several Poulsens in Magrath, but it is difficult to determine to which family Sarah belonged. See Magrath and District History Association, *Irrigation Builders*, 506–7.

133. Floyd and Clarice Godfrey, joint oral history, 8 May 1977.

134. The currant bush has spindly vines and produces a white or red berry from which jams and juice were preserved. The story of "The Currant Bush" was made famous by President Hugh B. Brown in his 1968 BYU commencement address. See "The Current Bush," *New Era*, January 1973.

135. Floyd and Clarice Godfrey, joint oral history, 8 May 1977.

## CHILDHOOD TRAGEDY

Leland and Clarice were joined by three more siblings, two younger brothers and a sister. Cyrus Henry, born 5 September 1909; Glen Charles, born 27 December 1911; and, fourteen years later, Melva Rose, born 17 March 1925. Transportation to and from school for four children magnified the difficulties. George tackled the problems head on. He rented a room in town from Grandma and Grandpa Sabey.[136] Now the children had only a short distance to walk.

Tragedy struck on 23 June 1916. Leland had come home thirsty and wanted a drink. He went to the cupboard and took what he thought was a bottle of currant juice, harvested from the backyard bushes. There were no labels on these home-bottled preserves. Unfortunately, instead of the sweet fruit juice he expected, the bottle contained a poison used to treat field potatoes, fertilizing the soil and killing the bugs. His body went into convulsions, and he died. There was no undertaker. So George placed Leland's body in the bedroom, covered him with bottles of ice, and spread pansy flowers over the body. Clarice remembered this scene as "about the most beautiful I had seen," but Leland's death was a catastrophe no one forgot. He was buried in the Magrath Cemetery.[137]

## MOVE TO TOWN

It was 1918 when George and Rose purchased a home in town, just two blocks east of the school and immediately south of the Godfrey's home. Clarice was now eleven years old. Their new home at 181 1st Avenue South was perhaps 1,500 square feet, at the corner of the block. The front door faced south. There were irrigation ditches running on the east and south sides of the lot. Across the gravel road to the south, over a larger ditch, and down the hill was the Pothole Creek. The Cards' visitors walked a short path north from the road across the lawn then up one small step and across a wooden sitting porch. Through the

---

136. To the children of small LDS towns, older people were often addressed as "grandma/grandpa" or "brother/sister." It was simply a term of endearment.

137. Floyd and Clarice Godfrey, joint oral history, 8 May 1977.

front screen door was the living room. Outside, around the eaves of the main house, there were wooden rain barrels. Rose, just as Eva Godfrey and other pioneers, used the soft rain water for washing her hair and watering her favorite flowers. The rainwater was soft and rich in nitrogen. Huge vegetable and flower gardens surrounded the Card home. The vegetable garden ran north and south, just west of the house. The flower garden was north of the house. The gardens were fun for the kids. What they did not eat in the summer their mother preserved, and anything left over was fed to the farm animals. Nothing went to waste.

### THE SPANISH FLU

While the tragic events of this global tragedy skipped over the Godfrey family, they targeted the Cards. Clarice was thirteen, the oldest of three siblings, with Melva on the horizon. The Spanish flu frightened everyone.[138] One day a person could be walking along the road, and the next day he or she would be dead. How did this disease spread so rapidly? No one knew. Was it an exotic disease brought home by soldiers who had served in foreign lands? Was it spread by the unsanitary condition of farmers' milk delivered from the farmer to every household and not always properly sanitized?[139] The fear of the disease was both physical and psychological, especially in the little farm towns. Being outside in town for any reason required cotton masks be worn over the mouth to guard against infection.

In Magrath, brave neighbors went into homes and cared for entire families who were sick. Home nurses tried natural remedies from their pioneer experience: mustard and onion plasters again. Heated remedies were spread on a cloth and laid on the body. Sometimes they were successful, sometimes not.

---

138. Kyvig, *Daily Life*, 139–40.

139. This idea actually spawned the creation of the paraffin paper bottle still commonly used today. A patent held by a little-known inventor whose primary work was in film and television. See Godfrey, *C. Francis Jenkins: Pioneer of Film and Television*, 85–88.

Amidst these fears, Clarice's mother, Rose, caught the disease. She was sick for an entire winter and almost lost her life.[140] Despite everyone being ordered to avoid contact, a nurse and neighbors stayed by her side. Brother Ammon Mercer, a member of the Magrath Ward bishopric, visited regularly and administered to her. "I think this was all that saved my mother's life."[141] People were warned to stay away from anywhere they might catch the flu, but Mercer and others ignored the warning to offer care and priesthood blessings. The flu subsided and routines were reestablished, but no one could say for certain where it came from nor why it left. The pandemic simply ended.

### WORK, FRIENDSHIPS, AND COURTSHIP

Clarice finished school through the eleventh grade. This was a common end to the education of children of the time. There were only a few students in the ninth- through twelfth-grade classes.[142]

Following her formal schooling, Clarice worked in the Jensen and Brothers Mercantile Company, one of the first stores in Magrath. It was a general store established by Charles Jensen and his wife, Allie. It sold a little of everything, from hardware to groceries. Clarice clerked and waited on the buyers. She liked her job, except for selling shoes. There was no instrument for foot measurement and proper fitting. The buyer simply tried on all the shoes available until a pair that felt comfortable was purchased. Clarice simply cringed when touching another person's foot. When she turned eighteen, Allie took her under her wing and

---

140. Floyd Godfrey, "The 'Flu' 1918–19," in "Life Stories," file of undated handwritten stories from the life of Floyd Godfrey.

141. See Clarice Card Godfrey, story in Godfrey Family Papers. Ammon Mercer served in the bishopric for twenty-three years. He was the counselor to Bishop Levi Harker, who was the first bishop of Magrath, serving thirty-two years, as well as two terms as mayor of the town. Magrath and District History Association, *Irrigation Builder*, 465–66, 490.

142. In 1913 there were twenty-one students attending in Magrath and only one in the twelfth grade. Magrath and District History Association, *Irrigation Builders*, 333–36.

trained her in finances and bookkeeping. It was a skill Clarice would take into her marriage.¹⁴³

Friends, fun, and dating were enjoyed after school and work. If a student missed school without an excuse, his or her parents would get a visit from the truant officer. Normally that was all it took to return them to class. While it might have been exciting to skip a class or two, they never missed work. Work was a family responsibility.

It was in the last two years of Floyd's schooling that he and Clarice began noticing each other. They had been neighbors, but Clarice's opinion of the roughshod Godfrey boys was not the highest. She never thought she would wed one of those ruffians. "If anyone had told me I'd marry a Godfrey, I would have slapped them silly."¹⁴⁴

Floyd and Clarice's dates revolved around dancing and the Empress Theater. They danced in Magrath's open air pavilion, in the assembly hall, and atop the old schoolhouse. Floyd was making the transition from working in the fields to working full time in the Magrath Trading Company, in addition to his job as evening projectionist at the Empress. It was said that whenever Clarice accompanied Floyd to the projection booth and reached over to give him a kiss, the old hand-cranked movies moved faster.¹⁴⁵ There was no hanky-panky in the booth. The movie had to keep moving, and Floyd's mother was right below in the ticket booth to make it so. Eva supported the growing relationship between Floyd and Clarice. As she sold movie tickets, if she came across a $2 bill ($26), Eva would place the bill on the floor in the projection booth, where she knew Floyd would find it and have sufficient funds to buy an ice cream soda after the movie. He had to have $1.35 ($17), as that was the price of a chocolate sundae. If Clarice's friend Janet did not have a date, she added to the cost. She would always accompany them if she didn't have a date. Neighbors often wondered which girl Floyd would marry.

---

143. Floyd Godfrey, "Great Events in My Life." This is Janet and Harold Boucher and Rose and Eldrid "Dad" Hudson. See Magrath and District History Association, *Irrigation Builders*, 470, 480–81. Also, handwritten letter from Rose Hudson to Floyd Godfrey, 7 April 1982, Godfrey Family Papers.

144. Floyd and Clarice Godfrey, joint oral history, 8 May 1977.

145. Floyd Godfrey, oral history, February 1977.

Jensen Brothers Mercantile Company, Magrath, Alberta. Courtesy Glenbow Museum.

### LIFE'S TRANSITION IN HISTORY

The Canadian families passed through significant historical transitions. Floyd's and Clarice's parents migrated northward on an open frontier in Canada with horse and buggy. Then the railroads opened the West to increased migration, with spur lines running north and south throughout southern Alberta, fanning agriculture and industrial growth. In Montana and southern Alberta, these interests were in mining and farming. While the railroads brought coal and industry to the consumers, they also brought settlers to areas once far removed. The Charles Ora Card, George Card, and Melvin Godfrey families utilized the new products that the railroads brought in.

The families of these pioneers witnessed the early days of the frontier West and particularly southern Alberta. They chased the cows down main street Magrath. New Mormon settlers brought irrigation and an economic stimulus. Floyd's father purchased one of the first automobiles in Magrath. He opened a new world of movies and local entertainment to his community. The automobile replaced the railroad spur lines for local transportation. Blood, sweat, tears—World War I, "the war to end all wars," took lives from every community. Another global threat would follow—the Spanish flu epidemic. The Roaring Twenties were a complete contrast—a revolution in morals and manners. It was party time for young Floyd and Clarice. They danced the years away and fell in love—just as the Great Depression arrived.

# THE MODERN CANADIAN WEST

CHAPTER 8

Foundations for modern families are laid in the footprints of their ancestors and the communities in which they lived. The horse-and-buggy frontier West was almost behind the times, and the modern West was just ahead. Family pioneers experienced civilizations in transition: from handcarts to horseback and to oxen- and cattle-drawn wagons. Uncharted trails became wagon roads and immigration and trade routes. The Industrial Age provided automobiles, new farm machinery, and a film and radio industry. It introduced the telephone and electricity into homes.[1] Railroads created faster transportation and trade. By the late 1800s, trains had become the first mass rapid transit system.[2] Families often

---

1. Kyvig, *Daily Life*, 27, 53, 91. Also, Ernest J. Wrage and Barnet Baskerville, *American Forum* (Seattle: University of Washington Press, 1960), 223.

2. In the United States, the Union Pacific and Central Pacific Railroads produced employment and transportation for thousands from Cache and Weber valley settlements. See Ricks and Cooley, *The History of Cache Valley*, 172–74, 182–85. The Union Pacific Railroad would eventually take over the Utah Central Railroad and the Utah & Northern Railroad. The Utah Central Railroad connected Ogden and Salt Lake. The Utah Northern (which is a separate railroad from the Utah & Northern Railroad) connected Ogden to Brigham City; Logan; Franklin, Idaho; Idaho Falls; Dillon, Montana; and the Montana mines. Leon-

used the rails,³ for even in those days it was certainly faster than the horse-drawn carriage. The Canadian Pacific Railway connected Canada, just as the Union Pacific connected the United States.⁴ The Canadian version of the golden spike was driven at Craigellachie, British Columbia, on 7 November 1885, just one year before Card, then forty-six years of age, would board for his famous trip from Kamloops, British Columbia, to Calgary, Alberta.⁵

The Roaring Twenties were exuberant years. They were a release from the earlier sufferings of World War I. During World War I and the Twenties, Floyd Godfrey and Clarice Card grew from children into working adults. They experienced the tensions of WWI, the terror of the Spanish flu pandemic, and the boisterousness of the 1920s. In contrast, the Great Depression hit like a hammer as the economy fell out from under the nations of the world. There was little cash, so barter and trade in kind became the manner of conducting small-town business. Salaries were cut, taxes went unpaid, and people, families, and governments found themselves struggling. Many of those employed before the stock market crash were making less than 50 percent of their previous wages, even four years later.⁶ These were the years that would launch the next family generation.

---

ard J. Arrington, *Great Basin Kingdom: An Economic History of the Latter-day Saints, 1830–1900* (Cambridge, MA: Harvard University Press, 1958), 257–92. In southern Alberta, the Galt Lines connected with the Great Northern lines in Shelby and Great Falls, Montana. Small towns throughout southern Alberta were Lethbridge and Calgary. See R. F. P. Bowman, *Railways in Southern Alberta* (Lethbridge: Lethbridge Historical Society, 2002), 36, map.

3. R. F. P. Bowman, *Railways in Southern Alberta*, 36.

4. See Pierre Berton, *The Last Spike: The Great Railway, 1881–1885* (Toronto: McClelland and Stewart, 1971). Also Robert G. Athern, *Union Pacific Country* (New York: Rand McNally, 1971); Frederick M. Huchel, *A History of Box Elder County* (Salt Lake City: Utah State Historical Society), 105–22.

5. Godfrey and Card, *The Diaries of Charles Ora Card: The Canadian Years, 1886–1903*, 14 October, 1886. See also, Claude Waitrowski, *Railroads across North America: An Illustrated History* (New York: Crestline, 2012), 146.

6. Kyvig, *Daily Life*, 209.

## WEDDING: THE GODFREYS AND CARDS

By 1926, Floyd had completed school; he was working at the Magrath Trading Company and the Empress Theater. He was saving his money as best he could and preparing for marriage. His only expenses were clothing and dating. Clarice worked as a clerk in the Jensen Brothers Mercantile Company.

Getting permission and preparing for marriage was nerve-racking, yet fun. By 1927, Melvin had started building his third home uptown on Main Street and was moving one last time. Word was getting out about Floyd and Clarice, and Melvin asked Floyd if they wanted the old Godfrey house after they were married. The answer was yes. Now Floyd just had to muster up the courage to ask Clarice's father.

Everyone could see the direction the courtship was headed, but Floyd was still nervous about approaching George Card. One spring morning, George went to his farm and came back to town with a team of horses so he and Floyd could plow the garden on the old Godfrey property for the summer garden. George was driving the team and Floyd was holding the blade deep into the soil as he turned the dirt and gathered his courage. He tried to work his question into casual conversation, but blurted it out: "Mr. Card, Clarice and I would like to get married. What do you think about that?" Floyd never forgot his response: "What in the hell do you think we're plowing this garden for, Floyd?"[7] And that was how Floyd received permission for Clarice's hand.

Floyd was twenty-one and Clarice was twenty when they married. Clarice had $27.40 ($360) in her savings. Floyd had his jobs at the trading company and the theater. The day before their wedding, 7 June, they caught the train to Cardston. Unusually heavy rain had been pouring for several days. As they rode, they listened to the railroad ties sloshing in the wet soil, splashing the water over the tracks as the ties sunk into the railbed. But Floyd and Clarice had no worries. Happiness, excitement, and anticipation were the emotions they shared. They were met at the Cardston Railway Station by Clarice's uncle,

---

7. Floyd Godfrey, oral history, January 1977, 3–5. Also, 20 March 1982, 18.

Joseph Y. Card. The day before their wedding was spent in preparation, obtaining their wedding license and visiting with Clarice's extended family—Joseph Y. Card, Hugh B. Brown, and Zina Card Brown.

On 8 June 1927, "they were joined together in the Holy Bonds of Matrimony according to the Ordinance of God and the Laws of the Province of Alberta at the Temple in Cardston." Joseph Y. Card performed the sealing ordinance, which was witnessed by James Hanson and William Henderson.[8] That evening, Joseph held a family reception at his home. It was a small family gathering but a joyous occasion. People were poor and could not give much to the newlyweds, but if Floyd and Clarice got even a dish towel as a gift, they were grateful, because they had nothing. As they were returning to Magrath the next day, a friend, "Dad" Hudson, sprinkled them with wheat as they stepped off the train. The round-trip to Cardston was their only honeymoon.

The young couple went directly to work and began preparing their home. They cleaned the old Melvin Godfrey house, 155 South First Street West. This home of Floyd's childhood would now be the first home of their family. They furnished it with borrowed hand-me-downs and homemade furniture. They had a couch, a table, two bow-backed chairs, a woodburning cook stove, a cupboard, a bedroom chest made of boxes, and a bed.[9] George gave them a cow and a calf for milk and beef. It was meager, but it was a beginning.

### A LOVING AND LEARNING PARTNERSHIP

Lessons of life and marriage progressed in the jubilant times of 1927, 1928, and into 1929. A year after they married, Floyd and Clarice

---

8. Marriage Certificate, license 5491, issued by Ira C. Fletcher, certificate in Godfrey Family Papers. A "sealing" in the LDS temple symbolizes the concept of an eternal marriage as opposed to this life only. Joseph Y. Card was the son of Charles Ora Card. James Andrew Hanson was son of Niels Hansen, one of Cardston's original pioneers. William Henderson came to Canada in 1898. Keith Shaw, *Chief Mountain Country*, 332–33, 338–39. See the Journals of Joseph Young Card, 8 June 1927, L. Tom Perry Special Collections.

9. Floyd Godfrey, "Great Events in My Life," from "Life Stories," file of undated handwritten stories from the life of Floyd Godfrey.

joined with friends and headed to the Raymond Stampede for a day of fun. Their savings had grown to $45 ($597), with which Clarice had hoped to purchase a bedroom dresser she needed. Their first dresser was made from cardboard boxes, wallpaper, and a cotton curtain with a mirror hanging from the wall. For the stampede, they thought they might use a little cash from their savings, so they took it all with them.

As they passed through the gates of the stampede grounds, walking along the circus sideshows, Floyd stopped to play a little "Crown and Anchor." It should be noted that the Crown and Anchor was a gambling concession. In this game, the player rolls the dice, and when the symbols on the dice match those on the playing mat, the player wins. If the symbol doesn't match, the player loses the bet. He won, tried it again, and then again. He worked their $45 up to having $85 ($1,126). The group strolled through the concessions and finally took their seats in the grandstands as the rodeo began. All the while Floyd's winnings were "burning a hole in [his] pocket," as he used to say. All he could think about was winning the cash to purchase the dresser. So he excused himself from the group, hurrying back to the Crown and Anchor.

Floyd ended up losing all of their savings! Dejected, feeling guilty and nervous, he slowly made his way back to Clarice, who was still watching the rodeo with their friends. He pondered just how he would tell her what he had done. When he told her, she cried and was not too happy with her husband. Floyd felt so deflated the next morning that he went to the Trading Company and made arrangements to purchase the dresser on credit, promising to pay $5 ($66) a month. Clarice got her furniture, and Floyd learned a valuable lesson.[10] They would later laugh at each retelling of the story.

Kenneth Floyd was born at home ten months after the wedding, on 28 April 1928. Dr. Douglas B. Fowler and nurse Sarah Polson attended the delivery. As Ken took his first breath, Nurse Polson hollered, "Come in here, Floyd, and see what you have been doing." The doctor appeared at the door, however, and directed the new father to "stay

---

10. Floyd and Clarice Godfrey, joint oral history, 8 May 1977.

out" in the kitchen.[11] All was well. Arlene Janet followed Ken sixteen months later on 13 September 1929. Both were born in Magrath. Floyd said that Arlene Janet was "our pride and joy. We sure did spoil her."[12] Less than a year after Arlene's birth, Clarice was in the hospital for the first time in her life to have her appendix removed.[13] Nonetheless, another daughter named Marilyn Rose was born three years later on 12 January 1932, with Lorin Card following not too long after on 22 July 1933. It was a busy beginning to their marriage. Within in six years, the couple expanded to a family of six. All of the oldest four children were born at home. Two more would surprise them later.

**COMMUNITY DRAMATICS**

Live local theater was a part of community entertainment. The Magrath Home Dramatics were under the direction of Louisa Ann Taylor.[14] Taylor directed a dozen or so actors and actresses, including Floyd, and they performed various three-act plays. It was a carefully selected group of young adults. Allowing too many people to participate resulted in goofing off that made control harder during rehearsals. Mrs. Taylor took her dramas seriously, and she expected the same from her actors and crews. The scripts were handwritten. Practice involved long weeks of memorization and rehearsal. Taylor always teased the lighthearted Floyd about practicing his lines: "When you learn your lines, please learn them correctly, so that you can cue the person following you. . . . Don't you know it is impossible for them to follow

---

11. Floyd Godfrey, oral history, January 1977, 34–35.

12. Floyd Godfrey, oral history, February 1977, 35. Fowler was Magrath's doctor from 1925 to 1936; Nurse Polson is said to have brought "hundreds of babies into the world." Magrath and District History Association, *Irrigation Builders* (Lethbridge: Southern Printing Company, 1974), 367, 506.

13. *Cardston News*, 22 May 1930, 1.

14. Magrath and District History Association, *Irrigation Builders*, 527. In Floyd Godfrey, "The Home Town Play," from "Life Stories," file of undated handwritten stories from the life of Floyd Godfrey, he indicates the director was "L. S." Taylor, but this is undoubtedly Louisa Ann.

you if you don't give the right cues?"¹⁵ Her reminders were necessary because Floyd was too good at improvising. Plays were enjoyable winter activities when life slowed on the farm.

Floyd enjoyed his part in community dramas, and sometimes he brought his family to watch. In one play, he was the general of an army. He had a uniform and a sword hanging at his side. He was to clash with the enemy in a climactic duel. Though makeshift wooden swords had sufficed in rehearsals, these swords were real, acquired from local veterans who had fought in real battles and who expected the swords returned. Floyd's opponent was a short fellow, his friend "Dad" Hudson. Dad Hudson had borrowed a long sword and scabbard. Floyd and Dad, the opposing general, approached each other to fight it out, delivering their lines with bold, exaggerated anger, challenging each other to draw the sword. Floyd was taller and swiftly drew his sword, but Dad Hudson suffered an equipment malfunction. His sword was so long and his arms were so short that he couldn't pull it out. Floyd could have "run him through ten times before he drew his sword." The audience broke into laughter; the actors were embarrassed, but everyone had a good time.¹⁶

Young Kenneth, who had just turned four years old, came to see a performance in which Floyd was the hero. The actors had scheduled a full dress rehearsal as a matinee. They watched through a small half-inch hole in the curtain as parents and sweethearts arrived, filling the auditorium. Children and families were specially invited to this afternoon performance. The actors dressed in costume, with the makeup artist having "really done his work well . . . with greasy paint and powder." Floyd did not think anyone would ever recognize him. The hero strutted confidently toward center stage as he delivered his lines. At just the right moment, as if on his own cue, little Kenneth got up from his mother's lap, walked straight to the front of the auditorium, looked

---

15. Floyd Godfrey, oral history, March 1982.

16. Floyd Godfrey, "The Home Town Play," from "Life Stories," file of undated handwritten stories from the life of Floyd Godfrey.

barely over the top of the stage, and hollered, "Hello, Daddy," in a voice heard throughout the hall. The crowd roared.[17]

Floyd and Clarice had a young family, but they still enjoyed going to dances and gatherings with friends who were also getting married. Floyd's participation in local dramatics continued, and they were active in their church. Between 1927 and 1935, Floyd was called to serve as the resident of the Young Men's Mutual Association, a local church program sponsoring youth activities and teachings.[18] He was ordained a Seventy, served as the Quorum of the Seventy secretary, and served as the secretary of the Melchizedek Priesthood committee.[19] He starred in local dramas and felt guilty about leaving Clarice alone with the children as he was off in rehearsals. However, she didn't mind too much because she was kept busy working in the Primary.

**THE GREAT DEPRESSION HITS HOME**

A month after Arlene's birth, the world of Floyd and Clarice changed drastically from the frivolity of the Roaring Twenties to the depths of the Depression. On 29 October 1929, the Great Depression hit families like a massive landslide. It buried every individual in unforgiving debt and hardship and choked the life and work from its victims. It was a catastrophe of international consequences, shaking the economy of every nation, state, and province. Alberta's per capita income dropped from $548 ($7,259) in 1928 to $212 ($3,710) by 1933, a drop of 61 percent.[20] Floyd's salary at the Magrath Trading Company was cut in

---

17. Floyd Godfrey, "The Home Town Play," in "Life Stories," Godfrey Family Papers. Also, Floyd Godfrey, oral history, February 1977.

18. An LDS Church "calling" is an invitation delivered by a church authority to assist in Church labors. The Church is supported by the voluntary, unpaid involvement in service and self-government. Ludlow, *Encyclopedia of Mormonism*, 248–49.

19. Certificate of ordination, 5 August 1935, in Godfrey Family Papers. A Seventy was a general priesthood office in the Melchizedek Priesthood. In 1986 the practice of local Seventies was discontinued and set aside for General Authorities.

20. Great Depression of Canada, http://www.yesnet.yk.ca/schools/projects /canadianhistory/depression/depression.html.

half, dropping to $0.18 ($3.15) per hour.[21] Four months before the crash, Floyd had started to build a new home at 145 South First Street West, south of Main Street and only a few doors south of his father's home.[22] This is the home where Marilyn and Lorin would be born. Floyd was twenty-three years old. Out behind the house, in the barn, they kept two cows. In the morning, the cows were milked and put out in the morning to graze with the city herd. The herdsman returned the cows each evening, and Clarice herded them back into the barnyard. If they weren't cooperating, she had to run up and down the alley trying to catch them. The cows provided milk for the family, and extra was sold to the neighbors. With the economic disaster settling in, debt and declining wages made it difficult for Floyd to pay even the interest on his home construction loan and the related property taxes. By 1935, he was asking the town to consolidate back taxes owed in the amount of $171.25 ($2,824).[23]

Floyd and Clarice almost finished their new Magrath home during these difficult few years. It was completely framed, roof and walls were in place. The outside was stucco and held tiny flecks of glass, giving it a reflective glitter. The family was anxious, and they moved in before the interior was finished. The children's Grandfather Godfrey gave them Hollywood movie posters to cover wall studs. They had no concern for the bare walls, but a movie poster was exciting, and no one else in town had them. There was a hole in the floor in one room where the children climbed down into the basement. There was a chemical toilet in the upstairs and likely one outside as well.[24] Still, paying the mortgage on the construction was a challenge for Floyd and Clarice during the Depression.

---

21. Floyd Godfrey's 1977 oral history indicates $.18 cents per hour. In his 1982 oral history, he indicated his salary was approximately $40 per month. To make these conflicting figures compute, Floyd's work week would need to approach fifty-five hours per week, which during the Great Depression may have been likely.

22. Magrath Town Council Minutes, 5 June 1929. Minutes reflect Floyd is working to purchase the land of Dora Coleman for his new home. Also, Lorin Godfrey, "A Touch of History," July 2008.

23. Magrath Town Council Minutes, 1 September 1935.

24. Correspondence from Arlene Janet Godfrey Payne, 11 October 2011.

Floyd and Clarice were not alone in their struggles. Values on a farmer's crops and a rancher's cattle hit rock bottom. It was impossible for many farmers to pay for expenses out of the meager returns from the crops, if they got any returns at all. Added to this economic upheaval, in 1930, southern Alberta was coping with drought conditions, and harvests were few. It was a time people could not forget but hoped they could. Alberta's stake president, Edward J. Wood, called for a day to be set apart for a "special fast for the preservation of our crops."[25] Church members were asked to abstain from food and drink while praying for moisture.[26] All local Cardston Seventies, including Floyd's brother Bert, were called to the temple for a special prayer circle.[27] "I don't know who was the mouth, but we were in there for about three hours.... I lived one-half block north of the temple. The rain was pouring down so hard that I was soaking wet by the time I got home, now that is an answer to prayer, my dear children."[28]

Life moved forward as the Great Depression directed. It was busy, and it was physical. During summer vacations from the trading company, Floyd borrowed the wagon from his father-in-law and drove the team north of Magrath about twelve to thirteen miles to Pothole Creek, where he dug coal for the winter. It was hard manual labor. A lump of coal as large as a kitchen table was maneuverable in the water, but when the second workers got it above water, its weight was immediately apparent. They broke it into manageable pieces with a pick and a

---

25. Journal of Edward J. Wood, June 1931, in Melvin S. Tagg, "The Life of Edward James Wood" (master's thesis, Brigham Young University, July 1959), 105–6.

26. An LDS stake is a geographic designation of several wards or congregations. Fasting is the voluntary abstaining from food while praying for the Lord's blessings. It was practiced in biblical and Book of Mormon times. In this case, it was a public fast, seeking the Lord's intervention in the drought. Ludlow, *Encyclopedia of Mormonism*, 500–502.

27. Prayer circles are a part of LDS temple worship, the practice dating back to biblical times. In this case, the prayer circle was formed for a special priesthood group, the members of the Seventy Quorum of the Alberta Stake. Except for the temple endowment, the practice of special prayer circles outside of the temple endowment were discontinued 3 May 1978. Ludlow, *Encyclopedia of Mormonism*, 1121–22.

28. Bertrand Richard Godfrey, oral history, February 1980.

shovel and threw it into the wagon box, then hauled it home.²⁹ This was a soft, dirty-burning coal that left a lot of ash, not the hard, long-burning coal of the nearby Lethbridge mines. But there were no complaints. The soft coal was available for the digging. So, with intensive heavy labor, Floyd hauled ten tons each year. This was sufficient to keep his family warm through the winter.

Hay and grain for their animals was hauled from the Card farm, where Floyd helped his father-in-law cut and stack it. He was paid for his labor in feed for his cow. Cattle was essential on every farm. Cows were a food supply—milk, cream, and a new calf each year that supplied the family with meat. Even Ken contributed, as he was now old enough to fill his wagon with fourteen quarts of milk and haul them to the train station, where he was paid $1 ($17). It was much-needed money, as Floyd was only earning $1.50 per day at the trading company.

Wheat from the Card farm was taken to the nearby Rockport Colony, where the Hutterites ground the grain into wheat and pancake flour.³⁰ If there was a charge for the service, it was probably an exchange in kind, meaning the Hutterites would take a part of the wheat in payment and grind it for themselves.³¹ Beef also came from the Card farm. Vegetables from their own garden were all tended to maturity, harvested, and preserved. Ice for perishable food was still dug from the creek. This time Floyd was not a spectator, as in his youth, but among those cutting, lifting, and hauling.

The year 1935 was particularly dry, another drought adding to the woes of the Depression. It was so dry that little hay was produced for the cattle, so Floyd improvised. He purchased some oat straw and filled his barn. Then he went to the Raymond Sugar Factory and bought sugar beet pulp and molasses. Two dollars ($34) loaded the wagon to the point that it was difficult for the horses to pull the load. The round

---

29. Floyd Godfrey, oral history, 20 March 1982.

30. Hutterites are a Christian people who adhere to traditional ways and live communally.

31. Floyd Godfrey, oral history, 20 March 1982. The Rockford Colony was formed not far from Magrath in 1918. See John A. Hostetler, *Hutterite Society* (Baltimore: Johns Hopkins University Press, 1974), 364.

trip took all day, the distance being ten miles from Magrath. He covered the pulp with straw to keep it from freezing in the winter months. When the cows were ready for feed, he placed a few pitchforks of straw in the manger, then poured a stinky quart of pulp over the hay. "The cows loved it," he recorded in his history. But it smelled, and it tainted the taste of the drinking milk. "After the cows had eaten, with the straw sticking to their noses, they looked like some strange creature from outer space with slick syrup and straw stuck all over their nostrils." They tried to lick it clean, but it seldom worked. It was a nonfattening diet for the cows, like the healthier hay, but it pulled his family through difficult winters. George Card's crop of sugar beets also produced a harvest of beet tops that were good cattle food. Floyd placed these in small piles all over his garden; each pile was just large enough for one feeding.[32]

Floyd kept his job at the trading company, and with the extra work, the family got along. Everyone in Magrath was living the same circumstances. Soup lines formed in the cities, and many people were on welfare. Floyd and Clarice thankfully were not. They were always proud of the fact that during their most difficult years, they "were never on [government] relief."[33] It was in the middle of the Depression when Floyd and Clarice began considering moving to Cardston.

### LIFE'S TURNING POINTS

Floyd's brother Bert was influential in convincing him to relocate his family from Magrath to Cardston. Bert had returned from his LDS mission, and he too struggled with employment, moving as work was available. He worked in one of the Magrath grain elevators until it closed because of the Depression. He moved to Cardston to operate the Cardston theater for Gordon Bremerton. He then moved up into Crows Nest Pass in Coleman, where he worked in the theater and the

---

32. Floyd Godfrey, "Cow and Beet Molasses," in "Life Stories," Godfrey Family Papers.

33. Floyd Godfrey, oral history, January 1977, 34.

mines. Later, he returned to Cardston and established his own store.³⁴ He sold lemons for $.25 per dozen from Godfrey's Groceteria. He had an ice cream parlor in the store, where his younger brother Douglas worked as a soda jerk.³⁵ Bert was also a sales representative for a Lethbridge funeral home.³⁶ He was active in the town business developmental circles and served as treasurer for the Cardston Board of Trade. Things were looking up for Bert in Cardston. By 1936, he was in a number of diversified fields. However, almost everyone was scrambling. He knew his younger brother Floyd was struggling in Magrath, so he reached out.³⁷

By 1937, the Depression was still in control of everyone's life, and World War II was approaching. Bert suggested that Floyd move to Cardston. "You can make a lot more money here than in Magrath," Bert had told Floyd.³⁸ Earl and Hal Peterson had just constructed a complex for Texaco Oil in Cardston at 195 Main Street. They built a new large warehouse and bulk storage facility, which included the service station.³⁹ So in March 1937, Floyd turned his Magrath home back to the Lethbridge lender, cleared his debt, resigned from the Magrath Trading Company, and moved to Cardston. He took the job of managing the Cardston Texaco Service Station, which still stands on the north Cardston hill across from the Cahoon Hotel, 211 Main Street.

---

34. Bertrand Richard Godfrey, oral history, February 1980. Bert Godfrey sold the Cardston Palace Theater to the Brewerton Brothers in 1927. The Brewertons would eventually purchase the Empress in Magrath and theaters throughout the small towns of southern Alberta. See Keith Shaw, *Chief Mountain Country*, 31–33.

35. "Seen and Heard," *Cardston News*, 22 March 1937, 1. A soda jerk was a person who operated the soda fountain in a store, serving flavored soda water and ice cream.

36. Advertisements, *Cardston News*, 20 October 1936, 4, 8.

37. *Cardston News*, November 1936, 1.

38. Floyd Godfrey, oral history, 1977.

39. Shaw, *Chief Mountain Country*, 439–40. There are several conflicting accounts of what drew Floyd to this job. His 1977 oral history suggests Bert Godfrey had the license for the station and wanted Floyd to "come and run it." At this writing, there was no evidence that this partnership ever existed or that Bert ever took an active part in the garage. Correspondence with Floyd's children, in March 2014, suggests that Floyd was working closely with the Petersons, who in 1944 purchased the station. Also, correspondence from Douglas Godfrey to author, 13 March 2014.

It was apparently a quick decision that caught the Magrath Trading Company staff by surprise. They promised him a "rip-roaring ding-buster party" as soon as he was available, "for there's no one who is entitled to it more that good old Floyd."[40] True to Bert's prediction, moving to Cardston more than doubled Floyd's wages, from $40 per month to $90 ($652 to $1,467).[41]

**CARDSTON AUTO SERVICE**

Old Floyd was thirty-one at this essential transition of his life. A month later, in the first week in May, Floyd made arrangements to move his wife and four young children to Cardston.[42] Kenneth was nine; Arlene, eight; Marilyn, five; and Lorin, three.

The advertisements began appearing in the *Cardston News* in mid-March: "Announcing New Management of Cardston Auto Service, Floyd Godfrey."[43] Douglas Godfrey said that "Floyd looked sharp in his Texaco uniform." The new job matched the standards Floyd maintained in the station, along with his quality of customer service and the work habits he had learned at the trading company. The operations of the station were oil changes, light mechanics, gasoline, and service. This service included filling the customer's tank with gasoline, checking the tire pressure and oil levels, and washing car windows. The station's advertising emphasized 100 percent efficiency. There were three or four employees. In less than a year, the business had shown an increase of 65 percent.[44]

Floyd was a progressive manager. He installed a new Alemite grease cabinet and a Lincoln grease gun.[45] The station grew beyond just

---

40. "Local and General," *Cardston News*, 16 March 1937, 6.
41. Floyd Godfrey, oral history, 20 March 1982.
42. "Local and General," *Cardston News*, 11 May 1937, 1.
43. Advertisement, *Cardston News*, 16 March, and 23 March, 1937, 3, 2.
44. Advertisement, *Cardston News*, 25 January 1938, n. p. Also, correspondence from Douglas Godfrey to author, 13 March 2014.
45. "Progressive Cardston" and "Local and General," *Cardston News*, 16 August 1938, 1. See advertisement, *Cardston News*, 14 September 1937 and 26 April 1938.

Cardston Auto Service, circa late 1940s. Courtesy of Glenbow Museum.

auto service. They sold automotive parts, batteries, and electronics; new Sparton radios for 1938 model cars; and even the "Norge Rollator Refrigerators." By 1939, the Texaco station was the agent for the new Pontiac automobiles. The *Cardston News* advertisements all concluded with the bold line "Cardston Auto Service, Floyd Godfrey, Phone 20." The number 20 was the phone number of the station.

As Floyd's family adapted to Cardston and the Texaco station grew, all the children pitched in. Ken helped clean the mechanics area; Arlene and Marilyn cleaned the toilets, sinks, mirrors, and floor; and Lorin flittered around or generally stayed home with their mother, which history says their older siblings did not much appreciate. Cleaning the restrooms was the "yucky job," so Floyd paid his daughters $0.25 ($4.08) to split between them when they did this job.[46]

---

Also, "Texaco Quality: The Best," *Cardston News*, 11 July 1939.

46. Correspondence from Arlene Janet Godfrey Payne, 31 December 2010. Godfrey Family Papers.

Like his children, Floyd did not enjoy the service station job. He was progressing, and business was expanding, but the Texaco regional management often popped in unannounced and headed back to where the mechanics were working. They fostered contention. If there was a single spot of oil on the floor, they hollered and cussed out the mechanics with whom Floyd worked. It was a needless show of authority that disrupted the operations.

The station opened early in the morning and remained open until all the other businesses in town—including the movie house—were closed, just to sell a few gallons of gas at 10 cents ($1.63) a gallon.[47] One evening as Floyd was closing up, a rough-looking character entered. Floyd told the gentleman that he was just closing and ready to lock up. The man responded that he just wanted to use the restroom, so Floyd waited for him outside the door. It had been a successful day, and Floyd had the cash in his pocket, ready to take home and then to the bank the following morning. When the fellow reappeared, Floyd locked up, but the man seemed to hang around a bit longer than Floyd thought normal. It was uncomfortable. Floyd started walking home, and the fellow followed for three blocks. Afraid a robbery was on the mind of the vagrant, Floyd offered a silent prayer and began to run. He made it home, and the frightening affair passed without incident. Thanks to an answered prayer and something extra in Floyd's quickstep, he was safe.[48]

Floyd missed the hardware business. He had worked ten years as a clerk at the Magrath Trading Company. In Magrath, Floyd and Clarice's families had all lived within a few miles, so the move to Cardston had not been taken lightly. However, if Floyd had stayed the course in Magrath, he might have lost his Magrath home and "worked for nothing all my life." In Cardston there were occupational options, growth, and opportunities for entrepreneurship.[49] The challenges of the Texaco station and relocating to Cardston were a major turning point for the

---

47. "The People History," http://www.thepeoplehistory.com/1937.html.
48. Floyd Godfrey, oral history, February, 1977, 2–3.
49. Floyd Godfrey, oral history, 20 March 1982.

family. The move to Cardston did not mean life became easy, just that there were more choices.

## COOMBS HARDWARE

Forest Wood pulled Floyd back into the hardware business. Forest was the son of Edward James Wood, who was the first Cardston Temple president.[50] He had opened a hardware store in 1928, almost a decade before Floyd arrived in Cardston. He had partnered with Mark A. Coombs until 1942, when he purchased the store but retained the same name, Coomb's Hardware.[51] Visiting the hardware store one day in the late 1930s, Forest invited Floyd to join him at Coombs Hardware. He offered him a job, and Floyd took it.

Coombs Hardware was a bit of a contrast to the Magrath Trading Company. In Magrath, Floyd had learned the importance of keeping the store clean, clear of clutter, and in order. Coombs Hardware was "anything but in order." So Floyd set about constructing new merchandise displays. As he thought himself "half a carpenter," he constructed new shelving, painted, and began to attractively arrange the store's inventory, which included everything from farm tools to fine china. Forest's father, Edward J. Wood, was the Alberta Stake president (1903–42), then the temple president with the dedication of the Cardston Temple on 26 August 1923.[52] Edward J. Wood, was so pleased with Floyd's work that he offered to help Floyd purchase eighty acres of land on the Glenwood Irrigations District if he would remain at the hardware store.[53] Floyd had a lot of respect for a man in the dual role as his stake president and temple president.[54] Floyd would stay in the store

---

50. Melvin S. Tagg, *The Life of Edward James Wood, Church Patriot* (master's thesis, Brigham Young University, 1959), 8–15; also, Edward James Wood, https://familysearch.org/photos/stories/1234555, accessed 5 January 2016.

51. Shaw, *Chief Mountain Country*, 520. Also, *Chief Mountain Country*, vol. 3, 127, indicated the sale to Wood was in 1943.

52. V. A. Wood, *The Alberta Temple: Centre and Symbol of Faith* (Calgary: Detselig Enterprises, 1989), 18–19.

53. Tagg, *The Life of Edward James Wood*, 103–25.

54. Tagg, *The Life of Edward James Wood*, 103–5.

for a few more years, but he was not interested in work of the farmer. From his youth, he had enjoyed the role of merchant.[55]

### CARDSTON IMPLEMENT COMPANY

In 1941–42, Floyd went to work for Kirk Lee. Lee had purchased the Cardston Implement Company. He had seen what Floyd had done for Coombs Hardware and asked him to do the same thing for him.[56] Floyd agreed. The implement company was a little different from Coombs in that it had small furniture on display on the second floor. Cardston Implement was a business fitting the "needs of your Home and Farm, Bringing the Spring into the Home," which meant an inventory of spring-filled chesterfields and sofas, electric washing machines, electric irons, wash boilers, tubs, tools, saws, rugs, hardware, and bicycles. By February 1942, Floyd had taken over as manager from Alf Strate.[57]

### THE BROWN HOUSE

The first Cardston home of Floyd and Clarice Godfrey was affectionately called "the Brown House," a rental up a small hill a half block from the northwest corner of Cardston Town Square. It was owned by a Mr. Gooding Brown, who lived next door. There were two rental units in the Brown House. Lilly Gregson Archibald, her daughter Donna, and several others lived in an adjoining modest unit during the years Floyd, Clarice, and family occupied the larger unit. It was a small house, but it accommodated the needs of their family. The four Godfrey kids slept in two double beds in the northwest corner room of the house. It was cold in the winter. Getting warm and ready for bed meant the children took their pillows out into the living room, at the north end of the room, where their dad stoked a red-hot fire to

---

55. Floyd Godfrey, oral history, 20 March 1982.

56. "Floyd Godfrey Manager 'IMP,'" *Cardston News*, 3 February 1942, 1; *Chief Mountain Country*, vol. 3, 129. Also, Floyd Godfrey, oral history, 20 March 1982.

57. "Good News," *Cardston News*, February 1944, 1. Also advertisement, *Cardston News*, 16 March 1944, 3.

last the night. They held their pillows toward the stove, a puffin-billy, letting them absorb the heat and then dashed into their beds, hugging the pillows. In the summer, they enjoyed the cool of sleeping on the porch. The only fear was of the wandering "Black Aces," which "scared the dickens out of us . . . [and] woke-us-up telling us they were 'going to get us' and take us somewhere."[58] The Black Aces were a group of young men, perhaps a year older than Ken, hoodlums of the day, bullies in today's vernacular. They dressed in black and cruised around neighborhoods frightening the younger children, climbing the walls of the temple, and acting a little more mischievous than usual. As the oldest, close to the Aces age, Ken knew who they were. He was unafraid and protected his younger sisters and brother. The Black Aces eventually faded, and home remained the family center for playing, cooking, and eating. Life was good. There was even an indoor bathroom in the southwest corner of this house.[59]

The barn and a root cellar were out back, just east behind the house. They were childhood magnets. Their Uncle Bert kept greyhounds in their barn along with their own cow and a few chickens. One of Ken's jobs was beheading the chickens, and he drafted Arlene and Lorin to hold the legs, trying to keep the victims steady on the chopping block. Then grabbing them before they ran, headless, underneath the chicken coop. The root cellar was just like the one they'd had in Magrath, except this one filled with water every spring.

Just out the kitchen door was a cesspool that smelled like an aging sewer. It was a septic tank, as there was no central town sewage-treatment system in town. So, if the home had an indoor bathroom, the sewage was stored in the tank, which was emptied periodically. Without a lid, it was dangerous. The wood sheet covering the pool was rotting. One day the kids' dog, Sport, fell in. As the children rushed to the hole, their mother saw them and hollered to stop. Otherwise, a little one of her own might have joined Sport in the pool. The dog was

---

58. Correspondence from Arlene Janet Godfrey Payne, 11 January 2011 and Lorin Card Godfrey, 29 March 2014; also, Kenneth Floyd Godfrey, oral history, 2013.

59. Correspondence from Arlene Janet Godfrey Payne, 11 January 2011, and Lorin Card Godfrey, 29 March 2014; also, Kenneth Floyd Godfrey, oral history, 2013.

rescued. Clarice gave it a bath, and the landlord covered the cesspool. Sport survived his fall into the sump, but he did not survive the passing cars he loved to chase. It is the way of childhood pets. Floyd consoled his children and promised they would have Sport in the hereafter, and soon another dog came into the family.

Home and community gardens were a significant means of food, especially during the Depression. Gardening was not a hobby; it fed the family. Community gardens in Cardston supplemented the large family garden plots that came with every house. The community garden was down near the Smith Dairy, along Lee's Creek. Every week during spring and summer in the Depression years, families planted, weeded, and harvested potatoes, corn, peas, and beans. The Church had a simple steam canning system people used to preserve the harvest. When corn was ready, the parents had to get it canned before the kids had eaten it all. For them the harvest included the following: cook the corn; add salt, pepper, and butter; then eat away. The family worked their part of the garden with a group of friends, all of whom were LDS and belonged to their neighborhood study group.[60]

The Godfreys' home garden at the Brown House was as large as their first Magrath home. Along the north end of the garden was a long row of gooseberries and chokecherry bushes—sour! But berry pies were Clarice's specialty. All the preserves from the harvest were stored in the cellar with the vegetables. The cellar was a challenge each spring when it filled with water. The kids didn't mind because they got into a galvanized iron wash tub, using it as their boat, and paddled across to the shelves, retrieving a bottle of fruit or the vegetables for their mother.

The family remained fiercely self-sufficient through the Depression and into World War II. Grandparents from Magrath visited, often bringing food as they could. The road went in both directions. They ate what they grew and grew what they ate. If they tired of beef, poultry, or pork, then they made a family outing of going fishing. They fished the Belly River where the irrigation water was diverted from the river into

---

60. Correspondence from Arlene Janet Godfrey Payne, 11 January 2011, and Lorin Card Godfrey, 29 March 2014.

Payne Lake for the eastern farm and ranch lands. The stream sported fresh mountain suckers that were so plentiful these fish could be scooped up into large wash tubs, beheaded, washed, and cut into small pieces, which were taken home and bottled. In theory, this variety of sucker was different from their bottom-feeding cousins found along the junction of Lee's Creek and St. Mary's River. These Belly River suckers were eaten with a milk-cream sauce filled with peas and butter. The children's description remains "yucky" even today, but in the Depression it was all they had, and they were happy to have it.[61]

There was a small garage at the side of the Brown House, but since Floyd had no car, the structure was a storage shed for coal and wood. The kids used the driveway as a small soccer field. A graveled street running north and south in front of the house was an extension of the driveway, adding to the neighborhood playground. Ken, Arlene, Marilyn, Lorin, and friends played baseball, soccer, and the childhood games of run-sheepy-run, tag, and hide-and-seek with the neighborhood. They built bonfires of dry autumn leaves, threw potatoes into the flames, and called it supper. There was a willow tree in front of the house to the side of the driveway. This was where Tarzan played.

## WORLD WAR II

World War II was a surreal experience, especially for the children. Families were glued to the new technology of radio, listening to the news of Edward R. Murrow; the speeches from the political leaders of the time, including William Lyon McKenzie King, Canadian prime minister; Winston Churchill, Great Britain's prime minister; and Adolf Hitler.[62] Radio had quickly become popular, and as it was brought into every home, it linked the small towns and large cities together in a common

---

61. Correspondence from Arlene Janet Godfrey Payne, 11 January 2011, and Lorin Card Godfrey, 29 March 2014.

62. Milo Ryan, *History in Sound* (Seattle: University of Washington Press, 1963). Speeches of these leaders were recorded by the British Broadcast Corporation, London and KIRO-CBS Radio, Seattle. These collections are today housed in the British War Museum, London, and the Milo Ryan Phonoarchive (National Archives, Washington, DC).

experience.[63] World War II was frightening and set everyone in action. Even the children contributed by collecting tinfoil from anywhere, including gum wrappers, to recycle into the war effort. They came home from school selling "poppies," which were pinned to the lapel of one's suit, shirt, or dress, with profits going to the war effort. They sold "War Saving Stamps" for 25 cents ($4.10). The stamps were glued into small booklets, and at the end of the war the bank reimbursed them along with interest. Schools practiced evacuation drills and taught children how to get under their school desks for protection against falling bombs. It was just practice. There were no bombs dropped, but air raid drills took place overhead at night. The town lights were shut off. A lone plane flew over the town from the Pearce Air Training Base, north near Fort Macleod. It dropped a "bright flair that seemed to light up the whole town." Within minutes, the squadrons followed, "hundreds of them" it seemed. They were noisy, flying low enough to almost touch the roofs of houses. It was nerve-racking as the family contemplated the reason for these activities, but "we all stood out on the front lawn and watched." When it was over, the town lights switched back on, and the children went hunting for the burnt-out flair.[64]

Ironically, the war also brought people together, as all were supportive. Families seldom ate anywhere but home. Their three regimented meals were breakfast in the morning, dinner at noon, and supper in the evening. The movies promoted the war effort and for the most part were entertaining and inspiring. Movie fans of the time were shocked with *Gone with the Wind*, when Clark Gable, as Rhett Butler, said, "Frankly my dear, I don't give a damn." Swearing was taboo, but the movie was certainly a success.[65]

---

63. Kyvig, *Daily Life*, 71–72.

64. Letters from Lorin Godfrey and Arlene Godfrey Payne, 12 and 13 June 2014, Godfrey Family Papers.

65. Letter from Arlene Godfrey Payne, 13 June 2011.

## CARDSTON HOME CENTRAL

The Brown House was Floyd and Clarice's first home in Cardston as they became established in the community, making the transition from the Depression to World War II. Floyd and Clarice lived there for five years. It was the childhood home of Kenneth, Arlene, Marilyn, and Lorin. Their growing years were spent in the two Magrath homes, the Brown House, and a new one under construction. It was the latter where two more boys, Donald and Robert, would join the Godfrey flock.

In September 1941, Floyd applied for a building lot permit just south of the Thomas S. and Annie Gregson's home. The lot cost $60 ($958).[66] Constructed during 1941–42, it remains standing today at 334 4th Street West. This was the family home for the next fifty years—from 1942 to 1992, home central for half a century.

The home was built by the hands of Floyd and Clarice, with the children helping as they could. Children cleared the debris from the property. Rusty cans were placed in a burlap gunny sack and hauled away. Floyd worked late into the night, when weather permitted, as the children watched from the Brown House for the bright electric light to go out at the construction site of their new home, knowing their father would soon return. Help came as well from the neighbors and church friends. Henry Noble dredged the basement with his team of horses. Alfred Schaffer and Brig Low aided roofing the house, and others shingled.[67] The first room constructed was the indoor bathroom, followed by the kitchen. The family moved in with only these two rooms completed. They lived on a rough floor, with nothing on the walls, just the raw 2 x 4 boards. Cardboard furniture boxes from the Cardston Implement Company were nailed to the walls, and before bedrooms were added, the walls were plastered with movie posters from their Grandfather Godfrey's Empress Theater in Magrath.

Floyd and Clarice saved their money, adding rooms as they could afford it. When the home was finished, it consisted of the front room

---

66. *Cardston News*, 16 September 1941, 1. Also Shaw, *Chief Mountain Country*, 326–27; Floyd Godfrey, oral history, February 1982.

67. Floyd Godfrey, oral history, February 1977.

Floyd and Clarice Godfrey, Cardston home. Courtesy of Marilyn Ockey-Pitcher.

and two bedrooms, one on each side of the bathroom, with the girls' room, to the east, still walled with movie posters and the master bedroom to the west. The boys slept in a small bedroom downstairs in the basement. There were bunk beds and a small closet built under the stairway where they hung their clothes. Upstairs, two back rooms were eventually added, a bedroom and sun room, plus a new rear entrance. This was part of the lifestyle of the times—a little at a time—neighbors helping neighbors and pay as you go.

The new house faced the town square to the west, and the Cardston Alberta Temple, almost in the backyard, was just to the east. The old clothesline was out the back door and down five steps. The loose wire strung with wet clothes ran between two short wooden poles, with six lines running parallel. Lugging a basket of wet laundry from the basement washing machine to the upstairs to hang them outside was a physical feat not for the faint of heart, but it was repeated by Clarice every Monday.

Godfrey home, backyard view, winter 1955. Courtesy of Godfrey Family Files.

Monday was laundry day every week on every calendar. Dirty clothes were dropped through a clothing chute in the bathroom. They fell into the dirty clothes bin in the basement. The bin's latched door opened, and the clothes fell onto a table for separating into whites and colors. Chips of soap from a homemade bar were added to the washing machine as it started. It was a new electrical model. Whites were washed first and afterward put through the wringer to squeeze out the water. After a rinse or two, the clothes were placed in a wicker basket; carried upstairs, outside, down the porch steps; and hung on the clotheslines east of the house. Floyd later constructed a closer entry on the east side of the house and stretched a long clothesline with a pulley system from which Clarice hung the washing to dry. This saved many paces and a few stairs. It was a nice change, out of the wind, where she simply stood on the porch, hung the laundry on the line, and rotated the lines on the pulley stretched from the steps over her summer flower garden to a tall pole at the other side of the yard. This was modernization. Monday's winter laundry was frozen solid, but it was somehow dry when brought into the house. One load at a time, all day long, with loads of sheets, towels, colored shirts, and work pants.

The gardening traditions continued in the new house, but now there were two gardens. Floyd's was the family vegetable garden. The first was just southeast, behind the barn. The plot itself was as long as the house, perhaps 30 x 60 feet. The noise of their father's early morning work woke the sleeping children. Floyd was a proficient gardener. Years later, when the barn was dismantled, the garden moved to the north of the house. While planting, Floyd would leave a small play circle in the middle of a dozen rows of corn where his children could play.[68] A month or two after planting, the corn towered above their heads as they played in their secret hideout among the spiraling stalks.

Clarice's garden was a beautiful bouquet of roses and honeysuckles and a burst of all kinds of flowers. She loved this garden. The tiny red-white bleeding hearts provided a delicate contrast against the majestic gladiolas. In summer, the aroma of her sweet peas filled the air. The honeysuckles could be pinched and eaten while weeding. Clarice even won a few prizes at the garden fair.

There was nothing unusual or ornate about the garden or the home. It was immaculately clean and full of love. Everyone was welcome! The doors were never locked, for there was no need. The exterior of the house was finished in white stucco and trimmed with a four-foot dark green strip at the base. The roof was a contrasting lead-based dark green paint. In the 1950s, a thirty-foot television antenna was raised. It pointed east toward Lethbridge and was anchored onto the roof. The house had a television! One channel was all that was needed for complete family entertainment: Disney nature films, cartoons, and wrestling from the Maple Leaf Gardens. A curious copper wire stretched from the antenna into the ground. Floyd explained to the children and his grandchildren that it was for lightning storms that thundered over the town from the foothills.

To the south of the house, during the 1950s, Floyd constructed a free-standing garage. A line of three crab apple trees stretched

---

68. Donald was born 17 July 1944 and Robert 7 May 1961. Certificate in Godfrey Family Papers.

between the house and the garage. The trees were white, with blossoms in the spring. Branches swung low and heavy with fruit by late summer. The fruit was small, delicately bite sized, and *sour*. The apples were enjoyable for the neighborhood children with a fancy for things tart. What the kids chose not to eat, the Hutterites from one of the nearby colonies were pleased to harvest for jam.[69] The garage never housed an automobile. Instead, it became a storehouse and was later renovated as a home for Grandmother Card. It was small and humble, clean, and even warm in the winter, allowing a grandmother to live close during her final years.

A line of ash trees and a small lawn separated the front of the house from the western edge of the property. These were stout little trees protecting the house from the persistent winds and the winter snow drifts. When the plow removed the snow from the street, it was piled on the west side of the road so high neither children nor drivers could see Town Square nor the trees. Children climbed up these piles of snow like young mountaineers.

Originally, an ornate wrought iron fence separated the house from the trees and the road. The heavy gates were always open to the new driveway. It seems someone kept backing into it, so the bent and snarled iron was finally removed. The front door to the house was generally "stuck" closed. It was warped by the snow, wind, and moisture, but it did not matter; it was used only by visitors anyway. Family and friends used the back door. Remodeling had moved the sunroom back door from the west and replaced it with a lilac bush outside. The door was relocated to the rear of the house, where an entrance and porch were added, protecting the entrance from the constant west wind. Five weather-beaten wooden steps at this entry had been painted green, but were so well worn, no one ever really noticed. There was a cast iron mud scraper sealed into the cement at the bottom of the steps. Here, the visitor, children, and parents scrapped the mud and snow from their boots before heading up onto a small porch leading to the entry.

---

69. The Hutterite colonies near Cardston were Raley, West Raley, Big Bend, and East Cardston. Hostetler, *Hutterite Society*, 362–65.

Winter storms drifted snow right to the top of this porch. Snow was caught in a small white lap-wooden fence between the house and the garage, with drifts as high as six feet and extending as far east as the barn. The results produced short sled rides or a good snowball fight between parents and children. Children, left to their own imaginations, dug passages in drifts where there was a quiet stillness within these safe worlds of snow and ice. The porch provided a resting place for children in the summer months. They would just sit there and visit with their mom or play with the dog—Fido, Pal, or Sport—friends that lived underneath the steps.

The porch led into an entry room. It was a 4-by-6-foot cubicle for hanging winter parkas and storing overshoes. It insulated the main house from the inclement weather and mud that might be otherwise tracked through. In the entry, the children defrosted their ears and shook off snow before entering the blanketing warmth of home. It was at this little entry where the children first called for "mother." There were never really any questions following the initial inquiry as to her presence. Children just wanted the comfort of knowing she was always there for them. If not, there was always a note of explanation on the kitchen table.

Once in the house, children huddled around the cook stove or sat on the oven door to warm up. Every morning started with Floyd as the first one out of bed, and he made the fire in the kitchen stove while singing, "You are my sunshine, my only sunshine."[70] It was a sad country song about a man whose wife had left him. Floyd repeated the chorus over and over. Modern appliances replaced the wood and coal-burning kitchen stove with an electric one and central heating. Central heating shot hot air from the furnace downstairs to the upstairs kitchen vent. Clarice's wide dress caught the heat blowing from the vents, so kids stood close, and she would cuddle them and laugh as they pushed and maneuvered for the warmest positions.

A barn was the second building on the property, southeast of the house. The haystack was immediately south of the barn. The pig pen

---

70. "You Are My Sunshine," by Jimmie Davie and Charles Mitchell, was first recorded in 1939.

was a muddy mess between the haystack and the wall of the barn. On the other side of the wall there was the chicken coop. At the north end of the barn were feeding and milking mangers for the cattle. The manure trough was in the middle of the barn. The oats, wheat, grain, and bailed hay were along the west side of the manger. The barn housed one or two cows, a pig, and the chickens. Each spring, Floyd brought home a box of little yellow chicks and placed them in the open oven to keep warm and adjust to home before they were sent to live in the chicken coop. Betsy was the family cow, a pet of sorts. She had one lone horn, but with it she could hook the gate or barn door and escape out, only to be recaptured and returned. At night, the manger was filled with hay, and in the cold winter the hay helped protect the animals. Manure rich in nitrogen was hauled from the barn to fertilize the garden. The cows were returned for milking each evening. The cows were bred to bear a calf each fall and were the winter meat.

The barn was all work and part play, depending upon age and the child's position within the family. Ken and Lorin did the milking and heavy barn work. As they filled the milk buckets, they squirted the barn cat and any passing young ladies they might have been trying to impress or annoy. The raw milk was placed in milk bottles and capped. A day later, the cream had risen to the top, and young Don now had the milk delivery responsibilities. He pulled his red wagon full of milk bottles to the waiting neighbors. Disaster struck one day when Lorin came home from school to water the cows. They had broken into the grain bin and lay on the barn floor bloated. Floyd, Lorin, and the veterinarian righted the cows and tried running them to force the gas out, but to no avail. Something was expelled, and it covered Lorin from head to toe, but the cows died, and they were dragged off the property.[71] It was a significant loss to the family in terms of income and nourishment, but new cattle were acquired. The daily opportunities for tending to the livestock and for milking, feeding, and watering the cows were

---

71. Lorin Godfrey, "The Barn," 1 November 2012, Godfrey Family Papers; also, Kenneth Floyd Godfrey, oral history, 2013.

always a source of debate among Floyd's sons. Debate persists to this day among eldest brothers as to who did most of the milking.[72]

As time passed, cows gave way to the milkman's daily delivery and eventually the grocery store. The family maintained the animals as a means of sustaining their daily living. Floyd kept hay for the cow outside in a haystack and brought it inside the barn dry to feed the animals. The hay was purchased by weight from the neighboring Blood Tribe farmers. If it had been a dry year, the cattle would get beet tops from the Magrath farms. Generally, on Thanksgiving Day, Floyd shook his two oldest sons from their slumber and headed to Magrath to load their borrowed truck with beet tops.[73] They hauled them back to Cardston and unloaded them in stacks placed around the garden. The beet tops were frozen by the time the cows got them, but that didn't seem to deter them at all. This Thanksgiving Day routine kept Kenneth and Lorin out of their mother's hair while she, Arlene, and Marilyn prepared the feast. After the beets had been unloaded, the men cleaned up, and grandparents, relatives, and friends arrived, and Floyd carved the turkey.

In 1954, their barn and garden land to the east of the house was donated for the building of the LDS Church Alberta Stake Center. The barn disappeared, and the garden was moved to a plot immediately north of the house. A wooden fence separated the Godfreys' and their neighbor's gardens. The old cat walking across wooden planks was good target practice for the young man with a rock in hand. When Kenneth's aim proved accurate, his father instructed him that he would go and have a talk with Grandma Annie Gregson.

In addition to the eastern property, Floyd and Clarice donated a strip of land along the south edge for an east–west roadway access. The ragweeds, into which children once tunneled, also disappeared. The east garden and barn became part of the new church building with a large parking lot. Sunday services were in the new chapel. Basketball, scout activities, dances, and a small theater stage resulted in a

---

72. Lorin Godfrey, "The Barn," 1 November 2012, Godfrey Family Papers.

73. Thanksgiving Day in Canada is a celebration of the harvest and occurs the second Monday in October.

Alberta Stake Center under construction, 1953-54; view from Godfreys' back porch; note the clothesline in the foreground and the outhouses left. Courtesy of Godfrey Family Files.

continuous flow of activity, since the stake center building was always open. Even after school, neighborhood children gathered for basketball. There were no uniforms. Teams were chosen and games played: "shirts" against the "skins."

The stake center's construction was a welcomed sacrifice for the entire neighborhood. Families happily donated their land. Clarice sewed the curtains for the large stage, and he started his own store, Floyd's Furniture, providing the carpet and the chairs. The days of barns and large lots in the town transformed into more home lots. It was a community and a neighborhood transformation. Everyone pitched in to help.

## CARDSTON ALBERTA TEMPLE

The most imposing structure in the neighborhood and in southern Alberta was and remains today the Cardston Alberta Temple of The Church of Jesus Christ of Latter-day Saints. It was constructed and dedicated in 1923, when Floyd and Clarice were teenagers living in Magrath. Their families were not directly involved in the construction of the temple, but they did teach their children the significance of this spiritual structure. Over the front door it reads, "The House of the Lord." The Cardston Temple sits on a small hill, just an echo away from the Godfreys' back porch, and Floyd's whistle would bounce off the granite walls as he called the children for supper. This edifice of religious worship centered around family life, community, heritage, cultural pride, and religious belief. Every week, Floyd and Clarice went to the temple, promising the children that when they were old enough they too could worship there. It produced a comforting spirit in the backyard. It was a symbol of profound history and cherished personal worship.

**CARDSTON TOWN SQUARE**

The Charles Ora Card Town Square had family and town history. The land owned by Charles was donated and set aside as a recreation park for Cardston. The center of the town's sports activities remains directly across the street, just west of the Godfrey home. It was originally surrounded by a wooden fence, then enclosed as a field with barbed wire. Today it is an open four-square block of recreational space. In the early years of the Godfrey family, it was simply a block reserved for baseball, tennis, and ice skating. If the neighborhood children were not in the gardens, running around the yards, or playing in the wilds of the ragweeds, they could be found across the street playing baseball. There was one baseball diamond at the southeast corner. Games were played both informally by neighborhood kids and competitively between church youth groups in the surrounding towns. Behind home plate stood a larger-than-life, weather-beaten, gray-green grandstand. It was a shady place to watch the games. The front of the grandstand was covered with chicken wire to protect the fans who sat on the wooden benches. The whole structure was about fifty feet wide and sat immediately behind home plate. The teams sat on several 2-by-6-inch benches strung along both the first-base and third-base lines. In all likelihood, no more than a few hundred spectators could have squeezed onto the stand. It was uncomfortable and slivery, but better than a ground blan-

Cardston Alberta Temple. Photo by Matthias Süßen.

ket on a hot summer day. Town workmen used the space underneath the grandstand for storage. The neighborhood children snuck into the darkness to smoke corn silk, thinking they were committing a great sin. The back doors were always locked tight, but the enterprising youngster was always able to find a loose board or crawl under the steps for entry. Miraculously, the stand never burned down. Today the field is beautifully developed with multiple ball diamonds and known as the Town Square.

The tennis courts were off right field to the north of the baseball diamond. There were three courts created with crushed red rock, and tattered nets. Whether the nets were abused or worn is unknown, probably both. They were surrounded by a twelve-foot-high fence that never seemed high enough. At night the children lay in bed and listened to the wind whistle through the courts like a song. Hearing the wind singing was an ever-present soothing sound; unless it blew the roof off the school's shop building. Even that was okay, though, because the kids would not have to go to school when a classroom had no roof.

Hockey and ice skating were winter sports at the northwest corner of the square. There was a freshwater spring that kept this corner of the field moist and sticky. Walking across it in the summer, a child could lose a shoe or boot yanking their foot from the mud. It was a good place to catch tiny frogs. In the winter it froze, transforming itself into a children's skating pond. Children sailed over the bumpy ice—mostly west to east as they unzipped their parkas, lifted them over their heads (like a sail), and skated to the east side of the ice. Once there, they'd drop their jackets, zip them up, fight the wind back to the west side, then sail back for another trip over the ice. The older boys took off their snow boots and put on their skates and practiced their hockey. They would lace two boots on the north end of the pond and two on the south and use them as their goal posts as they practiced for the NHL. Today, the bog has been drained and filled to make space for more baseball diamonds.

A five-foot-deep ditch once ran north to south along the west side of the park, attempting to drain the water, but more importantly, the high mud banks provided an imaginary world of childhood cowboy heroes: "Zorro," "The Lone Ranger," or "Lash LaRue." The running water at the bottom of the ditch heightened the imagination and the danger in this visionary world of play. The ditch ran for half a mile before it emptied into Lee's Creek.

This was the 1940s and 1950s neighborhood—the hub of the Godfrey family—the center of their earliest years in Cardston. Children ventured beyond the neighborhood, but only to hike Lee's Creek, swim up the creek to Bob's Hole or Slaughter Hole, go on a family picnic in Waterton and Glacier Parks, or visit extended family in Utah. The influence of people, places, and events within these few blocks was substantial. Within this neighborhood, children were protected, and teenagers were guided by mothers and fathers who taught high standards and expected discipline. Footprints were etched and molded from the seeds of this heritage, loving hands, time and experience, and were traced by the families who followed.

# SMALL-TOWN BUSINESS

CHAPTER 9

By the end of the 1930s, the Great Depression was passing, and the world was making the transition into World War II. The war caused social upheaval, but, at the same time, it was an economic revitalization. Canada was drawn into the war on 9 September 1939, in support of Great Britain and Europe. The war drew Canada into a critical position in the battle for the Atlantic and against the German air assaults, helping to grow the Canadian industrial manufacturing base.[1]

Farming, ranching, and other small-town businesses struggled but ultimately succeeded within the overarching tides of the nation's economy—war, drifting consumer whims, transportation, competition, the evolution of society, and in southern Alberta, even the weather. Agriculture remained central to southern Alberta life. Cardston was the center of a unique market defined by ranches, small settlements, and the First Nations people in the region. Mountain View, Waterton Park, and Twin Butte framed the west side; the Blood Reserve, Standoff, Hillspring, and Glenwood to the north; Raley, Woolford, Spring Coulee, Magrath, and Raymond on the east side; and Aetna, Kimball, Jefferson

---

1. Kyvig, *Daily Life*, 257. Also C. P. Stacey, "Second World War (WWII)," in *The Canadian Encyclopedia*, accessed 18 January 2016, http://www.thecanadianencyclopedia.ca/en/article/second-world-war-wwii/.

Del Bonita, and Owendale to the south. In-town enterprise included blacksmith shops, saddle shops, a printing office, grocery stores, hardware stores, and an early community theater featured in the Cardston Tabernacle.[2] In the beginning, Cardston was a growing hub. Common religious beliefs and life's challenges drew people together. Just a few families rolled into Cardston in 1887, but the population soon grew. Six years following the arrival of the first settlers, in 1893, the population was 593, and by 1901 it had 631 residents.[3] Today, the population has reached 4,167.[4] During the first few years, the growing land shortages in Utah contributed to the population growth in Cardston. The 1913 announcement of a temple in Alberta fulfilled the early pioneers' dreams and fostered growth.[5]

Transportation was key to the growth of Cardston. The settlers first came to Cardston in horse-drawn and ox-drawn covered wagons. Freight from the United States was hauled up the trail from Fort Benton, Montana.[6] The Lethbridge stagecoach even stopped at Cardston.[7] Democrat wagons—horse-drawn carriages—were the first personal means of transportation. As the region's transportation options grew from wagons, to railroads, and finally to automobiles, the distances between families, towns, and neighboring cities seemed to decrease. Business competition came knocking at the doors from the cities of Lethbridge and Calgary. The locally owned businesses always started small in Cardston and seldom grew beyond the region. They were simply passed from one generation to the next with little change. Some grew and were sold; Floyd's Furniture was one such entrepreneurial enterprise.

---

2. Shaw, *Chief Mountain Country*, 1:7, 38.

3. V. A. Wood, *The Alberta Temple*, 18.

4. Statistics Canada, *Cardston County, Alberta (Code 4803001) and Alberta (Code 48)* (table), *Census Profile*, 2011 Census, Statistics Canada Catalogue no. 98-316-XWE, Ottawa, http://www12.statcan.gc.ca/census-recensement/2011/dp-pd/prof/index.cfm?Lang=E.

5. V. A. Wood, *The Alberta Temple*, 25–27.

6. David L. Innes and H. Dale Lowry, *Lee's Creek* (Cardston, AB: Innes & Lowry, 2001), 6.

7. *Chief Mountain Country*, 3:102.

Floyd shovels snow in front of the store, 1950. Courtesy of Godfrey Family Files.

### FLOYD'S FURNITURE

World War II was just ending as Floyd's Furniture opened its doors. The transition to peacetime and then almost immediately into the Cold War was swift. Soldiers were returning home. Victory in Europe Day was celebrated Tuesday, 8 May 1945.[8] Cardston businesses were responding to change and were growing.

From the mid-1920s and into the 1930s, Floyd worked for the Magrath Trading Company. After that, he moved to Cardston and worked for Coombs Hardware, the Cardston Auto Service, and the Cardston Implement Company. Hardware was his interest and his trade. He had been offered land near Glenwood, but farming was not in his blood. The Cardston Implement Company, which sold furniture, interested him. Other businesses occasionally advertised limited pieces of furniture. The largest was Spencer's Hardware. During the Depression, it traded furniture for farm products, attracting those who had no cash—"Will trade a good piano for 100 bushels of wheat." It also advertised that they were willing to deliver the piano and take the wheat out of the bin as a part of the deal.[9] Furniture for sale in Cardston was spotty and an accessory to other business interests. But

---

8. "V-E Day Program," *Cardston News*, 8 May 1945.
9. Advertisement, *Cardston News*, 16 November 1937.

for Floyd, this was an opportunity. He wanted to branch out on his own, and the timing seemed right.

Spencer's Hardware opened in 1936 in the middle of the Great Depression. It was initially connected with the Cardston Implement Company, but it broke away and began operating under Cardston Hardware and Furniture. Within a year it was renamed Spencer's Hardware. In the mid-1940s, Floyd met with David D. Spencer, and Spencer suggested, "Godfrey, you go into the furniture business and I will quit selling it." Spencer had no interest in furniture; he wanted to sell hardware.[10] Floyd jumped at the suggestion to be independent and grow on his own initiative. He was an entrepreneur and confident in his abilities. The question was simply one of financing.

### CONSERVATIVE INVESTMENTS

Floyd and Clarice discussed the risks of owning their own business. They were somewhat anxious about the debt incurred. The financial exigencies of the Depression, the losses of their Magrath home, and the move to Cardston were still fresh in their minds and their wallets. They were excited about the prospects, but moved cautiously.

Floyd had just turned forty and Clarice thirty-nine. Their oldest child, Ken, was sixteen; followed by Arlene, fifteen; Marilyn, twelve; Lorin, eleven; Donald, two; and Robert, yet to come in 1951. Floyd drove to Magrath in his first car, a Model A Ford. He wanted his father's advice before he went to the bank. Melvin encouraged his son, "You can do it, Floyd; . . . now go do it." So Floyd set out to secure financing. The Royal Bank of Canada would only lend him $1,500 ($18,060), but Melvin agreed to match that with another $1,500, giving Floyd a capital of $3,000 ($36,120).[11] The reluctance of the bank was due to the

---

10. *Chief Mountain Country*, 2:36–37, 1:479. Also Shaw, *Chief Mountain Country*, 1:479. David D. Spencer was the older brother of Mark V. Spencer, sons of Mark Spencer and Janette James-Spencer. Also Floyd Godfrey, "Floyd's Furniture," in "Life Stories" file of undated, handwritten stories from the life of Floyd Godfrey. See Floyd Godfrey, oral history, 1982.

11. Figures vary in different documents. In "Floyd's Furniture," from his "Life Stories," the amounts borrowed were $1,500. In Floyd Godfrey's oral history, the fig-

fact that Floyd had no collateral. He had lost his Magrath home during the Depression and had just built a home in Cardston. However, the banker reasoned, "The way you have shown yourself on Main Street. . . . I'll lend you [the money]."[12]

The Canadian economy was growing due to World War II manufacturing, and permission to open Floyd's Furniture as a new household-furniture retail establishment came through the government Wartime Prices and Trade Board on 22 September 1944. Canada's manufacturing operations were transforming from defense to consumer goods, but the bureaucracy of war still held tight control over progress. It took time for the appropriate authorization and for Floyd to get organized. The formal business license was issued two years later on 31 March 1947 by the Province of Alberta Department of Trade and Industry, eight days after its officially advertised opening.[13] The actual opening was 21 March 1947. "The Store is now open for business in the premises above the Cardston News Office. A large selection of furniture is now on display and new shipments are arriving every day. The new phone number is 266."[14] Floyd was elated. He thought he might have done more with a larger investment and a bigger grand opening splash, even multiple stores over time, but funds were never available. He would start small and grow slowly.

### FURNITURE SHOWROOM OPENS

Floyd invested his start-up cash in three places: a building, inventory, and advertising. He first rented showroom space above the *Cardston News* building. Entering the store, customers ascended a steep stairway to the second floor. The interior was large and adequate for multiple

---

ure was $1,800 from his father and $1,000 from the bank. Totals thus ranged from $2,800 to $3,000.

12. Floyd Godfrey, oral history.

13. Wartime Prices and Trade Board, 7 March 1946, Order 414. Also Department of Trade and Industry, Government of the Province of Alberta, License H 1040, Floyd Godfrey (Floyd's Furniture), Godfrey Family Papers.

14. *Cardston News*, 21 March 1946, 8.

furniture displays, but there was just one small, square window—large enough to see only one chair from the street below. Floyd had the space; filling it with furniture was the next challenge.

Floyd took two approaches in creating inventory. First, he placed want ads in the *Cardston News*, letting the community know, "We Buy Used Furniture" and "We Do Upholstery."[15] He knew there was a substantial market for used furniture, and Clarence Olsen's upholstery shop was a quick walk from Floyd's Furniture.[16] Second, Floyd networked in national furniture manufacturing circles. His contacts at the Magrath Trading Company and the Cardston Implement Company were his introduction to furniture wholesalers. He wanted quality furniture: Simmons, Kroeler, McClary Appliances, Mason & Rich pianos, and La-Z-Boy. He ordered the furniture, and it soon began arriving. It was shipped from Vancouver, Calgary, and Toronto manufacturers via the Canadian Pacific Railway (CPR) to the Cardston Railway Station. Lawrence H. Jessen and Max Pitcher trucked it to the store. Jessen backed his delivery vehicle right up against the rear of the building, where the waiting Godfreys—Floyd, Clarice, Ken, Arlene, Marilyn, and Lorin—all climbed onto the roof of the *Cardston News* building and lifted the furniture up through the back door of the second floor into the showroom.[17] Carrying the furniture up to the back second-story rooms then down a few steps to the display area was a family affair. Clarice and the children worked right alongside Floyd, Jessen, and Pitcher.

Finally, Floyd had to charm the customers up the front staircase and into the store. The earliest promotions for the store were in the newspaper want ads. The two-to-three lines in the classified section continued for more than ten years. They always emphasized that the store sold used furniture and crafted new upholstery. There was a ready market for good used furniture among the disadvantaged who

---

15. Advertisement, *Cardston News*, 14 and 21 March 1946.

16. Lorin C. Godfrey to author, 8 April 2014, in author's possession. Also Shaw, *Chief Mountain Country*, 429.

17. Lorin C. Godfrey to author, 4 April 2014. Godfrey Family Papers, in author's possession. Also *Chief Mountain Country*, 2:326–27.

were living in Moses Lake on the Blood Reservation and returning soldiers who were establishing their first homes. Moses Lake was across the highway, immediately north of the town and adjacent to Highways two and five. Full-page, half-page, and smaller black-and-white display advertisements later targeted the townsfolk, ranchers, farmers, and the surrounding Blood Indian Reservation First Nations people.

By the mid-1950s, Floyd's Furniture's sales campaigns included use of direct mail and even radio. Newspaper readers were directed to check their mailboxes for flyers and in-store specials.[18] Full-page flyers were printed on a variety of colored paper and folded and placed in every mail box at the post office—one of the busiest buildings in town. Everyone had a PO Box, as there was no neighborhood or rural delivery. Being somewhat venturous, Floyd even advertised on the airwaves of CJOC-AM radio. At that time, it was the only radio station in the region and reached the entire district.

### GROWING THE BUSINESS

Wooden kitchen tables and chairs were the first furniture pieces sold. The solid set cost $89 ($1,078). Floyd remembered, "I must have sold a hundred of those" before manufacturers turned to chrome dinettes, a term synonymous with kitchen tables and chairs. The chrome dinettes trended toward sets with plastic tops and black, iron legs bent into a hairpin style. The newspaper announced the arrival of new chrome chairs and kitchen tables. A new two-piece "Bed Chesterfield [called a sofa and chair in US terms] sold for $165 [$1,999]; unfinished wooden end tables $3.95 [$48]; and a gold leaf framed round mirror, twenty-four-inch heavy plate glass, for $17.95 [$218] at Floyd's Furniture, Upstairs News Office, phone 266."[19] Net earnings for Floyd's Furniture in 1948 were $4,429 ($43,147). Floyd discovered that "you could sell

---

18. Advertisement, *Cardston News*, 29 July 1954, 1.

19. A "Bed Chesterfield" is a fold-out sofa with a mattress. See *Cardston News*, 11 April 1946, 1. Also Floyd Godfrey, oral history.

anything" to families relocating to southern Alberta.[20] The Godfreys were off to a strong start and in need of more showroom space.

The old bowling alley and pool hall building on the south block of Main Street became available in the early 1950s. It was next door to both the Mayfair Theater and Thad's Grocery, two businesses which drew traffic. The building's drawbacks became painfully obvious: it had only half a floor, no support braces for the roof, and had poor heating. The old furnace belched as much black soot as it did heat. Melting snow from the roof had to be shoveled to prevent possible collapse and leakage. Half of the floor was removed when Gordon Brewerton, the building owner, removed the bowling lanes, which left a long hole in the floor running the width of the building.[21]

Despite the drawbacks, the location gave Floyd significant advantages: approximately 20 percent more space on the ground floor—which was about forty feet wide and one hundred feet long—and two large display windows at street level. Folks driving past or walking into the movies or grocery store next door would see the new merchandise on display. Floyd felt the location was ideal. Brewerton wanted $75 ($677) per month for rent. Floyd's Furniture had spent almost five years on the second floor above the *Cardston News*. He wanted to expand, and he took the chance.

Furnishing the larger store, Floyd and Clarice moved every piece of inventory from the *Cardston News* building to the new location. It did not fill the expanded space, so they went to what would be the first of many national furniture shows in Toronto, Ontario, looking for the latest styles. Floyd and Clarice wandered through the exhibits and learned about the latest trends in design and home furnishings from national manufacturers and wholesalers. Their homework resulted in new products filling the front half of the store.

---

20. Floyd Godfrey, "Floyd's Furniture," in "Life Stories," file of undated handwritten stories from the life of Floyd Godfrey.

21. Lorin C. Godfrey, "A Touch of History," July 2008, Floyd and Clarice Godfrey Family Reunion presentation, Godfrey Family Papers. Gordon S. Brewerton was the builder who constructed the first motion picture theaters in Cardston—the Mayfair and Roxy theatres. At the time of this transaction he was also the Alberta Stake president, the Church authority in the region. *Chief Mountain Country*, 3:231–33.

## NATIONAL FURNITURE SHOWS

Over the years, the annual furniture show became both business and vacation time. Floyd and Clarice took the three-day train ride to Toronto, eating in the dining car and enjoying the scenery across Canada from the observation car. In Toronto, they stayed near the Toronto Exhibition Center on Lake Ontario or with their old Magrath friends Harold and Janet Boucher, and then took the streetcar to the show. The exhibit covered several large buildings with every Canadian manufacturer displaying and selling to retailers. It was three days of constant walking, making purchases for Floyd's Furniture and the people of Cardston. Shipments were scheduled throughout the year. Networking, as well as inventory, were important elements of the show, and over time Floyd got to know the leading manufacturers as well as their representatives with whom he would work for more than two decades. After each furniture show, Floyd and Clarice visited her sister Melva in Ottawa or the Cahoons in New York, who were friends from Cardston.[22] This became an annual routine as Floyd worked to stay current with trends and the trade. Sometimes their sons Ken and Lorin went along so they could learn the business.

At the 1964 furniture show, Clarice entered a contest that picked the best display, and she won an all-expenses-paid trip to Bermuda. The trip was the first time Floyd and Clarice had ever flown. It was a far cry from train rides and bumpy gravel roads. They spent two weeks on the tropical island. Both the *Cardston News* and the *Lethbridge Herald* picked up the story.[23] At home, the youngest son, Robert, suffered a contracted appendicitis attack and needed surgery. At the time, he was staying with Lorin, and with the help of his sisters, Marilyn and Arlene, they all nursed him back to health. There was no emergency phone call to Bermuda; those remaining in Cardston did not want to spoil their parents' once-in-a-lifetime vacation.

---

22. *Cardston News*, 13 January 1955, 1.

23. "Godfreys in Bermuda," unidentified newspaper clipping from the files of Floyd Godfrey, Godfrey Family Papers.

Near the end of the 1950s, Gordon Brewerton, the owner of Cardston's Mayfair Theater, informed Floyd that he wanted to sell the building, but Floyd reminded him that by contract Floyd had the rights of first refusal. Floyd quickly borrowed $11,000 ($87,522) from Lloyd Cahoon, promising to pay $100 ($796) per month at 6 percent interest. The sale was signed, sealed, and delivered 2 March 1961. Floyd was always proud of the fact that he "never missed a payment in those 100 months, a little over eight years."[24] He cleared the debt and felt free from its pressures.

The next building purchased was the grocery store, which shared a common wall with Floyd's Furniture. Guy Wilcox owned the grocery store, which he had sold to Thomas Thaddeus Gregson. It was Thad's Grocery from 1945 to 1953.[25] When Wilcox offered the building to Floyd, the agreement was for $6,000 ($52,760), a $500 ($4,397) down payment and, again, $100 per month.

The Brewerton and Wilcox buildings were aging, so Floyd renovated. He cut a doorway through the support wall between the two buildings, providing customer access and almost doubling his overall square footage. The display space in Thad's building was smaller, but the dirt-floor warehouse in back offered improved storage, and the front added a third large display window. Floyd acted quickly, installing updated heating and new wiring throughout the showrooms. He hung large fluorescent lights from the ceiling. They stretched about six to eight feet in length and around three feet wide, resembling flipped flat-nosed canoes and providing lighting for the displays. The roof was tarred, but still did not always hold back the weather. The heavy, wet snow caused the ceiling to creak with the weight as a warm Chinook wind turned snow into running water that slowly dripped through the ceiling. This created an immediate danger to the furniture below.

---

24. "Agreement," contract between the Mayfair Theatres and Floyd Godfrey, 2 May 1961, Floyd's Furniture Files, Godfrey Family History Papers. Floyd Godfrey, "Floyd's Furniture."

25. Shaw, *Chief Mountain Country*, 327, 510–11. Also *Chief Mountain Country*, 2:299–300.

All challenges were met, and the expanded space enabled Floyd's Furniture to buy a train car full of furniture. The savings were good, as the manufacturer often paid the freight bill. Renovations were costly, but they enhanced the attractiveness of the merchandise and the building, as well as taught the Godfrey children to work—there was always dusting and sweeping to be done. Floyd's Furniture's net earnings for 1953 were $6,091 ($53,560).

**BUSINESS WEATHER**

Business in a small town was small business. The opportunities for expansion were limited without opening new stores in other communities, but Cardston and the Church were still growing. The ranchers, farmers, Natives, and townspeople remained the foundation—a reality never far from Floyd's mind.

By 1951, just after Floyd had purchased his first building, his success bolstered his courage and trust with his wholesalers. His eldest son, Ken, was in Europe serving in the France Mission, and Floyd reasoned that the family would be blessed for Ken's service. Southern Alberta crops had never looked better. Taking a gamble, Floyd hesitantly approached Kroehler Furniture and Restmore Bedding and bought $9,000 ($81,794) in mattresses from Restmore and $11,000 ($99,970) in bedroom sets and front-room furniture from Kroehler. The crops were yet to be harvested, but they looked so promising, "just beautiful," and so, he placed the orders. Lots of new furniture was in route to Cardston; then it started to rain. It was only August and it "never stopped raining." The rain turned to snow, and "it never stopped snowing!" The crops were frozen, flattened, and rotted on the ground. It was not until spring the following year before the farmers desperately tried digging the frozen ground to rescue what little they could. Here, Floyd had "all this big debt on [his] shoulders," furniture packed in his showrooms, and farmers with no crops. He called his debtors and explained what had happened, and they encouraged him, saying, "You just keep hammering away and send us what money you can, and we'll keep taking care of you."²⁶ It was an atmosphere of grateful cooperation. Floyd staged a Christmas-extravaganza sale and paid the debtors as much as he could. Clarice pitched in and ran the store while he traveled ranch-to-ranch making contacts. The debts took six years to clear and almost put Floyd's Furniture out of business.²⁷ Through Floyd working directly with his wholesale distributors, who gave him leeway on payments, Floyd was able to dodge bankruptcy.

**CRAZY DAYS PROMOTION**

As business advanced, so did Floyd's involvement in the community. As a member of the Chamber of Commerce, he was part of a business development group on Main Street that organized events such as "Dollar Days," "Crazy Days," and promotions around the Dominion Day parades. These were small-town marketing tactics organized to bolster business, ideas hatched from the Chamber of Commerce. For Dollar Days, silver coins were stamped, and every merchant had to buy $100 or $200 worth to scatter throughout the community. The coins provided discounts on Main Street merchandise.²⁸

During one Crazy Day promotion, the Cardston merchants and Floyd's Furniture soaped all the windows using water and white Bon Ami (a powdered cleanser that is easily removed) and then covered all of the windows with brown butcher paper. For this sale, the stores did not open until 10 a.m., two hours later than the normal business day. Outside, the customers waited in anticipation. Inside, Floyd, Lorin, and the workers were busy tearing sheets of the brown paper and making torn price tags for everything, some with significant price reductions. During one sale, Floyd advertised a lamp for $1 ($8). First thing that morning, three women appeared at the door, headed straight for the lamp, and started arguing over it. One had hold of the lamp shade and the other two grabbed the stand. Floyd held off ringing up the sale

---

26. Floyd Godfrey, oral history, 31–33. In 1982, he reported these figures as totaling $20,000. His 1977 interview reported the totals at $21,000 to $22,000, 5.
27. Floyd Godfrey, oral history, 5.
28. Floyd Godfrey, oral history, 16–17.

for an hour or so as a cluster of shoppers enjoyed watching the hilarious competition. He finally gave his son Lorin the responsibility of handling the conflict. Names were written on small slips of paper and put into a bowl. Whoever drew his or her own name won the lamp. More profitable than $1 lamps were $99 ($796) Chesterfields desired by women who brought their husbands in tow. The women, liking the more expensive French provincials, opted for quality over savings and requested that their husbands write out the checks. One of the best window displays exhibited a friend of Floyd's, Alex Glenn, sound asleep in a La-Z-Boy chair. Floyd had covered him with a warm blanket, and Alex slept for a couple of hours. It drew a nice crowd.[29]

Floyd's Furniture was always a part of any community activity or celebration. During one parade celebration, Floyd dressed as a woman and paraded up and down Main Street as two tremendously embarrassed teenage sons tried to avoid eye contact with their father, who they pretended was a complete stranger. Floyd had fun and attracted attention. Even during the more serious Dominion Day parades, the store always participated with a float that advertised the latest in design, furniture, and appliances. The window display on these celebration days were critical as people lined the street, standing to see the parade and checking out what was in the store windows.

## CHURCH AND BUSINESS CLIENTS

Good service throughout his community evolved into meeting the needs of the growing number of LDS Church buildings across Canada and the development of business customers. This was a significant step forward from the customer base of local families. In 1958, Floyd learned that the Church wanted to buy three thousand folding chairs for its chapels across Canada and were requesting information from the T. Eatons Company of Canada. At that time, Eatons was Canada's largest retail department store and a significant competitor.[30] The

---

29. Floyd Godfrey, oral history, 42.

30. See Donica Belisle, *Retail Nation: Department Stores and the Making of Modern Canada* (Vancouver: UBC Press, 2011). In 1999, Eatons was purchased by Sears.

Eatons in Calgary was pursued because the Church was having difficulty getting furnishings across the border into Canada from United States manufacturers. An enterprising Floyd let the presiding bishop of the Church know that he too wanted to bid on the sale of the chairs. He claimed he could eliminate the import problem by providing Canadian products at a better price. He immediately contacted Royal Metal, a Canadian manufacturer, who insisted on an order of 3,100 chairs—one railcar load—but agreed to pay the freight. The cost was $6.35 per chair ($56), and Floyd had to provide the storage until the chairs were shipped throughout southern Alberta and across the country to the different chapels that were under construction. He built a garage next to his home, where the chairs were stored before they were needed and shipped.[31] This was a gigantic opportunity that could lead to other openings, but Floyd's Furniture was small, and Royal Metal wanted payment within thirty days. Floyd was anxious. He and Clarice traveled to Salt Lake, meeting directly with the Presiding Bishop Joseph L. Wirthlin. Floyd knew Wirthlin from Church association, but he did not realize Wirthlin did all the buying for the whole Church.[32]

Floyd left a trusted employee, Lynn Sommerfelt, in charge of the store and drove off to Salt Lake. When he and Clarice reached the Church Office Building, he paused; he was "in fact scared" to go in. Clarice gave him a loving nudge. "You are as good as they [your competition and the buyers] are now go in there." Floyd walked in, and Wirthlin was surprised to see him and said, "Well Floyd what can I do for you?" Floyd had done his homework in southern Alberta, surveying the chapels in the district and assessing their need for chairs. Wirthlin reviewed Floyd's report and responded, "Well the committee are meet-

---

31. "Application for Building Permit, Of the Town of Cardston," 26 August 1958, signed by Clarice C. Godfrey and initialed by Floyd Godfrey, Godfrey Family Papers.

32. There is a discrepancy in the oral histories of Floyd Godfrey in that he states "Bishop Burton" was a part of these transactions. In the "Biological Register of General Church Officers," there was no "Burton" at the helm when these transactions took place. Lorin Godfrey, Floyd's second son, who worked extensively with his father, reported "with certainty" it was Joseph L. Wirthlin as presiding bishop. Ludlow, *Encyclopedia of Mormonism*, 4:1631–51. Also Lorin C. Godfrey to author, 8 April 2014, Godfrey Family Papers.

ing upstairs now, let's try them." He called his secretary and asked that Floyd's order be taken into the meeting to "get it okayed." Ten minutes later, Floyd had an order for more than $19,000 ($166,898) worth of chairs.[33] He immediately called Royal Metal and gave them the order to ship. They sent Floyd an invoice, he sent it off to the Church, and the check came back ahead of the billing cycle.[34] In Floyd's personal history, he sketched a little drawing in the margins. It was a cloud. Written inside are the words "Cloud Nine." It was the beginning of many trips to Salt Lake City, as Floyd's Furniture was the only LDS furniture distributor in southern Alberta for two decades before new LDS merchants in Lethbridge began circling this prized customer.

Godfrey family folklore tells that Floyd Godfrey spent more time on his knees in the Cardston Alberta Temple than any other temple worker or administrator—he carpeted the temple on multiple occasions. He sold exquisite English wool carpets. One such order called for a carpet labeled "Heaven's Pile."[35] As the temple patrons stepped onto it, their feet sank in, and walking across the temple floor seemed more like floating. As the temple carpets showed wear, a call to the Presiding Bishop's office resulted in new floor coverings.

Renovations to the temple from 1961 to 1962 required carpet to be installed on granite steps. To accomplish this, a "smooth edge" was cut into one-inch pieces and fastened to both sides of the granite stairways with permanent adhesive. Today, "smooth edge" has a more appropriate name; it is called "tack board," which uses yardsticks with small tack nails hammered through at a forty-five-degree angle. Strips were fastened around the edges of a wall or staircase wherever the carpet was laid. The tacks pointed at right angles toward the wall to grip the fibers. Carefully cut, expensive carpet was stretched and wedged between the tack board and the wall, held in position by the opposing

---

33. The order of 3,100 chairs at $6.35 would have resulted in a wholesale purchase price of $19,685.

34. Floyd Godfrey, "Floyd's Furniture," in "Life Stories," file of undated handwritten stories from the life of Floyd Godfrey.

35. Floyd Godfrey, 1968 accounting book in which Floyd scratched estimates, diagrams, and possible sales, Godfrey Family Papers.

wall. The long hours kneeling on granite stairs and temple floors were painful. Floyd sacrificed comfort for the excellence he wanted and the result expected in the Lord's house.

Business clients of Floyd's Furniture included The Church of Jesus Christ of Latter-day Saints and motels in Cardston and Waterton. These were competitive bids, which had to total less than Eatons's bid. The inventoried order had to line up everything from kitchen pots, plates, pans, and utensils, to light switches, carpets, beds, and mattresses. These bids had to be detailed because, working on slim, competitive profit margins, one error caused the business to lose money.

Floyd was successful in getting the carpet contract for the prestigious Prince of Wales Hotel in the Waterton-Glacier International Peace Park, where he was also the victim of a little humor. His friend, Ted Weston, who was not a member of the LDS Church, hunted high and low for a camera so he could get a picture of Floyd laying carpet in the ornate hotel bar room. Floyd did not drink alcohol and would never be seen in a bar, except perhaps to lay carpet.[36]

**IN-KIND TRADE**

Like many small businesses, life in Floyd's Furniture was not always rosy. On occasion, it required marathon negotiations and a plan to pay a debt. If wholesale inventory was unavailable, a smaller merchant purchased items from the larger retailer in Calgary, creating the necessity of a small markup to stay competitive. These jobs were considered an investment toward future business. The wholesale price and retail markup on any furniture item in Floyd's Furniture varied depending on product quality, color, style, and manufacturer. Special orders were a little more expensive, but Floyd kept his pricing below big-city competitors. He stressed service and had a reputation for honesty and was therefore able to attract and retain customer loyalty. He made each customer feel that "they were the most important customers Floyd

---

36. Floyd Godfrey, oral history, 1982, 47.

ever had... [and] every customer felt the same."[37] Of course there were occasional complaints, but Floyd moved quickly to resolve any issues, and he was generally successful.

Floyd traded in-kind when times were difficult, when there was a mutual benefit, and when there was a need. He traded meat for a Chesterfield. He traded furniture for the services of a butcher and cold locker storage, for a delivery truck, and for a new blue Chrysler 300 with push-button transmission. Trading was a bedrock for making it easier for the customer as well as the store.

### SMALL BUSINESS CHALLENGES

Most of the significant challenges faced by Floyd's Furniture were weather and crop failures, but there were the occasional disputes, too. One of the more dramatic conflicts came when two women got into a physical confrontation in full view of the store window one day. One pushed the other and she fell through the display and landed in a recliner chair, which toppled over backwards with her legs flying in the air. Arbitration and cleanup were significant.

Floyd's Furniture was robbed on two occasions. Both incidents ended well. In the first incident, money was missing from the office and so Floyd reported the theft to the town police, who detained a young man. However, rather than file formal charges, Floyd suggested that the man "could work it out," and over the years this man "became very trustworthy, got married, and [became] one of his [Floyd's] best customers," right up to the time Floyd's Furniture was sold.[38] Floyd knew the man, but his name was never recorded in court or the family records. The second robbery ended when they found the whole unopened safe in a hay field. The safe was heavy, perhaps two feet by three feet of solid steel. The thieves got it out of the store but could not get it open.

---

37. Dahl Leavitt to Floyd Godfrey, April 1988, 82nd Birthday Celebration Collection, loose-leaf notebook in the Godfrey Family papers.

38. Floyd Godfrey, "Floyd's Furniture," in "Life Stories," file of undated handwritten stories from the life of Floyd Godfrey, Godfrey Family Papers.

## FIRST TELEVISION IN CARDSTON

One of the first television receptions in Cardston was in the display window of Floyd's Furniture in early October 1954.[39] Floyd cleared the window next to the Mayfair Theater and placed a small, black-and-white, twenty-one-inch receiver in the display, next to a water bucket for the rain dripping from the ceiling. The signal was coming from CHCT-TV Calgary, the first station on the air in Alberta. The Floyd's Furniture antenna was extended and pointed north in hopes the signal would reach 145 miles to the south. Floyd turned on the set and checked the screen. What he saw was "snow," matching the light flakes falling outside the window. He carefully worked the dials, tuning the signal. A ghost of an image appeared through the screen's snow. He twisted the dials some more as his family and onlookers watched patiently and expectantly, becoming excited at even the slightest outline of an image. A fuzzy image and muffled sound was the best they got, but it would not be long before stations appeared in Lethbridge, and Floyd, his children, and other Cardston families were watching Disney's nature movies and wrestling matches from the Maple Leaf Gardens in Toronto. A few years later, color was added by placing a clear sheet of special plastic over the screen. As the light passed through the filter, red, green, and blue colors appeared to give a vividness to the images. It was soon replaced by the real thing.

## FAMILY AND YOUNG EMPLOYEES

Floyd's Furniture was about more than financing a family and supporting employees; it was also about teamwork. Floyd and Clarice used the store to teach their children, to help others, and to come together. They taught by example. Clarice moved furniture when it was necessary, managed the books, and accompanied Floyd on buying trips to Vancouver, Calgary, and Toronto. When Floyd was asked to perform

---

39. Floyd's Furniture and Sunshine Industries were the first to have television receivers for sale in the area. Sunshine Industries was owned by Wilburn Van Orman, who owned a store along the Waterton Highway selling propane, appliances, and garage service.

Church or community service during store hours, she was at the store managing operations.

Lorin was younger and missed the Texaco Gas Station experiences of cleaning washrooms, but in his youth he delivered the daily *Lethbridge Herald* and eventually worked in the store longer than any other sibling. On his paper route one day, Lorin got caught in a dust storm so dark that he got lost. The dust was blinding, so he hid among the trees near his school. After a brief prayer, he heard someone calling, "Lorin, Lorin," and knew it was his dad, who had left the store to find his son. They waited out the storm and delivered the remaining papers together. Later, they dusted the furniture together.

Dust brought by the wind could always be found on top of the furniture. If there was no obviously pressing work, Lorin was taught to find something and keep busy—which in a furniture store always meant dusting. If the furniture was dust free, Floyd and a helper would rearrange the furniture, creating new window displays and presentation groupings around the floor of the store. Every one of Floyd and Clarice's children worked alongside their parents, learning work standards, honesty, ethics, service, and money management. In their younger years, the children had worked together at home and in the gardens just as their parents had done. At Floyd's Furniture there was the constant need to help with new displays, new arrangements in the windows, deliveries to and from the store, daily sweeps of both the floors and the sidewalk, and daily dusts of the furniture. At times it wasn't only Floyd's children that helped; he hired young men preparing for and returning from missions. Floyd's Furniture did more than put food on the table; it taught principles of living by example and experience. In 1949, Lorin was anxious to attend the first national Canadian scout jamboree in Ottawa, but he had no way of paying for it on his own. His dad offered to pay $100 ($986) toward this trip if Lorin would help unload a rail car full of furniture, which he did with his mother's and father's help. His earnings from carting furniture more than paid for his train ride.

Every young man employed by Floyd learned to work. Floyd hired a number of young men over the years: Brent Nielson, Robert Stringham,

Alvin Hatch, Dale Tagg, Lynn Sommerfelt, and each of his four sons. He treated them all like extended family. Dale and Lynn stayed longer than others, and Floyd trusted them with the store when he traveled. More than needing help at the store, Floyd enjoyed watching each young man grow. One day, Lynn came into the store and found blood on the floor. Startled, he asked what had happened. An embarrassed Floyd told him, "Never mind," and after Lynn had cleaned up the mess, Floyd admitted he was stapling a thick, clear plastic over the leaking skylights and had accidentally stapled his finger to the ceiling. Lynn "didn't dare laugh because he needed the job."[40]

Floyd reinforced the idea of making the best of your blessings in any situation. While carpeting the temple on one occasion, he cut the carpet incorrectly. Thus, Clarice was blessed with new carpet to cover the hardwood floors in her front room and dining room, and a new piece of matching carpet was ordered for the temple. Carpet laying was on-your-knees labor from start to finish, whether the laborers were in the temple, a chapel, or a home. Nothing went to waste, and making the best of your blessings was the standard.

The carpet incident was not the first time Clarice benefitted from store sales. She loved to host neighborhood club parties. Following these gatherings, a lady in attendance would frequently appear the next day in Floyd's Furniture wanting "something like Clarice had in her front room." At this point, that *something* would disappear from Clarice's home and she would visit the store feigning aggravation and pick out another. One time her new kitchen table even disappeared and her old, wooden, drop-leaf table sat in its place. She was not happy, but it was replaced. Clarice's home was a showroom, always full of the newest and the best furniture.

Floyd's Furniture employees were taught that work was challenging, rewarding, and fun. When delivering fine hardwood furniture, Floyd always reminded his employees, tongue in cheek, of the value of what they were moving, saying, "Don't scratch the furniture, your fingers will heal." He loved training new carpet installers. They were nor-

---

40. Lynn Sommerfelt to Floyd Godfrey, 13 March 1988, 82nd Birthday Celebration Collection, loose-leaf notebook in the Godfrey Family Papers.

mally assigned to lay the felt (now called padding) or carpet underlay, the depth of which gave the carpet its cushion. In the days of Floyd's Furniture, padding consisted of horsehair pressed into half-inch-thick sheets that was rolled up for transport, just as the carpet was. The sheets were not always smooth. Once this padding was down on the floor, with the carpet on top, a keen eye could identify lumps on the carpet surface. It was the felt layer's responsibility to take a fist-sized rubber hammer and beat the lumps flat. The start of the hammering was the cue for a friend, usually the lady of the house, to appear frantically yelling, "My canary, my canary, I've lost my canary . . . have you seen my canary?" At this point the entire crew, all in on the joke, looked over at the new hire, his rubber hammer frozen in midair. After the appropriate panic level registered on the unsuspecting worker's face, the entire crew and the lady of the house burst out laughing. The workers in training were most often Floyd's sons, a son-in-law, or someone he was trying to teach in his own version of a classroom. They learned and had fun.

**LEARNING BY THE SPIRIT**

One time, a teenage son walked hurriedly through the noisy back door of Floyd's Furniture from the display area into the warehouse area, only to see his father Floyd kneeling in the dirt and praying. The son stopped and backed out, quietly closing the squeaky storage-room door. Nothing was ever said, but the image was powerful. Many times Floyd "knelt in the back of the store" and poured out his heart.[41]

When his son Lorin was on his mission in South Africa, there came a month when Floyd and Clarice had no money. They had managed to get funds for earlier months, but this month they had nothing. Sales were insufficient, and it was two weeks before the mission payment was due. They were supposed to send the money early so it would arrive in Africa by the end of the month. They fasted and prayed for several days, but the deadline came and no money arrived. "It was a Monday

---

41. Floyd Godfrey, oral history.

morning and we waited in despair." Floyd had called on his outstanding accounts, people to whom he had sold furniture and trusted their credit. He had pushed for new sales, all to no avail. They did not know what to do, except trust in the Lord. As if on cue a fellow walked into the store that morning, "Floyd, I am ashamed of myself. . . . I've owed you this bill for four months." He gave Floyd the cash and then he and Clarice went immediately to the bank and the funds were off to South Africa that same day. The Lord had answered their prayers.[42]

## CHRISTMAS AT FLOYD'S FURNITURE AND HOME

Christmas was a special season at Floyd's Furniture, because it was busy and Floyd loved Christmas. He exemplified the principle of service, always cautioning against wants versus needs, and, of course, he taught the true meaning of the holiday at home and in his store. He would go to any length to bring Christmas to his family, his neighbors, and his store. Every year, Clarice spent the autumn months preparing Christmas candies, cakes, and puddings. Even the fruit cakes were savored. Most memorable were her homemade breads, rolls, cinnamon buns, chocolate candies, and English toffee. It was difficult for her to stay ahead of her kids, who would eat the candy out of the freezer as fast as she could make it. Floyd and his grandson Roy were playing pool in the basement, aware that Clarice had just placed some Christmas chocolates in the freezer. They knew it was strictly off limits, but they snuck upstairs to see if they could snatch a couple without her noticing. After they had eaten the first few without getting caught, they were trapped and got a stern lecture from Clarice as she turned her back to them and walked away with a smile.

The store was adorned with the spirit, smell, and excitement of the season. None of his children thought much of the extra sealed boxes sitting in the back of the warehouse that were loaded into the delivery truck on Christmas Eve. If asked about the boxes, Floyd would simply

---

42. Floyd Godfrey, oral history, 48–49.

suggest he had another delivery he had to make a little later. The store helped out Santa, delivering to family and customers.

Floyd knew his own daughters were Christmas snoopers. More often than not, the charge fell on Arlene, the oldest daughter. She liked poking around her presents and queried her brothers and sisters for hints. Unknowing little brothers were always more than happy to play along with the game until she figured out what gifts she was getting. One year, while Arlene and Marilyn were in their teens, a big parcel arrived addressed to them, "in care of Floyd's Furniture." It was from one of Floyd's eastern Canadian distributers and was labeled "do not open until Christmas." It had official manufacturing labels and was delivered by the Canadian Pacific Railway to Cardston. A CPR truck delivered it to the house, addressed to both sisters. They could hardly contain themselves. They grilled their father and mother endlessly. They and their friends rattled the long box endlessly, trying to assess its contents. The excitement built as Christmas morning approached. It was the first gift they opened: it was a kitchen broom. Floyd was a practical joker, but it remains uncertain whether the joke about the broom was rightly received. It has, however, produced laughter over the years of its telling. Floyd would frequently appear among the children and rattle the unknown gift contents of a paper bag around Arlene and Marilyn and say, "Oh, you are going to love this." Clarice was the only one to laugh and protecting her daughters responded, "Floyd, cut it out." Floyd was a tease and known as "the biggest kid in town."

The kids decorated the house and the store with colorful streamers and put up Christmas trees. The trees came from either Pole Haven, one of the farmers, or the lot next to Floyd's Furniture. On Christmas morning Floyd was the first one awake, or maybe he never slept. He grabbed pots and pans from the cupboard and went to each bedroom door, banging the pots loudly until all his children were wide awake. The smells of Christmas were already in the air. After presents were opened, Ken's electric train knocked over Arlene's new play cupboard and broke all of her dishes. Memories were not centered on the presents, but on the joys of spending the day together as a family. Relatives and friends arrived and gathered around an L-shaped table for dinner. Games and sharing filled the day and the Christmas dance filled the evening.

Floyd's Furniture's display windows were filled with rocking chairs, and cedar-lined hope chests were positioned near the door. The chairs were of every color and size imaginable. Entering the store, people were immediately hit with the smell of fresh cedar emanating from the hope chests. Every young lady wanted a hope chest so as to store items for her own future home, husband, and family. So Floyd offered a large selection. Christmas was a time of giving, sales, and service.

### CHRISTMAS EVE DELIVERIES

Many a Christmas Eve was spent delivering furniture until midnight. In this manner, whatever was delivered was a surprise for the wife, daughter, or entire family. In the early '60s, there was an extra-ugly Chesterfield that sat right behind the rockers. The colors were not complementary, contemporary, or Christmassy; they were dreary. It seemed this poor piece of furniture would remain in the store forever. The arctic wind was howling, and that meant a snow storm was coming. As one of Floyd's sons entered the warmth of the store that morning, he saw the ugly sofa and said, "Dad, you're going to have to haul that thing to the dump or give it away."[43]

Work was rushed on this day when a gentleman came into the store and sat on the ugly couch and began talking with Floyd. In this small town, everyone knew everyone, and it was generally the ladies who dragged their husbands into the furniture store. This man was alone and obviously intense. Floyd said the fellow was "headed to the city where he thought he'd have a better selection."

The last delivery of the day was done. It was getting colder, and a winter storm was predicted to come in from the north. It was past closing, and the man who had been there in the morning was again sitting on the ugly Chesterfield; this time he was all smiles. His wife was going to get the surprise of her life—a new sofa. Floyd smiled, "We have one

---

43. Donald G. Godfrey, "The Ugliest Chesterfield in the World," in *Seeds, Faith & Family History* (Queen Creek, AZ: Chrisdon Communications, 2013), 24–26.

more delivery, son," he said. "We need to go to Waterton." The gentleman from the morning had purchased the ugliest Chesterfield in the world. "Let's go now so we can get back early." That meant they would get back late, as driving in a blizzard was likely.

The wind howled as the ugly sofa was loaded into the truck. The snow had not yet started to fly, but the wind was picking up. The drive to Waterton, thirty miles west, was not particularly picturesque this day because it was too dark to see the mountains. Waterton is a village on the Canadian side of the border within the Waterton-Glacier International Peace Park. On this run, black clouds covered the stars, and the wind drove snow south over the highway.

As the delivery truck entered Waterton, the snowfall was getting heavy. "Let's hurry," Floyd urged. "We can make it home before the storm drifts over the road." The gentleman's family lived on Wildflower Avenue. The driveway had been cleared, and the snow was piled higher than the truck. The delivery moved quickly, but Floyd's son struggled at first to match the spirit of this little family, who could hardly wait for this ugly thing to be in their home. The excitement in the air completely muted thoughts of the approaching blizzard. In contrast to his son, Floyd had a broad smile on his face, his voice happy. Was it the final sale of this "special" sofa, or just Floyd's love of Christmas? It was likely both.

Then the unexpected occurred. There was something of a transformation. As the sofa was set into place, it became an integral part of one of the most beautiful Christmas scenes in memory. The children were jumping on and off the sofa while the mother sat at one end, near the Christmas tree, with tears streaming down her face. The father's face was radiant. The son thought, "What was the matter with these folks? . . . Couldn't they see this ugly thing?" No, they could not! Floyd carefully placed the gift in their home, exchanged pleasantries with the children, and rushed to put the chains on the truck for the drive back to Cardston. It was a Christmas picture to be remembered, as that ugly Chesterfield became the beautiful centerpiece of a family Christmas in the cold Rocky Mountains. Floyd didn't talk much on the way back. The father's gift of love for his family carried the Christmas spirit into their home. Floyd and his son both saw the transformation that love and joy bring.

Floyd's service was often given quietly. He helped those he could. Max's Fast Freight and the sheriff once went to a Native American woman's home to repossess a kitchen set, table, and chairs for the store.[44] The next day, Floyd and Max Pitcher returned the furnishing to the family's kitchen. Floyd felt she needed the furniture more than he needed the money, so he gave it to her.[45] This was not a common occurrence, but it happened more than once. He silently supported missionaries financially in the field and no one ever knew. People who accidentally discovered such evidence were sworn to secrecy.

There were many small acts of love and kindness. At times, Floyd let the Hutterite boys into the store and they quietly watched the marvel of television. They were not supposed to watch television, but they were so curious that Floyd let them in. He let Hutterite fathers into the store when all they wanted was to measure the fine wood furniture. After carefully making notes, they returned to their colony and made it themselves. He allowed First Nation mothers into the store where they headed to the back room for privacy to sit and nurse their babies or change a diaper. His kindness was silent and came from his heart.

**TOWARD RETIREMENT**

Floyd's Furniture fluctuated over the many years. It grew when crops were plentiful but wavered with the drought, the weather, growing interest rates, competition from the growing cities of Alberta, and the decline in personal banking. However, it served the Cardston district, the community, local business ventures, and the LDS Church in Canada. It trained Floyd and Clarice's children to make their way in the world. It taught others in the community about love and service as well as produced furniture for their homes.

---

44. This is Max Pitcher's Fast Freight, which delivered goods to Calgary from the neighboring cities.

45. Lorin Godfrey, "A Touch of History," July 2008, Floyd and Clarice Godfrey family reunion presentation, Godfrey Family Papers.

Floyd always hoped one of his sons would take over the business he had built. After Ken returned from his mission to France and got married, he worked for the store from 1952 to 1954. Lorin toiled for nearly a decade, from 1955 to 1963. He graduated from BYU and shared his market research that he thought would benefit Floyd's Furniture. Arlene, Marilyn, Donald, and Robert mostly dusted furniture.[46] Ken moved to Utah after a few years, and Lorin spent the longest working with his father. Arlene and Marilyn married local ranchers, and Donald and Robert were the only remaining youngsters at home, but they were not at the age that either could consider taking over the business. The larger communities of Calgary and Lethbridge grew increasingly easier to reach with automobiles, now the mainstay of transportation. It was difficult to stay increasingly competitive and attract new customers.

Floyd always felt if he had amassed greater collateral or could have borrowed more from the beginning, "perhaps $50,000" ($304,501), he could have launched a chain of stores. He sent Ken to Cranbrook with a truckload of furniture and tried to establish Floyd's Furniture in British Columbia. Lorin later explored Red Deer, Alberta, for opportunities. Nothing clicked. These were growing markets, which house multiple furniture retailers today, but the banks were not supportive. He asked each of his sons about taking over the Cardston business, but each headed onto different career paths. They had witnessed the burden of debt and knew the profits could not support multiple families. It was not to be. There simply was limited investment money. Floyd would later explain that he "had many ups and downs, but it was a happy time."[47]

Floyd's Furniture remained a small-town business. It did not make anyone rich, but it provided an income and the cornerstone for multiple

---

46. Ken married A. Naone Mason of Tremonton, Utah, on 27 December 1951; Arlene married Paul D. Payne of Mountain View, Alberta, on 25 January 1951; Marilyn married Eddie J. Ockey of Beazer, Alberta, on 8 September 1956; and Lorin married Ann Van Orman on 28 March 1956.

47. Floyd Godfrey, "Floyd's Furniture," in "Life Stories," file of undated handwritten stories from the life of Floyd Godfrey.

individuals' futures. The buildings were clear of debt and in the later years used as collateral for operational bank loans. The Godfrey home and property were paid in full. The family car and Floyd's Furniture's delivery truck were debt free. Floyd had repaid his father and debtors for their investments and trust in him. Profits were consistent, but a line graph would have shown a roller coaster ride for every year. The best year was 1961, when profits hit $9,404 ($78,823). The worst year followed in 1962 with a profit of only $2,499 ($19,686).[48] In contrast, Floyd's operational debts with the Royal Bank had increased steadily with parallel pressures as competition and interest rates simultaneously grew.

In 1968, Canadian Simpson Sears opened a major store in Lethbridge. Automobiles and trucks had shrunk the travel time between Floyd's small town and the cities. Customers now shopped from Cardston, Lethbridge, and Calgary—only short drives away. Floyd's Furniture found it increasingly difficult to compete. Some years he was just meeting interest payments on the operational loans. He could match or beat city prices for his furniture, but the city stores were lures offering the appearance of greater selection and better pricing. The same merchandise might have been available at Floyd's Furniture, but *perception* was winning the competition. Their effect on small-town business was to squeeze Floyd out. Increasing interest rates on bank loans were a progressively heavier load. Trust and reputation had been replaced by the necessity for collateral and cash.

Floyd was sixty-four and Clarice was sixty-three. Floyd's Furniture had sustained their family for almost twenty-five years. Floyd wanted to serve an LDS mission, which he had been unable to complete in his youth. Floyd's Furniture was a personal, family, and financial success, but he had a difficult decision to make. He consulted his children and his banker, who was also a personal friend. Floyd was six months away from turning sixty-five years of age, the date they had always planned to retire. He decided to sell.

---

48. "Floyd's Furniture Net Earnings, 1948–1970," Godfrey Family Papers.

Lorin was tending the store alone the day two men representing Macleods Hardware entered. They indicated interest in buying one of the Floyd's Furniture buildings. They left for lunch indicating they would return, and Lorin quickly found his father. Floyd was very interested, and the north store building was purchased in 1965. Not long after, Leland Prince negotiated the sale of the second building, and Floyd's Furniture closed on 20 October 1970.[49] It was like selling his heart. Steadying himself, Floyd realized that his heart belonged to his family, his church, and his community. Floyd and Clarice were looking to the future, not the past.

Floyd and Clarice entered the LDS mission home in Hawaii on 8 January 1972. Floyd's first sentence in his mission journal reads, "It is glorious to be here."[50] He and Clarice would later serve as the first mission couple in Taiwan.

---

49. Clarice Card Godfrey to Melva Card Witbeck, 15 October 1970, Godfrey Family Papers.

50. Missionary Journal of Floyd and Clarice Godfrey, 8 January 1972, 1, Godfrey Family Papers.

# SERVICE IN CARDSTON

### CHAPTER 10

The town of Cardston grew from the philosophical service traditions of The Church of Jesus Christ of Latter-day Saints. Dedication to the LDS Church meant dedication and involvement in one's community. Local Church officers served, and still serve, without financial compensation.[1] While believing strongly in the separation of church and state, members were encouraged to be involved in all kinds of government and civic affairs. Even though Cardston and southern Alberta had a limited industrial base, they shipped cattle and crops across Canada and around the world. One of their primary exports became human talent. It spread across Canada and into LDS leadership. Those in the general leadership of the Church from Cardston included N. Eldon Tanner and Hugh B. Brown in the First Presidency; Robert E. Sackley and William R. Walker in the Quorum of Seventy; Elaine Low Jack, Relief Society General President; and Ardeth Greene Kapp, Young Women General President. Cardston's famous citizens, those not associated with the LDS Church, included Herman Linder, Canadian rodeo champion; James Gladston, Canadian senator; George Woolf, jockey of the famous racehorse Seabiscuit; Fay Wray, King Kong movie star; and Rose Marie Reid, fashion designer—just to name a

---

1. Bruce Douglas Porter, "Church of Jesus Christ of Latter-day Saints," in Ludlow, *Encyclopedia of Mormonism*, (New York: Macmillan, 1992), 1:277, 281.

few. Many people from the area served as local mayors, state governors representatives in the House of Parliament and Congress, and presidential cabinet members, as well as in provincial legislative assemblies and courts.² Throughout Church history, members have pledged their time and talents, serving with integrity and honesty and working together for the mutual benefit of their Church, towns, and countries. They were taught to support leadership and each other for the greater good and to not give in to the temptations of ego and notoriety.

Just a few years after Floyd and Clarice Godfrey's marriage, and with two children at home, Floyd was appointed as a volunteer Magrath fireman.³ Later on, he ran in his first Cardston public election for the school board. They then had been married fifteen years, with four school-aged children: Kenneth (17), Arlene (16), Marilyn (12), and Lorin (11), with a fifth child on the way. The family survived through the Great Depression and World War II by moving from Magrath to Cardston in hopes of improved opportunities. Ambitious entrepreneurs, they started their own furniture business. In 1945, Germany surrendered, and the United States dropped atomic bombs over Japan, forcing its surrender. Before all this, the children in the Cardston schools had practiced war drills, had watched the Canadian Air Force planes scramble over their town at night practicing, had participated in food rationing, and had wholeheartedly supported the war efforts. Life would never be the same as it moved from the Great Depression and World War II, but it would improve. It was a time of change and service.

---

2. Porter, "Church of Jesus Christ of Latter-day Saints," *Encyclopedia of Mormonism*, 1:285–86. See also Ernest G. Mardon and Austin A. Mardon, *Alberta Mormon Politicians* (Edmonton: Golden Meteorite Press, 1992), 61–74; G. Homer Durham, *N. Eldon Tanner His Life and Service*, 50–90; Eugene E. Campbell and Richard D. Poll, *Hugh B. Brown: His Life and Thought*, 104–12; Shaw, "Government: Local, Provincial, Federal," in *Chief Mountain Country*, 3:159–86; and Shaw, "Citizens & Celebrities," in *Chief Mountain Country*, 3:229–64.

3. Minutes of the Meeting of the Magrath Town Council, 15 April 1935, Magrath Museum Files.

## CARDSTON SCHOOL DISTRICT

It was February 1944 when Floyd agreed to run for his first elective office. He was campaigning for the school board ballot with Percy C. Gregson, Brigham Y. Low, and Lyman M. Rasmussen.[4] Their campaign consisted of a few newspaper ads and word of mouth. They promoted a progressive, well-managed, and well-equipped school system cooperating with "parents, students, and taxpayers" with "no untried and expensive experiments." They were a slate of men well known in town, and all four were elected.[5]

The initial Cardston School District had been organized in 1894, shortly after the first pioneers arrived. It came under the rule of the Northwest Territories, and by 1944, the province of Alberta had control. The business of the school board was to draft an inclusion agreement with the St. Mary's Division, giving community schools a greater share in available funds and grants. In other words, the schools of Cardston were in financial difficulty.

Multiple rural schools popping up throughout the region had become a financial drain with a limited tax base. Local ranchers were moving their children into Cardston, where the student population was climbing and broader educational programs were available. Growing families and returning soldiers starting families all stressed the school budgets. It had become difficult for the town to pay its portion of the costs. When Floyd was elected to the school board, Lyman Rasmussen was chairperson. Floyd followed as the next school board chairperson, under which capacity he served for several years.[6]

---

4. Gregson founded the Foodland Grocery in 1940, Low owned a large ranch on Lee's Creek, and Rasmussen was a part owner in the Cardston Trading Company. Shaw, *Chief Mountain Country*, 327, 389–90. See also Shaw, *Chief Mountain Country*, 2:298–99, 426–27.

5. See "Ballots," "Vote," and "Election Results," *Cardston News*, 10 and 14 February 1944, n.p.

6. There are two Lyman Merrill Rasmussens listed in Shaw, *Chief Mountain Country*, 2:426–27. This is likely the son of the pioneers Lyman and Annie. Lyman Sr. passed away on 7 November 1947.

The new board's charge was to merge fifty-three small rural schools out of the St. Mary's River Division and create "nine centralized schools at Cardston, Hillspring, Glenwood, Mountain View, Del Bonita and Magrath." Floyd wrote that this reorganization was controversial and "took many, many long meetings and travel."[7] But with the cooperative representation of John S. Smith, a Cardston resident and financier, Floyd and John took the train to Edmonton to present their case in the provincial capital. Their position was simply that combining rural and town schools would provide a better education at a lower cost. The minister of education and the Alberta premier were supportive of Floyd and John's position. The Cardston schools were consolidated, and "education seemed to bounce ahead." The work of Smith, Godfrey, and Cardston board members remains the conceptual foundation of today's Westwood School Division #74.[8]

### LIONS CLUB AND CHAMBER OF COMMERCE

It was good citizenry that drew people into the public service organizations. By 1946, Floyd was a school board member and would soon become a director of the Cardston Lions Club International, a member of the Rotary Club, and a member of the Chamber of Commerce. The Cardston Lions Club was organized in November 1940 with the motto "We Serve." They promoted citizenship, good government, unification of people in friendship, and service without personal or financial gain. During WWII, the Lions of Cardston raised money for the Red Cross and the War Service Committee. By 1942, the Lions had committed to building a permanent community park along Lee Creek and a swim-

---

7. Shaw, *Chief Mountain Country*, 2:51–52; See also Shaw, *Chief Mountain Country*, 2:58–59; and "School Board," Floyd Godfrey notes and the Cardston Inclusion Agreement, Godfrey Family Papers.

8. Shaw, *Chief Mountain Country*, 2:51. See also "Smith Addresses Home-School Meet," *Lethbridge Herald* (16 March 1948), 5. John S. Smith was a businessman of considerable wealth and influence. He served on the St. Mary's Divisional School Board and later the Cardston School Board for twenty years. Shaw, *Chief Mountain Country*, 2:472–74. See also Floyd Godfrey, oral history, March 1982.

ming pool close to the center of town. Both have stood for more than six decades.⁹

The Cardston Chamber of Commerce was originally known as the Board of Trade. In 1948, the name changed to the Chamber of Commerce to promote trade and economic growth.[10] Floyd's brother Bert was a member of the board when he encouraged Floyd and Clarice's move from Magrath to Cardston. Years later, the new Chamber brought the town merchants together, including Floyd's Furniture, organizing and sponsoring economic development projects. There were blood-donation drives, "Paint Up, Clean Up, Fix Up" campaigns, and ever-present sporting events. Participation in these events attracted attention to the activities and traffic in the stores.[11] Over the years, Floyd's Furniture was listed among the various sponsors. In 1948 and 1953, art exhibits of school, local, and native artists were on display in the front window of Floyd's Furniture.[12] The Cardston 3rd Ward Explorers basketball team, coached by Ken Godfrey, brought home the winning trophy from Idaho. Coach Godfrey reported that the boys had won the sportsmanship trophy as well but were allowed to bring just one home. This basketball trophy too appeared in the window of Floyd's Furniture.[13] Floyd's Furniture, along with all the Main Street merchants, donated what they could to community development.

In 1962, Floyd was succeeded by Lloyd Gregson as president of the Chamber of Commerce, and Floyd became the planner of his most

---

9. Shaw, *Chief Mountain Country*, 2:165–66. See also "Cardston Lions Club Reorganized," *Cardston News*, 1 August 1946, 1.

10. Shaw, *Chief Mountain Country*, 2:118–22.

11. "Wanted: 300 Blood Donors," *Cardston News*, 22 November 1951, 5. This was repeated in the *Cardston News* on 24 July 1952, 6. See also advertisements "Beautify Canada by Beautifying Our Community," *Cardston News*, 20 May 1948, back page; "Art Exhibit," 19 February 1948, 2; and "Art Exhibits Held Here," 5 November 1953, 1; "Explorers Victorious Bring Home Cup," April 1952. In the "Floyd & Clarice Godfrey Family History: News Clippings," Godfrey Family Papers.

12. "Cardston District First Public Art Exhibition," *Cardston News*, 18 February 1948, 2. See also "Art Exhibits To be Held Here," *Cardston News*, 5 November 1953, 2.

13. "Explorers Victorious—Bring Home Cup," *Cardston News*, 3 April 1952, 1. The Explorers were a boys' group within the LDS Mutual Improvement Association.

memorable community service events: "Silver Dollar Days" and "Crazy Days." Gregson was a friend of Floyd's, was the owner of the Foodland, and was later the elder's quorum president in the Cardston Fifth Ward with Bishop Godfrey, so they worked well together. The "Silver Dollar Days" featured seventeen thousand legal tender silver dollars that were shipped to the Cardston Royal Bank. Merchants purchased these silver dollars, and they gave the silver dollars as change during a week of special sales. In a matter of three weeks, the coins were gone. The campaign stimulated business, the result illustrating "how fast money moves around." During "Crazy Days," merchants blacked out their windows and opened stores later than usual, offering discounted screwball sales items, pulling in customers. Men dressed as women, Milton Berle style, and pranced up and down the streets during the Cardston Rodeo Day parades, embarrassing every merchant's teenage son or daughter.[14]

The chamber's efforts saw the official opening of the new main street bridge over Lee's Creek in 1962.[15] South of the business district, it crossed over the creek on the southern leg of Alberta Highway 2 that ran from Grimshaw in northern Alberta and on to Calgary and Cardston, then to the borderline at Carway, Alberta, where it became the historic US Highway 89 south into Montana. It was a small bridge in a small town, but it meant a lot to the community's development along this historic drive. John Diefenbaker, the Canadian prime minister, and Hugh B. Brown, a member of the First Presidency of the Church and former Cardston resident, were invited to the celebration of Cardston's seventy-fifth anniversary in July 1962. Brown's wife, Zina, was one of the first children born in Cardston, and her father was Charles Ora Card.[16] Diefenbaker and the Browns were escorted to the Social Center in a horse-drawn carriage. Seated on the rostrum, Floyd, as president of the Chamber, was to conduct the meeting. He whispered to Brown, who was sitting beside him, "Brother Brown would you speak first?"

---

14. Shaw, *Chief Mountain Country*, 2:120–1.

15. "Scene of Official Bridge Opening," and "Godfrey Heads Temple Chamber," *Cardston News*, 1962, n.p., from "News Clippings," Godfrey Family Papers.

16. Campbell and Poll, *Hugh B. Brown: His Life and Thought*, 247.

Brown responded, "Brother Godfrey, nobody is ahead of the Prime Minister." Floyd immediately recognized the priority of dignitaries and introduced the Prime Minister, declaring that President Brown "set me straight."[17] It was an interesting learning curve for a new civic leader.

**CARDSTON TOWN COUNCIL**

On 24 February 1955, Floyd was nominated for the first time for a seat on the Cardston town council. He was on the slate with Albert Widmer, also running for a council position, and Henry H. Atkins, who was running for mayor.[18] They were up against the incumbents, Mayor Joseph S. Low and his councilors William G. Bennett and Willis A. Pitcher.[19] Both slates offered considerable community experience, and it was predicted to be a close election.[20] Low had served for two years and had been a councilman for eight. The incumbent's push was a continuance "for sound financial and progressive civic government." The competition, on the other hand, were all comparative newcomers. Atkins served on the town council before and was a successful merchant with an interest in public affairs and municipal business. Widmer and Floyd were completely new candidates. As a councilman nominee, Floyd promoted himself as active in the community, with years of service on the school board and as chair of the board. Widmer campaigned as a livewire citizen with experience as proprietor of the Center Service Company. The overall push for the Atkins, Widmer, and Godfrey campaign ticket was a "Vote for Natural Gas."[21] The new slate swept the election. The Cardston voters overwhelmingly wanted the Canadian Western Natural Gas Company as a utility. Now, with a new mayor and council, a significant step began on 17 March 1955,

---

17. Floyd Godfrey, oral history, March 1982, 39–40.
18. "Nominations," *Cardston News*, 24 February 1955, 1.
19. "Vote March 7," *Cardston News*, 3 March 1955, 8.
20. "Interesting and Close Election," *Cardston News*, 24 February 1955, 1.
21. "Vote for Natural Gas," advertisement, *Cardston News*, 24 February 1955, 3. See also "Vote March 7," advertisement, *Cardston News*, 3 March 1955, 8; and "Build Cardston," advertisement, *Cardston News*, 3 March 1955, 3.

when the last reading of the gas franchise bill was read and passed by the town council. Ironically, it was the last act of Mayor Low and the retiring council before the new officers were sworn in. The laying of the gas line between Lethbridge and Cardston began in the spring.[22] Floyd was appointed to the water, sewer, finances, and public welfare committees. He served three terms under Mayors Pitcher (1957–58) and Lyle Holland (1959–60). In 1961, Floyd ran for mayor but was soundly defeated by Robert Dennis Burt (1961–67). "It didn't bother me much. . . . Of course no one ever likes to get beat," but Floyd enjoyed serving. He loved his community.[23] In 1970, Floyd retired, took a hiatus from public service, and sold Floyd's Furniture. A year later, he and Clarice were on their way to Taiwan to serve an LDS mission there in the Republic of China (see chapter 12). Seven years later, he would be convinced to enter the political race again as a candidate for mayor.[24]

**CARDSTON MAYOR**

Nomination day for Cardston was on 19 October 1977. There was a flurry of activity that resulted in eighteen candidates vying for six town council positions and two candidates for mayor. Floyd Godfrey and Robert W. Russell were in the mayoral race.[25]

Russell was a noted physician.[26] He had served three terms on the town council and was a current member. His experience in former town councils had been in the late 1950s. Floyd was seventy-one, retired from twenty-five years in the furniture business and public ser-

---

22. "H. H. Atkins New Cardston Mayor" and "Work on Southern Albert Gas Line to Start This Spring," *Cardston News*, 10 March 1955, 1. The newspaper campaign advertisements are not clear which team—the incumbents or the newcomers—was the stronger supporter for natural gas. However, the newspaper reports cast the natural gas favor to the Atkins, Widmer, and Godfrey ticket.

23. Floyd Godfrey, oral history, March 1982, 39–40.

24. Shaw, *Chief Mountain Country*, 2:105.

25. Al Schindler, "Cardston Election Day, October 19th," *Westwind News*, 28 September 1977, 4.

26. Fred N. Spackman, "The Cardston Clinic," in Shaw, *Chief Mountain Country*, 2:74.

vice. He had recently spent almost two years in Taiwan, the Republic of China. He wanted to keep busy and return basically as a busy volunteer. He was anxious and a little uncertain when asked to run, but he made it "a matter of prayer," after which he moved boldly forward.[27]

Both candidates' platforms expressed concern over water, sewer, taxes, new development, and the debts left by the government's financial grants. The town's airstrip and agricultural facility had been constructed with such project grants to promote employment. However, at times, local autonomy was not always possible. Even when communities satisfied their portion of the grant, they were still "forced to pay interest until the end of the loan term."[28] Floyd's campaign differed only slightly from Russell's, adding desires to expand industry, improve communications, and upgrade the library. Speaking before the Cardston Rotary Club, he stressed the need for economic growth, tourism, job creation, library upgrades, improved communication, and closer relations with Glacier and Waterton parks, Macleod, Pincher Creek, the Native people, and the municipal district. He declared, "My life has been service to this community, Church and individuals. I have no axe to grind. I give you my time and experience."[29] His position was one of creating industry to trigger employment for the town's young people, many of whom moved away reluctantly because there was no work. "If we work together and make the town into a tourist destination, it could really grow," Floyd declared. Elected one of the first full-time mayors, he never passed up an opportunity to beautify the town and preserve its history. He wanted to see the town library expand into a regional center. "We need everyone working on the project," he urged. Perhaps the only significant difference between the two candidates was Russell's promise to "make the time commitment to serve the community," implying time away from his medical practice while Floyd's was

---

27. "LDS Drive Nets Large Voter Turnout," *Church News*, 10 December 1977, 7. See also Floyd Godfrey, oral history, March 1982.

28. "Mayor Concerned Over Government Grants," *Westwind News*, 8 November 1978, 2.

29. Rotary Club Address, October 1977. Draft in Godfrey Family Papers.

to devote "FULL TIME, I have the EXPERIENCE."[30] An interesting photo of both candidates appeared in the *Lethbridge Herald*, with Russell reading a medical file in his clinic and Floyd at home in his easy chair, reading the words of Confucius with a sly grin on his face.

On 26 October 1977, Cardston's turnout "broke all previous records," with virtually 90 percent of voters casting a ballot. Floyd Godfrey was elected to be the eighty-sixth mayor of Cardston.[31] Joining him on the town council were Rhea Jensen, Laurier J. Vadnais, Dale Lowry, Delbert L. Steed, D. Dahl Leavitt, and Lowell Hartley.[32]

The first order of town business was to become acquainted with the work of the prior council, then complete projects in progress with a smooth transition to new leadership. Primary among the ongoing projects were the spiraling costs of the water system and the effects of the new bypass road on tourism. Even before the new council was organized, Floyd reached out to the neighboring communities. He met with their leadership and opened lines of communication. He interviewed each council member, assessing backgrounds and interests for the various committees and assignments. Perhaps one of the most important of Floyd's mayoral leadership qualities was this assessment of his council and their appointments to various project committees, standing committees, and committee chairs. Once appointments were made, Mayor Godfrey let them do the work and got out of the way. He communicated with them, and when reports were turned into the council, he supported the committee recommendations. He did not seek the limelight or credit, and he pushed for progress and resolution.[33]

---

30. "Vote Godfrey for Mayor," advertisement, *Westwind News*, 12 October 1977, 3; emphasis in the advertisement.

31. "Cardston," *Lethbridge Herald*, 19 October 1977, from "Floyd & Clarice Godfrey Family History: News Clippings," Godfrey Family Papers. There is a difference in voter turnout reported between the *Lethbridge Herald*, which reported "nearly 90 percent," and the *Church News*, 10 December 1977, report indicating "an 80 percent voter turnout," 86th year placard in Godfrey Family Papers.

32. "Statement of Officer Presiding at Poll Accounting for Ballots—Town of Cardston," 19 October 1977, copy in Godfrey Family Papers. Al Schindler, "Cardston Election Results," *Westwind News*, 26 October 1977, 3.

33. Rhea Jensen, video history interview, 1996, Godfrey Family Papers.

Floyd Reading Confucius, mayoral campaign photo. Courtesy of Godfrey Family Files.

There were a variety of community activities that demanded the mayor's presence. One was the ribbon-cutting ceremony for the Cardston Mall, which opened the summer after the elections. Dale Tagg, who managed the anchor IGA grocery store, attended the debut. He had once worked at Floyd's Furniture, so there was a strong friendship already existing. The mall featured the IGA, Robinson's Clothing, Doug's Sports, and Topsy Fashion. It was expected to be the center of community shopping. However, plans for expansion were derailed years later with the opening of the Extra Foods store, and consumer traffic moved again. Mayor Godfrey was a strong supporter of "Hire-a-Student" week. It was an employment opportunity matching young people with jobs. The program brought together financial support from the federal, provincial, and local governments to help the youth find work. It linked employers to potential employees and assisted students in the particulars of writing a résumé and landing a job. In 1981, the mayor presented the Cardston Library Board with a Rotary Club check for $3,500 ($8,835), a partial payment of the total $10,000 ($25,244) committed the new library building. Plans for expansion of the library grew exponentially when the mayor and council decided to renovate the old town office building, creating much needed space for a new library.[34] A new town office was built, along with the reconstruction and development of the former community social center. The town council was temporarily housed in the provincial building on south Main Street as construction progressed.

From the beginning, Mayor Godfrey was described as a go-getter. He was actively engaged with every council committee, encouraging and "forwarding the cause of a better Cardston."[35] His communications and "Letters to the Editor" of the *Westwind News* continually encouraged the involvement of the electorate. "Now is the time, Let's do it," he proclaimed. He wanted to repair Cardston homes and purchase property and paint from local merchants. "Let's even out our own economy. Our [Canadian dollar] might be going down, but our determination and working ability is going up. . . . This town has strength, character and beauty. Let's be part of it and do it NOW."[36] A year later, Mayor Godfrey gave a similar message, along with a public report on town council activities, and concluded, "I see a Cardston with people eager to help. We have great youth, let us support them. They are the Cardston of tomorrow."[37] The mayor spoke at the Treaty 7 banquet, emphasizing the need for constructive relationships between Cardston and

---

34. "Cardston Mall Official Opened by Mayor," *Westwind News,* 23 August 1978, 2, 5; see also "Community Support Makes Hire-a-Student Week Success," *Westwind News,* 11 July 1979, 3; "Hire-A-Student Program," *Cardston Chronicle,* 27 May 1980, 1; and "Rotary Club Makes Presentation to Library," *Cardston Chronicle*, 14 October 1980, 1.

35. Gordon Brinkhurst, "New Mayor a Go Getter," *Westwind News* 26 October 1977, 3.

36. Floyd Godfrey, "Letter to the Editor," *Westwind News,* 13 September 1978, 2; emphasis in original.

37. Floyd Godfrey, "Letter to the Editor: To the People of the Town of Cardston," *Westwind News,* 21 February 1979, 12, from "Floyd & Clarice Godfrey Family History: News Clippings."

the Blood Indian Reserve. He stated that "it is only through friendship and being good neighbors that this goal will ever be reached."[38]

Mayor Godfrey traveled extensively throughout Alberta, cementing relationships and bringing new business to the town. With Clarice at his side, he was on the road to Calgary working with Caravan Industries, which had seemed interested in opening a small factory in Cardston. He made trips to Edmonton, where he met with Alberta provincial ministers. During his meetings with the minister of environment, they focused on the controversy over a much-needed sewage treatment plant, as well as erosion of the Lee's Creek waterbed and the Goose Lake Reservoir. In his meeting with the minister of transportation, they focused on the need for road improvements, the Cardston bypass, and possible bus service for the town. In his meeting with the minister of education, they dealt with representation on the local school board. Mayor Godfrey pitched to the minister of finance to acquire assistance in financing a clothing factory for Cardston. Finally, in his meetings with Premier Lockheed, the two men focused on communication and overall government. He attended small-town association meetings working to reach out. "All listened and promised to follow through."[39]

## CONTROVERSIAL POLITICS

No political organization is ever without its issues. Water supply, flood control, and sewer lines were among the early attention-getters in Floyd's administration. A 1979 study of Cardston's key water resource control had landowners in an uproar at the idea that the Goose Lake

---

38. "Chamber of Commerce Treaty 7 Banquet," *Westwind News*, 2 November 1977, 2. Treaty 7 was one of eleven agreements signed between the First Nations people and Queen Victoria. The agreement basically established today's Blood Indian Reserve north of Cardston. See also Alexander Morris, *The Treaties of Canada with the Indians of Manitoba and the North-West Territories* (Toronto: Willing & Williamson, 1880; Toronto: Coles Canadiana, 1971).

39. Journal of Floyd Godfrey, 5–7 June 1979, Godfrey Family Papers.

water reserves on the Lee's Creek basin might be dammed.[40] Those in favor felt it would allow greater flood control and "give the town a greater reservoir capacity." The system that was then in place gave Cardston "only eight weeks of water" in case of drought or a hard frost. The issue was further clouded by opponents who objected to the work of the environmentalists seeking to redirect the creek in efforts to cope with flood control. The council had commissioned a study fifteen months earlier and stated that a report from the engineers would be made public next month.[41] Sensitivity to the environment and the needs of the town kept the search for water at the forefront. The town finally commissioned Stanley Associates Engineering from Lethbridge to study and analyze costs.

The conflict over sewer treatment plants involved examining alternative updated methods of sewage treatment and the selection of a suitable site for the plant itself.[42] There was concern about keeping the citizenry fully informed and about the potential devaluation of property "less than a block away from a residential area." The citizens claimed they had not been informed. The council was hesitant to delay construction due to rising costs. However, there was delay and the plant was relocated.[43]

A new water resource and treatment plant was dedicated in 1978 at the west end of town. It pleased the environmentalists who wanted the Lee's Creek Basin and Goose Lake to be pristine. It held the potential for town growth, providing water for five thousand. The town had room to attract new residents, as its current population of 3,500 residents had been stable over the years.

---

40. "Goose Lake/Lee Creek Basin Planning Study," Town of Cardston, 1979–80, Godfrey Family Papers.

41. Brent Harker, *Lethbridge Herald*, 31 October 1979, 15, from "Floyd & Clarice Godfrey Family History: News Clippings."

42. "Proposal to Town of Cardston for Design Service for New Sewage Treatment Facilities," 5 December 1977, by Underwood McLellen & Associates.

43. Gordon Brinkhurst, "Citizen Irate Over Sewage Plans," *Westwind News*, 6 June 1979, 3.

The sewage treatment plant was christened on the east end of town in undeveloped flat land. Part of this development included the creation of a ballpark watered with treated effluent from the plant.

### FEDERAL GOVERNMENT, CARDSTON, AND THE BLOOD TRIBE

The most significant conflict occurred in July 1980 when Cardston was caught in the middle of the federal government and the Blood Tribe over disputed land agreements. Floyd received a late-night telephone call from local Mounted Police: "Sorry to wake you up at this hour, but we have troubles . . . we need you right away." There had been rumors of a group preparing for a conflict, "but perhaps they had something to say to him and he should listen." The First Nations people's claim was that Cardston was positioned on native land, and they wanted the Mormons out. The listening session escalated, dragged into hours, and then into days of arbitration with police, government officials, and First Nations people. Their tempers were prepared for violence, and the conflict came to a head when Highway 5, the tourist and local route to Waterton National Park and communities west, was blockaded with construction equipment by the tribe. Cardston locals knew their way through town and accessed Highway 5 by skirting the protestors from the road north of the rodeo grounds. The tourists heading to the park, on the other hand, were mystified and were unaware of any detour.

The protest blocked the Esso gas station emblazoned with signs reading "Mormons Go Home," and "You've Taken More Than Enough, White Man." News reporters arrived early on the scene in the morning to film the scene. Mayor Godfrey wondered where they had learned of the dispute so early, asking, "How did they know?"[44] The answer was that the protestors had invited the press. The Royal Canadian Mounted Police were called, and detachments from Cardston and Lethbridge gathered to remove the roadblocks and disperse the crowd. The protesters refused, scuffles broke out, Mounties made arrests,

---

44. Floyd Godfrey Notes & Prose, handwritten notes following the event, untitled and undated, Godfrey Family Papers.

First Nations protest, *Cardston Chronicle*, 29 July 1980. Courtesy of Mayor Floyd Godfrey Files.

and peace was restored.[45] John Munro, federal minister for Indian affairs, met with the Blood Band Council a week later in a closed meeting in Standoff at the headquarters of the tribe, located twenty miles north of Cardston. The Blood Band expressed six concerns: treaties, treatment at the Carway, the US border crossing, treatment in Cardston schools, treatment in hospitals, and the police dogs. Canadian federal authorities and the Cardston town council pointed to the 1883 Treaty 7, which established the reservation borders and noted that the Mormon settlers had not appeared until five years later, in 1887. Mayor Godfrey encouraged law and order in the resolution of the conflict, suggesting to the federal government that "Commitments made by Federal, Provincial or Municipal bodies, as well as those made by the Blood Band, should be honored . . . and would support the Blood Indians request of the Federal Government to have all commitment

---

45. "Tension High Over Weekend in Cardston," *Cardston Chronicle*, 29 July 1980, 1, 3.

made to them honored."⁴⁶ The mayor had executed his due diligence and immediately contacted Church headquarters, resulting in President N. Eldon Tanner sending records and titles that documented the property around Cardston.⁴⁷ He had the proof but did not need to use it. His response stressed that settling controversy needed to be within the boundaries of the law. Mayor Godfrey invited the Blood chief, Shot Both Sides, and members of the Blood Council to meet with the Cardston town council to air their dissatisfaction regarding treatment in schools and hospitals, but there was no reply.⁴⁸ The treatment of border agents was outside local control. A task force was immediately established to gather the facts and help resolve differences of opinion. The goals of the task force were to "generate understanding between all people concerned, provide information relative to education, hospitals and business concerns; and insure the safety, security and Human Rights necessary for the growth and cultural development of all people in this area."⁴⁹

Floyd always felt he had had a good relationship with the Blood Tribe. He seemed to recognize that changing their way of life "to the white man's way of life was very difficult for them" and not always what they wanted.⁵⁰ He knew they had been disadvantaged from the beginning by the American whiskey traders who smuggled alcohol into southern Alberta, long before the Mormons ever immigrated. Floyd found the First Nations people, who had traded at Floyd's Furniture, to be "very good people." He felt like he had friends on the reservation, so he was totally surprised and frightened when his life was threatened during the protests. The Mounties suggested he might want to consider a vacation until the discontent abated.⁵¹

---

46. "Minutes of the Regular Meeting of the Town Council," 29 July 1980, 3.

47. Floyd Godfrey, oral history, March 1982.

48. "Minutes of the Regular Meeting of the Town Council," 12 August 1980, 5. See also "Minister Meets with Bloods" and "Town of Cardston Makes Declaration," *Cardston Chronicle*, 5 August 1980, 1.

49. "Meeting of the Task Force for Indian Affairs," Town of Cardston, 21 August 1980.

50. Floyd Godfrey, oral history, March 1982, 57.

51. Floyd Godfrey, oral history, March 1982, 57.

Dr. Roy Spackman, the medical doctor treating the protestors, responded to the charge of aggressive canine behavior, calling the accusations "radical and misinformed" and created to attract media attention and enlist sympathy. Dr. Spackman reported that contrary to published newspaper reports, "there were no significant injuries" to anyone, and that there had been "no dog bites, no broken bones and no beatings." He called attention to the fact that the "beaten and bruised women on T.V. was a misleading charade of the highest order." The only significant injuries were "to the RCMP [Royal Canadian Mounted Police], and of this, the media has said nothing." He challenged the media to report truth.[52]

As in most media-generated events, the controversy subsided. The concerned parties met in discussion and the press moved on to other events.

### LEGACIES OF THE MAYOR

The real challenges of Mayor Godfrey's service began in placing the right person in the right place. Floyd was happy with his appointments. "They worked hard and long on their projects," and he supported their actions. In the first year, the new water system was completed. The mayor's only concern was the flow of water in dry years and cold winter months. He was concerned that provincial environmentalists, without notifying the town government, had started clearing the Lee's Creek watershed, which was the town's primary water source. After heated discussions, the town decided to monitor the creek and survey the base, which was accomplished "at no cost." Water was considered the town's most valuable commodity. With the cooperation of later authorities, workers were able to bring the erosion of the creek bed under control. The authorities paid for 75 percent of the costs, which included the costs for the Third Avenue Bridge. Roadwork included working on the town bypass, with a parking area for heavy trucks. Workers completed a large parking lot behind the post office. These workers also reinforced

---

52. R. R. Spackman, "Letter to the Editor," *Lethbridge Herald*, republished in the *Cardston Chronicle*, 26 August 1980, 2.

roads along the creek, supporting a part of flood control. Highway 2 improvements through the area facilitated travel between Calgary and Helena. As a part of this project, workers installed new lights along Main Street from the top of the south hill to the top of the north hill—again at no cost to the town. Workers also upgraded the roads to Fort Macleod and Waterton. They also constructed a new swimming pool, and the mayor hoped to see a solar panel on the roof of the building to heat the pool so that it could be utilized in the winter. Floyd envisioned it as part of the school sports curriculum. A revitalized Lions Park created a multiuse park for sports, community, and school. A new campground, patterned after the Glacier and Waterton centers, was opened on the south side of Lee's Creek. Tourism was considered a must, and a tourist hut provided local information for visitors.[53] However, progress on anything new slowed due to accelerating prices.

Mayor Godfrey traveled throughout the province, lobbying for cooperation among Cardston, the Waterton-Glacier International Peace Parks, Fort Macleod, Pincher Creek, and the surrounding area. He pleaded with them, "We sit between two parks and we should try to do something" to take advantage of this location. The council moved the town office to the Provincial Building while the library and the Social Hall were renovated into a new Town Center. He lobbied for small business development.[54]

### FROM TOWN SERVICE TO HOME SERVICE

Mayor Godfrey might have run for another term, but life had other plans. In all of Floyd's community and Church service assignments, his wife, Clarice, had been his ally at home and in his travels. In each of the official photos they were side-by-side, and if one looked closely, he or she could see that the two were holding hands. If Floyd traveled, she went with him, and she was always pleased when visiting dignitaries

---

53. Floyd Godfrey, "Work of a Council," Godfrey Family Papers.

54. "Mayor Report of Activity," 23 March 1979, handwritten text in Godfrey Family Papers.

recognized her, asking, "How are you, Mrs. Godfrey?"[55] When Floyd's obligations took him away from home, she never complained. She was supportive and was always there for Floyd. In fact, she was the inspiration of his life. When Floyd was reluctant to take on an assignment or step forward, she prodded him, saying, "You can do it; . . . you can do it." This encouragement was a key factor in Floyd's activities.[56]

It was following their Taiwan mission and during Floyd's mayoral occupation when Clarice's health began to deteriorate rapidly. She was a lifelong lover of sweets and suffered from high blood pressure and hardening of her arteries. She had undergone several surgeries, all leaving her body weak and in poor health.

Her parents had suffered from dementia. Medical care facilities were unavailable, and her father, George, was sent to what today is called the Centennial Centre for Mental Health and Brain Injury in Panoka, Alberta, for the last years of his life. This was painful for Clarice, who feared that this, too, was her fate. When her mother began to suffer the same symptoms, Floyd and Clarice converted the garage into a small one-bedroom home next door so that Clarice could care for her. It was a challenge, and she loved her mother but feared for herself. As Clarice's health waned, Floyd felt that his primary responsibility was to her. He left public service to care for his wife as she had cared for her parents. Clarice passed away on 16 December 1980.

---

55. Comment from the Alberta premier, in Floyd Godfrey, oral history, March 1982.

56. Floyd Godfrey, oral history, March 1982, 44–47, 64–65.

# CANADIAN GOSPEL SERVICE

CHAPTER 11

The Church of Jesus Christ of Latter-day Saints was built on the bedrock of pioneer service, and service was a part of the lives in both the Card and Godfrey families. Service is synonymous with work, worship, obedience, love, dedication, and sacrifice. People in Church organizations are called in administrative, teaching, and service assignments. At the same time, they continue their employment supporting and sustaining their own families.[1] Many members of the Church today serve one another in a variety of capacities ranging from missionary work, teaching children and young adults, administering the programs of the Church, and donating to fast offerings. Members are taught not just Church service, but community, military, and patriotic service.

Charles Ora Card's mission to Canada lasted sixteen years. The Card Ward was organized 15 June 1887, named the Card Ward on 6 October 1888, and a year later became the Cardston Ward. From 15 June 1887 until 9 June 1895 it was under the jurisdiction of the Cache Valley Utah Stake, which covered a huge territory north of

---

1. Doctrine and Covenants 4:2.

Logan, Utah, to an area in Canada that stretched east to Ontario and west to the Pacific. The Alberta Stake was created in 1895. At the end of World War II, Cardston reported having four wards. The population was swelling as young men returned from the military to farm and start their own families. The Cardston First and Third Wards' congregations met in the tabernacle on the northeast corner of the temple block, and the Second and Fourth Wards met in the Church social center, today's town center, just east of the courthouse.

When Floyd and Clarice Godfrey relocated from Magrath to Cardston, it was the middle of the Great Depression. Cardston was still geographically isolated, with the US border just south, the Blood Indian Reserve immediately north, the Rocky Mountains to the west, and empty prairies to the east. Southern Alberta was no longer open prairie; it was composed of tidy organized settlements dotting land from the foothills. The Depression was taking its toll. Grain previously expected to sell for $1.40 per bushel before the market collapsed would bring less than $0.77 per bushel.[2] By 1932, Waterton Lakes and Glacier National Park had become the Waterton-Glacier International Peace Park, but with the Depression, the number of visitors to Glacier sank from 10,182 before the stock market crash to 2,988 in 1932.[3] In 1930, adding to difficult times, hurricane-force winds destroyed Cardston buildings, trees, and roofs and damaged many homes.[4]

During the Depression, Edward J. Wood, the Alberta Stake president (1903–42), promoted expanding irrigation projects to help out communities.[5] In the 1930s, ranchers and farmers could not sell their cattle or their crops, but their Mormon heritage taught them to work

---

2. Keith Regular, *Neighbours and Networks: The Blood Tribe in Southern Alberta Economy, 1884–1939* (Calgary: University of Calgary Press, 2009), 152.

3. Ray Djuff, *High on a Windy Hill: The Story of the Price of Wales Hotel* (Calgary, Alberta: Rocky Mountain Books, 2009), 103; and Graham A. MacDonald, *Where the Mountains Meet the Prairies: A History of Waterton Country* (Calgary: University of Calgary Press, 2003), 13.

4. Shaw, *Chief Mountain Country*, 2:6.

5. Melvin S. Tagg, "The Life of Edward James Wood, Church Patriot" (master's thesis, Brigham Young University, 1959), 104–5; Shaw, *Chief Mountain Country*, 1:519–20; and Shaw, *Chief Mountain Country*, 3:137.

Cardston Temple and Tabernacle, 1927. Courtesy of Glenbow Museum.

cooperatively; so they did. There were community gardens where people shared, harvested, and bottled produce for the winter months. There was significant fasting and prayer for moisture. They were dependent upon each other, and they leaned on the Lord. Wood followed Charles Ora Card as the Alberta Stake president and later as the Cardston Alberta Temple president. He was a recognized leader of significant influence.[6] "The business world is in great commotion, but here in this sacred soil of the country which the Lord has given us, it will never refuse to yield something to sustain life," he wrote in his journal.[7] His advice was sought by everyone. He told people when to plant, when to harvest, when to buy, and when to sell.

---

6. Tagg, "The Life of Edward James Wood," 131–41.
7. Shaw, *Chief Mountain Country*, 1:520.

Heber J. Matkin, was a bishop when the Godfreys moved to Cardston and was a partner in the Cardston Trading Company.⁸ A spiritual man, he taught that blessings came as individuals lived the gospel, even during the depths of hardships. He taught patience with oneself and compassion for those with whom he served. He taught by the power of love, understanding the value of calm in times of trials. Bishop Matkin asked Floyd to accept a calling in the ward. Floyd responded, regretting that he was behind in his tithing. Matkin encouraged him, "You will do better . . . [when] you pay a full tithing." He and Clarice decided they would do so, and from that time forward, they never were behind, and their "blessings were many."⁹

**TEMPLE SERVICE**

In 1948, Floyd was called as a Cardston Alberta Temple ordinance worker. This meant he would administer the sacred ordinances of the temple and participate in the presentation of the endowment.¹⁰ The temple president, Willard Smith, encouraged Floyd with the kindness of his example and integrity. Smith was a member of one of the Godfreys' neighborhood study groups when he asked Floyd if he would serve. Floyd again expressed concern about his worthiness, to which Smith responded, "Well get yourself worthy because I want you to come." It was the beginning of a lifelong devotion working in the house of the Lord. Lifetime bonds were forged with friends and associates, coupled with the spiritual witnesses that strengthened their marriage and family. Floyd was a dedicated temple worker. He and Clarice attended regularly.

One winter evening, Clarice headed for the temple. It was snowing, and she had forgotten her temple recommend.¹¹ The recom-

---

8. Shaw, *Chief Mountain Country*, 1:405–6.

9. "Men of Greatest Influence," handwritten account in Floyd Godfrey, "Life Stories," Godfrey Family Papers.

10. See Alma P. Burton, "Endowment," in Ludlow, *Encyclopedia of Mormonism*, 2:454–56; and Allen Claire Rozsa, "Temple Ordinances," in Ludlow, *Encyclopedia of Mormonism*, 4:1444–45.

11. For further information about temple recommends, see Robert A. Tucker, "Temple Recommend," in Ludlow, *Encyclopedia of Mormonism*, 4:1446–47.

mend desk worker could not allow her to enter without it. The wind blew the snow around her as she walked home across the street and through the parking lot of the Alberta Stake building. She retrieved her recommend, returned, and entered the temple. She was frustrated with the desk attendant, whom she knew. She never again forgot her recommend.

The Godfrey children were not taught about the temple from sermons or lectures but from what they observed. They always knew it was time to get home when the lights in the room on the top floor of the temple came on. If they hurried, they could beat their parents home.

Floyd served in the Cardston temple for twelve years and was released on 27 January 1960.[12] He knew every part of the endowment dialogue and every ordinance. He expected the same of his children. While taking a son through his second temple experience, Floyd commented to him, "Now you can pay attention." His sons and daughters were listening. Everyone later followed his footsteps and served as temple workers in Cardston and Calgary, Alberta; Ogden and Provo, Utah; Seattle, Washington; Vancouver, British Columbia; and Gilbert and Mesa, Arizona. Collectively, his family served 127 years as temple workers, and several of his descendants are still serving.

### STAKE AND WARD SERVICE

Floyd and Clarice served in the Church all their lives. It was just a part of their lifestyle choices. Floyd worked in executive positions, wishing he could be "just a teacher." Prayer was constant at home and in Church callings. Family prayer meant kneeling together in the morning. Evening prayer was Clarice and Floyd holding hands as they knelt together before bedtime. Fast Sundays were long days of prayer, and the children might have had feelings of starvation.[13] Floyd was on the

---

12. Willard Smith was the second president of the Cardston Alberta Temple between 1945 and 1955. Floyd indicated he served for twelve years, which would make his initial calling in 1948. Letter from Lorin C. Godfrey, 13 October 2014, Godfrey Family Papers.

13. For more information on fasting and fast offerings, see Dawn M. Hills, "Fasting," Isaac C. Ferguson, "Fast Offerings," and Mary Jolley, "Fast and Testimony

Alberta Stake high council and attended regular prayer circle leadership meetings in the temple.[14] There the leaders of the stake prayed together for their community, for individuals, and for rain to water the crops. Perhaps the most important, Floyd also offered silent individual prayers, such as when he knelt on the dirt floor of the warehouse of Floyd's Furniture, or while he was on a long country drive or in the quiet bishop's office before an appointment.

Floyd's first calling in the Alberta Stake was as a member of the priesthood committee.[15] As such, he accompanied John H. Johansson, a high councilor, in touring the various wards on speaking assignments.[16] Floyd enjoyed public speaking even though he felt self-conscious about what he perceived as his limited knowledge. His lessons in dramatics gave his addresses a flair, and his constant love for the scriptures and good books gave him the knowledge. He was called to speak many times throughout his adult life.

As stake superintendent of the Sunday School, Floyd organized the first Sunday School on the Blood Reserve.[17] They held the inaugural meeting in a little cottage on the reserve. The First Nations wives wrapped their little ones in blankets and hung quilts between the corners of the room like hammocks. They would give them a little push and rock the babies back and forth while lessons were taught. At the first meeting ten were in attendance, and the branch continues today.

Superintendent Floyd's assignments facilitated the needs of all the wards in the stake, providing training materials and coordinating the administration of Sunday School and its teachings. He participated in several teacher training courses prescribed by the Church and shared these experiences to those with whom he worked. He enjoyed his Sun-

---

Meeting," in Ludlow, *Encyclopedia of Mormonism*, 2:500–502.

14. For information on prayer circles, see George S. Tate, "Prayer Circle," in Ludlow, *Encyclopedia of Mormonism*, 3:1120–21.

15. For more information about priesthood executive committees, see David C. Bradford, "Priesthood Executive Committee, Stake and Ward," in Ludlow, *Encyclopedia of Mormonism*, 3:1142.

16. Shaw, *Chief Mountain Country*, 1:364–65.

17. The Blood Indian Tribe Reserve is the largest reservation in Canada and is just north of Cardston. See Dempsey, *Mike Mountain Horse: My People the Bloods*, 1–5.

day School assignments because they gave him confidence in working with others.[18]

## CARDSTON THIRD WARD

The Cardston Third Ward was almost four decades in the making. On 14 February 1946, the First and Second Wards were divided, creating the Third and Fourth Wards.[19] At stake conference on 12 May 1946, Alma Orson Wiley was sustained and set apart as the bishop of the Third Ward, Ora LeRoy Nielsen as first counselor, and Floyd Godfrey as second counselor. All three were ordained high priests in the Melchizedek Priesthood and set apart by Joseph Fielding Smith of the Quorum of the Twelve Apostles.[20]

In the Third Ward, the Godfrey family grew. Clarice served as Relief Society president, with Beryl B. Shaw and Gladys C. Hall as counselors.[21] She was on the ward welfare committee, where she directed efforts to care for those in need. Floyd's bishopric responsibilities included working with the young men in the Aaronic Priesthood, managing the choir, and serving as the ward work director to help returning soldiers find employment. In 1949, he became the first counselor in the bishopric. Their eldest son, Kenneth, departed on his mission to France in March 1949. Their next son, Lorin, served as a teenager in his teachers quorum presidency as counselor and later as president. Once he became a priest, he served as the secretary in the

---

18. "Sunday School Board Entertained," *Cardston News*, 23 December 1954, 6; *Cardston News*, 23 June 1955, 4; "Taylorville," *Cardston News*, 21 July 1955, 3; and "Beazer," *Cardston News*, 17 April 1958, 4.

19. Certificate of Ordination, 12 May 1946, Godfrey Family Papers. See also "Cardston Third Ward, 1946," LR 1421-2, Church History Library. There is a discrepancy in dates of the division in the creation of the Third and later Fifth Wards. The first dates indicated February, and the second dates indicated April. All ward data comes from LR 1421-2. The change was likely announced in February and accomplished in April.

20. Floyd Godfrey had been ordained a stake Seventy in the Melchizedek Priesthood by Melvin J. Ballard on 25 August 1935; see Seventies certificate of ordination. Floyd was also ordained a high priest on 12 May 1946; see the second certificate of ordination, Godfrey Family Papers.

21. "Locals," *Cardston News*, 5 September 1946, 8.

priest quorum. Arlene was secretary of the Sunday School. Marilyn was seventeen, and young Donald was only six years old, with Robert still on the horizon.

In these days, sacrament meeting, Sunday School, and priesthood meeting were spread throughout the Sabbath day. Sunday School was the morning service, followed by priesthood, and sacrament meeting was held in the afternoon. The Relief Society, the Primary, and the Mutual Improvement Association meetings were held throughout the week.

### MARTIN HARRIS'S TESTIMONY

Bishop Wiley's goal at sacrament meeting was to produce a feeling of the spirit—a goal that produced memorable events. There were often prayers for rain. There would be a clear, sunny sky when the congregation strolled into the tabernacle and took their seats, but after the service, they exited in the rain.

During his time in the bishopric, Floyd witnessed the testimony of William Glenn, who had known Martin Harris, one of the three witnesses to the Book of Mormon.[22] The Glenn family were onetime neighbors of Martin Harris when the Glenn and Harris families lived in Wellsville, Utah. The Glenns had taken care of Harris during an illness, and they became personal friends. The Glenns then moved to Canada in 1897, and by the late 1940s they were in the Third Ward. The testimony of Brother Glenn was vivid: "I want you brothers and sisters to know that *I heard Martin Harris say that he saw the golden plates*." Harris's testimony of the Book of Mormon appears today as "The Testimony of the Three Witnesses" in the introduction to the Book of Mormon. Years later, Brother Glenn bore his own witness of having heard the words of Harris for himself. Brother Glenn made a direct, declarative statement of what he heard personally from Martin Harris. Those words reached into Floyd's heart, and Glenn's testimony strengthened more than one family's testimony over the generations.

---

22. Near the end of his life, Martin Harris lived in Harrisville, Utah. See "The Testimony of Three Witnesses," Book of Mormon; see also Rhett Stephens James, "Harris, Martin," in Ludlow, *Encyclopedia of Mormonism*, 2:574–76.

The gospel of Jesus Christ and his Church does make a difference in our lives and our testimonies over generations.²³

## ALBERTA STAKE CENTER

Thoughts for a new building to serve as the Alberta Stake Center began surfacing after World War II. The old tabernacle, on the northeast corner of the temple, had served as a meetinghouse and community center for almost forty-two years, but the sandstone foundations were crumbling. The social center had a chapel upstairs, but it was too small to accommodate expansion. A new building was needed and would be constructed just west of the temple. The land was donated by those who lived on it, and Floyd and Clarice provided manual labor in addition to part of their land. The first architectural drawing for the new building looked something like today's modern temples. A crowd gathered for the "Sod Turning Ceremony," but rain delayed the beginning of the excavation.²⁴

In accordance with Church practices at the time, members pitched in with donations and labor, coordinating their time and talents to see the new building finished.²⁵ As the bulldozers cleared land for the parking lot, the two youngest Godfreys, Donald and Robert, ages ten and three respectively, rescued a wild calico cat living in the curls of the rolled soil. They fed, befriended, and adopted the cat and named it "Tic-ity." Robert's young tongue just could not get around the word kitty, so "Tic-ity" stuck. Clarice sewed huge curtains for the stage in the gymnasium, which functioned both as an auditorium and a basketball court. Floyd's Furniture sold chairs used in the classrooms, in the gymnasium, on the stage for talent shows, at weddings, at social gatherings, and at conferences. By 1954 the new chapel was ready, and the old tabernacle sadly came down.

---

23. Floyd Godfrey, oral history, February 1977. See also Shaw, *Chief Mountain Country*, 319–20.

24. "First Sod Turned for Stake and Ward House," *Cardston News*, 7 June 1951, 1.

25. This happened all over the Church until building policies changes and ended the required local budget donations for new buildings.

After nearly seven years in the leadership of the Third Ward bishopric, Bishop Wiley and his counselors, Floyd Godfrey and Vernon Hall, were released on 14 December 1952. Fred N. Spackman was called as the new bishop. Floyd moved into a position with the stake high council under Gordon Brewerton, president of the Alberta Stake. The stake high council were the eyes and ears of the local Church.[26] They supervised, trained, and assisted local ward leaders and watched over their towns. By 1959, Kenneth, who had returned from his mission in France and Switzerland, was the Young Men Mutual Improvement Association president. Lorin, who had returned from his mission in South Africa, became the First Ward Young Men president. Donald was fifteen and was serving in his teachers quorum presidency. During this same time, Robert turned seven.

**CARDSTON FIFTH WARD**

On a 1964 visit to Cardston from Salt Lake, Elder Nathan Eldon Tanner called a meeting of the stake high council to discuss the creation of a new ward. Tanner was a counselor in the First Presidency of the Church and was there to reorganize the Alberta Stake. He called for Floyd Godfrey, interviewed him, and then called him to be the bishop of the Cardston Fifth Ward.[27] The Fifth Ward was organized by dividing the First and Third Wards. It was a powerfully spiritual experience as Floyd realized the responsibilities ahead in organizing a completely new ward.

Floyd Godfrey was ordained and set apart as bishop by Elder Tanner on 26 April 1964.[28] He led the newly created Fifth Ward with Donald G. Shaw and Myron Berry as his counselors. By this time, his children Kenneth, Arlene, Marilyn, and Lorin were married and were

---

26. For more information about stake high councils, see Stan L. Albrecht, "Stake," in Ludlow, *Encyclopedia of Mormonism*, 3:1411–14.

27. Cardston Fifth Ward, "Quarterly Historical Report, June 30, 1964," LR 1421-2, Church History Library. Floyd Godfrey's 1982 oral history is in error as he indicates that Joseph Fielding Smith was the visiting authority.

28. Bishop's Certificate, 19 May 1964, Godfrey Family Papers.

starting families of their own. Kenneth lived in Provo, Utah; Arlene in Mountain View, Alberta; Marilyn in Beazer, Alberta; and Lorin in Cardston, Canada. Donald was on a mission in Florida, and Robert was president of his teachers quorum.

Being new, the Fifth Ward needed total organization. Every ward position from teachers and leadership to youth organizations needed people to take responsibility. Floyd called the Relief Society women and the Melchizedek Priesthood men together. The discussion focused on starting the new ward. No one had any callings, and the ward itself "did not have a cent." Some people suggested that they throw parties to raise operational funds, but one wise elderly gentleman said, "No, we can each donate and give this new ward a start." The checks immediately started coming. The amounts on them ranged from a few dollars to one thousand dollars, and when the donations concluded there were almost $6,000 ($44,485) in the account. From this money, the ward ordered supplies, and the bishopric began assigning callings for people to staff the multiplicity of assignments. People readily accepted different assignments in the Relief Society, priesthood quorums, Primary, Sunday School, and Mutual Improvement Association programs. After the Fifth Ward's first year, the quarterly historical report indicated they had a "very successful period. The ward is well united and [people] willing to serve."[29] Floyd was completely dedicated. He loved the people of the Fifth Ward.

**MENTORING YOUTH**

Not all of a bishop's work is dedicated to administration shuffles. There are more important times when a bishop quietly mentors and advises as directed by the Spirit. A bishop would typically spend a good deal of time with the youth, and the Fifth Ward was no different. The ward leadership organized regular camps and social outings that strengthened the young adults. Some were simple fireside gatherings in members' homes that featured special speakers who engaged the young

---

29. "Quarterly Historical Reports" and "Manuscript History and Reports," Cardston Fifth Ward, LR 1421-2, Church History Library.

people in thought-provoking topics. Others were more elaborate, and the guests may have spoken around the fire during a campout in the mountains.

In 1967, nineteen young men joined Bishop Godfrey and his counselors on a horseback camp out in Waterton Park at Crypt Lake. In the mid-1920s, when Waterton Park's hiking trails were under development, one particular hike was called "Hell Roaring Falls."[30] This is a notorious hike on the eastern shore of the Upper Waterton Lake into the mountains and along high cliff sides. Even today, it is known as one of the Waterton-Glacier International Peace Park's most difficult treks. On this outing one of the horses fell over backwards and counselor Myron Berry, along with his horse, nearly slid down the mountain one thousand feet. It put a scare in the group and prioritized safety for the ride. Memories such as these produced guideposts in the lives of those teenage boys.

The ward navigated through its first five years. There were several conferences, funerals, and meetings. In spring 1967, President Tanner attended stake conference, and this generated record attendance since Tanner was a native of Cardston. Temple assignments and work increased. In the Fifth Ward, Donald Shaw was released as a counselor, and Kenneth D. Holland was sustained by the congregation to replace him.

### SPIRITUAL COUNSEL

Many tasks of a bishop simply require quiet service to those in need. A bishop is a spiritual and ecclesiastical leader, but he also helps provide assistance to those in poverty. The bishop makes assignments to assist the poor, keeping in mind that food and clothing are the greatest needs. The ward organized welfare suppers, from which they donated food. Furthermore, youth fund-raising activities also provided support for anyone in need. Young men were sent on missions, aiding those in

---

30. Djuff, *High on a Windy Hill*, 25. Today, Crypt Lake Trail is one of the most difficult trails in Waterton Lake National Park. See "Crypt Lake Trail: Inside the Park," *Waterton Lakes National Park*, http://mywaterton.ca/do/crypt-lake-trail/wat2d06cc9d678fdc690.

need in addition to proselyting. Generally, the families kept their own missionaries in the field, but if they were unable, support was always found within the ward.

Simple experiences touched Bishop Godfrey's heart and spirit. He tells the story of an elderly gentleman who was watching over a child: "Yes, I know of a man in this ward who waited for a boy two hours, while he [the boy] had the 'ride of his life' on the first [department store] escalator he had ever seen."[31] The boy went up and down the moving staircase, while the grandfatherly gentleman simply waited patiently. Memories and associations such as these built bonds of love and friendship.

Bishops quietly assisted the unselfish mothers and fathers of children who were contending with temptations or struggling at school. Bishop Godfrey's phone number was easily accessible to all young adults in their dating years. If they needed middle-of-the-night counseling or a ride home, they had his number. In those days, they would actually be required to dial a landline number. Names of people seeking the bishop's counsel, along with the counsel given, remained eternally confidential—not even Clarice knew who sought the counsel or what their needs were. Many meetings were personal and sensitive, coming from moments of individual trial. Bishop Godfrey provided spiritual guidance, which prayerfully directed individuals through difficult situations as they "held to the rod."[32] If professional counseling was needed, LDS Social Services provided assistance at the request of the bishop. Most members who called on their bishops were seeking strength to overcome temptations. Perhaps the Spirit had been lost to them, and visiting with the bishop brought its return.

Spiritual experiences are seldom forgotten and are kept quietly in the hearts of all those involved. One day, two parents came to Bishop Godfrey. They had four children and were struggling to make ends meet. Floyd called them "John" and "Mary" for the sake of confidentiality.

---

31. Floyd Godfrey, "Notes on 'T'—Talk Preparation," handwritten notes in three-ringed notebook, Godfrey Family Papers.

32. See 1 Nephi 8.

John was born and raised on a farm of the prairie provinces. He was a hardworking farmer who was taught to milk the cows in the morning before breakfast and then wrangle the horses, grease the wagon, and take the cows to pasture. These were the daily chores of farming the prairies. The family was not wealthy. As a boy, John longed for a pair of shoes and overalls, but his father and mother had no money, so he was not dressed like the other kids. He had no schooling, either. His father was rigid and strict, and too many times he vented his feelings onto his suffering child. As a result, there was conflict, but John worked hard under his father's constant pressure.

As John grew into his teenage years, he wanted to go to school, and he attended a one-room prairie schoolhouse, which stood by itself on a distant hill near the farm. As John grew, a beautiful young schoolteacher, Mary, secured a job at the school. She was dark and beautiful, with eyes that sparkled when she smiled. John's secret love for her was kept to himself. He was perhaps a year older than his teacher, but even still, he feared the ridicule of his classmates if they were to discover what was in his heart. The days and weeks passed and school would soon be over. John felt that Mary had feelings for him, too, but never a word was spoken. He wanted to ask her to the annual closing school dance and social. So, with all the courage the young student could muster, he asked Mary for a date—and she accepted.

Mary stayed at the little school for another year. She and John were together constantly. Getting to know one another, Mary mentioned something about her religion. She believed in God, and she expressed a belief that Joseph Smith was a Prophet. At first John was uneasy, but Mary was so honest and sincere that it was not long before he was baptized into The Church of Jesus Christ of Latter-day Saints. They were married and had children.

John and Mary moved to be with Mary's family and others of her belief. They purchased a small home. John found employment, but "not enough for their desires." House payments took most of his regular paychecks. Mary too found a job, but budgets were always tight.

Over time, little quarrels began, and then arguments arose between them. John would worry and Mary would cry. Differences between them grew until love seemed to disappear, replaced by anger. Kind words were replaced with criticism. Unforgettable words were spoken to the point where they decided to seek counsel from Bishop Godfrey.

Mary telephoned Bishop Godfrey, saying, "Bishop, we want to come over to your office *now*!" Floyd walked through the parking lot to his office, which was in the chapel behind his home. He went in and had a quiet word of prayer before the couple arrived. A soft yet persistent knock announced their presence, and they entered. It was obvious Mary had been crying, and John's face was fixed. The first words spoken were those of anger: "Bishop, we want a divorce!" There was a long pause as the couple waited for the bishop's reaction. Floyd surprised himself when he responded, "You fools, do you realize what you are doing to your children? You are teaching your children how to get a divorce." To John he pressed, "How long has it been since you took this woman in your arms and told her how much you love her?" To Mary he said, "How long has it been since you met John at the door after a long day's work and greeted him with a kiss, telling him you loved and appreciated him? Do you treat him like a groom?" And again to John, "Do you treat her like a bride, like you did just a few years ago?" The bishop could feel the anger radiating from the conflict as he said, "You [need] to exchange the anger for love if you want to be happy." The husband broke in, rebuking the counsel, "See, I told you he couldn't do anything about it."

Bishop Godfrey turned to Mary and asked her to tell him her story. Through tears and sobbing the story unfolded. John interrupted several times to assure his side was understood. After another long pause, Bishop Godfrey responded, "Let's pray about it. Would you like to kneel down with us and pray?" The wife responded affirmatively, but the husband retorted, "I will not kneel down!" Bishop Godfrey knelt, then the wife, her husband still standing. Bishop Godfrey prayed first. His own heart aching, he talked to the Lord as if the couple were not in the room. He asked for forgiveness to enter their hearts, for love between them to return, for blessings of love to be upon the children. He asked for their success and for increased budgeting in their lives.

He asked that they be able to talk out their problems. He talked to the Lord about repentance and love, children and unity. As he finished, he asked Mary to pray. Her tear-filled prayer expressed a deep love for her husband and sorrow for what had come between them. When she finished, the bishop again prompted John to pray. "Well, I guess so," he grumbled as he knelt down. Battling against the anger, John put love in its place. His prayer was a plea for help, and he was answered immediately as the Spirit moved him, and he, too, began to shed tears. The spirit returned during Mary and John's prayers. They stood, throwing their arms around each other and the bishop, all crying together, "The Lord has saved a marriage."

They had the foundation. They began planning together and as a family. John was offered a good job in a neighboring province, and the family moved. Several years passed, and Bishop Godfrey unexpectedly met Mary on the street. Her eyes and smile were sparkling with love. She told the bishop that two of their sons were on missions and their daughter was attending Brigham Young University. "Yes, Bishop, there is a reward, but not in dollars and cents, but in the Lord's blessings. . . . The Lord blessed those people . . . just at the right time."[33]

On another, easier counseling occasion, a middle-aged couple asked to see Bishop Godfrey in his office immediately. For those in need, it always needed to happen *now*. There was no postponing the immediacy of one's spiritual needs. The couple had been married for nearly two decades, and by all appearances they had a happy and successful family. They had married in the temple, and both of them had served in prominent ward positions. But for all of those years, they had carried a heavy burden. When they were married, they had lied to their bishop to get a temple recommend when they knew they had not been worthy to enter the temple. Throughout their entire marriage they had always felt guilty. "We want to get rid of this [guilt], how can we do it? . . . We were hypocrites and we want to clear this up with the Lord," they cried through their tears. "Let's kneel down and pray," the bishop suggested. He prayed first, asking the Lord to forgive the couple of their sins and lift their burden. The couple had been worthy in every

---

33. Correspondence from Floyd Godfrey, 2 July 1978; see also Floyd Godfrey, oral history transcripts, February 1977 and March 1982.

way, "doing the best they could" under the pressures of the guilt they felt. "We talked with the Lord really straight," the bishop wrote. Then the wife and husband prayed individually. Their hearts were poured out to the Lord, as they felt so ashamed. They prayed for a long time, but as they tearfully stood following their prayers, they threw their arms around each other. "Phew," the husband belted out. "Bishop, I feel so free!" The wife managed a smile through her own tears. The bishop felt impressed to tell them of the Lord's forgiveness. "I feel this and I know this by the authority that I hold as your bishop, I know the Lord has forgiven you." After all those years of guilt, their burdens had finally been lifted.[34]

This is how it went for Bishop Godfrey. There was a constant flow of organizing and reorganizing the ward callings, collecting and distributing tithes and offerings where needed, and teaching and counseling the youth, all punctuated with experiences of spiritual enlightenment during times of family counseling.

### PRIMARY AND RELIEF SOCIETY SERVICE

A bishop's wife is seldom without responsibilities. On the day Floyd was sustained as the bishop of the Cardston Fifth Ward, he paid tribute to the three main women of his life: his wife, Clarice; his mother, Eva; and his sister, Lottie.[35] Clarice grew up in a family in which she was the oldest living sibling. Her grandfather first settled Cardston, and his wife Zina Young Williams Card was the third Primary president of the settlement.[36] Clarice felt the strength of her heritage and was always active in Church. She witnessed the service brought to others and the power of the priesthood blessings, which came into her childhood home during the Spanish flu pandemic of 1918. She witnessed the quiet, spontaneous service her father offered to friends, neighbors, and especially the elderly. Her dad served without concern for his own finances, his time, or personal rewards.

---

34. Floyd Godfrey, oral history, 20 March 1982.
35. Letter from Eva Kay Harker Copieters, December 2012, Godfrey Family Papers.
36. Alice Crabtree, "Primary of the Alberta Stake," Cardston Museum.

In Church service, Clarice was involved with the Primary children. In her late teens, she taught the youngest children, playing games such as "London Bridge Is Falling Down" and "Drop the Handkerchief." In those days, there were no teaching manuals, so teachers simply taught basic gospel principles interwoven with fun. For a short time, she was the Primary organist, with Lottie Godfrey as music director. She enjoyed spending time with the twelve- to fourteen-year-old girls, who did not go on to the Young Ladies' Mutual Improvement Association (MIA) during those times. She served as the Magrath Ward Primary secretary for several years, spanning her young adulthood and her first seven years of marriage. After she and Floyd moved to Cardston, she remained in the Primary, serving as the stake Bluebird leader. The Bluebirds were a class of young girls. A few years later, she graduated from Primary with them, teaching in the MIA, assigned to the fourteen- to sixteen-year-olds.[37]

Clarice's name first appears in the Alberta Stake Primary history as a primary worker with Clara Coombs Stutz, and she served from 1931 to 1943. In 1953, she was again called as a worker and taught a girls' class, called the Larks, for the next three years. At a 1953 Primary baby show for young mothers and their new babies, Clarice received the Oldest Mother Award. She was forty-six, and her new son, Robert, got a balloon. Two years later, Donald was on the 1955 honor roll for perfect attendance in Primary. He was in the Primary Guides class.[38] From 1956 to 1959, Clarice was a counselor in the Primary presidency.

Clarice served in both teaching and administrative positions in the Primary. As a member of the Stake Primary presidency, she attended Primary conferences in Salt Lake City. There she received training from leaders as new programs were introduced throughout the Church. She mixed with Churchwide Primary leaders and Church authorities such as Sterling W. Sill, Marion D. Hanks, Harold B. Lee, Marion G. Romney, and Church President Joseph Fielding Smith. These were close-

---

37. Clarice Card Godfrey, "My Work in Church Organizations," *Floyd Godfrey Family Newsletter*, November 1993, 6–7.

38. "Primary History: Alberta Stake," Cardston Museum Archives.

quarter conferences, meaning groups met with Church authorities in small sessions, depending upon needs and their Primary responsibilities. Small sessions provided more direct inspiration and direction. Clarice always returned home with notes and newspaper clippings summarizing the events. "The Primary teacher's responsibility is to a child's need"; "Radiate the light"; "A child cannot be touched by light unless a teacher radiates it"; "The children must feel the warmth of the light"; "You radiate what you are and what you think"; "Look to the spirit of the Lord for strength." Enthusiasm, love, and ideas were shared with her classes and her fellow teachers.[39] And just as these devoted Saints would travel to Salt Lake City, several visitors would visit Cardston. When Primary presidencies ventured into Canada, they were hosted by the Godfreys.

Spread over a lifetime, Clarice served thirty years in the service of the Children's Primary Association. The formal award recognized "23 years," but at the bottom of the certificate, Clarice indicates an additional seven years of service.[40]

Clarice served as the Relief Society president in the Cardston Third Ward and as a counselor in the Cardston Fifth Ward Relief Society.[41] These positions forced her out of her comfort zone. As a teacher, she was comfortable with the girls and young women, but as a leader, she was front and center, traveling throughout the Alberta Stake and speaking at ward conferences. She also traveled south to Salt Lake City to learn from Church leadership, then returned to Cardston to report

---

39. Handwritten notes from within the program of the 52nd Annual Conference of the Primary Association of The Church of Jesus Christ of Latter-day Saints, 2–3 April 1958, Salt Lake City, Godfrey Family Papers.

40. "Locals," *Cardston News*, 5 September 1946, 8. See also Primary Association Service Award, presented to Clarice Godfrey, Godfrey Family Papers. The award date is likely 1954. LaVern W. Parmley was the Primary General President at the time. She served from 1951 to 1974. Her second counselor, whose signature also appears on the award, was Florence H. Richard, who served only from 1951 to 1953. See "Appendix 5: General Church Officers, A Chronology," in Ludlow, *Encyclopedia of Mormonism*, 4:1684.

41. "Record of Officers Sustained at the Annual Conference of the Cardston Fifth Ward," 11 May 1969, LR 14221-2, Church History Library. See also "Locals," *Cardston News*, 5 September 1946, 8.

to her ward.[42] She was far more comfortable out of the limelight, but she was a leader when the calls came to her. She wondered how she could ever take the place of some leaders she admired. The counsel returned, "Clarice, you are not, taking anyone's place, you are taking your own." And she said in the Relief Society she experienced "one of the happiest assignments I had been called to do."[43] She was in a new ward, with new sisters all working together.

The Cardston Third Ward Relief Society met in the old Cardston Scout House. In the winter, heat came from an old, smoky furnace in the basement. It filled the building with smoke, and the sisters opened up the windows to clear the air. The walls were dusty and likely had never been washed, so the sisters cleaned the building thoroughly. Clarice almost fainted when she was asked to help prepare a body for a funeral, but she was assisted by friends and was ready for the next occasion. She worked in the Third Ward Relief Society for five years until just before her last son, Robert, was born.

In 1946, with a two-year-old child in tow, she organized the Christmas celebrations for the combined Cardston First and Third Wards. The old tabernacle was decorated as she took charge preparing the party, welcoming the crowd, and conducting the program. At Cardston's celebration of the Relief Society's 106th anniversary, Clarice was mistress of ceremonies and delivered the welcoming speech for this and numerous other occasions.[44] In leadership she was highly visible, but she preferred the unsung accolades as she quietly and confidentially served and assisted families in need.[45]

Clarice did not like being out front, but she did like entertaining. Throughout the years, her and Floyd's home hosted Church groups, firesides, local Rook clubs, the "Lucky 14 Club," reading clubs, and

---

42. "Stake Primary Union Meeting," *Cardston News*, 9 May 1957, 6.

43. Clarice Card Godfrey, "My Work in Church Organizations," *Floyd Godfrey Family Newsletter*, November 1993, 6–7.

44. "Xmas Party Enjoyed," *Cardston News*, 19 December 1946, 2. See also "Celebrates 106 Anniversary," *Cardston News*, 1 April 1948, 3.

45. Correspondence from Arlene J. Godfrey Payne, 12 October 2010, Godfrey Family Papers.

study group meetings.[46] Church groups focused on service and study gatherings, social groups centered on card games, and other clubs focused on showing members' finest sewing skills and knit dresses. Floyd took the children to a movie if the party was for women only.

Church service was a part of both Floyd's and Clarice's lives from their days of young adulthood in Magrath and into their last days at Cardston. They held multiple positions of leadership and honor but were known primarily for their quiet, unfailing service. They would tell you their most significant service was to their family, to the people of the Cardston Third and Fifth Wards, and to their hometown—and soon the people of Taiwan would be included in that group.

---

46. These were all neighborhood clubs and informal gatherings of friends, all of whom were LDS.

# TAIPEI, TAIWAN

### Chapter 12

Floyd and Clarice Godfrey were the first missionary couple from the LDS Church to serve in the Republic of China.[1] An LDS *mission* has several meanings. First, the mission of the Church of Jesus Christ of Latter-day Saints is inviting all to come to Christ. Second, a mission is a designated geographical, ecclesiastical unit of the Church, somewhat akin to a stake where one has not yet been established. Third, a mission is a call to service, issued to individuals, by the First Presidency of the Church and the Church Missionary Department. Today, missionaries serve eighteen to twenty-four months, depending on age, gender, and assignments. Young men, eighteen years of age and older, serve at their own expense, two years in finding, teaching, and providing community service. Young women, nineteen years of age and older, and retired couples, typically serve eighteen months. Generally, married retired couples are assigned to humanitarian service, public relations, family history, Church visitor centers, mission offices, or basic leadership training.[2]

---

1. Floyd and Clarice Godfrey's mission call letters were not among the family papers. Their "Taiwan Mission" release certificate is dated 10 July 1973, Godfrey Family Papers.

2. For more information on missionary work, see Spencer J. Condie, "Missionary, Missionary Life"; Richard O. Cowan, "Missionary Training Centers";

## CALLING AND PREPARATION

Floyd and Clarice were called on a leadership training mission. In September 1971, they were visiting their son Lorin and his young family in Lacombe, Alberta. Before they left Cardston, their former bishop and current stake president, Fred Spackman, had asked them about going on a mission for the Church.[3] They wanted time to think it over, but it did not take them long. Ten days later, when President Spackman telephoned them in Lacombe, they told him they would be happy to accept a mission call. Floyd was particularly anxious, as he had always wanted to serve a mission. He felt like he had missed something by not going as a young man, but young men serving missions was not common at that time. His older brother Bert had gone, but Floyd and his younger brothers, Mervin, Joseph, and Douglas, had not. He and Clarice said, "We were not [going to be] sloughing the Lord's calling."[4] They had put their own sons on missions at great sacrifice and had quietly assisted other young men of Cardston over the years. Now it was their time.

They began preparing and started the process of serving a mission. They scheduled interviews with their bishop and stake president, and then they submitted their mission papers. Like all missionaries, they waited in anticipation for word of their assignment from Church headquarters. They started preparing their home and fiscal affairs for departure to wherever they were to be called. While they waited, there was much work to do. They wondered what they would they do with their Cardston home while they were in the mission field. They would also need to provide head shots for their passports. They needed their

---

Gerald J. Day, "Mission President"; and Dean B. Cleverly, "Missions," in Ludlow, *Encyclopedia of Mormonism*, 2:910–20.

3. Fred Spackman served as bishop of the Cardston Third Ward from 1952 to 1958 and as Alberta Stake president from 1971 to 1980. Floyd refers to him as bishop at the time of their calling because he had once been their bishop, but he was the stake president at this time. Correspondence from Randall P. Spackman to Donald G. Godfrey, 20 December 2014, Godfrey Family Papers.

4. Clarice Card-Godfrey to her sister Melva Card-Witbeck, 27 September 1971, Godfrey Family Papers, hereafter cited as the Godfrey/Witbeck Letters.

immunizations, some of which made Floyd very sick. Floyd sold his small fishing boat, their family car, and the aging Floyd's Furniture truck. They shared their daughter's farm truck as transportation for a few months while they waited. Arrangements were made to rent their home to a lady from Red Deer. And while all of this went on, Christmas was almost upon them.

**WHERE IS TAIWAN?**

On 12 October 1971, they received their call from President Joseph Fielding Smith to serve in the Taiwan Mission.[5] They were to report at the Salt Lake City Mission home on 8 January 1972, after which they would go to the Church College of Hawaii for eight weeks of language training. They were in shock and wondered where Taiwan even was!

They soon learned that Taiwan was a small island off the coast of mainland China. It was about the size of Vancouver Island off the southwest coast of British Columbia. Taiwan was approximately 250 miles long and 90 miles wide, and its population was 15,000,000. By comparison, Vancouver Island was the same length, only 50 miles wide, and had a population of a little more than 759,000 people, with more than half of those people living in the southeastern city of Victoria, BC, the provincial capital. Floyd and Clarice could not imagine they would be headed across the Pacific Ocean to a place so far away. Frightened by the unknown, they declared, "We decided we'd go anyway."[6] They were filled with anticipation, as they would be the first missionary couple to serve in this distant land.

---

5. Correspondence and Instructions, Missionary Committee and President Kenneth J. Orton, Asian-Pacific Language Training Mission, 12 October 1971, Godfrey Family Papers.

6. Floyd and Clarice recorded their mission experiences in the "Missionary Journal of Floyd and Clarice Godfrey," in letters they sent to their children, in the Godfrey/Witbeck Letters, and in the Godfrey oral history transcripts of 1977 and 1982. Clarice was the primary journal keeper, but both maintained entries in the same journal, and the authorship is noted via different handwriting styles. All collections come from the Godfrey Family Papers.

## PREPARING FOR DEPARTURE

People full of support, love, and concern began to surround them. Clarice's sister, Melva Card-Witbeck, who lived in Ottawa, worried about the difficulty of the Chinese language, the presence of the lingering Cold War, and the threat of communism. She also feared for their safety, with them being so close to mainland communist China. Clarice assured her that the Church would evacuate the missionaries in any emergency, and regarding learning the language she responded, "Our 7th Article of Faith says, 'We believe in the gift of tongues' . . . and we know this blessing we will surely need." [7] Suddenly, they had local speaking engagements in the Magrath and Cardston wards. On the second Sunday in December 1971, they were set apart by President Spackman, and their farewell sacrament meeting took place the day after Christmas on 26 December. After the meeting, a few friends gathered at their home for supper. A little lady from the old Cardston Fifth Ward approached Floyd, saying, "I want you to have this, Bishop." She sheepishly put a folded bill in his hand. Upon receiving this, Floyd remembered, "You know, she had folded a one-dollar bill about twenty times. It was no bigger than a dime and she put it in the palm of my hand." She could not afford a gift, but Floyd graciously received this one dollar as a cherished contribution. The overall financial support for their mission came from their retirement savings, which they acquired through help from their children and extended family, as well as from the sale of Floyd's Furniture.

### TRAGEDY STRIKES

Tragedies suddenly struck simultaneously that winter as Floyd and Clarice prepared to leave. A fourteen-year-old son of a friend, Olive Greninger, died in a tragic accident that resulted from children filling balloons with gasoline, one of which ignited when the balloon dropped from the child's hands. On 12 December, Rulon Harker, Floyd's brother-in-law, was attacked and murdered by an intruder who had broken

---

7. Godfrey/Witbeck Letters, 26 October 1971, Godfrey Family Papers.

into Rulon and Lottie's home in Magrath. The crazy interloper beat Rulon to death and left Lottie unconscious, thinking she too was dead. Lottie was rushed to the hospital. Floyd and Clarice were informed and left immediately for Magrath. They considered postponing their mission, but Lottie encouraged them to move forward. In one of Clarice's letters, she wrote, "It is going to be hard to leave Lottie, but she is planning on our going, which makes it a little easier."[8] They were sixteen days away from their intended departure. Along with all their normal preparations for their own departure, they now had funerals to attend, and their last Christmas in Canada for the next two years was only days ahead. Their house was a flurry of activity, and they were with Lottie every day, up until the moment they left for Salt Lake City.

Amid all of this scurrying, even the weather was uncooperative. There were eight inches of snow, the wind blew, and the temperature was negative twenty degrees Fahrenheit. The Hawaii Missionary Training Center almost sounded like a paradise, and in Taiwan it did not snow, except in the high mountains.

### MEETINGS WITH CHURCH AUTHORITIES

The first leg of their mission was to the Salt Lake City Mission home. Lorin took them to the airport in Calgary, and their son Kenneth picked them up in Salt Lake. Floyd and Clarice spent ten days visiting with Church authorities and getting instructions and counsel. They expressed their concerns to President N. Eldon Tanner about leaving Floyd's sister, and he assured them that all would be well at home. He encouraged them forward: "Why worry about the language?" he advised. "You are just young people and will have no problems." President Tanner was seventy-four at the time, and Floyd and Clarice were in their mid-sixties.[9] They knew President Tanner from his years in Cardston and throughout Alberta, so these were warm, loving sessions.

---

8. Godfrey/Witbeck Letters, 19 December 1971, Godfrey Family Papers.

9. Letter from Clarice Card-Godfrey to Lorin Card Godfrey, 6 January 1972, Godfrey Family Papers. See also G. Homer Durham, *N. Eldon Tanner: His Life and Service* (Salt Lake City: Deseret Book, 1982), 7–8.

They met the Church missionary committee chair, Ned Winder. As they were the first couple in Taiwan, he again offered special instructions on their responsibilities. They knew Winder, too, as he was the Florida Mission president during the time their son Donald served under him. They took time to attend the Ogden Temple, which had just been dedicated, and visited Clarice's aunts—Zina Card-Brown, Mary Christensen, and Lavinia Shurtliff—along with old friends Jay and Ada Cahoon; all welcomed the visits.[10]

In Salt Lake, family and friends came out en masse to exchange love before they departed for Hawaii on 8 January 1972. Their son Kenneth and his wife, Naone, took them to the airport along with their daughter, Patti. Floyd's brother Mervin, his wife, Velma, and even his sister Lottie Godfrey-Harker and friends all saw them off. Their good-byes were sad yet exciting. As all missionaries do, they wanted to walk backwards toward the plane, holding on to one last look at the people they loved, waving good-bye as they approached the aircraft.

**HAWAIIAN MISSION TRAINING**

The Mission Training Center in Hawaii was the second leg of their journey toward Taiwan. While at the Language Training Center, they studied Mandarin and lived in an apartment near the BYU–Hawaii campus. Putting first things first, Clarice found a place to get her hair done, so all was well. This was the continuance of a lifetime ritual that made her feel comfortable.

Hawaii was a drastic change from the Alberta winter. "This is a land of paradise," Clarice wrote.[11] At the MTC, a rigorous training schedule consumed their time. After they were up at 6:30 a.m., they ate breakfast, and the first study class began at 7:30 a.m. Their days were full of reading the scriptures in Mandarin, multiple language training classes, lunch hour at 11:30 a.m., and then back to class. Dinner was served at 5:30 p.m., after which they heard gospel lectures and more

---

10. Mary Christensen and Lavinia Shurtliff were George Card's stepsisters by Charles Ora Card's fourth wife, Lavinia Clark Rigby-Card.

11. Godfrey/Witbeck Letters, 14 January 1972.

language training pressed them until the 10 p.m. bedtime. "I thought at times [in my life], I was busy and had a hard time keeping up some days," Clarice remembered, "but I didn't know what 'busy' meant until we came here."[12]

Floyd and Clarice had not been in school since they were teenagers, so the scheduled rigors of the missionary training center were a challenge. During their first Friday in class, one of the leaders handed them a written gospel testimony in Mandarin, and told them there was a Chinese testimony meeting on Sunday and everyone was expected to stand and give their testimony in the language of the country where they were headed. To them this was a little like "handing a grade one beginner, a high school paper and saying memorize this," but the teachers tutored them and "tried to cram it into us."[13] They were the first senior couple at the mission training center that the Chinese instructors taught. The trainers usually had a primary focus on the young men and women. "Faster, faster and faster" the Chinese words came at them. "How could I learn? I can never remember, my head, it aches," Floyd cried. Then he remembered one word, "Hau," meaning "good." "That's it!" the instructor said. "My eyes light up. A smile comes to my face."[14] Their vocabulary grew one word at a time.

As their training progressed, Floyd and Clarice were separated from the two young missionaries also headed for Taiwan. The pressures eased somewhat as they worked at their own pace and focused on conversational Chinese. Their mission records are jam-packed with notebooks and study notes—words in English appearing in parallel columns with Mandarin interpretations, line their notebook pages.

It was a difficult two months, particularly for Clarice, as they struggled to learn the language, but they succeeded. The language came slowly, and by the time they left Hawaii, their vocabulary and

---

12. Godfrey/Witbeck Letters, 14 February 1972. See also Clarice Card-Godfrey to Lorin Godfrey, 22 January 1972.

13. Clarice Card-Godfrey to Lorin Card Godfrey, 22 January 1972. See also Mission Journal, 13 January 1972, 2.

14. Floyd Godfrey, "Jun Guo Haw," in *Just Mine* (Mesa, AZ: Chrisdon Communication, 1996), 41.

their confidence was growing; they were beginning to read, understand, and pronounce the words correctly. Clarice was always timid about expressing herself, even in English, but throughout their mission if Floyd needed a Chinese word, she always had it for him.

Their studies were punctuated with a few visitors and recreational breaks. Floyd's brother Douglas and his wife, Yolanda, and friends Bryant and Ruby Stringham and Alan and Lorna Van Orman, from Cardston, were holidaying in Hawaii. They enjoyed the Laie Hawaii Temple, the Polynesian Cultural Center, and the sunrise testimony meetings at the beach. They ventured into Honolulu, where they ate Chinese food and went to a Chinese movie. All these activities provided an enjoyable respite from the rigors of study.[15] In the Hawaiian Language Training Center they experienced love unheralded. Their teachers always went the extra mile. The young missionaries inspired them with the desire to continue. "The L. T. M. [Language Training Mission] was a training ground for spirit, body, and mind."[16]

### ARRIVING IN TAIWAN

The final leg of their preparations began 11 March as they departed Laie, Hawaii. This time, new friends and associates gathered to see them off at the Honolulu International Airport with more tears at parting. The plane was late leaving Hawaii because of a bomb threat. It had to be searched thoroughly before the passengers were allowed aboard. Finally, the plane was ready for the nine-hour flight to Tokyo, Japan, where there was a layover for the evening. Floyd and Clarice slept well at the Paradise Hotel. They boarded the last plane the next morning at 6:15 a.m. Three hours later they were on the ground in Taiwan!

---

15. The Laie Hawaii Temple opened in 1919, and the Polynesian Cultural Center opened in 1963. See Lanier R. Britsch, "Moramona: The Mormons in Hawaii," in *Mormons in the Pacific* (Laie, HI: Institute for Polynesian Studies, 1991).

16. Draft correspondence from Floyd Godfrey to Stoddard, n.d., from Church College of Hawaii Workbook, Godfrey Family Papers. Full names of individuals are provided where possible, but in keeping with missionary tradition, "Brother and Sister" is what appears, with few full names provided.

For a few moments, Floyd and Clarice thought they had landed with arriving royalty on the plane, but no, the airport celebration was for them. A large group of Church members and missionaries gathered for the welcome. There was a large three-by-twenty-foot banner waving, which read, "Welcome Missionaries." Photos were taken, and Clarice was given a dozen American Beauty roses, warming her heart from the start. She loved roses. The Taiwanese press was even in attendance. Their new mission president, Malan R. Jackson, and his wife, Linda, had orchestrated a warm welcome. After the celebrations ended and the group dispersed, Floyd and Clarice went to the mission home, where they stayed for a few days and prepared for their first assignment in Taichung, the Central Zone in the capital district of the mission.

Clarice found a beauty shop and hair parlor that was within walking distance of their home. When Sister Jackson visited, they went together, and if Clarice looked too much like Phillis Diller, Sister Jackson would comb her hair out for her "with half the population of the village watching the procedure," including President Jackson, Floyd, and the sister missionaries. By the end of their mission, the beautician had been schooled in the fine arts of Clarice's hair.[17]

### TAICHUNG, TAIWAN, HOME CENTRAL

Their new home was in the city center of Taichung. They lived at Tai Ping Lu #8-1, just three blocks from the elegant historic Taichung Memorial Temple.[18] Their home was small, accessed through a large gate out in the front yard. The gate was closed at night, but otherwise it was generally open. It had one bedroom, a "toilet room" with a tub, a small study, and a front room. Setting up housekeeping was the first challenge. The house needed a serious cleaning. Elders had previously lived in the home, and it took a week with lots of scrubbing to bring it up to Clarice's standards. The toilet room was scrubbed multiple times by missionaries, and even President Jackson pitched in physical work.

---

17. Clarice Godfrey, Missionary Journal, n.d.

18. "Brief Story of the Taichung Memorial Temple," 260, Li Shing Road, Taichung. Tourist pamphlet describing the temple, Godfrey Family Papers.

Taiwan Chapel, Floyd and Clarice, 1973. Courtesy of Godfrey Family Files.

Floors were mopped and waxed. The washing machine, all of thirty inches in diameter, was tested, and it worked. They had a wash pan and a wooden washboard if they wanted to wash their clothes by hand as their parents had done. The gas stove was a two-burner, and since Clarice was used to her modern electric, she cooked up "many burnt offerings," but she learned and no matter how her meals turned out, "the Elders and Sisters were happy to come and share . . . and thought it was a real treat."[19]

Setting up the household furnishings meant shopping. This, too, was a new experience. They could not just go to a department store or Floyd's Furniture and order needed furnishings. Instead, "you hunted in dozens of little stores. . . . These are small and dirty and 'out of our world,' [but they] will make anything you want."[20] Furniture was purchased, and slowly it began to feel like home. The Taiwanese were already reaching out and helping them get settled over the months. Their home became a gathering place. Missionaries, local Church people, Church administrative meetings, and their Saturday English class students all congregated at their apartment. Dinners of every kind were served, and the people were always welcome. Food and counseling were dispensed with every visit. Neighborhood little boys liked to come and play ball on their lawn, as they otherwise had only the street. It is likely Floyd played with them from time to time. He loved baseball.

Floyd and Clarice quickly fell in love with the Taiwanese people, who were so different. The Taiwanese people, too, were equally enthralled with the Canadian couple who brought a different culture and a strange language to their island. Floyd and Clarice were different from the Americans the Taiwanese had met at the US military bases on the island. These missionaries lived among the people. The people were all kind and tolerant as love and understanding grew among them.

Floyd and Clarice's responsibilities in Taichung were ministering to the people in the Taichung Central District. Floyd was set apart as a counselor in the district presidency, working with President Chen

---

19. "Missionary Journal of Floyd and Clarice Godfrey," 12–13. See also Clarice Card-Godfrey to Lorin Godfrey, 21 March 1972.

20. Godfrey/Witbeck Letters, 17 March 1972.

Hsiung Huang.[21] Clarice worked directly with their mission president in the women's organizations and got them properly structured. She trained people in Church procedures and facilitating the work. She even acted as the youth adviser for the girls' camp in the mountains of Taiwan and loved it. They trained in local branch and regional districts. Floyd likened it to the original establishment of the restored Church in the 1800s. The Lord did not give the Prophet Joseph Smith all his training at once. The task of training, "literally the making of a prophet," evolved over time. Faith was developed, foundations were established, obedience was taught along with earnest prayer, and a "sensitivity to things spiritual"[22] was learned. Similarly, the Church members and leaders of Taichung were taught "line upon line," a little at a time.

**TAIWANESE MISSIONARY LIFE**

Floyd and Clarice's first real missionary teaching opportunity came while they were interviewing to hire a maid. A young man knocked at the door wanting to know about the Church. It was their first contact, a referral from President Jackson. They talked, and "when they had just about run out of [all the] words" they could remember, the doorbell rang, and it was two elders who took over the teaching.[23] Two weeks into their experience, they hired a lady named Yu Tai Tai, who worked maintaining their home throughout their mission. She cooked, cleaned, and went to the market for them. She did a little laundry, as did Floyd and Clarice, before they decided to send it out. They were settled into their home and settling into their work.

Work started as they began touring the branches in the district. They spoke at the church meetings, as they were a new curiosity to

---

21. A district is equivalent to a stake, but under the administration of the mission president. Full names of the Taiwanese people are provided where possible, but they did not always appear in the mission journal, oral histories, notebooks, or correspondence.

22. Mission "Note Book," n.d. There are numerous unidentified study notebooks from Floyd and Clarice's mission. This reference appears to be from a yellow-covered notebook which contains Floyd Godfrey's talk drafts on the Restoration of the gospel.

23. Godfrey/Witbeck Letters, 17 March 1972.

the Taiwanese congregations. Floyd and Clarice's vocabularies grew as they interacted freely with both the men and women's organizations, organizing, calling leadership, and training leaders and teachers on how the work of the Church operated. "If they [Taiwanese leaders] would only read their handbook, it would be much easier," they wrote in their journal.[24] Most times, it took an example and quiet mentoring along with the handbook. There was no lack of things to be accomplished. They were always grateful for the patience of the Taiwanese, along with people from the American military branch at the nearby base, who knew a little more of the language and had access to traditional American food, like hamburger.

### ADMINISTERING TO THOSE IN NEED

The people and the land were growing on Floyd and Clarice. Friendships and relationships grew as mutual service was extended. Floyd administered to the sick by pronouncing a priesthood blessing upon the heads of the individuals requesting them.[25] A Sister Yen's son had contracted Yellow Jaundice; his skin and eyes were tinged yellow. Frightened, she asked Floyd if he would administer to her son. She knew Floyd was a high priest, and that gave her the expectation that he had all the experience in the world. Worried about her outlook, Floyd prayed privately for direction. Then, with Clarice and the boy's mother, they went to the hospital. Her son lay in an old unsanitary Taiwanese army hospital cot. "I put my hands on his head and I promised him to get well." He did! And he came home from the hospital.[26]

A healthy son positioned Floyd to provide a little marriage counseling with the boy's parents. The boy's mother had heart trouble,

---

24. "Missionary Journal of Floyd and Clarice Godfrey;" 19–20.

25. Administering to the sick is a practice dating back to Biblical traditions. See James 5:14–15. Today it is accomplished by anointing the head of the individual with a drop of oil, laying one's hands on the head, and offering a prayer in his or her behalf. See Nephi K. Kezerian, "Sick, Blessing the," in Ludlow, *Encyclopedia of Mormonism*, 3:1308–9.

26. Floyd Godfrey, oral history, 1977.

and stress was interfering with her own health. Floyd counseled her husband, reminding him that much depended upon his actions. A strong-willed husband would only increase the pressure on her health, delaying her recovery. Floyd's directions strengthened the couple's relationship, and her health improved dramatically. Sister Yen became a constant in the Godfrey home, always helping Clarice.

On another occasion, a Sister Pan was experiencing difficulty in childbirth. She had been in labor for four days, and her husband called Floyd frantically, "Brother Godfrey, I've got to have you come over and give my wife a blessing, they [the hospital] can't do anything for her." Floyd went immediately. He and Brother Pan prayed together, and Floyd laid hands on Sister Pan's head, giving her a special blessing. Two hours later a beautiful baby was born.

Another challenge they faced was the traditional religious culture of Taiwan. Sister Pan's mother was a strict Buddhist. After the priesthood blessing and birth of her son, her mother had come to their home to help her daughter. Sister Pan did not think her mother would even enter the living room with Floyd, a Christian, present. Yet, Floyd wanted to ask if she would kneel in prayer with them. He walked out of the room, over to the mother and asked. She replied, "No, no, no; . . . she wouldn't come." Gently, Floyd said, "You believe in the great Buddha and we believe in God, maybe *they both* will bless [this family], why don't you come and kneel in prayer [with us]." Finally, the Buddhist grandmother came, and they knelt down together "with we Christians . . . and had a prayer for her daughter and her baby, which was just wonderful." Immediately, Brother Pan, the new father, wanted a blessing. This is the way it went in their mission. Priesthood blessings provided comfort as well as healing. Members came regularly to their home asking for blessings and advice in their callings. These blessings resulted in miracles produced by love, service, and God's will.

### LEADERSHIP TRAINING

Floyd and Clarice were leadership training missionaries. Like the proselyting missionaries, they taught new investigators as the opportunity arose. If someone appeared at their door, generally referred by those at the mission home or from their weekly English class, they taught until their Chinese vocabulary ran out, and at that same moment, the missionaries always seemed to miraculously appear. However, they spent the majority of their time in leadership training at all levels from the district presidency to the children's Primary programs. Floyd was called as a counselor in the Taichung Branch presidency, and Clarice worked directly with the Relief Society, the Young Women, and the children's programs. They represented the mission president in all of these local activities. They worked with individual leaders, mentoring them in the simplest of Church procedures: district presidency, high council, branch presidencies, and auxiliary organization training. Discouraged leaders soon became enthusiastic participators as Floyd and Clarice made the tasks of administration seem less daunting. More than once they wished the people would read the handbook. Nevertheless, Floyd and Clarice taught by example, walking individuals through their assignments, teaching as they walked side by side.

Floyd and Clarice referred to their Taichung home as "Grand Central Station," with the hustle and bustle of people constantly coming and going. There schedules primarily consisted of interviews, district presidency meetings, branch presidency meetings, and additional meetings. Sometimes President Jackson and his wife stayed with Floyd and Clarice, just to get away from their own office and relax for a few days. The Jacksons always left more assignments to be done, whether they were training meetings to educate new leaders; interviews for baptism or for leadership callings; releases from callings; or personal counseling interviews for leaders, missionaries, and members. These were all invited conducted to their home. When the weekly English class lost their library room to reconstruction, they also met in Floyd and Clarice's home.

The Taiwanese people thought highly of Floyd and Clarice. They wanted Floyd's personal blessings, which he often administered in his home. He ventured out to administer to the sick as needed, and they would come back to his home for more. Counseling sessions for people who had challenges in their lives were regular occurrences, along with missionary and district leadership blessings.

If they were not at a meeting at home, they were in conferences and branch meetings throughout the district. Floyd and Clarice spoke and taught on all such occasions. Their lessons and speeches were of basic scriptural teachings, talks written carefully verbatim in case translation was needed. Lessons often focused on Church procedure and leadership training; the speeches focused more on fundamental doctrines of the restored Church. The challenges were often unique. To convert a Buddhist individual to Christianity meant teaching about Christ. Once Christ was accepted, there came the unique understanding that Christ had a Father in Heaven. Finally, a complete understanding of the Holy Ghost and the nature of the Godhead was needed. A concept many American members of the Church take for granted was very new to the Taiwanese.

Floyd and Clarice loved the Taiwanese people. Was their mission all easy? Of course not. One of the significant challenges was cultural adaptation. Chief among these was the important, sometime serious, tradition of *saving face*. To be released from a Church position in the American tradition means that a new calling will likely be coming soon. In the Taiwanese culture, a release left an individual feeling they had lost social status. Good Taiwanese members sometimes left the Church after they had been released, simply to save face. Similarly, auditing Church records for tithes, offerings, and building donations were delicate. If an individual felt they were not trusted, they could lose face. It was an issue throughout every aspect of the Church. One mother was ready to let her daughter die after the daughter became pregnant out of wedlock. The daughter told her mother she was pregnant, and to save face, her mother gave her daughter so many sleeping pills that it put the daughter and her unborn baby in great agony, threatening their lives. Her father rushed her to the hospital. Saving face was a part of the culture and acculturation.[27] With each calling Floyd extended, he stressed an eventual release and the likelihood of

---

27. Clarice Godfrey, Missionary Journal, 30 May 1973.

a new calling. In the Church, it is not where you serve, but how you serve.

The district and branches grew as individuals became involved, one individual, one project, and one family at a time. Floyd and Clarice regularly visited members who had not attended church recently. People were sought out and activated. In doing so, they encouraged them individually, in the gospel, and in marriage and family. They reached out, and people reached back. Floyd and Clarice went into the homes of the humble farmers as well as the affluent business people. They helped clean houses and care for the children as they taught. Boxes of clothing for children and adults were distributed. They helped members find employment, which was not easy because the Buddhist and Catholic employers shunned members after a conversion to the Mormon faith. Individuals and families were always invited to activities. They often held "onto their hearts and their tears" in this most personalized level of service.[28]

Their first Christmas in Taiwan was with the missionaries and young people of the district, filling two hundred bags of candy and cookies for children at the School for the Blind. They had visited the school earlier and were touched as blind children played in an orchestra and performed for them. The school rooms were filled with Braille texts. On the tour, one little boy took Floyd's hand and felt his wedding ring. The child was curious as to what it was on his hand. He kept feeling, holding onto Floyd's hand and his heart. The children gave them a bushel basket full of sweet Mandarin oranges as they left, and the youngsters gathered around the bus, applauding. On Christmas Eve, Floyd and Clarice returned with the missionaries and young people from the branch with bags of goodies. Christmas was a beautiful, clear seventy-four degrees Fahrenheit.

Floyd and Clarice's home was always crowded. Brother Chin Kou Ehen, who owned a local flower shop, kept fresh orchids in their home, and that pleased Clarice. Each time he visited, he brought fresh flowers and potted plants, leaving the inside and outside of their home fresh and

---

28. Clarice Godfrey, Missionary Journal, 1 December 1972.

beautiful. People loved the Godfreys. Clarice noted that "when we walked in, people seemed to almost change, as all put themselves out to shake hands; . . . we seemed to give them a lift."[29]

### BUILDING THE TAICHUNG CHAPEL

One of the highlights of Floyd and Clarice's mission was the completion of the chapel in Taichung. Work had progressed slowly before their arrival, as it was difficult to raise the funds and coordinate construction. President Jackson was upset at the lack of progress and put Floyd in charge. The needs and finances were assessed. A building fund committee was organized, and Floyd encouraged contributions. The missionaries were already donating, but "this chapel should be built by the people who use it," he suggested. The Relief Society was asked to furnish the kitchen, and the Sunday School was asked to supply blackboards and visual aids.[30] Communications throughout the district began immediately; funding was developed, and Floyd took an almost daily taxi ride to the chapel, encouraging the contractors in their progress.

Floyd was given permission to hold the first meeting on Sunday, 26 November 1972 because the building was almost complete. The meeting was a central district conference. They rented chairs, carried them into the church, and set them in the chapel. A piano rented for the meeting was picked up immediately after the service. The priesthood was organized, eighty men were called to the Melchizedek Priesthood and sustained as elders, and a counselor in the district presidency and an elders quorum president were called and sustained. The Relief Society, Mutual Improvement Association, and Primary were all completely organized for the first time! It was crowded, but "never has there been a finer spirit in a meeting." President Jackson attributed the success of the

---

29. Clarice Godfrey, Missionary Journal, 16 February 1973.

30. Assessment from Floyd Godfrey to the mission office, 4 January 1973, Godfrey Family Papers.

Taiwan School for the Blind, 1972. Courtesy of Floyd Godfrey Mission Photos.

building and branch organization to the work of Elder and Sister Floyd and Clarice Godfrey. The Church in Taiwan was growing!³¹

## KE-LIAO CONGREGATION JOINS THE CHURCH

A rare and memorable experience in the mission field occurred toward the end of the year. On 19 November 1972, President Jackson was invited to the town of Ke-Liao by Wang, a Protestant minister, to speak to his congregation. Wang had felt a need for religion in his village and had, some ten years earlier, founded a new church utilizing the Bible as his guide. He taught the basic elements of Christian brotherhood, baptism by immersion, and tithing. He was now wanting to sell his land and church building to the LDS Church.

The reason quickly became apparent. He knew about the Church because his daughter, just fifteen years old, had been taught the gospel and wanted to be baptized. The young lady had met the Mormon

---

31. Floyd Godfrey, Missionary Journal, 27 November 1972.

elders on the street of Koashuing where they were passing out invitation cards for a branch open house. The elders noticed the shy youngster as she ran up, grabbed a card, and ran away. She kept coming back, and finally the elders were able to make contact and teach her the gospel. At first, her parents refused to let her be baptized, but she persisted. After several attempts, she was discouraged. The elders suggested the three of them have a special fast with prayers in her behalf. When the girl returned to her parent's small town, she discovered that her parents had recently committed to baptism and, of course, gave their daughter permission. Her prayer was answered, but that is not the end of the story.[32]

Reverend Wang had been impressed with the lifestyle changes his daughter had made as she associated with the Church. So when other churches expressed an interest in purchasing his property, he wanted The Church of Jesus Christ of Latter-day Saints to take over. He had a congregation of nearly 170 people. In November, President Jackson spoke to the faithful, about eighty in attendance. He taught the fundamentals of the gospel and felt they had been favorably received.

After his first meeting with Reverend Wang, Jackson returned to mission headquarters and immediately contacted Church headquarters in Salt Lake City, recommending to the missionary department that the little church and property be purchased. Several trips were made from Taipei to the village. On 28 March, Jackson received approval and the funds.

On 1 April 1973, at the close of the Protestant Church meeting with eighty of the congregation in attendance, the minister stood and announced, "I am going to be baptized into the Mormon Church this next Saturday. How many of you are coming with me?" Then Wang addressed the group, "We were all baptized this same way, but now I know I had no authority to do the baptizing."[33] Fifty followed him and were baptized. His daughter was baptized first. A new branch was organized. A teenage girl had set the example. The new missionary

---

32. Clarice Godfrey, Missionary Journal, 9 April 1973.

33. Clarice Godfrey, Missionary Journal, 9 April 1973. See also Clarice Card Godfrey to Lorin Godfrey, 13 April 1973, Godfrey Family Papers.

couple to serve in this branch were the second couple to come to Taiwan—Jack and Iona Mendenhall, friends of the Godfreys.³⁴

## THE TAIWANESE PEOPLE

Floyd and Clarice saw the Taiwan people as a hustling and bustling culture with motorbikes speeding down the roads, sometimes hauling a family of four all on one bike. Taiwan was a land with high mountains, lush forests, and rolling western plains that were full of rice paddies, water buffalo, and fruit orchards. Cities to the north were industrial and drove the national economy. The Taiwanese were a determined people, hungry for education and always inquiring about other countries. Masses of children crossed the roads walking to the schools, stopping all traffic. They were hardworking students, well-dressed, groomed, and ambitious—all under the watchful eye of their parents. The Chinese from the mainland spoke Mandarin and were usually the business people. The native Taiwanese worked manual labor and lived in both the cities and countryside. Craftsmen carved camphor wood, teak wood, marble, and jade.³⁵ Using only nimble fingers, a scythe, a sharp knife, and a brush, they passed down the art of carving through centuries. Today these smaller items are sold to the tourists. Carvings adorned all the furniture. They were clever and keen in their business dealings, but the desire was for life and family, not for the accumulation of money. "They bartered more for the pleasure than for the money."³⁶

Rice was the basic food of all Taiwanese. Beautiful rice fields covered the countryside. It was grown everywhere on the mountain terraces, on the plains, and on any vacant lot in the city. Neighborhood gardens reflected neighbors helping neighbors. Water was directed

---

34. Malan R. Jackson, Taiwan Mission President to Taiwan Mission missionaries, 10 April 1973, Godfrey Family Papers. See also Godfrey/Witbeck Letters, 16 April 1973, Godfrey Family Papers. Sources differ as to the number baptized. This correspondence indicates fifty of eighty were baptized and another forty-one were baptized later.

35. The camphor tree is a large evergreen from the laurel family. Teak wood is a hardwood that was used in early ship building.

36. Floyd Godfrey, Missionary Journal, 4 September 1973.

from one garden paddy to another, from neighbor to neighbor, making efficient use of the rain. As rice starts growing, it looks like a blade of grass. As it matures, it can reach two feet in height and looks more like bromegrass or oats. When ripened, it turns brown and is cut by hand and stooked. Neighbors gather, and the harvest is done by hand. Baskets of the grain are carried to the threshing box to extract the seed, which is sacked and carried to the end of the field, where it is picked up and hauled to the mill or the market.

The mountain people lived on any flat spot where a building would fit. They had large families, and the children worked alongside their parents. They planted apple and peach trees on the hillside terraces. Gardens included squash and melons. The yards were full of chickens and the inevitable dog. Water buffalo pulled the plow that cultivated the land. Their homes were small cottages, with low roofs and one main door. In the center of the house was a wood or charcoal fire with a pot hanging above it for cooking. Clothing was scant because of the hot temperatures, but if they got cold, they just added another shirt during the winter. They used a drag shovel or a bamboo pole with heavy shoulder baskets on each end to carry their harvests and crafts to the city markets. The mountain people did the physical work all over the island. They are a proud people, pushed back into the mountains because over the centuries they refused to yield to their conquerors. They worshiped their ancestors, the river, a three-thousand-year-old tree, and the sky.

### CITIES OF TAIWAN

Cities were a contrast to the countryside. Floyd describes the Taiwan city streets as always buzzing with action. Mobile street merchants used their bicycles with a box on the back piled high with goods for sale. The merchants resembled the old-fashioned American "Fuller Brush" salesman with dusters and mops of all kinds sticking out of a box.[37] The butcher displayed meat out in the open, on top of the box.

---

37. See Gerald Carson, *The Fuller Brush Man* (New York: American Heritage, 1986).

The vegetable lady, always clean, slowly walked the street, ringing a bell. People heard the merchant's bell and came out of their homes. The fish lady moved faster, trotting along with a crossbar over her shoulders, balancing two baskets of fish.

The city businessmen of the island lived in small homes with the amenities of a gas plate for cooking and a small refrigerator. Their homes were furnished with handmade furniture, a couch, and sleeping mats. They owned their own transportation, which was usually a small motor bike. There were shops with the owners inside, creating the items people wanted to buy. The larger shops were perhaps 375-square feet, with items for purchase everywhere. They exercised daily at 6 a.m. for an hour before work in the city park near Floyd and Clarice's home and were often joined by Floyd.[38] Work days started at 7 a.m. and did not end until 11 p.m. Large metal doors completely covered the front of the store front shops and were all closed at night.

The men and women all worked to support their families. However, on the day of the Dragon Boat Festival, the women all get off work. The legend has it that a famous Chinese poet, a government minister, was drowned while out fishing. In his honor, in the springtime on this festival day the women take the day off work, prepare food and wrap it in bamboo leaves, and then take it to the sea where it is placed on the waves to feed the honored man.[39] Missionaries all celebrated along with the people of the nation.

**ISLAND TRANSPORTATION**

Transportation for the Taiwan missionaries and the people was primarily by bicycle. Everyone owned a bike. The motor bikes were only for those few who could afford them. Taxis were small cars, Datsun or Volkswagen in size, but there were many. Wait a few minutes for an eager driver, and the missionary could get across town for $0.35 ($1.98). The cars were in good running order, and the horns worked

---

38. Godfrey/Witbeck Letters, 30 August 1972.

39. Floyd Godfrey, "Five Year Diary," 15 June 1972. See also the journal of Floyd Godfrey, "Taiwan Is," November 1986, Godfrey Family Papers.

exceptionally well. Whichever driver had the loudest horn and the internal fortitude had the right-of-way on any road. There were few traffic lights, even in the city centers. Two kinds of trains moved people all over the island. They ran on an exact schedule. The first trains were comfortable, air conditioned, and carpeted, and depending on the length of the ride, tea or dinner would be served. The second inexpensive train was different: crowded, standing room only, and people, parcels, and chickens all crammed in together. It stopped at almost every crossing. Floyd and Clarice utilized all means of transportation, but they did not own a bike. They walked, took a taxi, or rode the trains.

Trucks were plentiful and used in construction. They were an anomaly created by ingenious workers. The engine was up front and mounted between two wheels. The back wheels were chain driven. The vehicle was controlled by motorcycle-style handlebars. "This little workhorse will haul two tons of gravel, cement," bamboo poles for scaffolding construction, or whatever is needed. There was a canopy over the driver's seat to protect him from the rain or the sunshine. The government used the modern four- to six-ton trucks.[40] The common worker modeled anything to fill a need. If a motor-driven vehicle was unavailable, an ox or a cow was hitched to a wagon to pull the load.

The Taiwanese builders are artists at their work. Beautiful modern buildings were found in every city. A building under construction was covered with bamboo scaffolding, the bamboo sometimes five inches in diameter. It always made Floyd stop and stand and look in amazement. The bamboo was tied together using reeds and surrounded the entire building, sometimes as high as five stories. Builders climbed the scaffolding like ants on a tree. They carried rock, brick, tile, tools, and construction supplies in baskets on their shoulders as they worked.

### LIFE'S TIME WINDS DOWN

As the end of Floyd and Clarice's mission approached, in July 1973, they were anxious, and they were sad. "I can't believe I'm here. This

---

40. Floyd Godfrey, Missionary Journal, 5 September 1973.

great land far away from home. . . . I can't believe a small bashful boy of long ago has come this far." And they had to say goodbye "as we now leave your door."⁴¹ Thirty to forty people gathered at the train station to see them off. They held up the train as everyone said their personal goodbyes. "It was hard to leave," and they "cried all the way" from Taichung to Taipei, where another crowd came to the airport in Taipei, and tears poured again.⁴²

### HOME IN CANADA

Floyd and Clarice were back home in Canada. The adjustment was reversed, as they stepped back into the Canadian culture they had left to serve their mission. It was just as difficult to come home as it was to leave for Taiwan, but they were surrounded by three of their family members, namely "Rob and the girls" (Robert, Marilyn, and Arlene). They visited Kenneth, now in Brigham City, Utah; Lorin in Kitchener, Ontario; and Donald in Tucson, Arizona, during their transition to normalcy. They spoke in the wards and stakes of Southern Alberta. Floyd always sat in the middle of the chapel, singing the hymns in Mandarin Chinese at the top of his lungs. He had no fear or embarrassment. He liked to show off. They were now a new anomaly at home, just as they had been in Taiwan.

Clarice's health began failing her. Floyd cared for her as long as he could. A friend and family doctor, Alan Van Orman, and family doctor Fred Spackman advised Floyd that the toll of Clarice's healthcare on him was putting his own life in danger. She passed away just eight years after their mission on 16 December 1980.

### LIFE'S LONELY TRAVELS

Floyd was lonely. He would drive to his daughter Marilyn's ranch, sometimes twice daily. Upon arrival, he was unsettled and he would

---

41. Floyd Godfrey, *Just Mine*, 43–44.
42. Godfrey/Witbeck Letters, 22 July 1973.

drive back home. It was a tough transition made a little easier by more service jobs.

Three months after Clarice's passing, the Canadian Census Bureau put Floyd to work visiting the ranchers and farmers of southern Alberta. His time was immediately taken in training and preparation. He attended preparatory classes in Lethbridge, then hired fifteen people who would work with him. The Census Bureau knew Floyd could get into the homes and acquire the data the government was unable to obtain. It was a hectic four months before the census was brought to a close. "I am supposed to be retired . . . [but] I don't believe a person ever quits, [when] there is always so much to do," Floyd wrote.[43] The work kept him busy, but there was pressure getting it completed, and not all people were cooperative with the census takers.

Working kept Floyd active. A year later, he was contacted by the Federal Farm Bureau and asked to help them administer a survey on the use of energy in farming. In 1983, he was a member of the Cardston Historical Society and a year later, president of the society. This was a volunteer assignment, but a job he enjoyed as they worked together to establish and open the Cardston Museum. "Why do I accept these jobs?" he asked himself. "I seem to want to be working for our community and church," was the response to his own question.[44] In his church service, Floyd had taught the high priests group priesthood lessons for twelve years.[45] These jobs kept him active, but it was not long before he started looking around for female companionship.

**TAIWAN TEMPLE MISSION**

Floyd's eyes wandered to the widow ladies of his neighborhood. Friends and family had limitless suggestions as he looked about nervously, like a teenage kid again. In July 1981, Floyd mustered the courage to call Amelia "Olive" Aldrige Crooks (1929–2007) on the phone. Olive's

---

43. Journal of Floyd Godfrey, 21 June 1901.
44. Journal of Floyd Godfrey, 10 February 1984.
45. Journal of Floyd Godfrey, 25 March 1985.

husband had passed away in 1980, and Floyd had been watching her working in her garden as he mustered his courage. He called and asked her to dinner. She was hesitant and said, "I can't, I'm picking strawberries, and I have to finish mowing the lawn." Never one to take "no" for an answer, Floyd suggested he'd be over in twenty minutes to pick her up.[46] Their first date was supper at the Kootney Lodge in Waterton Park. A month later they went for Chinese supper and out to see the movie, "The Fox and the Hound." Dating continued until September, when Floyd kissed her goodnight and asked her to marry him. Olive was in shock! They both visited their families and by mid-month, "I was on cloud nine." Olive continued, "Floyd and I drove to Waterton."[47] It was a quiet civil marriage in the Cardston Alberta Temple on 26 September 1981.

Floyd and Olive traveled extensively. He introduced her to his family, who were now scattered: his son Kenneth in Brigham City, Utah; his daughter Arlene in Spanish Fork, Utah; Lorin in Penticton, British Columbia; and Donald in Tucson, Arizona. Left close to home were his daughter Marilyn in Beazer, Alberta, and his son Robert in Calgary, Alberta. Floyd loved to travel, and he wanted to show his new bride the world. They made several trips to Hawaii.

In Hawaii, Floyd engaged in conversation with friends at the language training mission where he learned that the new Taipei Taiwan Temple needed temple workers. The Taiwan temple had just been dedicated on 17 November 1984. That was the catalyst for the second Taiwan mission. It was a temple mission from 1985 to 1986. On 12 April 1985, he received a letter from the Taiwan Temple president asking if he would come and serve. Floyd was thrilled, but he had to wait for the official calling to make its way through proper Church channels, which tested Floyd's patience. Olive was nervous about living in such a differ-

---

46. Journal of Floyd Godfrey, July 1981. See also *Floyd Godfrey Family Newsletter*, November 1992, 5.

47. From Olive's journal, in Kathy Layton and Don Godfrey, *Remembering . . . Amelia "Olive" Aldridge Crooks Godfrey* (Mesa, AZ: Chrisdon Communication, 2004), 54.

ent land, but Floyd encouraged her.⁴⁸ On 3 June 1985, the formal call came from President Spencer W. Kimball. They were temple ordinance workers. Three months later, Floyd was called as a sealer on 9 September 1985, and President Kimball conferred authority on him—meaning he had the authority to perform eternal marriages in the temple.⁴⁹

Within a few months he was called to serve on the high council in the Taipei East Stake. His assignment was as temple representative in the stake, and he worked specifically with the American Branch. He traveled to promote temple participation and was the link for the American Branch to the stake leadership. Like all temples, there were days of quiet and days they worked fourteen hours. They performed all the ordinances for the patrons and were supervisors, in their turn. Olive described Floyd as "one of the big shots" because he had been in Taiwan before. He knew people, the language, and liked to visit.

Floyd and Olive were invited to Taichung in November 1985 to participate in the rededication of the Taichung chapel. A new addition was added to what Floyd had helped build in 1971–73. "It was like a homecoming," but the city had grown so much he did not recognize his old neighborhood. The home where he and Clarice lived had been replaced by a high-rise apartment complex. It was an emotional experience seeing all the old friends. Floyd was asked to speak at the dedication, and he struggled through tears. "For the first time since I married Olive, I felt like Clarice was beside me," he said at the rostrum of the chapel. The services were concluded, and they went for a roast beef dinner at the National Hotel. As the orchestra played "Somewhere My Love," Olive squeezed Floyd's hand. "I am a happy and content man. . . . Thank you Lord," he wrote.⁵⁰

---

48. Correspondence from Floyd Godfrey, 29 April 1985, Godfrey Family Papers.
49. Ordinance card documenting the confirmation, Godfrey Family Papers.
50. Journal of Floyd Godfrey, "Taichung," November 1986.

Floyd and Olive Godfrey at Taiwan Temple, 1983. Courtesy of Floyd Godfrey Mission Photos.

## "THE NIGHT I WRESTLED WITH SATAN"

Not all of Floyd and Clarice's or Floyd and Olive's mission experiences passed without challenge. There was the intensity of language study, the frustration of looking for the right Chinese word in conversation and for expressing the principles of the gospel. However, even in their trials there was never a moment when they were not loving, serving, and learning. Floyd was particularly determined to conquer disappointments the night he wrestled with Satan.

It was 7 January 1987. Olive was in Canada attending her daughter's wedding. The day before, Floyd had been in meetings with Robert L. Simpson, a former counselor in the Church Presiding Bishopric, an assistant to the Twelve Apostles, and currently a member of the Quorum of the Seventy. Floyd was at a spiritual high as he sat in the temple with them and knelt at the altar. "He is truly a man of God," Floyd wrote. He was enjoying the spirit of the day, wishing Olive could be with him, and watching, learning, and listening to Simpson.

The next morning, Floyd cooked hot cakes for breakfast and was proud of himself. He cleaned the stove before the ants took it over. He worked through a smoggy day and ended it at a wedding supper for a friend. He wasn't feeling well. His doctor had told him to rest his eyes and let them recover. He had been having trouble reading and was told not to read for a month to let his eyes recover. This was difficult for a man who had loved reading all of his life and who never stopped studying the Chinese language.

It was night, and Floyd went to bed, trying to sleep. His mind began to fill with "wrong things, bad things," and "[He] could not sleep." He tossed and turned, and yet these terrible thoughts kept coming back. At 3 a.m. he got up, trying to reorient his mind. He took a hot bath, but that made no difference. Every time he tried, the thoughts returned. "I was disgusted with myself for letting such awful things come into my mind, but I could not shake the thoughts . . . loaded with all kinds of terrible answers which were full of revenge."

Suddenly Floyd thought, "I am the master. . . . 'Satan, by the authority of the priesthood I hold, get out of here.'" He lay back on his bed very tired and went immediately to sleep. He slept "like a baby for the next 5 or 6 hours." The thoughts were cleared from his mind, and he realized, "I have help if I just ask," and he did.[51]

### FROM TAIWAN TO CANADA

Floyd's age and his health began to show toward the end of his second mission in Taiwan. It was painful to walk; laying all that carpet throughout his life, stretching it across the floors of the Cardston Alberta Temple on his knees, and his use of the "knee-kicker" was now taking a toll. He had repeated this in the Taiwan Taipei Temple when the newly installed carpet began to shrink. During a regular temple maintenance closure, he took charge and fixed the problem. He was

---

51. Floyd Godfrey, Missionary Journal, 5 and 7 January 1987. The title of this unit appears in Correspondence, 26 November 1987.

in the hospital for bronchitis for a few days, given excellent care from doctors he knew, and given priesthood blessings for his well-being. He never complained; he just tried to recover and keep on working.

Floyd and Olive served almost two years. They were released twenty-one months later on 7 March 1987.[52]

---

52. See Journal of Floyd Godfrey, 12 April 1984, 26 June 1985, and 7 March 1987. Floyd writes 1984 in the first entry of the journal, but it is likely 1985.

Part 4

# IN THEIR FOOTSTEPS

# FOOTPRINTS

## Chapter 13

The Mormon pioneer families of the nineteenth century were common folks living extraordinary lives. However, they were not immune to historic turmoil that threatened them; the anti-Mormon mobs of Illinois drove them from Nauvoo, and the US marshals chased them into hiding. Eventually, they fled to Canada, looking for freedom, work, and a better life; these were foundations of their legacies. Their children were raised in the rich lands of the Canadian west. These children were born in the early twentieth century, and their families were ranchers and farmers with horse-drawn plows; they planted and ate what they harvested. The children and grandchildren of the original pioneers faced turmoil in a similar fashion. World War I frightened them. In 1919, during the Spanish Flu Pandemic, a Card family almost became one of the statistics. In the Roaring Twenties, it was hard to imagine that the generation of young adults who had kicked up their heels, dancing the Charleston, were only to have their hopes dashed by the Great Depression. Soon after, World War II forced rationing. Did the children and grandchildren of these pioneers face difficulties? Of course they did. However, the posterity of the pioneers overcame their challenged by following in the righteous footsteps of their ancestors.

**LEGACIES OF THE GODFREY FAMILY**

"I believe my greatest desire is to have the spirit of the Lord with me always,"[1] Floyd Godfrey wrote. Floyd and Clarice's sensitivity

---

1. Floyd Godfrey, Taiwan Temple Mission Journal, 20 August 1985.

to the Spirit increased as they worked at it and grew with it. They were deeply spiritual, and throughout their lives they were very much in love. They were both raised to uphold the standards of The Church of Jesus Christ of Latter-day Saints, and the same followed in their own home. Their children never heard a cross word pass between parents. Children might have been tempted to sass their mother occasionally, but before the words spilled out, they were cut off by their father, who taught love and respect. Floyd and Clarice loved the Cardston Fifth Ward, and the ward loved them back. "I remember Floyd as a pillar of spiritual strength," wrote Maurine Stanford, a neighbor, friend, and member of the ward. "He was a humble man,"[2] she continued. Floyd's spirituality and his basic philosophy can be summed up in one epigram: "To thine own self be true. And it must follow, as the night the day. Thou canst not then be false to any man." His children heard that so often they thought it was scripture until they read Shakespeare's *Hamlet*.[3]

Floyd and Clarice loved the Cardston Alberta Temple and taught their children the same. Although he was reluctant at first, Floyd was a temple worker who served for many years. He encouraged his children to keep their covenants, to learn from the symbolism, and to feel the spirit of the temple. He held strong to his own temple covenants and promises. Floyd and Clarice's six children continued in their parents' footsteps, each serving as temple workers. Collectively, that service totals more than a hundred years. Elder and Sister Godfrey loved the Chinese people and never lost touch with friends and associates in Taiwan. After their first mission to Taiwan, Floyd could hardly wait to return. They had the Cardston temple in their backyard and both the Cardston and Taiwan temples in their hearts.

Floyd was a confident man; Clarice was a quiet, elegant woman. Floyd stood for integrity; Clarice stood for a strong work ethic, humility, and love. And although they had personality differences, they

---

2. "In Remembrance: Floyd Godfrey," Funeral Services and Cards, Godfrey Family Papers.

3. William Shakespeare, *Hamlet*, act 1, scene 3, lines 79–81.

treated each other as equals and with respect. Clarice set the tone of her home; she loved children. Her own were priority, but she served in the children's organizations of the Church for almost forty years. After she passed away, Floyd was lonely. Lying in his bed one evening, he cried out, "If only Clarice could come back." Just at that exact moment, his bedroom lit up so bright that it scared him. He pulled the covers over his head and said, "I didn't mean it," and the light disappeared. He wondered, "Had a car just turned around outside?" He saw a light, but heard nothing.[4]

Floyd and Clarice enjoyed their time together, and it is in these times their spirit was the strongest. Floyd and Clarice also enjoyed their time with others. They often led out in public, taking center stage. Their home was open for any occasion. Friends, family, and church colleagues were often invited over for an evening. How so many people squeezed into their little home at one time remains a puzzle, but they did, and they were happy.

They enjoyed their gardens. Gardening was a way of life. In childhood, their pioneer parents ate what they planted, and if the crops were poor, they went without. Gardens were lifelines of sustenance and provided opportunities to acquire good work habits that passed through generations. Floyd planted the seeds, and Clarice preserved the harvest. Even as the necessity of gardens faded during their lifetime, they continued planting. Every spring Clarice planted new flowers, and every fall she harvested the bulbs for the next spring planting. All of their children learned to garden, and each tended their own gardens as their own families grew.

Floyd and Clarice taught their children to work at home and at Floyd's Furniture. Dusting Floyd's Furniture was as critical as pulling weeds in the garden. Clarice taught her daughters how to embroider and darn socks when holes appeared in the heal or the toe. She was known for the artistry of projects she created with her hands, which were given to others at Christmas or in times of need. A lady's handkerchief with a simple crocheted border communicated love when it

---

4. Eva Kay Harker-Copieters, letter, December 2012, Godfrey Family Papers.

was inserted within a birthday card. A knit wool sweater kept children and grandchildren warm. Whatever the challenge, they taught, "You can do it!"

While his children were growing up, Floyd taught with a never-ending vault of epigrams, songs, and poems. He did not lecture. He did not speak an unkind word or raise his voice in anger. He would cut off any conversation where his children started to say anything critical of anyone. "Let us all speak kind words to each other" is a line from a popular LDS hymn that he sang to underscore what he taught.[5] These acts of self-control were monumental accomplishments. They must have been mountains for him to climb, but ones turned to gold in his family.

Floyd and Clarice took their church assignments seriously as they taught in the wards throughout the Alberta Stake and the Taiwan Mission by mentoring and engaging in fundamental gospel sermons. Floyd and Clarice's teachings revolved around hard work, ethics, honesty, and basic Christian love. They taught by example. Floyd wrote, "Communicate with your family, for it gives you unity and strength. Keep the lines of communication open that all may understand and love. . . . Build yourselves. . . . Control yourselves . . . Be at the helm of your own ship. It is very simple, my children, just follow the Lord's commandments."[6]

In the early years, the Godfreys and Cards traveled by wagon, and in Floyd and Clarice's childhood, people seldom traveled more than a few miles from their farms. Throughout their adult lives, they watched the modern world of gasoline automobiles, trains, and planes close the distance of those places once so far away. Travel for the adult Floyd and Clarice was for work, fun, exploration, and relaxation. At the drop of a hat they made trips to Salt Lake City, San Francisco, New York, and Toronto—visiting friends and family, mixed with a little furniture business. They once took both sets of their parents on extended journeys through eastern Canada to Ottawa, Ontario. They then went down to

---

5. "Let Us Oft Speak Kind Words," *Hymns*, no. 232.
6. Floyd Godfrey, Missionary Journal, 24 February 1983.

the United States through Ohio and onto the Grand Canyon in Arizona. All six climbed into the car, and off they went.

Floyd was called "Wrong Way Corrigan" by close friend Alma Wiley. Corrigan was a 1930s pilot who took off from New York, headed for Long Beach, and ended up in Dublin, Ireland.[7] Similarly, during the 1950s, Alma indicated he was going to pick up a son who was returning on a ship from a Church mission abroad. His ship was docking in San Francisco. "Well, you know Floyd has heart trouble," Alma wrote, "[and] it started to swell, tears came into his eyes and he said, Bishop, I have a new car and I have just got to get away from my business, let me take you." And off they went. "San Francisco here we come." But Floyd first traveled to Mesa, Arizona; then west to San Diego; and finally north up the Pacific Coast to the Bay Area, and then back to Cardston with Alma's missionary. On another occasion, Alma and his wife were invited by Floyd to ride to Edmonton with him and Clarice. This time they were going to Edmonton via a circular route through eastern British Columbia, stopping at Radium Hot Springs, Lake Louise, the Columbia Ice Fields, Jasper Park, and then northeast back toward Edmonton.[8] Traveling music was a humorous pastime wherever they went and when children went along on any vacation. Songs like "The Bear Went over the Mountain" and "Alfalfa Hay" were sung repeatedly until the tired little passengers gave out.

Floyd had a wonderful sense of humor. He was a tease, sometimes too much of one. In Floyd and Clarice's relationship, if his gregariousness was on the brink of going too far, it was Clarice who became the teacher saying, simply, "Floyd," and he settled right down. It was not so much what she said, but the way and the particular tone of her voice that balanced him. Clarice had a sense of humor as well. She could get the best of him only on April Fools' Day when she instigated the jokes before he realized it was a day of games. Any time could be turned into a humorous time. A winter's toss of a snowball or Christmas games produced laughter. During summer's Waterton Park family reunions,

---

7. See Douglas Corrigan, *That's My Story* (New York: E. P. Dutton, 1938).
8. Alma Wiley, "Dear Bishop Godfrey," letter in the Godfrey Family Papers.

Floyd put watermelon rinds into the coffee pots because he didn't want his brothers drinking coffee. His humorous approach reminded them of their childhood standards. His actions taught his children, who always laughed at their father's shenanigans. Unfortunately for him, his grandkids inherited the jokester gene. While lying on the sofa during a regular visit to his daughter's Mountain View ranch home, his oldest granddaughters asked him innocently to "please lift his leg up" so they could measure him for a coffin. They had their mother's sewing tape measure in hand, and they looked innocent enough. Floyd's eyes were closed; he was only half paying attention, half napping, as he lifted his leg to a 45-degree angle. Then he suddenly bolted from the couch like his pants were on fire. Those loving little girls had poured ice water down their grandfather's leg.

One day, when he was visiting family in Tucson, Arizona, Floyd's children and grandchildren concocted a little plan "to get Grandpa." They were taking him to a special steak restaurant; Floyd loved a good steak dinner. Three grandkids, who might have been ten or eleven at the time, built up the excitement of the evening, telling Grandpa about this special place they were taking him to eat. All kept a straight face. They dressed in their Sunday best. The boys wore their white shirts and ties. The girls wore dresses and were ready to go. The kids kept passing Grandpa's bedroom and asking, "Are you ready? Have you got your *tie* on yet?" He was pleased at the attention and love from his "sweet little grandkids," as he later described the event. At last, parents, grandparents, and kids all piled into the car and drove to an old cowboy restaurant called Pinnacle Peak in a shopping area of Tucson called Trail Dust Town. As they entered the restaurant, Grandpa Floyd didn't seem to notice the hundreds of ties cut and hanging from the walls and ceiling. Nor did he notice that his son and three grandsons had snuck into the restroom and removed their ties. He did not know, of course, that if you wore a tie to this restaurant, the waitress would show up with scissors, cut it off, and staple it to the wall.

The family was seated and looking at menus, kids nervously trying to contain their giggles when the waitress suddenly appeared grabbing Grandpa Floyd's tie and giving it an upwards jerk. In one hand, she was holding his tie and ready to hang him; in the other she had what was like a great big pair of carpet scissors. "You want this tie?" she declared, as she pulled on it. "Take it off or lose it!" she continued. "That's my only Chinese silk tie," Floyd declared with a surprised look on his face. Then, he suddenly realized he'd been duped by his grandkids. He rescued the tie; it was saved. All had a wonderful meal and a memory of a good time with Grandpa Godfrey.[9]

Stories of family, stories of his childhood, or stories from the scriptures always taught a principle, even without the sermon. Floyd loved a good story and had the ability to laugh at himself. "Don't play with the matches" was an important lesson. One day as he was preparing for a barbeque, Floyd opened a small box of matches he kept in the cupboard, and they all fell out on the ground. He never carried matches on his person, but he dutifully picked them all up and put them in his front pants pocket. He forgot about them until he was on an errand to pick up some groceries at the Cardston Mall. He got out of the car, put his keys in his pocket and was looking over the fruit counter when his pants began to smoke. The car keys had sparked the matches, and his pants were on fire! He started to take his pants off, but realized he could not do that with all the people in the store who were now watching. In a flash, he dug the matches from his pocket and flung them out over the grocery aisle, smoke still pouring out of the hole in his pants. While one customer screamed, he was doing the "fast chicken on a hot plate dance." A crowd had gathered to watch the action, and they were laughing hysterically, "including [his] own wife Olive." Floyd's pride was seared, but the only burn was to the hole in his pants. "I didn't know you could move that fast," Olive laughingly remarked.[10]

Floyd's Furniture was the family business for almost twenty-five years. It grew from a small upstairs loft into the largest store on Main Street. Floyd and Clarice rode together all over the southern Alberta countryside as he called on the local ranchers, selling furniture or even trading a Chesterfield (a couch or sofa) for a cow. Clarice staffed

---

9. Donald G. Godfrey, *Seeds, Faith & Family History* (Queen Creek, AZ: Chrisdon Communications), 121–23.

10. Journal of Floyd Godfrey, 23 August 1983.

Floyd's Furniture alone when he was involved in a Church assignment. It might have grown into a chain store, but there was insufficient financing to take it further than Floyd had come.

Floyd was a dedicated town servant. He was elected to the school board and became board president. He was among those who brought a troubled school budget under control. And in doing so, he established the foundations of the educational structure in the district. In the Rotary and Lions Clubs, he worked to beautify the community and strengthen its economic development.

Floyd's most significant community service was as a member of the town council and as mayor. Projects brought natural gas into Cardston, new water-treatment resources, and a sewage-treatment plant. The Lion's Park was redesigned and upgraded with neighboring campgrounds. A park building was constructed with accommodations for large groups and family reunions. The "old folks" Chinook Center Villa was expanded and modernized. A new swimming pool was designed, expanded, and constructed. Floyd was a major supporter of the Remington Carriage Center, today a dynamic tourist attraction. Plans for a new library and new council offices in the Civic Center, the old "Social Center," were the building blocks of his leadership. Floyd spent a short time as a member and the president of the Cardston Historical Society. He led the way in the preservation of the municipal courthouse, eventually transforming it into a museum under the management of the historical society. He was a continual promoter of historical preservation and beautification projects. Floyd was a team builder who did not chase the public stage; he gave his council members their spot in the light. Clarice was always by his side when he traveled for the town.

### HOPES FOR THE FUTURE

As Floyd's life drew to a close, there were many things he still wanted to accomplish. He wanted to visit his children and grandchildren again, pilot a plane, build a new home, and work again in the temple. He continued studying Mandarin, wanting to be perfectly fluent, even when there was no one who understood. He wanted to write. He still loved the scriptures, good books, and poetry. "Life is good," he wrote, "we all have our setbacks . . . but cheer the happy moments."[11] "What can I do at 80 years old?" he asked himself. He could not believe he was that old. "I can smile . . . , be kind . . . , love my wife and children. . . . I can do a kind deed."[12]

Floyd and Clarice lived beautiful lives. Everything was not always rosy, but they did love their "roses" and looked for them in life. Floyd always wondered what life would bring, but it was today, not tomorrow, that was his priority. "To-Day . . . I have a difficult time with detail. I like the big bands. Sometimes I yearn for a Rolls Royce (dreamer). I never seem to worry about money. I love to swim (in a warm pool). I like to ride my bicycle. I hate this arthritis in my left knee (my companion for 40 years). I love modesty. I like pretty women (unless they smoke). I abhor drunkenness. I love the countryside. I love the blue sky and Old Chief Mountain. I respect my many friends, all races. Today is good!"[13]

**FLOYD'S PASSING**

The following is a letter Floyd wrote to his children of his hopes for the future. His hopes were not of notoriety, nor positions of wealth and influence. His hopes were for his family's future, their faith, and love:

Dear Children: If I should die tomorrow, I would feel that I have succeeded in life . . . if I have planted in your hearts an earnest desire to love your God, love your fellow man, and a firm testimony of the Gospel. If in some way I had taught you to be honorable men and women. And if, I have taught you the wisdom of thrift in time and money.

I hope I have planted humility in your hearts, that you are earnest when you kneel before your Lord and repent, then rise with a new determination.

I hope mother and I have shown you that a family is no place for contention and that we have taught you, in our small way, to seek the Master's hand and to know that herein is real inner peace and happiness.

I hope I have taught you to have faith in yourselves and the future. Then and only then will I feel content as you walk in my footsteps.

    Love, Your Dad[14]

---

11. Journal of Floyd Godfrey, 23 October 1985.
12. Journal of Floyd Godfrey, 27 November 1985.
13. "Today," Journal of Floyd Godfrey, 7 January 1986.
14. Godfrey, *Just Mine*, v.

Floyd's health ebbed slowly after his second mission in Taiwan. His knees gave him pain, yet he was on them working the carpet of the new Taipei Taiwan Temple. His eyesight was fading; the doctors told him to rest, but this was not easy for a man who loved reading. Cancer began creeping into his body. He was honored by the Lion and Rotary Clubs for his life of service. He reached out to his extended family, and he was a part of their lives to the end. He was a positive and spiritual influence to those with whom he served from Magrath, the Cardston Third and Fifth Wards, the Cardston Alberta Temple, the town of Cardston, and Taiwan.

Floyd Godfrey passed away 11 April 1992 at eighty-six years of age.

# EPILOGUE

"History turns on small hinges, and so do our lives," said LDS President Thomas S. Monson.[1] Indeed, that is as true as any singular gospel principle. Our destiny is determined by the choices we make. Sometimes, it is those little, tiny, teensy, and small decisions that shape a life. There are always choices that might have been, both within the destinies of those who lived before, as well as decisions made in our own lifetimes.

*What if* . . . the 1800s whaling ship captain in the English harbor had not decided to take young stowaway Joseph Godfrey with him on his ship? In those days, there were alternatives for stowaways, including slavery or death. The captain could have chosen to return the young lad to his father, but the decision was to take the boy in and care for him. The captain virtually adopted young Joseph, making him his cabin boy. Joseph worked for decades on the seas, learning independence and even medical practices of the day as a member of the ship's crew because there were no doctors on board the vessel. It is a fact that Joseph had an abusive father, but it is an error to see Joseph as an eternal victim. His time aboard the ship set the foundations for a lifetime. He and a shipmate, George Coleman, became part of the Canadian Loyalist's Army. Later, they were among those who joined The Church of Jesus Christ of Latter-day Saints. Joseph and George were among the bodyguards of the Prophet Joseph Smith. They were driven from their homes in Nauvoo by mobs. Joseph Godfrey trekked

---

1. Thomas S. Monson, "Follow The Prophets," *Ensign*, January 2015, 5.

across the plains with his own family and another friend. Joseph settled in North Ogden, where some attribute the naming of Mount Ben Lomond to him. A large family evolved, and Joseph became known as a man of love and compassion to all in need. The whole of North Ogden attended his funeral.

*What if*... Charles Ora Card had decided that he had had enough? Hounded by the US marshals, he hid out in the attics of the Logan Tabernacle, in friends' homes, and in the bushes along the Logan River. For his own protection, he carried a gun, which he kept holstered. Even at the dramatic point of his capture by the marshals, he was prompted not to draw the pistol. What if he had drawn it? Charles had challenged the Edmunds-Tucker Act, gone to trial, and was acquitted. It was a miracle he was not convicted. *What if* he had been convicted and sentenced to the Yuma Territorial Prison?

Charles's wives and children were already suffering. He was suffering, but he was also determined. He set out with plans for Arizona, but a prophet, John Taylor, asked him to explore the British territories for a place of settlement and peace. It was a much different direction than he had intended, but he was obedient. On this sixteen-year mission, he established the foundations not only for his family but for the Latter-day Saints in Canada. He created irrigation systems, roads, and communication systems for the entire region. Where would the Card family and the LDS Saints of Canada be today without his sacrifice and his conquering of his human frailties and temptations?

In the next Godfrey generation, *what if*... the North Ogden family farm had been inherited by Melvin Godfrey, Joseph's youngest son? He expected the farm to be his, but it was not to be. The probate courts divided the choice property, leaving Melvin without a means of support for his new wife and their first-born son. They emigrated to "Starve Valley" in the dead of winter and later to Canada, again arriving in the middle of another brutal blizzard. Melvin was among the first pioneers of Magrath, Alberta. As the town marshal, Melvin brought law to the little community. He worked with the town council to bring electricity to the village. He established the town's first silent movie theater and hosted the first exhibitions of radio in the region. He loved Magrath and worked throughout his life for its modern improvements.

In the next generation, *what if* . . . the Great Depression had not occurred? Only a fraction of people over the world were positioned to avoid the economic devastation.[2] There is no question the Godfrey families were victims of the resulting hardships. The movie theater substituted cash tickets for "tickets in kind," meaning that patrons brought potatoes and eggs as admission. Floyd's wages were cut by the Magrath Trading Company. Food for his family came only from his garden and the Card farm. They dug coal for cooking and heating from the banks of Pot Hole Creek. Floyd was a new father with a growing family, building his second home, and he was about to lose that home to debt. He sold it, paid the debt, and followed his brother Bert to Cardston.

*What if* . . . Floyd and Clarice had not moved to Cardston? In Cardston, Floyd built his third and last home. He became a religious and civic leader, a member of the Alberta Stake high council, a bishop, town councilor, mayor, and unflinching community servant. *What if* . . . he and Clarice had not gone to Taiwan?

*What ifs*—these are rhetorical and somewhat speculative questions of history. They do, however, illustrate those small hinges that become turning points of heritage. The Godfreys and the Cards had come a long way since the seagoing vessels and the wagon treks across the plains to the Great Basin and then north into Canada. Each generation experienced their challenges thrown against their testimonies and lives. Each made their own decisions that directed not only their own lives but lives to come.

These are the footprints within which the communities of Cache Valley, North Ogden, Magrath, and Cardston stand today. The family heritage was a transition, bringing family from seventeenth-century England to America, then through the Revolutionary and Civil Wars. The Godfreys and the Cards joined a new religion. The Mormons were persecuted and driven from the United States because of their

---

2. For the effects of the Great Depression, see Frederick Lewis Allen, *Since Yesterday: The 1930s in America, September 3, 1929 to September 3, 1939* (New York: Harper and Row).

beliefs. In Utah, the American government came after them again. Some moved north into Canada, seeking a better life. The Godfrey and Card families witnessed the transition of the country, the abolition of slavery, and the creation of a more stable union; they witnessed the railroads uniting the East and West in both the United States and Canada. They participated in the transition of the Wild West into the modern West. Their immigrations had been by oxen and horse teams on nonexistent roads. Their lives ended driving gasoline automobiles on paved freeways. They experienced the historical eras that birthed the electronic media, telephone, train, and plane.

The Godfrey-Card heritage is one of American and Canadian originals. The first in new lands with new visions of life, liberty, and freedom. They were among the first to leave footsteps for their heritage to follow. "Though times and circumstances have changed, the principles for facing trials and successfully living together as a caring and prospering community under God have not changed," said President Dieter F. Uchtdorf.[3] So it was with our pioneers; so it is with those of us today. We learn as we walk in their footsteps.

---

3. Dieter F. Uchtdorf, "All Is Well," *Ensign*, July 2015, 4–6.

# SELECTED BIBLIOGRAPHY

**BOOKS**

Allen, Frederick Lewis. *Only Yesterday: An Informal History of the 1920s*. New York: Harper and Row Publishers, 1964.

Arrington, Leonard J. *Brigham Young American Moses*. Urbana: University of Illinois Press, 1986.

———. *Great Basin Kingdom: An Economic History of the Latter-day Saints 1830–1900*. Salt Lake City: University of Utah Press 1993.

———. *History of Idaho*. Vol. 1. Moscow, ID: University of Idaho Press, 1995.

———. *The Mormon Experience: A History of the Latter-day Saints*. Urbana: University of Illinois Press, 1992.

———. *The Presidents of the Church*. Salt Lake City: Deseret Book, 1986.

Arrington, Leonard J., Feramorz Y. Fox, and Dean L. May. *Building a City of God: Community and Cooperation Among the Mormons*. Urbana: University of Illinois Press, 1992.

Ashton, Paul and Hilda Kean, eds. *People and Their Pasts: Public History Today*. New York: Palgrave Macmillan, 2009.

Athern, Robert G. *Union Pacific Country*. New York: Rand McNally, 1971.

Bates, Jane Eliza Woolf, and Zina Alberta Woolf Hickman. *Founding of Cardston and Vicinity—Pioneer Problems*. Cardston, Alberta: William L. Woolf, 1960.

Belisle, Donica. *Retail Nation: Department Stores and the Making of Modern Canada*. Vancouver: University of British Columbia Press, 2011.

Bitton, Davis. *Guide to Mormon Diaries and Autobiographies*. Provo, UT: Brigham Young University Press, 1977.

Bowman, R. F. *Railways in Southern Alberta*. Lethbridge, Alberta: Lethbridge Historical Society, 2002.

Bradley, Martha Sontag, and Mary Brown Firmage Woodward. *Four Zinas: A Story of Mothers and Daughters on the Mormon Frontier*. Salt Lake City: Signature Books, 2000.

Briggs, Asa. *Social History and Human Experience*. Cedar City, UT: Grace A. Tanner Center for Human Values, 1984.

Britsch, R. Lanier. *Moramona: The Mormons in Hawaii*. Mormons in the Pacific Series. Laie, HI: Institute for Polynesian Studies, 1991.

Burton, Pierre. *The Great Depression, 1929–1930*. Toronto: McClelland & Stewart, 1990.

———. *The Last Spike: The Great Railway, 1881–1885*. Toronto: McClelland & Stewart, 1971.

———. *The National Dream: The Great Railway, 1871–1881*. Toronto: McClelland & Stewart, 1970.

Butler, Ann M., and Kenneth L. Holmes. *Covered Wagon Women, I: Diaries and Letters from the Western Trails, 1840–1849*. Lincoln: Bison Books, University of Nebraska Press, 1995.

Campbell, Eugene, and Richard D. Poll. *Hugh B. Brown: His Life and Thought*. Salt Lake City: Bookcraft, 1975.

Cannon, George Q. *The Latter-Day Saints' Millennial Star*. Liverpool: George Q. Cannon, 1863.

Card, Brigham Y., Herbert C. Northcott, John E. Foster, Howard Palmer, and George K. Jarvis, eds. *The Mormon Presence in Canada*. Edmonton: University of Alberta Press, 1990.

Cardston Company of Daughters of Utah Pioneers. *Alberta Stake Tabernacle Marker Dedication*. Cardston: Cardston Company, Daughter of Utah Pioneers, 2006.

Chisholm, Anne, and Michael Davie. *Lord Beaverbrook: A Life*. New York: Knopf, 1993.

Clymer, Floyd. *Floyd Henry's Wonderful Model T, 1908–1927*. New York: McGraw-Hill, 1955.

Cook, Tim. *No Place to Run: The Canadian Corps and Gas Warfare in the First World War*. Vancouver: University of British Columbia Press, 1999.

Dempsey, Hugh A. *Indian Tribes of Alberta*. Calgary: Glenbow Museum, 1997.

———. *Mike Mountain House: My People the Bloods*. Calgary: Glenbow Museum, 1989.

———. *Red Crow: Warrior Chief*. Saskatoon: Fifth House, 1995.

den Otter, A. A. *Civilizing the West: The Galts and the Development of Western Canada*. Edmonton: University of Alberta Press, 1992.

Djuff, Ray. *High on a Windy Hill: The Story of the Price of Wales Hotel*. Calgary: Rocky Mountain Books, 2009.

Duerger, David. *The Mysteries of Godliness: A History of Mormon Temple Worship*. San Francisco: Smith Research Associates, 1994.

Durham, Homer G. *N. Eldon Tanner: His Life and Service*. Salt Lake City: Deseret Book, 1982.

Emery, Edwin. *The Press and America: An Interpretative History of Journalism*. Englewood Cliffs, NJ: Prentice-Hall, 1962.

Essham, Frank. *Pioneers and Prominent Men of Utah*. Salt Lake City: Western Epics, 1966.

Ford, Thomas. *A History of Illinois*. Urbana: University of Illinois Press, 1995.

Glassburg, David. *Sense of History: The Place of the Past in American Life*. Amherst: University of Massachusetts Press, 2001.

Godfrey, Donald G. *C. Francis Jenkins: Film and Television Pioneer*. Urbana: University of Illinois Press, 2014.

Godfrey, Donald G., and Brigham Y. Card. *The Diaries of Charles Ora Card: The Canadian Years, 1886–1903*. Salt Lake City: University of Utah Press, 1993.

Godfrey, Donald G., and Kenneth W. Godfrey. *The Diaries of Charles Ora Card: The Utah Years, 1871–1886*. Provo, UT: Religious Studies Center, 2006.

Godfrey, Donald G., and Rebecca S. Martineu-McCarty. *An Uncommon Common Pioneer: The Journals of James Henry Martineau, 1828–1918*. Provo, UT: Religious Studies Center, 2008.

Godfrey, Floyd. *Just Mine: Poetic Philosophy*. Edited by Donald G. Godfrey. Mesa, AZ: Chrisdon Communications, 1996.

Godfrey, Kenneth W. *Logan, Utah: One Hundred Fifty Year History*. Logan, UT: Exemplar Press, 2010.

Gomery, Douglas. *A History of Broadcasting in the United States*. Malden, MA: Blackwell Publishing, 2008.

Greenwell, Jeanette Shaw, and Laura Chadwick Kump. *Our North Ogden Pioneers, 1851–1900*. Ogden, UT: Watkins Printing, 1998.

Harker, Cary, and Kathy Bly. *Power of a Dream*. Magrath, Alberta: Keyline Communications, 1999.

Hibbert, Christopher. *Queen Victoria: A Personal History*. London: Harper Collins, 2000.

Hill, Donna. *Joseph Smith: The First Mormon*. New York: Doubleday & Company, 1977.

Hilton, George W. *American Narrow Gauge Railroads*. Stanford: Stanford University Press, 1990.

Hostetler, John A. *Hutterite Society*. Baltimore: Johns Hopkins University Press, 1974.

Huchel, Frederick M. *A History of Box Elder County*. Salt Lake City: Utah State Historical Society, 1999.

Hudson, James A. *Charles Ora Card: Pioneer and Colonizer*. Cardston, Alberta: Hudson, 1963.

Innis, David L., and H. Dale Lowry. *Lee's Creek*. Cardston, Alberta: Innes & Lowry, 2001.

Jenson, Andrew. *Encyclopedic History of the Church of Jesus Christ of Latter-day Saints*. Salt Lake City: Deseret News, 1941.

Junkunis, Franklin J. "Urban Development in Southern Alberta." In *Southern Alberta: A Regional Perspective*, edited by Franklin J. Junkunis, 74–85. Lethbridge: University of Lethbridge Press, 1972.

Koroscil, Paul M. *The British Garden of Eden: Settlement History of the Okanagan Valley, British Columbia*. Burnaby, British Columbia: Simon Fraser University, 2003.

Kyvig, David E. *Daily Life in the United States, 1920–1940*. Westport, CT: Greenwood Publishing, 2002.

Kyvig, David E. and Myron A. Marty. *Nearby History: Exploring the Past Around You*. 3rd edition. Nashville: The American Association for State and Local History, 2010.

Layton, Kathy, and Donald G. Godfrey. *Remembering . . . Amelia "Olive" Aldridge Crooks Godfrey*. Mesa, AZ: Chrisdon Communications 2004.

Ludlow, Daniel H., ed. *Encyclopedia of Mormonism*. 5 vols. New York: Macmillan Publishing, 1992.

MacDonald, Graham A. *Where the Mountains Meet the Prairies: A History of Waterton Country*. Calgary: University of Calgary Press, 2003.

MacEvan, Grant. *Frederick Haultain: Frontier Statesman of the Canadian Northwest*. Saskatoon, Saskatchewan: Western Producer Prairie Books, 1985.

MacInnes, C. M. *In the Shadow of the Rockies*. London: Rivingtons, 1930.

Magrath and District History Association. *Irrigation Builders*. Lethbridge: Southern Printing, 1974.

*Magrath's Golden Jubilee*. Magrath, Alberta: n.p., 1949.

Mardon, Ernest G., and Austin A. Mardon. *Alberta Mormon Politicians*. Edmonton: Golden Meteorite Press, 1992.

McClintock, James H. *Mormon Settlement in Arizona: A Record of Peaceful Conquest of the Desert*. Phoenix: Phoenix Manufacturing Stationers, 1921.

Moffitt, John C. *The History of Education in Utah*. Salt Lake City: John Clifton Moffitt, 1946.

Mountain Horse, Mike. *My People the Bloods*. Calgary: Glenbow-Alberta Institute and Blood Tribal Council, 1989.

Morris, Alexander. *The Treaties of Canada with the Indians of Manitoba and the North-West Territories*. Toronto: Willing & Williamson, 1880. Reprint, Toronto: Coles Canadiana, 1971.

Musser, Charles. *The Emergence of Cinema: The History of Motion Picture to 1907*. Berkeley: University of California Press, 1994.

Nelson, Lowry. *The Mormon Village: A Pattern and Technique of Land Settlement*. Salt Lake City: University of Utah Press, 1952.

Oaks, Dallin H., and Marvin S. Hill. *Carthage Conspiracy: The Trial of the Accused Assassins of Joseph Smith*. Urbana: University of Illinois Press, 1975.

Owram, Doug. *Promise of Eden: The Canadian Expansions Movement and the Idea of the West, 1856–1900*. Toronto: University of Toronto Press.

Peterson, Ross F. *A History of Cache County*. Salt Lake City: Utah State Historical Society, 1997.

Pratt, Parley P. *Autobiography of Parley Parker Pratt*. Salt Lake City: Deseret Book, 1950.

Ramsaye, Terry. *A Million and One Nights: A History of Motion Picture*. 3rd ed. New York: Simon and Schuster, 1964.

Randall, Frank Alfred, and John D. Randall. *History of the Development of Building Construction in Chicago*. Chicago: University of Illinois Press, 1999.

Regular, Keith. *Neighbours and Networks: The Blood Tribe in Southern Alberta Economy, 1884–1939*. Calgary: University of Calgary Press, 2009.

Richard, Kent F. *A Family of Faith*. Salt Lake City: Deseret Book, 2013.

Ricketts, Norma Baldwin. *The Mormon Battalion: U.S. Army of the West, 1846–1848.* Logan: Utah State University Press, 1986.

Ricks, Joel E., and Everett L. Cooley, eds. *The History of a Valley.* Logan, UT: Cache Valley Centennial Commission, 1956.

Riggs, Ransom. *Miss Peregrine's Home for Peculiar Children.* Philadelphia: Quirk Books, 2011.

Roberts, Richard C., and Richard W. Sadler. *A History of Weber County.* Salt Lake City: Utah State Historical Society, 1997.

Romney, Thomas Cotton. *The Mormon Colonies in Mexico.* Salt Lake City: University of Utah Press, 2005.

Ryan, Milo. *History in Sound.* Seattle: University of Washington Press, 1963.

Samuel, Raphael. *Island Stories: Unraveling Britain.* London: Verso, 1998.

Shaw, Keith, ed. *Chief Mountain Country: A History of Cardston and District.* 3 vols. Cardston, Alberta: Cardston Historical Society, 1978, 1987, 2005.

Slater, Michael. *Charles Dickens: A Life Defined by Writing.* London: Yale University Press, 2009.

Smith, Joseph. *History of The Church of Jesus Christ of Latter-day Saints.* Salt Lake City: Deseret Book, 1946.

Snyder, Louis L., and Richard B. Morris. *A Treasury of Great Reporting.* New York: Simon and Schuster, 1962.

Soone, Conway B. *Ships, Saints and Mariners.* Salt Lake City: University of Utah Press, 1987.

Sterling, Christopher H., and John Michael Kittross. *Stay Tuned: A History of American Broadcasting.* Mahwah, NJ: Lawrence Erlbaum Associates, Publishers, 2002.

Strong, Josiah. *Our Country: Its Possible Future and Its Present Crisis.* New York: American Home Missionary Society, 1885.

Swinton, Heidi S. *To the Rescue: The Biography of Thomas S. Monson.* Salt Lake City: Deseret Book, 2010.

Waitrowski, Claud. *Railroads across North America: An Illustrated History.* New York: Crestline, 2012.

Walker, Ronald W., Richard E. Turley Jr., and Glen L. Leonard. *Massacre At Mountain Meadows.* New York: Oxford University Press, 2008.

Warrum, Noble. *Utah Since Statehood: Historical and Biographical.* Vol. 2. Salt Lake City: S. J. Clark, 1919.

Ward, Donald B. *The People: A Historical Guide to the First Nations of Alberta, Saskatchewan, and Manitoba.* Markhan, Ontario: Fifth House, 1995.

Wetherell, Donald G., and Irene R. A. Kmet. *Town Life: Main Street and the Evolution of Small Town Alberta, 1880–1947*. Edmonton: University of Alberta Press, 1995.

Wheeler, Seager. *Profitable Grain Growing*. Winnipeg: Grain Growers' Guide, 1919.

Willing, Gale. *Fielding: The People and the Events That Affected Their Lives*. Logan, UT: Herff Jones, 1992.

Wrage, Ernest J., and Barnet Baskerville. *American Forum: Speeches on Historic Issues, 1788–1900*. Seattle: University of Washington Press.

Woodfield, Floyd J. *A History of North Ogden: Beginnings to 1985*. Ogden, UT: Empire Printing, 1986.

## ARCHIVES, LIBRARIES, AND MANUSCRIPT COLLECTIONS

Church History Library, Salt Lake City.

Family Files, North Ogden Historical Museum, Ogden, Utah.

Family History Library, Salt Lake City.

Galt Museum and Archives, Lethbridge, Alberta.

Glenbow Archives, Glenbow Museum, Calgary, Alberta.

LDS Genealogical Library, Cardston, Alberta.

L. Tom Perry Special Collections, Harold B. Lee Library, Brigham Young University, Provo, Utah.

Magrath Museum, Magrath, Alberta.

Provincial Archives of Alberta, Cardston Museum, Edmonton, Alberta.

University of Glasgow Special Collections, Glasgow, Scotland.

Weber County Second District Court Probate Case Files, Utah State Archives, Salt Lake City.

## ARTICLES

Campbell, Eugene E. "The Mormon Gold-Mining Mission of 1849." *BYU Studies* 1, no. 2 (Autumn 1959–Winter 1969): 19–31.

Christy, Howard A. "Weather, Disaster and Responsibility: An Essay on the Willie and Martin Handcart Story." *BYU Studies* 37, no. 1 (1997–98): 6–74.

Godfrey, Donald G. "Zina Presendia Young Williams Card: Brigham Young's Daughter, Cardston's First Lady." *Journal of Mormon History* 23, no. 2 (Fall 1997): 107–27.

Grinnell, George B. "The Crown of the Continent." *Century Magazine* (September 1901): 660–71.

Hartley, William G. "Mormons and Early Iowa History (1838–1858): Eight District Connections." *The Annals of Iowa* 59 (Summer 2000): 217–60.

Hinckley, Gordon B. "Faith of the Pioneers." *Ensign*, July 1984, 3.

Humphries, Mark Osborne. "Paths of Infection: The First World War and the Origins of the 1918 Influenza Pandemic." *War in History* 21, no. 1 (2013): 55–81.

Johnson, Alex, and H. Joan MacKinnon. "Alberta's Ranching Heritage." *Rangelands* 4, no. 3 (June 1982): 99–102.

Monson, Thomas S. "Follow the Prophets." *Ensign*, January 2015, 5.

Morgan, Dale L. "The State of Deseret." *Utah Historical Quarterly* (1940): 65–251.

Walker, Newell R. "They Walked 1,300 Miles." *Ensign*, July 2000, 44–49.

Walker, William R. "Fortifying Faith with Ancestor's Stories." *Church News*, 13 April 2014, 20.

## GOVERNMENT DOCUMENTS

"Goose Lake/Lees Creek Basin Planning Study, Town of Cardston, 1979–80." Town of Cardston.

"Judge Melvin Godfrey, Court Cases, 1946." Magrath Museum.

Magrath, Alberta Town Council Meeting Records. Magrath Museum.

Minutes of the Town of Cardston Council, 1980. Town of Cardston.

Proposal to Town of Cardston for Design Service for New Sewage Treatment Facilities, 1977. "Survey of Cardston." Industrial Development Branch, Department of Industry and Development, 1963. Province of Alberta.

## UNPUBLISHED DOCUMENTS

Hansen, John A. "The History of College and Young Wards, Cache County, Utah." Master's thesis, Utah State University, 1968.

Mitchner, Alyn E. "William Pearce: Father of Alberta Irrigation." Master's thesis, University of Alberta, 1985.

Colman Family History, including short stories and oral histories. Magrath Museum.

Ellen Clair Weaver Shaeffer Family Papers. Includes short stories.

Floyd and Clarice Godfrey Family Papers. Includes journals, diaries, letters, and short stories.

Letters of Clarice Card Godfrey to Melva Card Witbeck, 1959–86. Godfrey Family Papers.

Pearl Card Sloan Family Papers. L. Tom Perry Special Collections, Harold B. Lee Library, Brigham Young University, Provo, UT.

JoAnn Sloan Rogers Family Papers. L. Tom Perry Special Collections, Harold B. Lee Library, Brigham Young University, Provo, UT.

Life Histories of the Wives of Charles Ora Card, Card Family publication, 1978. L. Tom Perry Special Collections, Harold B. Lee Library, Brigham Young University, Provo, UT.

Lorin Card Godfrey Family Papers, private collection.

Marilyn Rose Godfrey Ockey Pitcher Family Papers, private collection.

Martha Mitchell Family Papers. Includes short stories.

Mary Ellen Godfrey Meacham Family Papers. Includes short stories.

## PAMPHLETS

"Brief Story of the Taichung Memorial Temple." N.d.

McIntyre, William H., Jr. "A Brief History of the McIntyre Ranch." Lethbridge, Alberta: n.p., 1947.

## ORAL HISTORY INTERVIEWS FROM GODFREY FAMILY PAPERS

Bertrand Richard Godfrey, interview by Burt Godfrey family, 1980.

Clarice Card Godfrey, interview by Donald G. Godfrey, 1977.

Floyd Godfrey, interview by Donald G. Godfrey, 1972.

Floyd Godfrey, interview by Donald G. Godfrey, 1977.

Floyd Godfrey, interview by Donald G. Godfrey, 1982.

Floyd Godfrey, interview by Donald G. Godfrey, 1988.

Mervin Godfrey, interview by Floyd Godfrey, 1982.

Rhea Jensen, interview by Donald G. Godfrey, 1996.

# INDEX

## A

Alberta Canada. *See* Cardston, Alberta; Magrath, Alberta; southern Alberta, Canada
Alberta Stake Center, 280–81, 343–44
alfalfa, 197–98
Allen, Andrew L., 160
Allen, Simeon, 151, 156
Allen, Warner H., 160
Alston, Louisa, 219
*Amazon*, 47–48
Atkins, Henry H., 321
automobiles, 192, 201–2, 264–67

## B

badger, 184
barn, 201
baseball, 82–83, 231
baths, 95
bear, 215

Bear Lake Valley, 55–56
Beaverbrook, William Aitken, 219
Beeman, Norman T., 240
bell tower, in Magrath, 79–80
Belly River, 270–71
Bennett, John H., 85
Bermuda, 293
Bingham, David, 67
Bingham, Rulon, 87–88
Birdneau, Sarah Jane "Sallie," 115–17, 118, 156–58, 167–69
Bishop, John M., 41
bishops' storehouse, 20
Black Aces, 269
blessings, for sick, 369–70
Blood Tribe, 132–33, 152, 329–32, 340
Boggs, Lilburn W., 12
Booth, Ann, 111n34
Booth, Emma, 111n34
boxing matches, 204
Bradshaw, Richard, 221

Brewerton, Gordon, 292, 294
Bristol Harbour, 3
Brown, Hugh B., 225, 320–21
Brown, James, 140
Brown, Zina Card, 320
Brown House, 268–71, 273
Buchanan, James, 23

## C

Cache Valley
    Card family settles in, 108–11
    Charles Ora Card as prominent leader in, 111–13
    Charles Ora Card leaves, 135–38
    Charles Ora Card returns to, 153–54
    Charles Ora Card's influence on, 160–61
    growth of, 173–74
    as successful settlement endeavor, 128
Calgary, Alberta, 147–48
Cameron Falls, 215–17
Campbell, Nancy, 111n34
Canada Day (Dominion Day), 228, 231, 296–97
Canadian Overseas Expedition Force, 225
Canadian Pacific Railway, 131–32, 138, 191–92, 252
Canadian Pacific Railway Bridge, 75–76
cane, of Charles Ora Card, 114–15
Card, Abbie, 164–65
Card, Charles Ora, Jr., 116, 117, 119, 167

Card, Charles Ora, Sr.
    and birth of George Cyrus, 173
    called to settle in Canada, 128, 135–38
    capture and escape of, 125–26
    as caring father, 163–65, 175
    childhood of, 104–5
    completes exploration mission, 151–53
    and construction of Logan Temple, 170–71
    death of, 171–72
    emotional trials of, 166–67
    and exploration of British Territory, 139–44
    and irrigation of southern Alberta, 73
    legacy of, 160–61, 402
    missionary work of, 113–15
    ordained as seventy, 108
    persecution of, 124–25
    as prominent leader in Cache Valley, 111–13
    protects Sallie from public humiliation, 167–69
    recruits settlers for southern Alberta, 154–55
    returns home following exploration mission, 153–54
    and settlement of southern Alberta, 62–63, 132, 133, 149–51, 155–60, 194, 195
    settles in Cache Valley, 109–10
    tender heart of, 161–63

Card, Charles Ora, Sr. (*continued*)
  travels with family, 165–66
  treks to Utah, 106–7
  wives of, 115–23, 155, 165–66
Card, Clarice. *See* Godfrey, Clarice Card
Card, Cyrus William, 102, 103–11, 162, 163, 168
Card, Edgar George, 176
Card, Elisha, 101–2
Card, George Cyrus
  approves Clarice's engagement, 253
  birth and childhood of, 164, 165, 173–75
  community involvement of, 183
  as disciplinarian, 242
  education of children of, 242, 244
  final years of, 334
  generosity of, 182–83
  marriage of, 176–77, 179, 181–82, 187
  moves into town, 244–45
  personality of, 183–84, 186
  as pioneering farmer, 182
  relationship between Rose and, 187
  and settlement of southern Alberta, 195–96
  temptations and trials of, 175–78
Card, Joseph Y., 253–54
Card, Lavantia, 164
Card, Leland, 186, 244
Card, Matilda Francis, 163
Card, Orson Rega, 119, 163–64
Card, Pearl, 164–65
Card, Polly, 107, 162

Card, Sarah Jane "Jennie," 115–16, 117, 119, 156–58, 167, 168
Card, William (1722–85), 101
Card, William (1793–1864), 102, 104
Card, William Fuller (1787–1846), 102, 104
Card & Son Sawmill, Lath, and Shingle Mill, 109–10
Cardston, Alberta
  agriculture and enterprise in, 285–86
  Church units in, 335–36, 341–42
  Godfreys relocate to, 262–64
  location of settlement site in, 149–51
  service in, 315–16
  settlement of, 194
  sewer treatment plant in, 328–29
  town square in, 282–84
  water supply in, 327–28, 332
Cardston Alberta Temple, 281–82, 299–300, 338–39, 392
Cardston Auto Service, 264–67
Cardston Chamber of Commerce, 319–21
Cardston Fifth Ward, 344–45
Cardston Implement Company, 268
Cardston Lions Club International, 318–19
Cardston Mall, 325
Cardston School District, 317–18
Cardston Third Ward, 341–42
Cardston Ward, 335–36
Card-Witbeck, Melva, 360
carpet, 299–300, 304–5
cars, 192, 201–2, 264–67

cat claim, 48–49
cattle
  during Depression, 261–62
  herding privately owned, 259
  herding stray, 78–79
  keeping, 280
  milking, 279–80
  shipped to Magrath, 196–97
Census Bureau, 382
cesspool, 269–70
Charles Ora Card Town Square, 282–84
chewing tobacco, 236
Chicago Canal, 9
chicken, stolen, 81
child labor, 3, 4
children
  and antipolygamy acts, 42
  education of pioneer, 38–42
  Melvin Godfrey's dealings with mischievous, 80–82
  taught responsibility, 206–11
  during Victorian Age, 4
*Chimborazo*, 31
Chin Kou Ehen, 373–74
choices, impact of, 401, 403
Christmas, 231–33, 306–10, 373
Church of Jesus Christ of Latter-day Saints, The
  as Floyd's Furniture customer, 297–300
  service in, 335–38
Civil War, 10
clothes, washing, 95, 207–8, 275–76
coal and wood shed, 200

coal digging, 260–61
Cochrane, Matthew H., 130, 158–59
Coleman, George, 8–15, 16, 401
Coleman, George Moroni, 56–57, 85
Coleman, Moroni, 15, 16, 21–22, 56–57, 62
College Ward School, 177
community gardens, 270, 336–37
community theater, 256–57
Coomb's Hardware, 267–68
cows. *See* cattle
Crazy Day promotions, 296–97, 320
Crooks, Amelia "Olive" Aldrige, 382–84
Crookston, N. W., 169
Crown and Anchor, 255
curfew, in Magrath, 79–80

## D

dances, 52, 229–30, 239
Davis, Edward Joseph, 41
debates, 24
democrat wagon, 140
Dickens, Charles, 3
Dickenson, Canfield, 114
Diefenbaker, John, 320–21
diphtheria, 235
discipline, in schools, 40
Dominion Day, 228, 231, 296–97
drought, 236, 260, 261
Duckworth, Mary Ann, 50–51
dugouts, 16–17, 199
Dunn, Thomas James, 19–20, 21

# E

Easter, 231
Eatons, 297–98
Edmunds Act (1882), 42, 124
Edmunds-Tucker Act (1887), 42, 124, 134, 154
education
    Charles Ora Card as proponent of, 112
    of Clarice Card Godfrey, 242–44
    of Floyd Godfrey, 222–29
    of pioneer children, 38–42
    of Rose Elizabeth Plant, 175–76, 180–81
"Electric, The," 85
electricity, 88–89
Ellsworth, Edmund L., 107
Ellsworth Company, 106–8
Empress Theatre, 84–93, 236
extermination order, 12
Exum, E. W., 126

# F

fast
    for mission funds, 305–6
    for rain, 260
firearms, 205
First Nations peoples
    Eva Jones's experience with, 59
    first Sunday School among, 340
    Joseph Godfrey and, 23, 25–26
    land dispute between federal government and, 329–32
    missionary work among, 193
    in Northwest Territories, 131
    Sarah Ann Price and, 30–31
    and settlement of southern Alberta, 132–33, 152
fishing, 270–71
Fletcher, Mark, 169
Floyd's Furniture
    challenges of, 295–96, 301
    Christmas at, 306–10
    Church and business clients of, 297–300
    community service rendered by, 319
    Crazy Day promotions at, 296–97
    family and young employees at, 302–5
    financing for, 288–89
    first televisions sold at, 302
    Floyd's retirement from, 310–13
    genesis of, 287–88
    growth of, 291–92, 294–95
    and legacy of Godfrey family, 397–98
    and national furniture shows, 293
    opening of, 289–91
    operations of, 300–301
folding chairs, 297–99
Ford, Thomas, 12
forgiveness, 350–51
Fort Macleod, 148
fur trading, 130

## G

Galt, Alexander T., 65, 71, 73, 134
Galt, Elliot T., 65, 71, 134
gardening, 270, 276, 336–37, 393
ghost, seen by Eva Jones, 51–52
Gibson, John W., 41
Glenn, Alex, 297
Glenn, William, 342
Godfrey, Albert, 13
Godfrey, Arlene Janet, 184, 256, 265, 307, 342
Godfrey, Bertrand Richard
    birth of, 53
    childhood of, 58–59, 66–67, 78–79, 197
    leaves Magrath, 238
    Melvin rescues, 213
    moves to Cardston, 262–63
    receives Christmas present, 233
    works at Empress Theatre, 90
    wrecks car, 202
Godfrey, Clarice Card. *See also* Taiwan and Taiwan Mission
    and Alberta Stake Center, 343
    childhood of, 239–42
    Church service of, 339–42, 351–55
    courtship of, 229, 247
    early marriage of, 254–55
    education of, 242–44
    employment of, 246–47
    final years and death of, 333–34, 381
    and Floyd's Furniture, 288, 292–93, 296, 298, 302–3, 304
    Great Depression's impact on, 258–62
    holiday celebrations of, 306
    home of, 268–71, 273–81
    legacy of, 391–98
    marriage of, 253–54
    moves to Cardston, 262–64
    prays for mission funds, 305–6
    temple service of, 338–39
Godfrey, Donald, 343, 352
Godfrey, Douglas, 90, 92, 197, 206–7
Godfrey, Eliza Jane, 13
Godfrey, Fanny, 5
Godfrey, Floyd. *See also* Floyd's Furniture; Taiwan and Taiwan Mission
    and Alberta Stake Center, 343
    baptism of, 218
    as bishop of Fifth Ward, 344–51
    and Cardston Chamber of Commerce, 319–21
    as Cardston mayor, 322–33
    childhood of, 78–79, 197–98, 203, 204–6
    Church service of, 339–42
    community service of, 316–34, 382, 398
    and community theater, 256–58
    contracts infection, 234–35
    courtship of, 247
    early church experiences of, 218–19
    early marriage of, 254–55
    education of, 222–29
    employment of, in Cardston, 264–68
    final years and death of, 398–400
    following Clarice's death, 381–82
    Great Depression's impact on, 258–62

Godfrey, Floyd (*continued*)
    holiday celebrations of, 231, 306–8
    home of, 268–71, 273–81
    honesty of, 221–22
    kindness of, 310
    legacy of, 391–98, 403
    and Lions Club, 317–19
    marriage counsel given by, 347–51, 369–70
    marriage(s) of, 253–54, 383
    Melvin rescues, 213–17
    Melvin's relationship with, 211–12
    moves to Cardston, 262–64
    prays for mission funds, 305–6
    pulled teeth of, 235–36
    retirement of, 310–13
    returns to Taiwan, 383–87
    serves on Cardston school board, 317–18
    serves on Cardston town council, 321–22
    taught responsibility and work, 206–11
    teenage social life of, 229–30
    temple service of, 338–39
    works at Empress Theatre, 90
Godfrey, James, 13
Godfrey, Jeremiah, 54, 83
Godfrey, John, 33
Godfrey, Joseph
    childhood of, 4–6
    children of, 24
    church and community service of, 19–21
    context of life of, 10
    conversion of, 11–12
    death of, 27
    eightieth birthday of, 26–27
    estate of, 53–54
    humanitarianism of, 25–26
    Josephine and Melvin Godfrey and, 37
    legacy of, 401–2
    and Mormon Battalion, 13–15
    names Mount Ben Lomond, 18–19
    persecution experienced by, 35
    remarries, 21–22, 32–33
    Richard Jones and, 50
    as sailor, 6–8
    settles dispute with Native Americans, 23
    settles in North Ogden, 16–18
    travels and settles in United States, 8–10
    treks to Utah, 15–16
    trials of, 12–13
Godfrey, Josephine, 37, 39
Godfrey, Joseph (son of Melvin), 78–79, 90, 92, 197, 214–16
Godfrey, Josiah, 56, 65–66, 83
Godfrey, Kenneth Floyd, 201, 255, 257–58, 269, 311, 344
Godfrey, Lorin Card, 256, 303, 305–6, 311, 313, 341–42, 344
Godfrey, Lottie, 82, 197, 204, 231, 232, 361
Godfrey, Margaret Barrows, 4, 5
Godfrey, Marilyn Rose, 256, 265, 307

Godfrey, Melvin
    baseball as favorite pastime of, 82–83
    birth and childhood of, 37–38
    businesses owned by, 84–93, 196
    courtship and marriage of, 44–46
    early marriage of, 52–53
    education of, 38–42
    encourages Floyd to start business, 288
    as father, 205–6, 211–17, 227
    holiday celebrations of, 232–33
    homes of, 203–6, 238
    legacy of, 402–3
    legal responsibilities of, in Magrath, 77–82
    loses family farm, 53–55
    as Magrath constable, 68
    moves to Canada, 34, 61–69
    moves to Star Valley, 55–61
    pulls Floyd's teeth, 235
    service of, in Magrath, 74–76
    settles in southern Alberta, 195
    teaches children responsibility, 206–11
    young-adult difficulties of, 42–44
Godfrey, Mervin, 78–79, 197, 214–16, 235, 238
Godfrey, Norris, 93–94, 197
Godfrey, Parley Melvin, 61, 66–67, 69, 197
Godfrey, Robert, 293, 343
Godfrey, William, 4, 5, 6
Goose Lake, 327–28
grain, harvesting, 208–9

Great Depression, 237–39, 252, 258–62, 336–37, 403
Gregson, Lloyd, 319–20
Gregson, Percy C., 317
Greniniger, Olive, 360
guns, 205

## H

handcarts, 105–6
Harker, Orin, 86
Harker, Rulon, 360–61
Harris, Martin, 342–43
harvesting, 208–11
Haultain, Frederick, 133
hay, harvesting, 209–10
Haynes, John C., 143–44
healings, in Taiwan, 369–70
healthcare, 234–36, 240, 245
Hell Roaring Falls hike, 346
Hendricks, Charles, 138–39
Hendricks, John W., 138–39
Hendricks, William D., 139, 140–52
Herbert, Jane, 117
holidays, 228, 230–34, 296–97, 306–10, 373
honesty, 221–22
Hood, Ben, 222
horses, 43, 78–79, 202–3
Hudson, Dad, 254, 257
Hudson's Bay Company, 130, 138
humor, 395–97
Huntington, Oregon, 44
Hyde, William F., 140
Hyde, William, Jr., 113–15

## I

ice, harvesting, 204–5
imperialism, 193
Indians. *See* First Nations peoples
irrigation, 73, 113, 133–34, 161, 178. *See also* water supply
irrigation ditches, 198–99

## J

Jackson, Linda, 365
Jackson, Malan R., 365
Jacobs, Henry Bailey, 11n27
Jacobs, Zebulon W., 182
Jensen, Allie Rogers, 69
Jensen and Brothers Mercantile Company, 246
*Jersey*, 29–30
Jessen, Lawrence H., 290
Johnson, Michael, 156
Johnston, Albert S., 23
Jones, Alice Louis, 176
Jones, Eva
    church service of, 96
    community involvement of, 97
    courtship and marriage of, 45–46
    early marriage of, 52–53
    family of, 46–50
    fears fire, 50
    gives birth to Douglas, 206–7
    goes camping, 214–16
    holiday celebrations of, 231–32
    homes of, 203–6
    household routines of, 93–96

Jones, Eva (*continued*)
    influence of, on children, 217–18, 222
    moves to Canada, 61–69
    moves to Star Valley, 56, 57–60
    personality of, 46
    relationship between father and, 50–51
    sees ghost, 51–52
    supports Floyd and Clarice's courtship, 247
    works at Empress Theatre, 89
Jones, Richard, 45, 46–51

## K

Kamloops, British Columbia, 146–47
Ke-Liao congregation, 375–77
Keogan, Michael, 144–45
Keokuk, Iowa, 30
Kimball-Lethbridge Canal, 113
Kroehler Furniture, 295–96

## L

laundry, 95, 207–8, 275–76
Lee, Kirk, 268
Lee's Creek street bridge, 320
Lee's Creek watershed, 332
Lindsay, J. H., 54
Lions Club, 318–19
Logan Temple, 170–71
Low, Brigham Y., 317
Low, Joseph S., 321

## M

Magrath, Alberta
  childhood in, 196–99, 203–6
  Godfrey family moves to, 194–95
  Great Depression's impact on, 237–39, 252, 258–62
  healthcare in, 234–36
  holidays in, 230–34
  homes in, 199–203
  Melvin Godfrey moves to, 61–69
  recreation and entertainment in, 82–93
  settlement of, 65, 74–77
  Spanish flu pandemic in, 245–46
Magrath, Charles Alexander, 71, 73, 134
Magrath Agricultural Fairs, 197–98
Magrath Band, 228
Magrath Home Dramatics, 256–58
Magrath Trading Company, 211, 221–22, 238, 263–64
Malad, Idaho, 52–53
Mandarin, 362–64
marriage counseling, 347–51, 369–70
Martineau, James Henry, 36n2
matches, 397
Matkin, Heber J., 338
McDonald, Duncan, 145–46, 149
McIntyre, William, Jr., 72
McIntyre, William, Sr., 72
McIntyre Ranch, 72–73, 196–97
medicine, 234–36, 240, 245
Melody Theatre, 92–93
Mercer, Ammon, 246
Merkley, Alva, 204–5

Mexican-American War, 13–15
milking, 279–80
missionary work, 357. *See also* Taiwan and Taiwan Mission
  among First Nations peoples, 193
  of Charles O. Card, 113–15
mission funds, 305–6
Monson, Niels, 156
Mormon Battalion, 13–15
Mormon Underground, 124, 125–26, 164–67
Morrison, Henry, 158
Mount Ben Lomond, 18–19
Mountie, 80
movies, 85–90, 207, 236
Movie Theater, 85
mustard plaster, 234–35

## N

Nauvoo, Illinois, 11–12
New England, Card ancestors in, 101–2
North Ogden
  debates in, 24
  education in, 38–42
  Jones family settles in, 48–49
  Joseph Godfrey's church and community service in, 19–21
  Joseph Godfrey settles in, 16–19
  Price family moves to, 32
  relationship between Native Americans and residents of, 23–24
Northwest Territories, 129–32, 138–49. *See also* southern Alberta, Canada

## O

Old Baldy, 78–79, 202–3
Order in Council of 1881, 130, 131
Oregon Trail, 35–36
outhouse, 200

## P

packet vessel, 47
Painter, George, 117
Painter, Sarah Jane, 112, 117–18, 163, 166, 170, 175
Pan, Sister, 370
Parkinson, William C., 153–54
Parson, Naomi, 46–47, 49
patriarchal blessings, of George Cyrus Card, 174
Pearce, William, 133
persecution, 11–12, 28, 35–36, 42, 120, 123–27, 134–36, 164–68
Picture Butte, Alberta, 92–93
pigeons, 223–24
pioneer(s)
    Card family as, 105–8, 162, 182
    determination of, 196
    education of children of, 38–42
    Jones family as, 47–48
    Joseph Godfrey as, 15–26
    lifestyle of, 191
    persecution of, 35–36
    Plant family as, 179–80
    Sarah Ann Price as, 28–34
    transportation methods of, 191–92

Pitcher, Marilyn Godfrey Ockey, 111n34
Plant, Henry, 179–80
Plant, Rose Elizabeth
    church and community service of, 186–87
    education of children of, 242
    final years of, 334
    marriage of, 179–82
    moves into town, 244–45
    personality of, 186
    raises poultry, 184
    relationship between George and, 175–76, 177, 187
    stricken with Spanish flu, 246
Plant, Sarah Harris, 179–80
plural marriage
    of Charles Ora Card, 115–23, 155, 165–66
    of Cyrus Card, 111n34
    of Joseph Godfrey, 21–22, 26, 32–33
    persecution due to, 35–36, 42, 120, 123–27, 164–68
    of Richard Jones, 49
    and scattering of Mormons, 134–36
potatoes, 89
Pothole Creek, 205
Poulsen, Sarah, 243
prairie wildfires, 77–78
pranks, 395–97
Pratt, Parley P., 107–8
prayer
    of Eva Godfrey, 67
    in Floyd and Clarice Godfrey's family, 339–40

prayer (*continued*)
    for healing of Mervin Godfrey, 235
    for lost watch, 204
    for mission funds, 305–6
    for rain, 260, 340, 342
Prescott, Ontario, 8n16
Preston, William B., 124
Price, Ann, 22, 32
Price, Jane Morgan, 28, 31–32
Price, Jeremiah, 27–28, 31–32
Price, John, 32, 52–53
Price, Josiah, 28, 29
Price, Sarah Ann, 22, 26, 27–34, 35, 54
priesthood blessings, 369–70
Primary, 218–19
Prince of Wales Hotel, 300

## R

radio, 91–92, 271–72
railroad(s)
    Canadian Pacific Railway, 131–32, 138, 191–92, 252
    impact of, 36–37, 191–92, 251–52
    Melvin works on, 44
    in Taiwan, 380
    and travel between Canada and U.S., 63
    travel by, 61–62, 63
rain, 106, 245, 253, 260, 340, 342
Ramsel, Benjamin, 116–17, 169
Rasmussen, Lyman M., 317
rattlesnake, 201
Raymond Stampede, 255
readers, 40

rebaptism, 44
Red Crow, Chief, 132–33
Reeves, Ann Elizabeth Eliza, 9–10, 11, 15, 17, 21
Reeves, Eunice, 9
Reeves, James, 9
Reeves, Mary, 9–10, 11, 13, 15, 16, 21–22
Rega, 150
Restmore Bedding, 295–96
revivalism, 10
rice, 377–78
Rich, Charles C., 55–56
Richard, Charles C., 167
Richards, Franklin D., 155
Ricks, Joseph, 156
Ricks, Thomas E., 156, 158
Rigby, Lavinia Clark, 120–23, 155
Rigby, Mary Clark, 121
Rigby, William F., 121, 122, 155–56
Ririe, Alfred, 221
Ririe, Elmer, 219
Rogers, Jo Anne Sloan, 111n34
Rolapp, Henry H., 167
root cellars, 201
roustabout, 210–11
Royal Canadian Mounted Police officer, 80
Royal Metal, 298–99
Russell, Robert W., 322–24

## S

Sabey, William, 240
Sabey family, 240–42

Sabin, Sarah, 102, 104
Salt Lake Temple, 163–64
Satan, Floyd's wrestle with, 385–86
saving face, 372
sego lily bulbs, 21n57
septic tank, 269–70
sewing machine, repossession of, 212
sheepherder's wagon, 60
sheep herding, 60
Shoshone, 59
shotgun, 205
sick, administering to, 369–70
silent movies, 85–87
Silver Dollar Days, 320
slavery, 102
Smith, John S., 318
Smith, Joseph, 12, 114
Smith, Orson, 127, 151
Smith, Thomas X., 158
Smith, Willard, 338
Sommerfelt, Lynn, 304
sourdock, 20–21n57
southern Alberta, Canada. *See also*
  Cardston, Alberta; Magrath, Alberta
  Card completes exploration mission in, 151–53
  characteristics of, 129
  childhood in, 196–99, 203–6
  George Cyrus Card moves to, 177–78
  holidays in, 230–34
  homes in, 199–203
  irrigation of, 73, 113, 161, 178
  lack of conveniences in, 184–86
  location of settlement site in, 149–51, 155–60

southern Alberta, Canada (*continued*)
  McIntyre Ranch in, 72–73
  Mormon exploration of, 138–49
  public schools in, 222–29
  recruitment of settlers for, 154–55
  settlement of, 65, 71–72, 74–77, 132–35, 192, 194–96
Spackman, Fred, 358, 381
Spackman, Roy, 332
Spanish flu pandemic, 236, 245–46
Spencer's Hardware, 287, 288
Sport, 269–70
Star Valley, Wyoming, 55–61
Stone, Sarabette, 111n34
Strong, Josiah, 193
swimming, 205

### T

Tagg, Dale, 304, 325
Taichung chapel, 374–75
Taipei Taiwan Temple, 383–84
Taiwan and Taiwan Mission, 357
  arrival in, 364–65
  calling and preparation for, 358–59, 360
  city atmosphere in, 378–79
  completion of Taichung chapel in, 374–75
  conversion of Ke-Liao congregation in, 375–77
  delayed departure to, 360–61
  departure from, 380–81
  getting settled in, 365–67
  leadership training in, 370–74

Taiwan and Taiwan Mission (*continued*)
  life in, 368–69
  location of, 359
  people in, 377–78
  priesthood blessings in, 369–70
  responsibilities in, 367–68
  return to, 383–87
  training for, 361–64
  transportation in, 379–80
Tanner, Nathan Eldon, 344, 361
Taylor, John, 77, 128, 137–38
Taylor, John W., 73
Taylor, Louisa Ann, 256–57
teeth, 235–36
television, 276, 302
temple(s)
  Card prays for son in, 163–64
  Cardston Alberta Temple, 281–82, 299–300, 338–39, 392
  Floyd and Clarice's service in, 338–39
  impact of, in Charles Ora Card's life, 170–71
  Logan Temple, 170–71
  Salt Lake Temple, 163–64
Texaco station, 264–67
theater, 256–58
tie prank, 396–97
tithing, 338
tobacco, 236
Toomer, Idell Jane, 218–19
touring politicians, preachers, and performers, 102–3
transcontinental railroad, 36. *See also* Canadian Pacific Railway
transportation. *See also* railroad(s)
  and growth of Cardston, 286
  in Taiwan, 379–80
Trott, Caroline, 5
Tuttle, Sarah, 104, 162–63

**U**

ugly Chesterfield, 308–10
Union Pacific Railroad, 191–92
United Order, 110
United Order Manufacturing and Building Company of the Logan Second Ward, 110
Utah War, 23

**V**

Victorian Age, children during, 4
visiting teaching, 96

**W**

Walter, Archer, 107
Walwork, Margaret, 50
watch, prayer for lost, 204
water supply, 327–28, 332. *See also* irrigation; wells
Waterton-Glacier International Peace Park, 213–17, 333, 336
wells, 200–201
West, Jane, 41–42
Weston, Ted, 300
westward expansion, railroad's impact on, 36–37

whale hunting, 6–7
wheat, 261
Wickham, Elizabeth, 45, 46, 49–50
Widmer, Albert, 321
Wilcox, Guy, 294
wildfires, 77–78
Wiley, Alma, 395
Wilhelm II, Kaiser, 225–26
Williams, William W. "Willis," 14
Williams, Zina Young, 119–20, 155, 166
Winder, John R., 45–46
Winder, Ned, 362
*Wings*, 87–88
Wirthlin, Joseph L., 298–99
Wood, Edward J., 267, 336–37
Wood, Forest, 267
Woodruff, Jessie, 52
Woolf, Golden, 227
World War I, 193, 224–26
World War II, 271–72, 285, 287, 316

# Y

Yen, Sister, 369–70
Young, Brigham, 22, 108
Young, Zina, 119
Young, Zina D. H., 166
Yu Tai Tai, 368

# Z

Zundell, David E., 139–52

# ABOUT THE AUTHOR

Donald G. Godfrey, PhD, is a professor emeritus of the Walter Cronkite School of Journalism and Mass Communication at Arizona State University. He was the recipient of the Mormon History Association's Christensen Best Documentary Award in 2007. He is an LDS and media historian whose articles on Mormon history have appeared in the *Journal of Mormon History*, the *American Review of Canadian Studies*, *Pioneer*, *This People*, and the *Ensign*. He is the author of many books, notably *The Diaries of Charles Ora Card: The Canadian Years* and *The Utah Years*, as well as biographies on *Philo T. Farnsworth: The Father of Television* and *C. Francis Jenkins: Film and Television Pioneer*. Godfrey is a past president of the Broadcast Education Association, former editor of the *Journal of Broadcasting & Electronic Media*, and past president of the

National Council of Communications Associations. He is the founding director of the ASU School of Journalism's doctoral program. He is the 2017 BEA recipient of the Lifetime Achievement Award in Scholarship. He is retired and writing from his home in Arizona.